Diego Rivera and Juan Rulfo
Post-Revolutionary Body Politics 1922-1965

LEGENDA

LEGENDA is the Modern Humanities Research Association's book imprint for new research in the Humanities. Founded in 1995 by Malcolm Bowie and others within the University of Oxford, Legenda has always been a collaborative publishing enterprise, directly governed by scholars. The Modern Humanities Research Association (MHRA) joined this collaboration in 1998, became half-owner in 2004, in partnership with Maney Publishing and then Routledge, and has since 2016 been sole owner. Titles range from medieval texts to contemporary cinema and form a widely comparative view of the modern humanities, including works on Arabic, Catalan, English, French, German, Greek, Italian, Portuguese, Russian, Spanish, and Yiddish literature. Editorial boards and committees of more than 60 leading academic specialists work in collaboration with bodies such as the Society for French Studies, the British Comparative Literature Association and the Association of Hispanists of Great Britain & Ireland.

The MHRA encourages and promotes advanced study and research in the field of the modern humanities, especially modern European languages and literature, including English, and also cinema. It aims to break down the barriers between scholars working in different disciplines and to maintain the unity of humanistic scholarship. The Association fulfils this purpose through the publication of journals, bibliographies, monographs, critical editions, and the MHRA Style Guide, and by making grants in support of research. Membership is open to all who work in the Humanities, whether independent or in a University post, and the participation of younger colleagues entering the field is especially welcomed.

ALSO PUBLISHED BY THE ASSOCIATION

Critical Texts
Tudor and Stuart Translations • *New Translations* • *European Translations*
MHRA Library of Medieval Welsh Literature

MHRA Bibliographies
Publications of the Modern Humanities Research Association

The Annual Bibliography of English Language & Literature
Austrian Studies
Modern Language Review
Portuguese Studies
The Slavonic and East European Review
Working Papers in the Humanities
The Yearbook of English Studies

www.mhra.org.uk
www.legendabooks.com

VISUAL CULTURE

Visual Culture reflects the dynamism of a vibrant and fast-growing field which showcases the interdisciplinary nature of research in Modern Languages and the Humanities more generally. The series publishes cutting-edge monographs and edited collections on any aspect of global visual culture from the Middle Ages to the present day. In line with this expansive scope, areas of interest include photography, advertising, memorials, urban visual studies, installation and performance art, commercial art and design, museum and gallery studies, and text-image relations in a variety of media and contexts.

APPEARING IN THIS SERIES

1. *Reimagining History in Contemporary Spanish Media: Theater, Cinema, Television, Streaming*, by Paul Julian Smith
2. *The Integrity of the Avant-Garde: Karel Teige and the Biography of an Ambition*, by Peter Zusi
3. *Diego Rivera and Juan Rulfo: Post-Revolutionary Body Politics 1922-1965*, by Lucy O'Sullivan
4. *Memory of the Future: Holograms and Digital Afterlives*, by Silke Arnold-de Simine
5. *Seeing in Tongues: Modern Languages and Visual Culture*, edited by J. J. Long and Edward Welch
6. *Intermedia in Italy: From Futurism to Digital Convergence*, by Clodagh Brook, Florian Mussgnug and Giuliana Pieri

Managing Editor
Dr Graham Nelson, 41 Wellington Square, Oxford OX1 2JF, UK

www.legendabooks.com

Diego Rivera and Juan Rulfo

Post-Revolutionary Body Politics 1922-1965

Lucy O'Sullivan

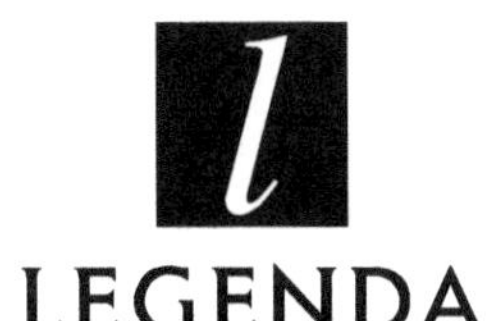

Modern Humanities Research Association
Visual Culture 2
2022

Published by Legenda
an imprint of the Modern Humanities Research Association
Salisbury House, Station Road, Cambridge CB1 2LA

ISBN 978-1-78188-878-0 (HB)
ISBN 978-1-78188-914-5 (PB)

First published 2022

Copy-Editor: Dr Ellen Jones

CONTENTS

ACKNOWLEDGEMENTS

I am immensely grateful for the many forms of support I have received while writing this book. Firstly, I owe my greatest debt to María del Pilar Blanco for the invaluable guidance and encouragement she provided while I completed the doctoral thesis on which this book is based at Trinity College, Oxford. From her meticulous feedback on incoherent early drafts to her practical advice on teaching and career planning, she consistently went above and beyond the role of supervisor and I cannot thank her enough for everything she has done for me. As an undergraduate at Trinity College Dublin, I was lucky enough to find a mentor in Ciaran Cosgrove, who encouraged me to pursue a PhD and to consider opportunities further afield.

In its earlier life, this project benefitted greatly from the detailed and insightful comments provided by my generous viva examiners, Olivia Vázquez-Medina and Claire Lindsay. I am very grateful to the anonymous reader commissioned by Legenda for carefully reviewing this manuscript and to colleagues at the University of Birmingham such as Khadija von Zinnenburg Carroll, Charlotte Ross and Kate Ince who kindly provided feedback on specific sections. Camilo Chiappe Bejar also deserves a special mention for his last minute assistance with the most awkward translations. I would also like to sincerely thank the librarians at Oxford and Birmingham for providing me with access to so many books and articles, as well as Dylan Joy at the Benson Latin American Collection at University of Texas and the Bodleian Imaging Team for providing high quality images of rare illustrations. I am also most grateful to Graham Nelson and Carolin Duttlinger at Legenda for their editorial work on this book.

I would like to express my enormous gratitude to my family (immediate and extended) for their support. To my dad, Peter O'Sullivan, for inspiring an early love of literature and for patiently proofreading various drafts over the years. To my mum, Penny Hayes, who first introduced me to Hispanic literature and who has fostered my curiosity and creativity in so many ways over the years. Her unique sensitivity and perceptiveness has encouraged me to see the beauty in everyday things. And to my brother Max, for sustaining us all with his wit and kindness and always being such a stable presence. This book is also dedicated to my grandmothers, Phyllis O'Sullivan and Yvonne Hayes, who were both great lovers of literature and art in their own ways. I would like to thank my friends in the UK, Ireland and elsewhere for their constant encouragement and for generally being wonderful humans, and my adopted English parents, Patrick and Chantal, for providing a home away from home in England. Finally, I could not have finished this book in one piece without Ralph Marnham, who has brought so much love and laughter into my life.

Sections of Chapter 2 were originally published by the University of London Press and by the *Journal of Latin American Studies* in the following form:

'The Politics of the In-Between: The Negotiation of Urban Space in Juan Rulfo's Photographs of Mexico City" in *Creative Spaces: Urban Culture and Marginality in Latin America* (University of London Press, 2019), pp. 31–54

'Diego Rivera and Juan O'Gorman: Post-Revolutionary Architectural Anatomies', *Journal of Latin American Cultural Studies*, 28 (2019), 253–75

All translations are my own unless otherwise stated.

LIST OF ILLUSTRATIONS

LIST OF ILLUSTRATIONS

INTRODUCTION

Post-Revolutionary Body Politics

The catalogue for a 1964 exhibition of works by the geometric abstract painter Pedro Coronel at the Galería de Arte Mexicano in Mexico City includes the following description of his visual imagery by the writer Juan Rulfo:

> Sus figuras yacen como aplastadas y gimientes en la tortura de la desesperación o huyen casi sin forma hacia un horizonte de tinta. La imagen de nuestro tiempo: el hombre cuyos goznes han sido rotos y cuyas deslavadas arterias se mueven aferrándose al vacío en contorsiones casi macabras.[1]
>
> [His figures lie crushed and groaning in the torture of despair or flee almost formlessly towards an inky horizon. This is the image of our time: the man whose joints have been broken and whose faded arteries grasp at the void in almost macabre contortions.]

For readers familiar with Rulfo's literary works, these elusive and grotesque figures suggest a striking affinity with the unusual bodies inhabiting his earlier short story collection *El Llano en llamas* (1953) and novel *Pedro Páramo* (1955). The significance of this parallel is illuminated by Rulfo's assertion that Coronel's troubled bodies constitute an expression of the present historical moment, that they are 'the image of our time'. From the mid-1950s, Coronel had been associated with the informal Ruptura movement, led by the iconoclastic José Luis Cuevas, which actively deconstructed the heroic revolutionary visual language that had been configured by the state-sponsored muralists during the 1920s and 1930s. In the aftermath of a violent armed conflict (1910–1917) that resulted in widespread human devastation, the robust and resilient bodies surging forth from the epic visual works of the muralists, and most strikingly those of Diego Rivera, provided a compelling fantasy of collective rehabilitation and progress for a divided and debilitated nation. As lasting social change failed to materialise over the subsequent decades, however, discontent rippled through the cultural sphere, prompting writers and artists to configure an alternative corporeal language to express the failure of the revolutionary project.

This book traces evolving narratives of revolutionary nationhood across the domains of literary and visual culture by engaging in an interdisciplinary and comparative examination of the corporeal images and metaphors presented in the visual and literary works of two of Mexico's most canonical cultural figures of the twentieth century: the muralist, painter and illustrator Diego Rivera (1886–1957) and the writer and photographer Juan Rulfo (1917–1986). This project began with a curiosity to better understand the origins and lifecycle of the deteriorating, unstable and grotesque bodies populating so many mid-century artworks, from the paintings of the Ruptura generation to the literary texts of Rulfo, Carlos Fuentes and others. How was this imagined national body constructed in the early post-revolution period? What were the conditions that brought about its subsequent transformation? In an attempt to answer these questions, this book analyses specific works produced by Rivera and Rulfo between 1922 and 1965. By examining their visual and textual corporeal images against the shifting political, intellectual and cultural backdrops of their respective periods, it furnishes a multimedia history of the imagined construction and dismemberment of the revolutionary nation from the euphoria of the reconstruction phase to the era of widescale disenchantment beginning during the Miguel Alemán administration (1946–1952).

Rivera and Rulfo cut strikingly different figures within the post-revolutionary cultural landscape, both in terms of their physical persona and aesthetic corpora. While the larger-than-life Rivera, who forged a robust workman-like public image during the 1920s and 30s, painted over 6000m² of wall over the course of his career, the total creative output of Rulfo, whose reticence and physical fragility was often noted by interviewers and biographers, amounts to a collection of short stories, a slim novel and a modest portfolio of published photographs, screenplays and other writings.[2] Composed from different media, their oeuvres stand as monuments to two distinct moments in Mexico's cultural history. The most visible member of the muralist movement that dominated the cultural field during the 1920s and 30s, Rivera continues for many to be Mexico's, and perhaps Latin America's, preeminent artist. His early murals captured the utopian spirit of the immediate post-conflict period by projecting a Janus-like vision of a Mexico positioned between an idealised collective past and a progressive proletarian future. Writing in 1925, the intellectual Pedro Henríquez Ureña celebrated Rivera's frescoes as 'el mejor símbolo del México actual' [the best symbol of contemporary Mexico], while the philosopher Samuel Ramos described his imagery as a revelation 'de nuestra auténtica existencia mexicana' [of our authentic Mexican existence].[3] Since the publication of his two major literary works, Rulfo has been identified as an equally definitive interpreter of Mexican reality. Emerging from the sceptical intellectual climate of the 1950s, his bleak literary portraits of a decaying rural universe comprehensively dismantled the myths of revolutionary unity, order and progress that had been enshrined in Rivera's epic national portraits. Rulfo's novel, considered by Fuentes to be the highest expression of Mexican literature in the twentieth century, was praised by contemporary critics for capturing 'lo propio y singular de México' [that which is characteristic of and unique to Mexico] and 'una atmósfera inconfundible de mexicanidad' [an unmistakable atmosphere of Mexicanness].[4]

Despite both being considered synonymous with post-revolutionary national identity, the works of these two figures have never been examined together. This book offers the first comparative analysis of Rivera and Rulfo and the first substantial intermedial exploration of their oeuvres, incorporating both well-known and previously overlooked essays, murals, illustrations, photographs, films and literary texts. Reading their artistic corpora together draws out a shared preoccupation with the body that sheds light not only on its function as a critical political signifier in their works, but also on how the ideas of nation and revolution were conceptualised — literally and figuratively — in primarily corporeal terms during this transformative period in Mexican history. Locating Rivera's and Rulfo's literary and textual representations within Mexico's evolving post-revolutionary intellectual environment, and the broader constellation of thinkers and artists that shaped the national imaginary during these years, I analyse their distinct corporeal languages to trace a history of aesthetic and intellectual interpretations of post-revolutionary nationhood from the 1920s to the 1960s. By adopting a chronologically broad and interdisciplinary framework, *Post-Revolutionary Body Politics* explores the intimate yet underexamined links between artistic and intellectual activity during this period and contextualises Rivera's and Rulfo's output within the ongoing dialogue between visual and literary forms that defined post-revolutionary cultural production. To lay the foundation for this discussion, my introduction will provide a historical overview of the Porfiriato, the fragmented revolutionary conflict it provoked, and the theatre of political and intellectual activity in Mexico from the 1920s to the 1960s. This historical survey will be useful for illustrating how the Porfirian regime continued to haunt Mexican politics and culture after 1920, a phenomenon I address throughout this book.[5] It will also draw attention to the intersections between notions of corporeality and interpretations of national identity that emerged in political discourse and artistic production during these decades of societal transition.

The Porfiriato and Mexico's Many Revolutions

Understanding the series of complex historical events commonly referred to as the 'Mexican Revolution' necessarily leads us back to the late nineteenth century and the dictatorial regime of Porfirio Díaz. After distinguishing himself among the successful liberal forces of Benito Juárez during the French Intervention (1862–1867), General Porfirio Díaz was elected president in 1877 and returned to power again in 1884, following a four-year interregnum by Manuel González (1880–1884). Following the turmoil of the post-independence period, Díaz's presidency ushered in an era of unprecedented stability known as the 'Pax Porfiriana'. During this period, public policy was influenced by the Científicos, a small circle of technocrats whose positivist philosophy aligned with the regime's principles of social order and progress and provided the basis for its Comtean-inspired motto of 'Order and Progress'. By championing gradual societal change over radical transformation, these thinkers ideologically justified Porfirian authoritarianism.[6] Drawing from Comtean and Spencerian interpretations of society as a living organism, prominent Científico Justo Sierra employed biological analogies to explain this model of societal development:

> La sociedad, como todo organismo, está sujeta a las leyes necesarias de la evolución [...] Es decir que en todo cuerpo, que en todo organismo, a

> medida que se unifica o se integra más, sus partes más se diferencian, más se especializan, y en este doble movimiento consiste el perfeccionamiento del organismo, lo que en las sociedades se llama progreso.[7]
>
> [Society, like every organism, is subject to the necessary laws of evolution ... That is to say that in every body, in every organism, the more unified and integrated it becomes, the more distinct and specialised its parts become, and it is through this double movement that the organism undergoes a process of continuous improvement, which in societies is called progress.]

While this imagined 'social organism' evolved rapidly during the Porfiriato due to the regime's emphasis on export-led economic growth, foreign investment and industrialisation, Sierra also conceived social evolution through a racial prism, identifying the mixed-race subject as the dynamic component of Mexican society and advocating the assimilation of indigenous communities to further collective advancement. Such theories of racial progress can be linked to efforts to promote physiological improvement through the public health initiatives of the late nineteenth and early twentieth centuries.[8] Spencerian social evolutionism also influenced Sierra's belief in educational reform as a means of correcting social ills and he promoted a secular public school system based on positivist tenets during his time as Minister of Public Instruction and Fine Art (1905–1911).

In cultural terms, the Porfiriato was a cosmopolitan urban regime that relied heavily on visual forms of representation to forge a coherent national image. Positivist thought informed the regime's utilitarian conception of painting as an expression of social progress, a view encapsulated in the dictum 'Verdad, Belleza y Utilidad' [Truth, Beauty and Utility].[9] The reliance on visual media to illustrate Porfirian societal advancement was consistent with positivism's faith in scientific observation as the basis of human knowledge. Underlining the importance of positivism as a philosophical context for visual culture, Jenks notes Comte's emphasis on the role of the 'observer' in discovering and understanding phenomena in the social world. This perceived link between seeing and believing, he claims, provided the basis for a 'perceptual and literal view of reality' that demanded a 'cultural sharpening of the senses'.[10] This outlook is reflected in the late-nineteenth-century paintings of José María Velasco, regarded by his student Rivera as the world's finest artist, who articulated Díaz's national vision of 'Order and Progress' by employing a pictorial style of 'positivist naturalism' to depict Mexico's industrialising landscape with almost scientific precision.[11] During the regime, maps, illustrated encyclopedias, as well as emergent visual technologies such as photography, played an equally central role in communicating the achievements of Porfirian modernisation both domestically and internationally.

Despite dramatic infrastructural development, the progressive veneer of the Porfiriato faded with the increasing centralisation of political power and repression of dissent. The benefits of modernisation were experienced only by a relatively small metropolitan elite and the majority of Mexico's land lay in the hands of wealthy landowners who overworked and underpaid peasant labourers. In his critique of the regime in *Los grandes problemas nacionales* (1909), Andrés Molina

Enríquez condemned this disproportionate growth of the Porfirian 'social body':

> Por ahora, nuestro cuerpo social es un cuerpo desproporcionado y contrahecho, del tórax hacia arriba es un gigante, del tórax hacia abajo es un niño. El peso de la parte de arriba es tal, que el cuerpo en conjunto se sostiene difícilmente [...] Sus pies se debilitan día por día. En efecto, las clases bajas día por día empeoran de condición y, en la última, en la de los indígenas jornaleros, la dispersión ha comenzado ya.[12]
>
> [For now, our social body is disproportionate and misshapen, from the thorax up it is a giant but from the thorax down it is a child. The weight of the upper half is such that the body struggles to support itself as a whole ... Its feet grow weaker by the day. In effect, the conditions of the lower classes are worsening by the day and in the very lowest class comprised of indigenous labourers the dispersion has already begun.]

Molina Enríquez's diagnosis was echoed in *La sucesión presidencial en 1910*, a book published in 1908 by landowner Francisco Madero who would play a pivotal role in the next chapter of Mexico's history. Madero declared his candidacy for the 1910 elections as the leader of the anti-re-election party after Díaz intimated in an interview published in the US magazine *Pearson's* that the nation was ready for democracy. Díaz ordered Madero's arrest and retained the presidency in a fraudulent election. During his exile in Texas, Madero published the Plan de San Luis Potosí (1910), in which he declared himself the legitimate president and called for an armed insurrection, setting in motion the first phases of the Revolution. Although Madero's planned revolt was a failure, rebel troops mobilised by Pancho Villa and Pascual Orozco scored a decisive victory against Federal forces during the Battle of Ciudad Juárez (1911), forcing Díaz into exile. Following the interim presidency of Francisco León de la Barra, Madero successfully ran for president in 1911.

However, the modest reforms guaranteed by Madero, particularly those relating to land distribution, failed to satisfy revolutionaries seeking radical social change. Emiliano Zapata, leader of the Ejército Libertador del Sur, denounced him as a traitor in his Plan de Ayala (1911). Madero faced opposition on several fronts and in 1913 he and his vice-president José María Pino Suárez were murdered as part of a *coup d'état* led by Victoriano Huerta. Huerta was challenged almost immediately. The conservative Venustiano Carranza, who had supported the Madero regime, gathered an army of fighters who united with the forces of Villa and Álvaro Obregón to defeat Huerta and his federal troops in June 1914. The Convención de Aguascalientes of that year aimed to unify these disparate groups but in fact served to further entrench political divisions, resulting in the formation of two groups: the Convencionistas, headed by Villa and Zapata, and the Constitucionalistas led by Carranza and Obregón. Although Carranza seized power in August 1914, fighting between the two factions continued. While the battle against Villa and Zapata raged on, Carranza, with the assistance of Obregón, devised a new charter modelled on the liberal reform constitution of 1857 as the blueprint for a new revolutionary society. Carranza assumed the presidency in 1917, but like Madero, displayed a conservative attitude towards the implementation of social, and particularly agrarian, reform. When Obregón, a widely respected general of the Revolution, launched his presidential manifesto in 1919, Carranza endorsed the candidacy of Ignacio Bonillas, triggering a movement to overthrow the president that resulted in his assassination in 1920. Following the brief interim presidency of Adolfo de la Huerta, Obregón assumed office in November 1920 and set about consolidating the regime through a national reconstruction project that prioritised socio-political stability, economic growth and public education.

For Octavio Paz, the Revolution represented 'la súbita inmersión de México en su propio ser' [the sudden immersion of Mexico in its own being], a moment of profound self-awakening and self-reflection that would trigger an intense phase of national redefinition.[13] The transition from the Porfirian to post-revolutionary intellectual landscapes is best represented by the activity of the Ateneo de la Juventud, a circle of thinkers formed by José Vasconcelos, Alfonso Reyes, Pedro Henríquez Ureña, Antonio Caso and others, that converged around the art journal *Savia moderna* at the beginning of the century. Although by no means a homogenous group, the members of the Ateneo were united in their criticism of the positivist doctrine that had provided the philosophical foundation of the Porfiriato. The group's most direct link to the Revolution was through Vasconcelos, who had acted as editor for the pro-Madero journal *El Antirreeleccionista*. The Ateneístas hailed the Revolution as a 'nuevo despertar intelectual' [new intellectual awakening] that would liberate Mexico from positivist dogma and allow it to embrace a new humanistic framework.[14] As the conflict raged, Reyes spoke of the intellectual revolution that was unfolding away from the battlefield:

> Es la hora de los guerrilleros y de los políticos; pero unos y otros solo pueden aportar soluciones provisionales y crear equilibrios poco duraderos. Solo la obra de la cultura, construyendo lentamente un ideal nacional y descubriendo los caracteres propios de una tradición, puede lograr el bien definitivo de un pueblo.[15]
>
> [It is the hour of guerrilla fighters and politicians; but they can only provide provisional solutions and create temporary harmony. Only the work of culture, by slowly constructing a national ideal and discovering the specific characteristics of its heritage, can achieve the definitive good of a nation.]

In a similar vein, Henríquez Ureña claimed in 1925 that 'mientras la guerra asolaba el país [...] los frutos de nuestra revolución filosófica, literaria y artística iban cuajando gradualmente' [while the war was devastating the country... our philosophical, literary and artistic revolutions were gradually crystallising].[16] These statements echoed Sierra not only in emphasising the role of lettered men in the project of national transformation, but also in advocating a more gradual process of societal transformation through ongoing cultural reform. Such parallels reveal how, despite defining themselves in opposition to the philosophical currents of the previous century, the Ateneístas in many ways adhered to the models of their Porfirian predecessors.[17]

If, as Alan Knight contends, the nation-building initiatives of the 1920s and 1930s, did little more than 'pump red blood' into an 'anemic corpus of ideas', this was most strikingly, and appropriately, apparent in the physiological metaphors used by thinkers and politicians to articulate the concepts of nation and revolution.[18] During the armed conflict and its immediate aftermath, the Revolution was portrayed as a moment of collective rebirth. Already in the midst of the fighting, Reyes described Mexico as a nation that was gaining bodily consciousness ('quería ejercitar sus propias manos y saberse dueño de sus músculos'), while Minister of Public Education José Manuel Puig Casauranc (1924–1928), speaking in 1925, promised that the country emerging bloodied from the armed conflict would be rehabilitated by the 'virtud preciosa de renacimiento' [precious virtue of rebirth].[19] By the end of that decade, however, descriptions of this new revolutionary national body paradoxically began to echo the ideals of 'orden y progreso' [Order and Progress] that had shaped the Porfirian social organism. Adhering to the Hobbesian conception of the body politic as an anatomical entity encompassing all the subjects of the Commonwealth, the educator Moisés Sáenz stressed the need for internal cohesion within the 'national body':

> Los partidos políticos y la organización de grupos funcionales dentro del cuerpo nacional deben reconocer ante todo el respeto a los hombres y marchar de acuerdo con los dictados de la cooperación y de la solidaridad. Las masas de México deben ser despertadas, rehabilitadas, habría que decir, redimidas — tal es el extremo en que viven —, y luego habrá que proceder a su organización. Organizar dentro de una unidad mayor, orgánica también, que es la nación: patria para todos.[20]
>
> [Political parties and the organisation of functional groups within the national body must recognise, above all else, respect for all men and march to the dictates of cooperation and solidarity. The masses of Mexico must be awakened, rehabilitated and one would have to say, redeemed — so extreme are the conditions in which they live — and then it would be necessary to address their organisation. To organise them within the larger organic unit that is the nation: a homeland for all.]

During the 1930s, organic imagery was used to conceptualise both the nation and the Revolution, emphasising the dynamic and progressive nature of the latter. Echoing president Lázaro Cárdenas's (1934–1940) definition of the Revolution as 'un conjunto indivisible de aspiraciones populares que no se estanca sino que vive en orgánico movimiento de renovación' [an indivisible set of popular aspirations that never stagnates but lives in an organic movement of renewal], the prominent leftist intellectual Vicente Lombardo Toledano described it as a self-renewing living entity that was inseparable from the bodies of the masses:

> La revolución es una cosa viva, en marcha perpetua, que no sucumbe, que no se agota, que renace incesantemente [...] La Revolución se crea cada minuto, cada hora, cada día, cada año, en la entraña misma de las masas que no han alcanzado aún su liberación definitiva.[21]
>
> [The Revolution is a living thing, constantly in motion, which never surrenders or tires but which is constantly being reborn... The Revolution comes into being every minute, every hour, every day and every year, in the very entrails of the masses who have not yet achieved their complete liberation.]

This projection of the revolutionary nation as a unified, orderly and progressive organism can be linked to the theories of racial miscegenation that were integral to post-revolutionary nationalism in the early 1920s. Despite insisting that 'entre las ideas de entonces y las de hoy, media un abismo' [a gulf separates the ideas of yesterday and today], Vasconcelos and the other Ateneístas promoted concepts of racial hybridity that echoed the *mestizo*-centric ideologies of Sierra and Molina Enríquez.[22] In his seminal text *La raza cósmica* (1925), Vasconcelos outlined a process of racial and cultural synthesis that would give rise to a unified and superior 'cosmic' race in Latin America. Vasconcelos's projection of the *mestizo* body as a metaphorical site of post-revolutionary national transformation began to translate into real public health and social engineering policies during the 1920s and particularly the 1930s, which sought to actively reshape real Mexican bodies by promoting secular education and hygiene. Discourses of *mestizaje* were complemented by the state-endorsed *indigenista* movement led by the anthropologist Manuel Gamio, who served as director of the Departamento de Antropología in the early 1920s and as Under Secretary of Education in 1925. Initially shaped by Gamio's major publications *Forjando patria* (1916) and *La población del valle de Teotihuacán* (1922), the *indigenista* movement that flourished in Mexico from the 1920s to the 1940s promoted the incorporation of indigenous peoples into the mainstream *mestizo* population and the celebration of indigenous culture as the basis of an authentic *mexicanidad*.

Cultural Narratives of Revolution

In the immediate aftermath of the Revolution, President Obregón (1920–1924) initiated an ambitious reconstruction project that sought to rehabilitate the nation in not only economic and infrastructural but also cultural terms. In 1921, he appointed Vasconcelos as Minister of Public Education to spearhead the project of forging a new nationalist identity. Inspired by the ambitious cultural campaign launched by Anatoly Lunacharsky as the Commissar of Enlightenment (1917–1929) in the early days of the Soviet Union, Vasconcelos set about implementing a nationwide literacy campaign and transforming the Secretaría de Educación Pública (SEP) into an incubator for cultural projects. Faced with a fragmented and largely illiterate populace, Vasconcelos turned to visual art as a universally accessible medium through which to shape a distinctive and cohesive post-revolutionary *mexicanidad*. As the journal *Savia Moderna* had proclaimed in 1906: 'El arte es vasto, dentro de él cabremos todos' [art is vast, we will all fit within it].[23]

While the so-called novel of the Revolution started to gain momentum in the mid-1920s, following renewed interest in Mariano Azuela's *Los de abajo* (1915), state patronage of the visual arts and persistently low literacy rates secured painting's status, as Paz put it, as 'la hija de la revolución' [the daughter of the Revolution].[24] During the early reconstruction phase, the artistic landscape was dominated by the artists Diego Rivera, José Clemente Orozco and David Alfaro Siqueiros, who were recruited by Vasconcelos to lead a state-funded public mural programme that would become a central pillar of the government's cultural regeneration project. The 1923

'Manifiesto del Sindicato de Obreros Técnicos, Pintores y Escultores', which was signed by all three artists, declared a revolution in aesthetic values, rejecting the elitism of easel painting in favour of a genuinely popular and monumental form of revolutionary art. Encompassing the dual meanings of the verb *ilustrar* [to illustrate, to educate], the muralists' early works performed a powerful didactic function by articulating national themes through a broadly legible representational visual language. During the early 1920s, the murals' elevation of peasants and workers to the status of national protagonists provided something of a pictorial analogy to the populist rhetoric of post-revolutionary nation builders, while their reinvigoration of pre-Columbian themes and aesthetics dovetailed with the *indigenista* revival of interest in vernacular art.

The relationship between the muralists and the government was, however, a complex and often unstable one. Obregón viewed muralism as a political tool for projecting Mexico as a culturally sophisticated modern nation while also promoting domestic inter-class consensus. Alongside its other educational and cultural initiatives, these public works provided the nascent state with a means of encouraging popular consent and thus distancing itself from the dictatorial Díaz regime. Although Mexican muralism came into being as a state-funded project, the fledgling regime lacked a coherent cultural policy and was in no position to co-opt the artists into acting as spokespersons for official ideology.[25] On this point, Mary K. Coffey identifies muralism as an expression of what she terms 'official culture', but describes this as a 'collective process, formed slowly through the endeavours of multiple agents, often with competing agendas and intentions'.[26] From the outset, Vasconcelos granted considerable creative freedom to *los tres grandes* and their relationship with the state oscillated between collaboration and confrontation throughout the 1920s and 30s.[27] Although all three muralists signed the 1923 manifesto, this initial consensus did not provide the basis for a coherent and unified artistic movement. Each artist approached questions of national identity from unique thematic and stylistic angles and their aesthetic and ideological agendas diverged considerably in response to shifting domestic and international political developments in the years that followed. The assumption that the muralists were capable of imposing a singular state-endorsed national vision onto a heterogenous public is further complicated by issues of reception. While there is little concrete evidence of who exactly had access to these works, contemporary claims regarding their genuinely popular nature have since faced considerable scrutiny. Although muralism projected itself as an art of the masses and for the masses, the location of many of these works within urban municipal buildings rendered them largely invisible to those sectors of the population they claimed to address. While photographic reproductions of the murals appeared in state-funded publications distributed in rural areas, these often cropped, black and white images failed to capture the rich colour schemes or complex spatial dimensions of these works. Furthermore, as Vaughan has pointed out, there was no systematic effort on the part of the government to educate the public as to how these images should be read.[28] As a result, the murals provoked varying and unpredictable responses. Even in the capital, the unorthodox pictorial style of the murals and their allegedly sacrilegious and pornographic content drew fierce criticism in conservative circles, leading to the defacement of Siqueiros's and Orozco's frescoes by students at the Escuela Nacional Preparatoria in 1924. Despite these oversights and obstacles, the muralists remained to the forefront of debates regarding national culture in the 1920s and early 30s and produced some of the most widely disseminated and durable images of Mexico's new post-revolutionary society.

While government patronage did not predetermine the content of their works, some of the muralists' earliest state-commissioned works exploring themes of racial mixing bear traces of Vasconcelian thinking. A prime example of is Rivera's *Creación* (1922), where theories of racial miscegenation and contemporary metaphors of national rebirth converge to form a *mestizo* creation myth. The visual metaphor was of particular relevance to Rivera, who consciously echoed the contemporary rhetoric of national regeneration by describing his homecoming to Mexico in 1921 as a kind of personal and artistic renaissance.[29] After completing his artistic training at the Academia de San Carlos in Mexico City under the direction of Porfirian academic painters such as Velasco and Santiago Rebull, Rivera had been awarded a government scholarship by Sierra in 1905 to study art in Europe. During his time in Paris, he established important links with prominent artists including Modigliani, Matisse and Picasso and began working predominantly within a cubist idiom. Already closely connected to Vasconcelos as a member of the wider artistic circle of the Ateneo, Rivera responded to the Minister's rallying call for artists to return to Mexico and rejected cubist abstractionism in favour of a robust and visually coherent style that could theoretically communicate national themes to a largely illiterate audience. During the early 1920s, Rivera strived to further align himself with the Revolution by claiming to have joined Zapata's forces and to have even colluded to assassinate Díaz.[30] These attempts at self-mythification proved effective and by the early 1920s, the muralist was regarded as the living embodiment of the institutionalised Revolution within the public sphere. Writing in *El Nacional* in 1922, the journalist Francisco Navarro declared: 'La revolución tiene en este momento, dos representantes supremos, encarnación viviente de sus ideales: Plutarco Elías Calles en lo político. En la senda del arte, el ventrudo Diego Rivera' [The Revolution currently has two supreme representatives who are the living embodiment of its ideals: Plutarco Elías Calles in politics and the potbellied Diego Rivera in the field of art].[31] While Rivera's relationship with the state was often strained, he maintained the strongest institutional links of *los tres grandes* throughout his career. Not only was he entrusted with the symbolic task of decorating the interior of the SEP (1923–1928) by Vasconcelos, but he continued to receive state commissions under Obregón's conservative successor Plutarco Elías Calles (1924–1928), whose lack of support for Siqueiros and Orozco prompted their departure to the U.S.

For the philosopher Samuel Ramos, Rivera's greatest contribution to Mexican art was 'tomar como asunto esencial de la pintura al hombre mismo' [to take man himself as the essential subject of painting].[32] Building on his initial efforts in

Creación, a mural I discuss in detail in Chapter 2, Rivera developed a figurative visual language to explore national themes that harmonised with contemporary organicist metaphors of national regeneration and the *mestizo* fantasy of a collective corporeal future characterised by stability, unity and progress. The muralists sought to embody these revolutionary corporeal ideals, projecting themselves as 'hombres de acción, fuertes, sanos' [strong and healthy men of action].[33] Rivera's vision of the Revolution as a 'gran fenómeno biológico' [great biological phenomenon], as I will demonstrate in Chapter 3, achieved its clearest expression in his fresco cycle at Chapingo (1924–1927) where a series of visual metaphors interlink the process of social revolution with the development of human life.[34] As Ramos notes, Rivera's marked 'privileging of the body' through the use of strong lines and solid three-dimensional forms was exemplary of a wider corporeal focus in contemporary art that can be easily perceived in works from the 1920s and 30s by Ramón Alva de la Canal, Ángel Zárraga, Fermín Revueltas, Agustín Lazo, Julio Castellanos and many others.[35] During this period, Rivera also established the model for the committed revolutionary artist. Conceptualising this social function in highly physiological terms, Rivera described the artist as:

> Un ser dotado de un sistema neuroglandular y de un aparato ocular que beneficia la actividad de su oficio, cuyo agente no es sino un aparato receptor, conductor y retrasmisor de las aspiraciones, los deseos y las luchas de las masas.[36]
>
> [A being equipped with a neuroglandular system and an ocular apparatus that aids him in his work, agents that are nothing more than conductors capable of receiving, channelling and transmitting the aspirations, desires and struggles of the masses.]

The muralist consolidated his political profile by forming the left-wing artistic collective known as the Sindicato de Obreros Técnicos, Pintores y Escultores with Siqueiros and Xavier Guerrero, and securing his position on the executive committee of the Partido Comunista Mexicano (PCM) in 1923. During the same decade, Rivera contributed to various left-wing Latin American organisations such as the Liga Anti-Imperialista de las Américas and the ¡Manos fuera de Nicaragua! Committee. Already a well-established figure within the European avant-garde community, Rivera played a key role in internationalising the muralist movement from the late 1920s onwards through his collaborations with the Soviet constructivists and commissions in the United States. It was in 1929, in the midst of this transitional phase in Rivera's career, that he married Frida Kahlo. The early years of their relationship were dominated by travel and the couple soon became the focus of international attention. Rivera's U.S. commissions during the 1930s served a diplomatic function in ameliorating North-South tensions in the wake of the Great Depression; however, his collaborations with capitalist patrons inevitably provoked accusations of ideological inconsistency from his fellow artists. By 1929, Rivera had been excommunicated from the PCM for accepting state-funded projects and the directorship of the Escuela Nacional de Bellas Artes, and in 1934 Siqueiros penned a devastating critique of the artist in an article entitled 'Rivera's Counter-Revolutionary Road'.[37] Alienated in varying degrees from Mexican communists, Stalinists and American capitalists, Rivera found himself politically isolated for much of that decade.

Rivera would come to embody many of the contradictions of the institutionalised Revolution into the 1940s. Although he continually projected himself as stridently communist and condemned the use of art to uphold the bourgeois status-quo, he spoke admiringly of the conservative and unapologetically capitalist president Alemán and accepted his invitation to act as a co-director of the Comisión Nacional de Pintura Mural alongside Orozco and Siqueiros in 1947.[38] Such collaborations demonstrate how, as Greeley argues, later administrations were more concerned with establishing a symbolic alliance with the muralists to uphold the state's revolutionary credentials than directly funding their artistic projects.[39] Even during the early 1950s, when muralism was facing mounting opposition from vocal critics such as Cuevas, Rivera continued to profess his adherence to the ideological principles of the 1923 manifesto.[40] The artist's unwavering utopianism is reflected in the late mural *El pueblo en demanda de salud* (1953). Painted a year after he was diagnosed with testicular cancer and four years before his death from heart failure, the mural presents scenes of medical advances from pre-Hispanic Mexico to the present day framed on the left-hand side by a phallic Tree of Life. Although impressive in its technical execution, the mural reveals the thematic and stylistic stagnation of Rivera's later works, which eschewed contemporary domestic politics in favour of the well-trodden themes of indigeneity and pan-American cooperation.

Rivera's shift away from the overtly revolutionary subject matter that had dominated his earlier murals can be largely attributed to the inescapable collapse of its social ideals towards the middle of the century. Although Cárdenas's acceleration of land distribution, implementation of social reform and nationalisation of the oil industry established him in the eyes of many as the most faithful interpreter of the Revolution's social principles during the 1930s, his administration also consolidated a corporatist form of government that bound peasant and workers' organisations to the state. Cárdenas's progressive agenda was also characterised by socialist education and a *desarrollista* [developmentalist] impulse that promoted domestic industrialisation and state-intervention in the economy. Cardenista social reform lost its momentum in the late 1930s and the presidency of Manuel Ávila Camacho (1940–1946) continued this transition towards a more conservative interpretation of revolutionary principles based on unity and economic progress that laid the foundations for the 'Mexican Miracle', a period of significant economic growth spanning roughly from 1940 to 1970. The trajectory of the Revolution during the Alemán administration (1946–1952) and thereafter might best be understood by returning to the term's etymological roots in the Latin verb *revolvere*, meaning 'to roll back'. With the reincarnation of the Partido de la Revolución Mexicana (PRM) as the Partido Revolucionario Institucional (PRI) in 1946, the Revolution entered an 'institutional' phase that echoed Porfirian rhetoric in its emphasis on social order and economic development. The PRI began an extended phase of political hegemony during that decade, combining repression and co-optation with a veneer of democratic legitimacy to establish what Mario Vargas Llosa famously described as a 'perfect dictatorship'.[41] As modernisation was matched by an increasingly pronounced class divide under Alemán, it became clear that the events of 1910–1917 had failed to bring about the desired radical change to the economic or social structure of the nation. Economic disparity increased under Alemán who also moved to neutralise peasant and worker unions. Increasing state repression of popular movements under Adolfo López Mateos (1958–1964) and Gustavo Díaz Ordaz (1964–1970) culminated in the government's brutal response to student protesters in the Tlatelolco Massacre of 1968, exposing an irreparable rift between revolutionary rhetoric and reality.

These mid-century developments prompted dramatic reassessments of the revolutionary body politic amongst intellectuals and artists. By the late 1940s, the organicist analogies employed by Cárdenas and Lombardo Toledano to describe the progressive and unifying impact of the Revolution had been replaced by the metaphors of corporeal decline used by Mexican thinkers to describe the collapse of its ideals. In his 1947 essay 'La crisis de México', the economist Daniel Cosío Villegas compared the Revolution to a dying patient whose condition was deteriorating day by day.[42] His language of bodily failure was echoed by sociologist José Iturriaga, who diagnosed the Revolution as gravely ill in 1947, and Silva Herzog, who asserted in 1949 that 'la revolución dejó de ser, murió calladamente sin que nadie lo advirtiera' [the Revolution ceased to exist, it died quietly without anyone noticing].[43] In 1950 the *Excélsior* columnist José R. Colín carried out a final post-mortem analysis in his article 'La Revolución Mexicana: R.I.P.', where he claimed that, like every living phenomenon, the Revolution had reached its 'fin obligado, biológico' [inevitable, biological end].[44]

Reflecting on the legacy of the Revolution in 1950, Paz echoed these metaphors of physiological deterioration by describing post-revolutionary demagoguery as an illness in the political system that had generated an atmosphere of distrust amongst intellectuals.[45] While Cosío Villegas and Herzog debated the disintegration of the Revolution's social and political ideals, thinkers like Paz began to explore the deeply ingrained insecurities engendered by the nation's historical experiences. Building on Ramos's psychoanalytic study of the Mexican's 'inferiority complex' in *El perfil del hombre y la cultura en México* (1934), thinkers linked to the intellectual circle known as the Grupo Hiperión (1948–1952) such as Leopoldo Zea, Emilio Uranga, Jorge Portilla and Luis Villoro engaged in a more self-reflexive and introspective exploration of national identity through existentialist, hermeneutical and phenomenological lenses.[46] In his writings, Uranga conceptualised this inward-looking approach as a form of ontological 'auscultation' that involved 'carefully listening to the internal processes of the human body'.[47] The group launched this phase of philosophical inquiry with a series of lectures in 1949 centering around the question 'Qué es el mexicano?' These thinkers were heavily influenced by José Goas, a prominent Spanish philosopher and disciple of José Ortega y Gasset who, along with several liberal *émigrés* who had fled the Spanish Civil War (1936–1939), profoundly enriched Mexican intellectual life from the late 1930s onwards. Zea and Uranga viewed cultural nationalism as an obstruction to collective self-awareness and development and sought to forge a non-essentialist and universal philosophy.[48] Following Ortega's assertion that 'el hombre no tiene naturaleza, sino historia' [man does not have nature, but rather history], the writings of the Hiperión philosophers sought to deconstruct totalising descriptions of national identity and stressed the dynamic and changeable nature of Mexican existence.

This wave of intellectual reassessment reverberated in artistic spheres throughout the 1950s. While a reduction in government funding for artistic initiatives resulted in fewer state commissions for the muralists during the 1940s, by this time the heroic and self-assured pictorial idiom crafted by *los tres grandes* in the 1920s had begun to jar with the socio-political realities of the Camacho and Alemán eras and was gradually giving way to the more abstract and introspective visual style of the Ruptura artists. Parallel developments became apparent in photographic practices from the 1920s to the 1950s, with Manuel Álvarez Bravo and his disciples Nacho López and Héctor García crafting what Erica Segre has described as a more provocative visual aesthetic founded on 'ludic self-reflexivity, experimentation and self-doubt'.[49] In the realm of cinema, the Nuevo Cine movement also emerged in the 1960s, challenging the visual identities established during the previous cultural nationalist phase of film production by configuring a more experimental and socially-engaged aesthetic.

The Decline of Muralism and the Rise of Literature

Despite these shifts in visual culture, the most significant challenge to the aesthetic model of the muralists was posed by a new generation of mid-century writers.[50] Cuevas situated the Ruptura aesthetic within a broader critical intellectual and artistic tradition shaped by figures such as Paz, Fuentes and Carlos Pellicer and it was two writers, Paz and José Revueltas who most emphatically echoed his criticisms of the muralist movement.[51] Writing in 1959, Paz reflected on the development of a new national literature that was defined primarily by its critical stance:

> Por arte mexicano se entiende a menudo la pintura. Es cierto que poseemos en esta rama grandes artistas como Rufino Tamayo, al cual, por otra parte he consagrado varios estudios. Pero según mi opinión los talentos más originales aparecen hoy en el sector literario [...] Lo que me parece interesante en la nueva generación es su anticonformismo [...] Nuestra moderna literatura es una literatura crítica.[52]
>
> [Mexican art is often understood to refer to painting. It is true that in this field we have great artists such as Rufino Tamayo, to whom I have devoted various studies. But in my opinion, the most original talents can today be found in the field of literature... What I find interesting about the new generation is its non-conformity... Our modern literature is a critical literature.]

Cultural developments in the 1940s and 50s provided favourable conditions for this literary revival. The steady growth of the publishing industry, thanks in part to the assistance of recently arrived Spanish intellectuals who had fled the Spanish Civil War, along with increasing facilities for higher education and the expansion of the middle class, provided greater opportunities for the dissemination and reception of literature. The arrival of literary magazines such as *Revista mexicana de la literatura*, founded by Fuentes and Emmanuel Carballo in 1955, and other journals like *Novedades*, *Siempre!* and *México en la cultura* opened new spaces for writers and literary commentators to contribute to debates on Mexican culture and nationalism.

By the end of the decade, literature's dethronement of the visual arts had become a topic of discussion in critical circles. In an article published in 1959 in a literary supplement edited by Uranga, Antonio Rodríguez observes:

> Asistimos pues, en estos momentos a un desplazamiento de posiciones rectoras. Hace treinta años la pintura dominaba al conjunto [...] En tanto que la pintura se ha vuelto anodina, sorda y muda, la literatura comienza a hablar, y a hablar con vigor, asumiendo ahora la actitud heroíca que aquella ya no se siente muy dispuesta a mantener.[53]
>
> [We are currently witnessing a shift in the positions of dominance. Thirty years ago, painting dominated the field... While painting has become dull, deaf and mute, literature has started to speak, and to speak energetically, assuming the heroic attitude that painting seems unprepared to maintain.]

Pointing to key figures such as Rulfo and Juan José Arreola, Rodríguez echoes Paz in attributing the increasing relevance of literature to its engagement with 'los problemas actuales, palpitantes y candentes del país' [the nation's most burning contemporary issues].[54] This more critical mode of literary expression had started to take coherent form during the 1940s with the publication of Revueltas's *El luto humano* (1943) and Agustín Yáñez's *Al filo del agua* (1947). Mirroring the psychoanalytic dimension of Ramos's study, these writers utilised interior monologue and multiple perspectives to create psychologically complex portraits of provincial communities before and after the Revolution. These innovations laid the foundations for the works of a new generation of writers from the 1950s onwards, including Rulfo, Fuentes and Elena Garro, who rejected the realist style of earlier narrators of the Revolution such as Mariano Azuela and Martín Luis Guzmán and drew from the narrative strategies of Anglo-American modernists to communicate a more indirect critique of its failings.

For Fuentes, Rulfo's lyrical and deeply metaphorical novel marked a turning point in this cycle of literary works focusing on the Revolution, bringing to a decisive close the realist phase initiated by Azuela.[55] Fuentes situates his contribution within a broader shift in twentieth-century Spanish American letters towards a more interrogative mode: 'se inicia un tránsito del simplismo épico a la complejidad dialéctica, de la seguridad de las respuestas a la impugnación de las preguntas' [a transition begins from epic simplism to dialectical complexity, from the security of answers to the impugnation of questions].[56] In line with the more self-reflexive and critical stance towards questions of national identity adopted by contemporary thinkers, and particularly those of the Hiperión circle, Rulfo's anti-narrative literary aesthetic founded on fragmentation, ambiguity and ellipsis, encouraged readers to actively re-read and reconfigure Mexico's post-revolutionary national narrative.[57] For Monsiváis, this participatory aspect of Rulfo's challenging text marked the development of a truly democratic style of literary expression: 'al no consentir ninguna Interpretación Definitiva, obliga a la renovación democrática de las constancias de lectura' [in refusing to privilege any single Definitive Interpretation, it demands the democratic renewal of rereading].[58] By repeatedly insisting on this anti-didactic aspect of his work, Rulfo seemed to consciously rail against the totalising political statements that had characterised art of the previous decades and particularly the works of the muralists. Although the writer admitted his opposition to the PRI, he never aligned himself with any political party and professed his total ignorance of political matters.[59] In his typically evasive manner, Rulfo simultaneously hinted at and denied the existence of any political content in his work:

> No quise hacer una literatura social, no fue afán de denunciar, menos de testimoniar un hecho, simplemente la forma en que han caído o han quedado ciertos sitios después de la llamada 'Revolución Mexicana'. Debido a esto se me ha llamado a veces anti-revolucionario [...] a mí la Revolución Mexicana no me interesa, ni me interesa en sí si fue buena o fue mala. Como no viví esa Revolución, no conocí sus consecuencias, ni las conozco todavía.[60]
>
> [I did not want to write social literature, it was not out of a desire to denounce, or to bear witness to an event, but to simply portray the way certain places have fallen or remained after the so called 'Mexican Revolution'. As a result, I have sometimes been called anti-revolutionary... The Mexican Revolution does not interest me, I am not interested in whether it was good or bad. As I didn't experience that Revolution, I never knew its consequences, I still don't.]

Despite Rulfo's professed lack of interest in the Revolution's outcomes, the surreal dreamscapes depicted in his texts are unmistakably rooted in a bleak post-revolutionary environment. Writing in the 1960s, John Brushwood claimed that it was impossible 'to understand recent Mexican fiction without knowing that the country had passed through a social revolution that did not create utopia'.[61] By presenting a cast of debilitated, spectral and grotesque *campesinos*, Rulfo's literature echoes the revisionist assessments of Cosío Villegas and others by articulating the collapse of revolutionary utopianism in primarily bodily terms. The corporeal language of societal crisis developed in these works from the mid-1950s reverberates in the literature of Elena Garro and Rosario Castellanos and most powerfully in the eponymous protagonist of Carlos Fuentes's novel *La muerte de Artemio Cruz* (1962), whose degenerating body metonymically stands in for the failed revolutionary nation.

The disturbing portrait of rural life presented in Rulfo's literature drew inspiration from his own traumatic childhood, which unfolded against the violent backdrop of the Cristero War (1926–1929). Rulfo was born into a family of wealthy landowners in 1917 in southern Jalisco, although the precise location of his birth remains somewhat nebulous. Following the death of his father in 1923, he was sent to an orphanage in Guadalajara along with his brother Severiano, where he would learn of the death of his mother four years later. He moved to Mexico City in 1935 and secured a post in the Departamento de Migración thanks to a recommendation from none other than future president Manuel Ávila Camacho. Working alongside

Manuel Gamio, Rulfo was responsible for the registration of immigrants and foreigners.[62]

This undemanding bureaucratic post enabled Rulfo to devote his time to writing and to immerse himself in the intellectual and artistic milieu of the capital. Although his lack of qualifications prevented him from enrolling at university, Rulfo satisfied his intellectual curiosity by attending lectures at the Facultad de Filosofía y Letras in the UNAM. Here he would have developed a keen understanding of contemporary philosophical and artistic developments listening to intellectuals such as Antonio Caso, Alfonso Caso, Carlos González Peña, the existential philosopher Adolfo Menéndez Samará, the Hiperión thinker Eduardo García Máynez and the art historian Justino Fernández, one of Mexico's most authoritative contemporary commentators on the muralist movement.[63] In the literary gatherings held in the café of the Mascarones building, Rulfo became acquainted with Paz and the poets Alí Chumacero and Jorge González Durán. It was during these meetings that Rulfo also came into contact with the works of Contemporáneos, a group of artists and thinkers who posed the most significant opposition to the cultural nationalism of the muralists during the 1930s.[64]

After a period working as an immigration agent in Guadalajara from 1941 to 1945, Rulfo returned to Mexico City, where he found employment with the tyre manufacturers Goodrich Euzkadi and married Clara Aparicio, with whom he had four children. While traversing the country as an itinerant salesman for Goodrich, Rulfo honed his camera skills and began publishing his first photographs.[65] The writer's literary career was transformed by the receipt of two grants from the Centro Mexicano de Escritores (CME), founded in 1951 by Margaret Shedd with support from the Rockefeller Foundation which enabled him to publish *El Llano en llamas* and *Pedro Páramo* and brought him into contact with literary luminaries such as Juan José Arreola and Castellanos, as well as the Hiperión philosopher Jorge Portilla.[66] Rulfo's stories and reviews of his works subsequently appeared alongside contributions from these writers and thinkers and others such as Uranga, Zea, Cosío Villegas and Paz in *La revista de literatura mexicana* and *La gaceta del fondo de cultura económica*.

While his two principal works initially received a mixed reception, they soon cemented his status within Mexico's literary firmament. Rulfo subsequently entered an extended period of literary silence. Although he continually alluded to two works in progress during the 1960s to appease journalists, a novel entitled *La cordillera* and a short story collection called *Días sin Floresta,* neither were published.[67] Rulfo survived a period of financial hardship following the publication of *Pedro Páramo* thanks to assistance from the Colegio de México from 1956 to 1958 and a series of short-term posts at other government institutions such as the Comisión del Papaloapan in Veracruz (c. 1955–1957), the library of the Sociedad Mexicana de Geografía y Estadística (c. 1958–1959) and the state-sponsored television station Televicentro in Guadalajara (c. 1960–1962). During the 1960s, Rulfo explored an alternative creative outlet in cinema, but ultimately devoted himself to anthropology. The writer joined the publications department of the Instituto Nacional Indigenista (INI) in 1962 and remained there until his death in 1986.

Reading Rivera and Rulfo Together

Rivera's and Rulfo's professional biographies reflect the complex and often contradictory links that developed between thinkers and the post-revolutionary state during this historical period. Like many of Mexico's most notable societal commentators in the twentieth century, both men developed their artistic interpretations of the Revolution's legacy while working within the folds of the post-revolutionary government. While Rivera publicly aligned himself with the government towards the beginning and end of his career, Rulfo occupied a more marginal position within the state apparatus, assuming a series of minor bureaucratic posts to sustain his family and literary ambitions. Rulfo's unlikely employment history reflects Nicola Miller's assertion that:

> Spanish American intellectuals remained bound up with the interventionist state even when they defined themselves in opposition to it — not only because they were often dependent upon it for employment, but also because it offered the only route to the realization of their visions.[68]

Rulfo was by no means an exception in this regard. While mid-century writers increasingly questioned the achievements of the institutionalised Revolution either through their prose or contributions to public debate, many remained reliant on state support. The works of Rulfo, Fuentes and Castellanos were published in the Letras Mexicanas series launched by the state-funded publishing house Fondo de Cultura Económica in 1952 and institutional recognition played an important role in consolidating their canonical status. Rulfo and several other writers also went on to accept positions in government institutions. Paz, who advocated a critical function on the part of the intellectual, held a string of diplomatic posts, while Yáñez worked as a speech writer for López Mateos and Fuentes briefly served as ambassador to France under Luis Echeverría (1970–1976).

Aside from demonstrating the professional links that continued to bind artists to the state, these collaborations underline the extent to which artistic, intellectual and political activity were fundamentally intertwined after the Revolution. For Fuentes, this politicisation of the role of the artist was an inevitable result of the lack of a functioning civil society: 'En un país sin información oportuna o verdadera, la cultura llena el vacío. Una línea de Octavio Paz dice más que todos los ramplones discursos del PRI' [In a country deprived of timely or reliable information, culture fills the gap. A line by Octavio Paz says more than all of the PRI's vulgar speeches].[69] The sheer number of post-revolutionary artists and writers who contributed to debates on national issues highlights the need for a sufficiently broad definition of the intellectual in this historical context as 'almost anyone who writes, paints, acts, teaches and speaks out', to borrow Jorge Castañeda's formulation.[70] The wide-ranging output of writers such as Reyes, Castellanos, Paz and others attests to the particularly strong bond between intellectual and artistic activity in Mexico during these decades. In evaluating Rivera's and Rulfo's specific contributions in this regard, Jeffrey Goldfarb's definition of intellectuals as 'those who use their expertise, their access to special knowledge, and their capacity to manipulate symbols, for broader purposes' is perhaps the most useful for my purposes.[71]

Over the course of their careers, both artists cultivated a profound understanding of Mexican culture and history that would shape their artistic production. An inexhaustible public speaker and prolific essayist, Rivera established himself as an outspoken commentator on Mexican art, politics and architecture in the public sphere from the 1920s to the 1940s, earning him the title of 'el filósofo del pincel' [the philosopher of the paintbrush].[72] Although Rulfo's links to contemporary intellectual activity are less immediately obvious, he was, according to Carlos Blanco Aguinaga, one of the best-read men in Mexico and amassed a substantial body of writings on topics as diverse as painting, photography, history, architecture and anthropology.[73] In addition to the cultural expertise they developed through personal research, Rivera and Rulfo also came into direct contact with some of the most prominent artists and thinkers of their times. Throughout this book, I demonstrate how this 'special knowledge' informs their aesthetic visions. In focusing on the specifically corporeal nature of the 'symbols' employed by both artists to articulate their respective interpretations of the Revolution and its legacy, I explore how a central trope of revolutionary identity was forged and dismantled during these critical decades.

In examining Rivera and Rulfo as landmark figures of twentieth-century Mexican culture, it is essential to acknowledge the role of gender in consolidating their canonical status and enduring legacies. While the muralists rose to prominence against the backdrop of a cultural reconstruction project that explicitly linked revolutionary progress with male vigour and virility, Emily Hind has convincingly demonstrated how male writers such as Rulfo also benefitted from a cultural system that disproportionately valued the intellectual contributions of men.[74] Working along similar lines, Sarah Bowskill revealed how the post-revolutionary literary canon was shaped by a predominantly male elite that possessed the authority to consecrate certain texts and discard others.[75] The fact that Rivera and Rulfo continue to be revered as cultural icons must thus be considered reflective not only of the significance of their contributions, but also of the discriminatory mechanisms and power structures that shaped canon formation during these decades.

Body Politics

The use of organicist metaphors to conceptualise social organisation and the distribution of power has deep historical roots in western philosophical thought. First developed in Plato's *Republic* (381 BC) and restated by Aristotle in his *Politics* (350 BC), the analogy of the body politic again provided the structural basis for the political theories proposed by medieval Catholic theologians such as Saint Augustine and Thomas Aquinas, who conceived of society as a unified body of hierarchically and interdependently arranged social organs. The body politic trope emerges again in modern discourses on state formation such as Hobbes's discussion of the formation of the commonwealth in *Leviathan* (1651) and in Herbert Spencer's Lamarckian conception of society as an evolving living organism during the mid-to-late nineteenth century.

During the latter half of the twentieth century, theorists working with the field of cultural studies began to reassess the political status of the body, focusing not on its function as a metaphorical expression of socio-political structures, but rather on its position within various societal power networks. Responses to this question have been so numerous and varied in their theoretical and disciplinary approaches that Terry Eagleton feared in the early 1990s that there would soon be 'more bodies in contemporary criticism than on the fields of Waterloo'.[76] This 'corporeal turn' was inaugurated in the 1970s with Michel Foucault's influential account of the disciplinary mechanisms regulating individual bodies ('anatomo-politics of the human body') and entire population-species ('biopolitics'). Foucault's projection of the body as an 'inscribed surface of events' paved the way for feminist inquiries into the discursive production of gender by Hélène Cixous and Luce Irigaray and, later, Judith Butler. The postmodernist interpretation of the body as a social construct proposed by Foucault and Butler was countered by theorists looking to redirect attention to the sensuous 'lived' body such as Maurice Merleau-Ponty and Pierre Bourdieu. The field of body studies has provided particularly fertile ground for revaluations of female corporeality by thinkers such as Julia Kristeva and Elizabeth Grosz, who followed the work of Mary Douglas in exploring the dangers located on the margins and boundaries of the body. Challenging the docility of the Foucauldian subject, Grosz insisted upon the unfixity of the body and its transformative capacity: 'As a political object, the body is not inert or fixed [...] if it is a social object, the body can be redefined, its forms and functions can be contested and its place in culture reevaluated or transformed'.[77]

Despite the significant divergences between these theoretical perspectives, they share a common concern with the inherently political nature of the body. *Post-Revolutionary Body Politics* takes as its starting point the assumption that artistic representations of the body, like their material counterparts, are not neutral but are inevitably inscribed within certain power dynamics. Following Grosz's interpretation of the body as a locus for the construction and contestation of meaning, the four chapters of the book examine Rivera's and Rulfo's allegorical uses of the body within the specific historical context of their production to demonstrate how they function as sites for the inscription and reconfiguration of certain narratives of revolutionary nationhood.

My discussion is guided by the following questions: What aesthetic and symbolic languages are used to compose these bodies? What conditions contributed to their formation? What can they tell us, more broadly, about how the concepts of revolution and nation were interpreted and conceptualised in political, intellectual and cultural terms during these periods? To answer these questions, I interpret the concept of the 'body' both literally (through close readings of visual and literary composition) and figuratively (as it is employed as a metaphor for the Mexican body politic). My analysis of these artworks focuses primarily on the formal aspects of Rivera's and Rulfo's corporeal imagery, but also spotlights the particular demands made on the body of the viewer or reader by their chosen media. Situating these works within the wider ambit of cultural debates on post-revolutionary identity, I examine how their images relate to the corporeal metaphors that were employed by contemporary intellectuals and politicians to conceptualise revolutionary national identity, as well as the physiological and behavioural ideals that were imposed on real Mexican bodies through the state's public health campaigns. By establishing connections between these different bodies, the book will shed light not only on the political dimensions of both artists' visual and textual corporeal visions but also on the broader 'body politics' of the post-revolution period, that is, the centrality of bodies, both imagined and real, to post-revolutionary formulations of nationhood.

In my readings, I explore how the body functions as a key site for the articulation of ideological and aesthetic concerns, either by upholding or destabilising certain interpretations of national identity or raising questions about the very possibility of narrativising the Revolution and its legacy. On this second point, I am particularly interested in how the chosen media of both artists enable them to present the body in varying degrees of legibility. Rivera's use of the body as a symbolic carrier for national themes must be understood in light of the didactic objectives of the muralist movement. If, as Benedict Anderson writes, the concepts of 'nation, nationality, nationalism [...] have proved notoriously difficult to define', the universal accessibility of the body as a metaphor of identity provides perhaps the most powerful means of visualising our 'imagined communities'.[78] As we accept the body as 'an irreducible sign of the natural, the given, the unquestionable', corporeal images possess a unique capacity to naturalise particular socio-political structures or sets of relations.[79] The image of the body provided Rivera with an effective and efficient means of communicating a set of new societal values to a theoretically broad social audience and presenting these concepts as inherent and self-evident. By fashioning a coherent visual idiom that incorporated elements of neo-classicism, post-impressionism and social realism, and by integrating both real historical bodies and longstanding nationalist bodily tropes into his works, the muralist consistently maximised the legibility of the body as a symbolic carrier. With this in mind, I explore how the Riveran body, to borrow Foucault's phrasing, can be read as 'an inscribed surface of events' in relation to contemporary nation-building discourses. By fully contextualising his works within the complex historical context of their production, I demonstrate how Rivera's formal preoccupation with corporeal fixity, unity and discipline speaks to wider political and intellectual anxieties regarding the future of the post-revolutionary nation during the 1920s and 1930s. Alongside the optimistic rhetoric of the Ateneístas and leftist thinkers such as Lombardo Toledano, Rivera's bodily imagery, which frequently verged on a kind of corporeal utopianism, was fundamentally aspirational, articulating the possibilities of a revolutionary process that had not yet come to fruition in the 1920s and 1930s. Furthermore, despite projecting the body as a locus for collective revolutionary transformation, Rivera's insistence on the principles of unity, order and progress in his composition of individual and collective bodies reveals a paradoxical line of continuity with Porfirian interpretations of the social organism.

Rivera's reliance on corporeal images to stabilise certain interpretations of revolutionary nationhood in the precarious years that followed the armed conflict supports Elaine Scarry's claim that in moments of societal crisis the 'sheer material factualness' of the human body is harnessed to imbue even the most fragile cultural constructs with an aura of 'realness' and 'certainty'.[80] As Sue Best warns, however, it is precisely when the body is invoked as a means of stabilising a particular ideological construction that it is most vulnerable to reformulations. Following from Douglas's claim that that boundaries of the body 'can represent any boundaries which are threatened or precarious', she asserts that:

> The use of the body-model indicates the demand or desire for a clear limit or boundary — it seems to bestow, or at least to promise, precisely this — and yet it is when the body is invoked that the boundary is probably most uncertain.[81]

As literature rose to a position of cultural prominence in Mexico towards the middle of the century, writers began to the expose the fragility of the corporeal models that had been formulated within the visual sphere. Focusing on descriptions of corporeal fragmentation, spectrality, overflow and mutation, I explore how Rulfo's literary works dramatise the gradual decomposition or unfixing of a resurgent national body that was constructed by nation-building intellectuals and artists such as Rivera during the early post-revolution period. If, as Rivera's biographer Bertram Wolfe claimed, the muralist 'painted what the Revolution should be, what it should have become', Rulfo's corporeal imagery unrelentingly confronts us with the realities of its outcomes from a disenchanted mid-century viewpoint.[82] By situating his works within the revisionist decades of the 1950s and 60s, I consider how the instability and indeterminacy of the Rulfian body addresses this moment of societal crisis and opens up the possibility of reconfiguring and reimagining the national image. In addition to highlighting how Rulfo's literary works subtly redraw the boundaries of the body through descriptions of corporeal decomposition and overflow, my analysis also breaks new ground by examining how the underexplored elusive human subjects of his photographs, who resist immediate visualisation, play an equally subversive role in destabilising narratives of post-revolutionary unity and progress. Like his literary texts, these works call into question the body's stability as a site of meaning by problematising its legibility. I argue that, in keeping with the mid-century spirit of scepticism, Rulfo's corpus signals a shift towards a more challenging and interrogative body aesthetic that opens up questions regarding national identity rather than providing answers.

In tracing these shifts in bodily representation, my intention is not to frame Rivera as a state-controlled propagandist or Rulfo as some kind of anti-establishment radical. While I analyse specific visual and textual images as a means of illuminating both artists' particular views on the Revolution and its legacy, my discussion also draws out contradictions and inconsistencies that characterised the political agendas and aesthetic visions of both men. Furthermore, rather than examining their corpora in a vacuum, I embed these readings within wider debates on national identity to explore how their works were shaped by different artistic, political and intellectual currents and how they both responded and contributed to specific imagined constructions of the nation during these transformative decades.

Although, as W. J. T. Mitchell argues 'there are no "purely" visual or verbal arts', it is necessary to consider how the broad differences between these forms contribute to Rivera's and Rulfo's distinct corporeal imaginaries.[83] Echoing the spatial-temporal distinction between painting and poetry proposed by Lessing, Arnheim concludes that 'a pictorial image presents itself whole, in simultaneity. A successful literary image grows through what one might call accretion by amendment'.[84] On the level of corporeal representation, these general distinctions suggest why the static and total nature of the visual image might prove most effective in articulating absolutist depictions of the body politic and why, as Hillman and Maude assert, the mutable and fluctuating nature of literary representation has made it the preferred medium for pre-modern and modern representations of its collapse into dysfunction. It is this 'unbinding of all kinds of fixity', they argue, that establishes the literary body as 'a locus of socio-political resistance'.[85] By attending to the specific formal dimensions of Rivera's and Rulfo's works, my readings explore not just why but also *how* this imagined national body transitions in general terms from a state of stability and coherence to one of breakdown and flux within the artistic sphere from the 1920s to the 1960s.

While studies by Elsa Muñiz and Beatriz Urías Horcasitas, have highlighted the centrality of the body to the post-revolutionary project of nation-formation, critics have only recently turned their attention to the bodies crowding Mexico's contemporary artistic and literary landscapes.[86] The most significant incursion in this field is Rebecca Janzen's *The National Body in Mexican Literature: Collective Challenges to Biopolitical Control*, which examines literary representations of bodies that challenge state-promoted models of nationhood in twentieth-century Mexico, with one chapter to devoted to Rulfo's novel.[87] As Janzen's discussion is restricted to a purely literary analysis of the period spanning from 1940 to 1980, the chronologically broad framework of *Post-Revolutionary Body Politics* provides a substantially expanded analysis of how literary and visual practitioners articulated political concerns through the body and, crucially, how these corporeal narratives evolved from the 1920s to the 1960s. David S. Dalton's more recent *Mestizo Modernity: Race, Technology, and the Body in Postrevolutionary Mexico* explores the relationship between race formation and technology after the Revolution by examining representations of the hybridised indigenous body in murals, film and literature from the 1920s to the 1970s.[88] My book further extends both the interdisciplinary reach and thematic focus of Dalton's research by examining the use of corporeal metaphors and images across diverse spheres of artistic production including muralism, illustration, architecture, literature, photography and cinema and by analysing these representations from race, gender and class perspectives.

In the field of Rulfian scholarship, the most significant contribution of recent years is Amit Thakkar's *The Fiction of Juan Rulfo: Irony, Revolution and Postcolonialism*, which utilises postcolonial theory to examine how Rulfo's irony operates in relation to the rhetoric of the post-revolutionary state.[89] While I adopt a similarly historicist approach, I diverge from Thakkar by contending that Rulfo communicates this critique primarily through his representation of the body. I further build on Thakkar's intervention by offering a more comprehensive historical account of the cultural context that helped shape Rulfo's aesthetic and political vision and by examining how this manifests itself across his entire oeuvre. While the contributors to Nuala Finnegan's and Dylan Brennan's *Rethinking Juan Rulfo's Creative World: Prose, Photography, Film* widened the lens of Rulfian studies by considering his experimentation with visual media, analyses of the content and form of his photographic and cinematic works remain thin on the ground.[90] *Post-Revolutionary Body Politics* seeks to redress this oversight by reading Rulfo's literature alongside his overlooked photographic and cinematic material and establishing intermedial connections between these works. Contrary to previous approaches, I also analyse Rulfo's photographs within the professional context of their production, exploring how his works for the government funded Comisión del Papaloapan and the state-owned railway company Ferrocarriles Nacionales de México subtly contradict the ideals of national unity and progress they were intended to project.

Book-length studies and edited collections analysing Rivera's muralism have tended to focus on his U.S.-based projects or to examine his works within a broader evaluation of Mexican muralism.[91] As a corrective to these approaches, I provide detailed and comprehensively contextualised readings of both canonical and overlooked murals and illustrations produced by Rivera in Mexico and the U.S. during the 1920s and 30s and offer the first comprehensive comparative analysis of his works alongside literary texts and other visual media. In this way, the book looks to expand the disciplinary scope of studies examining the cultural negotiation of post-revolutionary identity during these decades, which have tended to approach the question from art-historical or literary perspectives. Rick López and Mary K. Coffey expertly evaluate the contribution of visual culture to the state's nation-building project, focusing respectively on the rejuvenation of vernacular aesthetics and the intersections between muralism and didactic museology.[92] More recently, Stephanie J. Smith and John Lear have analysed the links between visual art and revolutionary politics during the first half of the twentieth century.[93] In the literary domain, Ignacio Sánchez Prado's *Naciones intelectuales* has examined 'la producción de estrategias intelectuales contrahegemónicas' [the production of counterhegemonic intellectual strategies] in Mexican literature from 1917 to 1959, laying the foundations for subsequent literary studies such as Janzen's.[94] Although, like Thakkar, Sánchez Prado states that literature provided 'espacios alternativos de imaginación de la nación' [alternative spaces for imagining the nation] to those created by visual media such as muralism and cinema, he does not discuss these earlier aesthetic models in depth.[95]

Through the use of a multimedia framework, this book works against a critical tendency to compartmentalise post-revolutionary literary and visual artists within separate historical periods and disciplinary silos, providing a wide-ranging and much needed cartography of post-revolutionary artistic activity.[96] By applying an integrated intermedial approach that brings together 'visual and verbal structures in a single, sustained thought', my project draws inspiration from Lois Parkinson Zamora's *The Inordinate Eye* (2006), which traces the development of baroque aesthetics in Latin America through an integrated analysis of painting, sculpture, architecture, and literature from the pre-Conquest period to the present.[97] For

Zamora, this interartistic comparative methodology reflects the porosity of the boundaries separating visual and verbal artistic creativity and criticism in Latin America, a historical 'mobility of media' that she traces back to the pictographic and ideographic systems of the Maya. This methodological strategy is particularly crucial for examining the post-revolutionary cultural environment in Mexico, which saw multiple collaborations between visual and literary practitioners (with the most notable early examples being the Estridentistas and the Contemporáneos) and interventions by numerous writer-artists, such as the poet and muralist Aurora Reyes and the sculptor, painter, poet, and songwriter Isabel Villaseñor. Throughout this period, artists and thinkers also consistently contributed to debates outside their discipline and painting, photography and literature were frequently compared within broader discussions of national culture. Rivera and Rulfo are prime examples of this interartistic fluidity. Hailed as the 'poeta épico' [epic poet] of the muralist movement, Rivera stated that his visual narratives at the SEP had been inspired by Azuela's prose and frequently incorporated textual elements into his murals such as lyrics and political banners to clarify their narrative content.[98] For his part, Rulfo, a photographer and cineaste who wrote knowledgeably about the work of Ruptura artists such as Coronel and Alberto Gironella, infused his literature with such a rich visual texture that early reviewers of the novel described him as a painter.[99] In the post-revolutionary context, the application of an interdisciplinary approach also spotlights the manner in which visual and literary media performed broadly different political functions from the 1920s to the 1960s, with changing social conditions, most significantly literacy and mounting political discontent, enabling literature to supersede public muralism as the dominant mode of socially engaged art within the post-revolutionary cultural landscape.

By assessing the creative contributions of Rulfo as a writer, photographer and cineaste and Rivera as painter, architect and theorist of art, I thus aim to furnish a textured and multifaceted account of their aesthetic visions and of post-revolutionary cultural production more broadly. By comparatively examining this artistic activity within a chronologically broad framework, *Post-Revolutionary Body Politics* provides an expansive diachronic examination of Mexico's evolving post-revolutionary cultural and intellectual landscapes from the 1920s to the 1960s. In this way, the book contributes to the field of post-revolutionary cultural history by bridging the gap between two periods that are often studied in isolation: the decades of national reconstruction immediately following the conflict and the lesser-studied modernising period of the 'Mexican Miracle' spanning from the 1940s to the 1970s. Beyond the domain of Mexican and Hispanic Studies, this research will be of interest to researchers examining the mobilisation and politico-symbolic implications of bodily images and metaphors in other historical contexts and to those pursuing interdisciplinary inquiries into representations of national identity that bring diverse media into dialogue.

The book is divided thematically into four chapters, each of which are composed of two subsections. In each chapter, I offer close readings of specific visual and literary texts, setting my analysis against a detailed historical backdrop drawn from print media, correspondence and previously unexamined archival materials.

By examining these representations through a range of theoretical lenses, *Post-Revolutionary Body Politics* traverses a theoretical history of the body, from Foucault's discussion of the disciplinary strategies introduced in the eighteenth and nineteenth centuries to the alternative corporealities imagined by Deleuze and Guattari in response to twentieth-century capitalism. Across the four chapters, I follow a broad evolution in representations of the body, as it transitions from a state of stability, legibility and cohesion in Rivera's murals and illustrations of the 1920s and 1930s to one of precariousness, ambiguity and flux in Rulfo's literary, cinematic and photographic works post-1950. By situating this process of corporeal transformation within the specific historical context of these decades, I demonstrate how the body can be viewed as a significant symbolic field for understanding and exploring post-revolutionary intellectual, cultural and political change.

Chapter 1 centres on the theme of collective memory and the narratives of political and ethnic unity that were constructed in the decades following the conflict's military phase. The first section examines how the literal and figurative historical bodies presented in Rivera's and Rulfo's works reflect evolving historiographical perspectives on the Revolution from the 1920s to the 1950s by endorsing or problematising the notion of a unified and intelligible historical narrative. The second section turns to the myths of ethnic solidarity that were promoted through the *indigenista* movement. I examine how Rivera's murals and Rulfo's photographs propose alternative ways of visualising the indigenous body that shed light on broader shifts in intellectual debates on indigenous and *mestizo* identity during this period.

Chapters 2 and 3 draw from Foucault's theorisation of biopolitics to consider how the Porfirian ideals of 'Order and Progress' were paradoxically projected onto real and imaginary Mexican bodies after 1920. Chapter 2 traces the rise and fall of the state's citizen-formation project by examining the interplay between architectural and anatomical forms in Rivera's and Rulfo's works. I read these images in the specific context of the post-revolutionary state's efforts to create a rational and disciplined populace through the implementation of social engineering strategies and a disciplinary functionalist mode of public architecture. The first section examines how Rivera articulates the post-revolutionary 'return to order' by configuring a rational architectonic human body and by drawing on functionalist architectural concepts to establish a link between spatial and bodily discipline in his muralism. The second part goes on to explore how these ideals of bodily and spatial stability and order are unsettled in Rulfo's novel and mid-century photographs of Mexico City, which respectively foreground ruinous bodies and an indeterminate mobile populace that slips between the crevices of the urban landscape.

Chapter 3 examines both artists' work in light of the gendered framework of (re)productive citizenship that was promoted by post-revolutionary politicians and intellectuals to propel national development. In the first section, I examine how Rivera's murals and Rulfo's short stories present alternative perspectives on the possibilities and outcomes of industrial development by conceptualising the technologised male body in terms of corporeal enhancement or perceptual crisis. The latter part of the chapter attends to the reproductive models of female citizenship that were promoted by the state to ensure the order and future prosperity of the nation. I consider how the negotiation of these restrictive concepts of womanhood during the period spanning from the 1920s to the mid-1950s is reflected in the transition from fixed to fluid female corporeal landscapes in Rivera's and Rulfo's works.

Turning to the representation of collective bodies, Chapter 4 investigates how the peasant mass was conceptualised in post-revolutionary intellectual and political discourses of rural reform and national unity. Setting close readings against the backdrop of the sacralisation of revolutionary politics that occurred after 1920, the first section explores how both artists utilise biblical metaphors to convey the peasantry's receptiveness or resistance to the state's secular education campaigns of the 1920s and 1930s. Moving on to a comparative discussion of Rivera's mural *El reparto de tierras* (1924) and *La fórmula secreta* (1965), the experimental short film on which Rulfo collaborated with the director Rubén Gámez, I consider how these works draw from Renaissance and baroque aesthetics respectively to visualise the peasant mass as a political entity.

Notes to the Introduction

1. Juan Rulfo, quoted in Alberto Vital, *Noticias sobre Juan Rulfo, 1784–2003* (Mexico City: Editorial RM, 2004), p. 169
2. David Craven, *Diego Rivera: As Epic Modernist* (New York: G.K. Hall, 1997), p. 1. Among others, Ernesto González Bermejo observed that Rulfo possessed 'un cuerpo menudo, de apariencia frágil' [a thin and fragile-looking body]. Juan Rulfo, 'La literatura es una mentira que dice la verdad: Una conversación con Ernesto González Bermejo', in *Toda la obra*, ed. by Claude Fell (Paris: ALLCA XX, 1996), 462–69 (p. 462).
3. Pedro Henríquez Ureña, 'La revolución y la cultura en México', in *Ensayos*, ed. by José Luis Abellán and Ana María Barrenechea (Madrid: ALLCA XX: 2000), pp. 254–61 (p. 261); Samuel Ramos, 'Diego Rivera', in *Obras completas III: Estudios de estética*, ed. and intro. by Raúl Cardiel Reyes (Mexico City: UNAM, 1991), pp. 41–74 (p. 42).
4. Alí Chumacero, 'La primera novela de Juan Rulfo', *La Gaceta del Fondo de Cultura Económica*, 15 March 1955, p. 3; Emmanuel Carballo, 'Arreola y Rulfo, cuentistas', *Revista de la Universidad de México*, March 1954, p. 29.
5. In this sense, my research builds on Mauricio Tenorio-Trillo's study of Mexico's participation in the world fairs from 1889 to 1929, which also highlights continuities between the pre- and post-revolution periods. Mauricio Tenorio-Trillo, *Mexico at the World's Fairs: Crafting a Modern Nation* (Berkeley: University of California Press, 1996).
6. Meri L. Clark, 'The Emergence and Transformation of Positivism', in *A Companion to Latin American Philosophy*, ed. by Susana Nuccetelli and others (Oxford: Wiley-Blackwell, 2009), pp. 53–67 (p. 61).
7. Justo Sierra, 'Positivismo político', in *Obras completas*, vol. 1 (Mexico City: UNAM, 1977), pp. 238–39, (p. 238).
8. For a detailed discussion of these policies, see Claudia Agostini, *Monuments of Progress: Modernization and Public Health in Mexico City, 1876–1910* (Calgary: University of Calgary Press, 2003).
9. Fabiola Martínez Rodríguez, 'Representing the Nation: Art and Identity in Porfirian Mexico', *National Identities*, 15 (2013), 333–55 (p. 333).
10. Chris Jenks, 'The Centrality of the Eye in Western Culture: An Introduction', in *Visual Culture*, ed. by Chris Jenks (London: Routledge, 2002), pp.1–25 (p. 5–6)
11. Tenorio-Trillo, p.114.

12. Andrés Molina Enríquez, *Los grandes problemas nacionales* (Mexico City: Imprenta de A. Carranza e Hijos, 1909), p. 221.
13. Octavio Paz, *El laberinto de la soledad* (Mexico City: Fondo de Cultura Económica, 1959), p. 134.
14. Henríquez Ureña, p. 255.
15. Alfonso Reyes, 'Literatura Mexicana', in *Obras completas I: Cuestiones estéticas, Capítulos de literatura mexicana* (Mexico City: Letras Mexicanas: Fondo de Cultura Económica, 1996), p. 467.
16. Henríquez Ureña, p. 258.
17. In tracing these lines of intellectual continuity, it is worth noting that Sierra himself sponsored and attended the first cycle of lectures held by the Ateneo in 1910. Alfredo A. Roggiano, *Pedro Henríquez Ureña en México* (Mexico City: Facultad de Filosofía y Letras, UNAM, 1989), p. 113.
18. Alan Knight, 'Popular Culture and the Revolutionary State in Mexico, 1910–1940', *The Hispanic American Historical Review*, 74 (1994), 393–444 (p. 431).
19. Alfonso Reyes, 'Pasado inmediato', in *Pasado Inmediato y otros ensayos* (Mexico City: El Colegio de México, Fondo de Cultura Económica, 1914), pp. 3–64 (p. 6); José Manuel Puig Casauranc, *Páginas viejas con ideas actuales* (Mexico City: Talleres Gráficos de la Nación Editorial, 1925), p. 75.
20. Moisés Sáenz, *México íntegro* (Lima: Imprenta Torres Aguirre, 1929), p. 263.
21. Lázaro Cárdenas, 'Mensaje a la nación del Presidente de la República', in *Palabras y documentos públicos de Lázaro Cárdenas: 1928–1970*, ed. by Javier Romero (Mexico City: Siglo Veintiuno Editores, 1978), p. 226; Vicente Lombardo Toledano, 'La Revolución Mexicana de ayer y la de hoy', *Futuro*, 3 (December 1936), p. 1.
22. José Vasconcelos, 'Don Gabino Barreda y las ideas contemporáneas', in *Conferencias del ateneo de la juventud*, ed. by Juan Hernández Luna (Mexico City: UNAM, 1984), pp. 97–113 (p. 111).
23. 'En el umbral', *Savia Moderna: Revista mensual de arte*, 1 March 1906, p. 1.
24. Octavio Paz, 'Los muralistas a primera vista', in *Obras completas de Octavio Paz: Los privilegios de la vista*, vol. 4 (Barcelona: Galaxia Gutenberg, 2001), pp. 709–15 (p. 709).
25. Rick A. López, *Crafting Mexico: Intellectuals, Artisans, and the State After the Revolution* (Durham, N.C: Duke University Press, 2010), p. 20.
26. Mary K. Coffey, 'Mural Art and Popular Reception: The Public Institution and Cultural Politics in Post-Revolutionary Mexico', in *La imagen política: XXV Coloquio Internacional de Historia del Arte*, ed. by Cuahtémoc Medina (Mexico City: UNAM, 2006), pp. 362–72 (p. 372).
27. Siqueiros recalled: 'No había nadie que nos dijera "Haz esto y ahora esto otro"' [There was no one telling us "do this and now do that"]. David Alfaro Siqueiros, quoted in Desmond Rochfort, *Pintura mural mexicana: Orozco, Rivera, Siqueiros* (Mexico City: Limusa, Grupo Noriega Editores, 1993), p. 21.
28. Mary Kay Vaughan, *The State, Education and Social Class in Mexico* (De Kalb: Northern Illinois University Press, 1982), p. 265.
29. Diego Rivera, 'Volver a nacer', in *Palabras ilustres, 1886–1921*, ed. by Roberto Pliego and others (Mexico City: Editorial RM, 2007), pp. 367–68 (p. 367).
30. Diego Rivera, *My Life, My Art: An Autobiography (with Gladys March)* (New York: Dover Publications, 1957) p. 50; Diego Rivera, *Confesiones*, ed. by Luis Suárez (Mexico: Editorial Grijalbo, 1975), p. 111.
31. Francisco Navarro, 'México y Diego Rivera', *El Nacional*, 2 March 1922, p.3.
32. Ramos, p. 58.
33. José Clemente Orozco, *Autobiografía* (Mexico City: Ediciones Era, 1999), p. 64.
34. Diego Rivera, 'Los primeros murales', in *Arte y política* ed. with notes by Raquel Tibol (Mexico City: Grijalbo, 1979), pp. 49–54 (p. 51).
35. Ramos, p. 50.
36. Diego Rivera, quoted in Alfredo Cardona Peña, *Conversaciones con Diego Rivera (el monstruo en su laberinto)* (Mexico City: Editorial Diana, 1980), p. 35
37. David Alfaro Siqueiros, 'Rivera's Counter-Revolutionary Road', *New Masses*, 29 May 1934, p. 17.
38. Manuel Espejel y Álvarez, *Miguel Alemán, biografía de su obra: Reportaje de la acción constructiva del régimen* (Mexico City: Taller Gráfico de la Nación, 1952), p. 51.

39. Robin Adèle Greeley, 'Muralism and the State in Post-Revolutionary Mexico', in *Mexican Muralism: A Critical History*, ed. by Leonard Folgarait and others (Berkeley: University of California Press, 2012), pp. 13–16 (p. 27).
40. Diego Rivera, 'La cuestión del arte en México', in *Palabras ilustres*, pp. 305–22.
41. Mario Vargas Llosa, 'La dictadura perfecta', in *Desafíos a la libertad* (Madrid: El País, 1994), pp. 171–76.
42. Daniel Cosío Villegas, 'La crisis de México', *Cuadernos Americanos*, March–April 1947, p. 30.
43. José Iturriaga, 'México y su crisis histórica', *Cuadernos Americanos*, May–June 1947, pp. 21–37; Jesús Silva Herzog, 'La revolución mexicana es ya un hecho histórico', *Cuadernos Americanos*, September–October 1949, p. 10.
44. José R. Colín, 'La Revolución Mexicana: R.I.P', *Excélsior*, 21 November 1950, p. 5.
45. Paz, *El laberinto*, p.142.
46. Samuel Ramos, *El perfil del hombre y la cultura en México* (Buenos Aires: Espasa-Calpe Argentina, 1951).
47. Emilio Uranga and Carlos Alberto Sánchez, *Emilio Uranga's Analysis of Mexican Being: A Translation and Critical Introduction* (London: Bloomsbury Academic, 2021), p. 75.
48. Anne T. Doremus, *Culture, Politics and National Identity in Mexican Literature and Film, 1929–1952* (New York: Peter Lang, 2001), p. 159.
49. Erica Segre, *Intersected Identities: Strategies of Visualisation in Nineteenth- and Twentieth-Century Mexican Culture* (Oxford: Berghahn Books, 2007), p. 158.
50. On the cultural 'rivalry' between visual and literary avant-gardes during the earlier decades of the 1920s and 30s, see Manuel Gutiérrez Silva, 'Aesthetic Rivalries in Avant-Garde Mexico: Art Writing and the Field of Cultural Production', in *Pierre Bourdieu in Hispanic Literature and Culture*, ed. by Ignacio M. Sánchez Prado (Basingstoke: Palgrave Macmillan, 2018), pp. 87–131.
51. José Luis Cuevas, 'La cortina del nopal', in *Ruptura 1952–1965: Catálogo de la exposición, Museo de Arte Alvar y Carmen T. de Carrillo Gil* (Mexico City: Museo Carrillo Gil, 1988), pp. 84–91 (p. 91); Paz, 'Los muralistas a primera vista'; José Revueltas, 'Escuela Mexicana de Pintura y novela de la revolución', in *Cuestionamientos e intenciones* (Mexico City: Ediciones Era, 1978), pp. 241–74.
52. Octavio Paz, 'En París, encuentro con Octavio Paz', interviewed by Claude Couffon, *La Gaceta del Fondo de Cultura Económica*, March 1959, p. 5.
53. Antonio Rodríguez, 'Literatura contra pintura: La pintura mexicana a la zaga de la literatura', *Claridades Literarias: Suplemento Cultural de los Jueves*, April 1959, p. 2.
54. Ibid., p. 2.
55. Carlos Fuentes, *La nueva novela hispanoamericana* (Mexico City: Editorial Joaquín Mortiz, 1969), p. 15.
56. Ibid., p.13.
57. Stephanie Merrim has previously linked Rulfo to the Hiperión on the basis of *Pedro Páramo*'s existential concerns. Stephanie Merrim, 'The Existential Juan Rulfo: *Pedro Páramo*, Mexicanness, and the Grupo Hiperión', *MLN*, 129 (2014), pp. 308–29.
58. Carlos Monsiváis, 'Sí, tampoco los muertos retoñan. Desgraciadamente', in *La ficción de la memoria: Juan Rulfo ante la crítica*, ed. by Federico Campbell (Mexico City: UNAM, 2003), pp. 187–202 (p. 187).
59. Juan Rulfo, 'Juan Rulfo examina su narrativa', in *Toda la obra*, pp. 451–62 (p. 459).
60. Juan Rulfo, quoted in Vital, *Noticias sobre Juan Rulfo*, p. 206.
61. John Brushwood, *Mexico in its Novel: A Nation's Search for Identity* (Austin: University of Texas Press, 1966), p. 16.
62. Fernando Benítez, 'Conversaciones con Juan Rulfo', in *La ficción de la memoria: Juan Rulfo ante la crítica*, ed. by Federico Campbell, pp. 541–50 (p. 544).
63. Roberto García Bonilla, *Un tiempo suspendido: Cronología de la vida y la obra de Juan Rulfo* (Mexico City: CONACULTA, 2008), p. 88.
64. Steven Boldy, *A Companion to Juan Rulfo* (Woodbridge: Tamesis, 2016), p. 13.
65. Ibid., p.17.
66. Eduardo Lizalde, *Nueva memoria del tigre: Poesía, 1949–2000* (Mexico City: Fondo de Cultura Económica, 2005), p. 20.
67. Rulfo's short novel *El gallo de oro* was finally published in 1980.

68. Nicola Miller, *In the Shadow of the State: Intellectuals and the Quest for National Identity in Twentieth-century Spanish America* (London: Verso, 1999), p. 6.
69. Carlos Fuentes, 'Aclarar los humos del pasado, volver el pasado presentable', interviewed by Margarita García Flores in *La cultura en México*, 27 August 1969, p. iii.
70. Jorge Castañeda, 'The Intellectual and the State in Latin America', *World Policy Journal*, 10 (1993), 89–95 (p. 89).
71. Jeffrey Goldfarb, *Civility and Subversion: The Intellectual in Democratic Society* (Cambridge: Cambridge University Press, 1998), p. 30.
72. José D. Frías, 'La obra genial del pintor Diego M. Rivera', *El Universal Ilustrado*, 19 February 1924, p. 18–19.
73. Carlos Blanco Aguinaga, 'Prólogo', in García Bonilla, pp. 13–17 (p. 16).
74. Emily Hind, *Dude Lit: Mexican Men Writing and Performing Competence, 1955–2012* (Tucson: The University of Arizona Press, 2019).
75. Sarah Bowskill, *Gender, Nation and the Formation of the Twentieth-Century Mexican Literary Canon* (New York: Routledge, 2017).
76. Terry Eagleton, 'Peter Brooks on Bodies', in *Figures of Dissent: Critical Essays on Fish, Spivak, Žižek and Others* (London: Verso, 2003), pp. 129–35 (p. 129).
77. Elizabeth Grosz, 'Notes Towards a Corporeal Feminism', *Australian Feminist Studies*, 5 (1987), 1–16 (p. 3).
78. Benedict Anderson, *Imagined Communities: Reflections on the Origin and Spread of Nationalism* (London: Verso, 2006), p. 3.
79. Annette Kuhn, 'The Body and Cinema: Some Problems for Feminism', in *Writing on the Body: Female Embodiment and Feminist Theory*, ed. by Katie Conboy and others (New York: Columbia University Press, 1997), pp. 195–207 (p. 199).
80. Elaine Scarry, *The Body in Pain: The Making and Unmaking of the World* (New York: Oxford University Press, 1985), p. 31.
81. Mary Douglas, *Purity and Danger: An Analysis of Concepts of Pollution and Taboo* (London: Routledge, 2018), p. 116; Sue Best, 'Sexualizing Space', in *Sexy Bodies: The Strange Carnalities of Feminism*, ed. by Elizabeth Grosz and Elspeth Probyn (London: Routledge, 1995), pp. 181–94 (p. 183).
82. Bertram Wolfe, *The Fabulous Life of Diego Rivera* (London: Barrie & Rockliff, 1968), p. 160.
83. W. J. T. Mitchell, *Picture Theory* (Chicago: The University of Chicago Press, 1994), p. 4–5.
84. Gotthold Ephraim Lessing, *Laocoon: An Essay Upon the Limits of Painting and Poetry*, trans. by Ellen Frothingham (Boston: Roberts Brothers, 1887); Rudolf Arnheim, *Visual Thinking* (London: Faber, 1970), p. 249.
85. David Hillman and Ulrika Maude, 'Introduction', in *The Cambridge Companion to The Body in Literature* (Cambridge: Cambridge University Press, 2015), pp. 1–9 (p. 5–6).
86. Elsa Muñiz, *Cuerpo, representación y poder: México en los albores de la reconstrucción nacional, 1920–1934* (Mexico City: Universidad Autónoma Metropolitana, 2002); Beatriz Urías Horcasitas, *Historias secretas del racismo en México (1920–1950)* (Mexico City: Tusquets, 2007).
87. Rebecca Janzen, *The National Body in Mexican Literature: Collective Challenges to Biopolitical Control* (New York: Palgrave Macmillan, 2015).
88. David S. Dalton, *Mestizo Modernity: Race, Technology, and the Body in Postrevolutionary Mexico* (Gainesville: University of Florida Press, 2018).
89. Amit Thakkar, *The Fiction of Juan Rulfo: Irony, Revolution and Postcolonialism* (Woodbridge: Tamesis, 2012).
90. Nuala Finnegan and Dylan Brennan, eds., *Rethinking Juan Rulfo's Creative World: Prose, Photography, Film* (London: Routledge, 2016).
91. Examples of the first approach include Anthony W. Lee, *Painting on the Left: Diego Rivera, Radical Politics, and San Francisco's Public Murals* (Berkeley: University of California Press, 1999); Leah Dickerman and others, *Diego Rivera: Murals for the Museum of Modern Art* (New York: Museum of Modern Art, 2011) and of the latter: Leonard Folgarait, *Mural Painting and Social Revolution in Mexico, 1920–1940: Art of the New Order* (Cambridge: Cambridge University Press, 1998); David Craven, *Art and Revolution in Latin America, 1910–1990* (New Haven: Yale University Press, 2002);

Anna Indych-López, *Muralism Without Walls: Rivera, Orozco, and Siqueiros in the United States, 1927–1940* (Pittsburgh: University of Pittsburgh Press, 2009); Alejandro Anreus and others, eds, *Mexican Muralism: A Critical History* (University Park: Pennsylvania State University Press, 2006); Roberto Cantú, ed., *Mexican Mural Art: Critical Essays on a Belligerent Aesthetic* (Newcastle: Cambridge Scholars Publishing, 2021).

92. López, *Crafting Mexico*; Mary K. Coffey, *How a Revolutionary Art Became Official Culture: Murals, Museums, and the Mexican State* (Durham: Duke University Press, 2012)

93. Stephanie J. Smith, *The Power and Politics of Art in Postrevolutionary Mexico* (Chapel Hill: The University of North Carolina Press, 2017); John Lear, *Picturing the Proletariat: Artists and Labor in Revolutionary Mexico, 1908–1940* (Austin: University of Texas Press, 2017)

94. Ignacio Sánchez Prado, *Naciones intelectuales: Las fundaciones de la modernidad literaria mexicana, 1917–1959* (Indiana: Purdue University Press, 2009), p. 5.

95. Ibid., 16.

96. In this way, my research seeks to further develop the interdisciplinary approach employed in book-length studies exploring specific post-revolutionary artistic and cultural developments by scholars such as Rubén Gallo, Tatiana Flores and Dalton. While these books draw examples from literature, painting, photography, film and architecture, they largely confine their discussion of distinct media to separate chapters and those by Gallo and Flores focus exclusively on the early post-revolutionary decades. Rubén Gallo, *Mexican Modernity: The Avant-garde and the Technological Revolution* (Cambridge, Mass: MIT, 2005); Tatiana Flores, *Mexico's Revolutionary Avant Gardes: From Estridentismo to ¡30–30!* (New Haven: Yale University Press, 2013)

97. Lois Parkinson Zamora, *The Inordinate Eye: New World Baroque and Latin American Fiction* (Chicago: The University of Chicago Press, 2006), p. xix.

98. Isidro Fabela, 'Diego Rivera: Ensayo en miniatura', in *Diego Rivera y los escritores: Antología tributaria,* pp. 73–75 (p. 74); Xavier Moyssén Echeverría, *La crítica de arte en México, 1896–1921* (Mexico City: UNAM, 1999), p. 267.

99. Rubén Salazar Mallén, 'El mensaje en la obra', *El Universal,* 21 June 1955, p. 3; Renato Molina Enríquez, 'Un libro de México: *Pedro Páramo*', *Boletín Bibliográfico de la Secretaría de la Hacienda,* 15 August 1955, p. 2; Juan Rulfo, interviewed by Elena Poniatowska, 'Charlando con Juan Rulfo: Voz de la tierra en llamas', *Excelsiór,* 15 January 1954, p. 7.

CHAPTER 1

Usable Pasts: Bodies of History in Post-Revolutionary Mexico

'Para tener confianza en el porvenir se necesita tener un culto del pasado'.
[To have faith in the future, one must have a cult of the past]
— 'La patria reconocida', *El Partido Liberal*, February 2, 1889.[1]

Mexico emerged from a chaotic revolutionary struggle to face an uncertain future. Already geographically, ethnically and culturally fragmented at the beginning of the twentieth century, its internal disunity was further exacerbated by the bitter factionalism of the armed conflict. To quote Alan Knight, in 1910 Mexico was:

> Less a nation than a geographical expression, a mosaic of regions and communities, introverted and jealous, ethnically and physically fragmented, and lacking common national sentiments; these sentiments came after the Revolution and were (notwithstanding some theories to the contrary) its offspring rather than its parents.'[2]

Confronted with the task of converting a debilitated and divided country into a stable unified nation in the tumultuous decades that followed the conflict, the post-revolutionary state returned to the nation-building strategies of the Porfirian regime which, as suggested by the above epigraph, sought to secure the nation's future through the construction of foundational historical narratives. While the victors of the Russian and French Revolutions declared a radical rupture with the past, post-revolutionary nation-builders established themselves as the custodians of a collective history rooted in the country's pre-Columbian origins and recent revolutionary experience.

Situating my analysis within the broader network of political and intellectual discourses that contributed to the construction of these imagined historical communities, this first chapter examines how the 'historical bodies' presented in Rivera's and Rulfo's works uphold or unsettle certain myths of ethnic and revolutionary unity and continuity that were propagated after 1920. Drawing from a multimedia archive encompassing muralism, literature and photography, I explore the multiple representative dimensions of the body in these contexts. By reading painted and photographic depictions of recognised political figures and indigenous subjects alongside metaphorical literary images of the body, I explore how both artists employ the human form both literally and figuratively, as a concrete 'body in history' and an allegorical 'body of history'. Through a comparative reading of representations of the indigenous body in selected murals by Rivera at the Palacio Nacional (1929–1935) and the SEP (1923–1928) and Rulfo's critically neglected mid-century photographs of the Mixe community in Oaxaca, the second part of the chapter traces the intellectual and aesthetic transformations of post-revolutionary *indigenismo*, a state-sponsored political and cultural initiative that sought to forge collective memory around the notion of a shared indigenous past. Before moving on to that analysis, the first section explores how the literal and figurative historical bodies depicted in Rivera's Palacio Nacional triptych and Rulfo's 1955 novel *Pedro Páramo* reflect evolving historiographical perspectives on the Revolution from the 1920s to the 1950s by endorsing or problematising the notion of a unified and intelligible historical narrative.

Part I: Historiographical Hauntings: Collective Memories of the Revolution

Playing on the common etymological root of the words corpse/corpus, Michel de Certeau establishes a link between the body and historical writing in *The Writing of History* (1975) by metaphorising historiography as an act of entombment. Reflecting on the totalising historiographical models developed in nineteenth-century France, he presents the historian as a mortician who summons the dead only to silence them by placing them in monumental 'scriptural tombs' (*tombeaux scriptuaires*).[3] De Certeau explains how historical writing memorialises these dead bodies 'on the condition that they remain forever *silent*' and separates 'what can be understood and what must be forgotten in order to obtain the representation of a present intelligibility'.[4] He attributes this emphasis on intelligibility, and the link it implies between knowledge and visuality, to the fact that modern historiography developed alongside the scientific study of anatomy. Just as modern medicine fixes the body as a 'legible picture' to be mastered through observation, historiography presents the past as a *corpus* of knowledge, 'a silent corpse', to be deciphered.[5] However, de Certeau also hints at the possibility of an alternative embodied past, an opaque 'other' that eludes the historian: 'a murmur [...] that seduces and menaces our knowledge'.[6] Introducing an ethical dimension to this spectral past, de Certeau describes how those previously silenced voices return to fill the gaps in official history: 'These voices whose disappearance every historian posits, which he replaces with his writing—"re-bite" (*re-mordent*) the space from which they were excluded'.[7]

De Certeau's metaphorical account of the suppressed voices of the past rising up from their tombs to haunt the present resonates with Rulfo's portrayal of collective memory of the Revolution as a chattering cemetery in the fictional post-revolutionary village of Comala. Written during an early revisionist phase in mid-century historiography of the Revolution, the polyvocal chaos of *Pedro Páramo*, in which conflicting and inconclusive recollections compete for dominance, troubles the master historical narratives that were discursively and artistically constructed in the immediate aftermath of the conflict.[8] During the intense nation-building period of the early 1930s, this vision of a singular and coherent revolutionary past achieved its most powerful aesthetic expression in Rivera's triptych *Epopeya del pueblo mexicano* at the Palacio Nacional, a panoramic national portrait that configures Mexico's deceased and living revolutionary leaders in the form of a single corporeal monument. The polyphonic disquiet of Rulfo's novel and the muralist's symbolic disinterment of the revolutionary dead reflects Blanco and Peeren's assertion, echoing de Certeau, that historiography functions as 'a form of haunting — of the past haunting the present as much as the present haunting the past'.[9]

Offering the first detailed analysis of their works against the backdrop of evolving post-revolutionary historiographical debates from the mid-1920s to the mid-1950s, the first section of this chapter traces the imagined construction and dissolution of the state's univocal revolutionary narrative, from Rivera's projection of the Revolution as a unitary pantheon of heroes in the Palacio Nacional to Rulfo's conceptualisation of collective memory as a cacophonous graveyard in *Pedro Páramo.* De Certeau's critique of nineteenth-century historiographical practices from a revisionist poststructuralist perspective in the latter half of the twentieth century is useful for mapping the transitions of the post-revolutionary historiographical landscape, which saw the totalising and distinctly Porfirian representational strategies of the 1920s and 1930s gradually give way to mid-century philosophical debates regarding the limitations of historical knowledge. As de Certeau structures his argument around the idea of the *tombeau*, a term referring both to the symbolic burial site constructed through historical writing and a commemorative work of art, his discussion is particularly appropriate for examining the intersections between historiography and artistic production. Employing this concept, I read the central panel of Rivera's triptych and Rulfo's novel as two distinct visual and textual *tombeaux* or historiographies of the Revolution that narrate the past through the body in different ways. I contend that changing perspectives on the nature of historical interpretation and representation from the 1920s to the 1950s can be perceived on the level of bodily legibility in the works of both artists. While Rivera's strategy of visually narrating the Revolution through a cast of emblematic historical bodies upholds the distinctly nineteenth-century notion of the past as an intelligible corpus of knowledge or a 'legible picture', to recall de Certeau, Rulfo's elusive spectres embody the zeitgeist of mid-century historiography by articulating contemporary anxieties regarding the limitations of historical knowledge.

Official History and the Revolutionary Pantheon

De Certeau's interpretation of history as a discourse about dead bodies that can no longer speak for themselves is useful for setting the aims of official historiography of the Revolution during the early post-conflict decades, which symbolically resurrected and memorialised its deceased leaders in an effort to suppress their competing voices and present the Revolution as an indivisible movement. Mirroring the fractured composition of the nation at the time of its outbreak, Knight states that the Revolution itself was 'many revolutions', a fragmentary struggle characterised by 'profound national divisions — ethnic, ideological, regional, factional and class-related'.[10] A key aspect of the so-called 'psychological phase' of the Revolution launched by president Plutarco Elías Calles was an attempt to quell revolutionary factionalism by inculcating a singular account of these events in the national consciousness.[11] In manipulating collective memory to secure political legitimacy, the post-revolutionary state paradoxically followed the example of Porfirian liberals, for whom 'a comprehensive nationalist history was the *sine qua non* both for the consolidation of the nation and as a proof of stability and civilization'.[12] Even more striking was the manner in which official post-revolutionary historiography recycled the totalising representational models of the previous regime, forging its revolutionary narrative around an imaginary pantheon of heroes that embodied the unity and continuity of Mexico's recent political past.

By the mid-1920s, Madero, Zapata, Ricardo Flores Magón and Felipe Carrillo Puerto were dead, providing the state with a cast of revolutionary figures whose memory could be moulded according to current political needs. As Benjamin notes, in the immediate post-conflict period, the politically and regionally fragmented nature of the Revolution gave rise to a 'babel of commemorative ceremonies, statues and tombs' devoted to individual martyrs.[13] Efforts to integrate these multivocal expressions of revolutionary memory into a single state-organised programme of memorialisation began in earnest under Calles who promoted the concept of a singular *familia revolucionaria* comprised of the nation's past and present revolutionaries. Following the assassination of Obregón, Calles established the Partido Nacional Revolucionario (PNR) in 1929 with the aim of incorporating competing factions into a single political entity and further efforts were made to unite the revolution's historical and contemporary representatives in the public imagination through commemorative ceremonies and official propaganda. This project of revolutionary conciliation was also pursued through the historical writings of figures such as Emilio Portes Gil, interim president from 1928 to 1930, whose account of the Revolution offered 'una interpretación colectiva e impersonal de los héroes' [a collective and impersonal account of the heroes].[14] This commemorative and discursive construction of a unified and historically continuous revolutionary 'pantheon of heroes' drew direct inspiration from official historiography during the Porfiriato, when dead political bodies enjoyed potent political afterlives. Florescano notes that during the regime:

> Se creó el panteón de héroes venerado en el calendario cívico: Cuauhtémoc, Hidalgo, Morelos, Melchor Ocampo, Benito Juárez, Ignacio Zaragoza, Porfirio Díaz [...] La presencia de estos patriotas en diferentes etapas de la formación del país expresaba la unidad y continuidad de la nación a pesar de las vicisitudes de la historia.[15]
>
> [A pantheon of heroes was created and celebrated in the civic calendar: Cuauhtémoc, Hidalgo, Morelos, Melchor Ocampo, Benito Juárez, Ignacio Zaragoza, Porfirio Díaz ... The presence of these patriots in different stages in the country's formation expressed the unity and continuity of the nation despite the vicissitudes of history].

Under Díaz, this illustrious collective was most frequently resurrected in the form of images which, as Martínez Rodríguez notes, enjoyed a privileged position in Porfirian nation-building processes due to their capacity to effectively 'represent complex historical narratives, and to convey abstract notions'.[16] In the Introduction I noted the regime's reliance on visual culture to forge the image of a progressive Mexican nation and this was particularly evident in its efforts to construct a coherent historical narrative. This visual impulse manifested itself in historical works tracing Mexico's historical and cultural evolution such as Vicente Riva Palacio's multivolume encyclopedia *México a través de los siglos* (1884), which boasted over two thousand images, and later, the profusely illustrated volumes of Sierra's *México su evolución social* (1900–1902). This link between visuality and historical knowledge in Mexican positivist historiography can be understood in light of Comte's application of the empirical-observational methods associated with the natural sciences to areas of social science such as historical research, as well as a strong reliance on philosophical and cultural models originating in France, where visual forms of historical representation had flourished after the Revolution.[17] Other forms of visual expression such as stamps, posters and public displays played an equally important role in constructing collective memory of Mexico's political history during the 1910 celebration of the Independence Centennial.[18] Commemorative memorabilia associated with this event adhered to the contemporary pictorial convention of depicting the liberal pantheon, comprised of Díaz, Hidalgo and Juárez, amongst others, as a gallery of individual bust portraits.

Nineteenth-Century Visions of History in The Palacio Nacional

After 1920, such graphic forms of historical narrativisation assumed new form in the epic works of the muralists which functioned as new visual monuments to the nation's shared revolutionary experience. While all three artists engaged thematically with the nation's past, Rivera's encyclopaedic vocabulary of historical images established him in the eyes of some intellectuals as 'el mejor historiador que ha tenido México' [the best historian Mexico has ever had].[19] Rivera's historical vision extended beyond the artistic domain, inspiring historians such as Alfonso Teja Zabre to create what were described as 'Dieguesque' histories of Mexico.[20] Teja Zabre openly acknowledged Rivera's influence and included reproductions of his murals in his *Breve historia de México* (1935), the first textbook with a strong revolutionary focus to be circulated in primary schools.

Although Rivera established himself as the definitive visual historian of the early post-revolution period and vocally rejected Porfirian culture, his visual strategies of historical representation were deeply indebted to nineteenth-century Mexican and French models. This contradiction should come as no surprise given that the muralist received his formal training at the turn of the century at the Academia de San Carlos, an institution that closely adhered to European, and particularly French, artistic standards and played a central role in visually reconstructing Mexico's past along official lines. As Martínez Rodríguez has pointed out, during the Porfiriato, close links between the government and official institutions such as the academy were solidified through the commissioning of historically themed and commemorative artworks that aligned with the state's official narrative.[21]

Rivera continued to work within this model for his state-sponsored mural *Epopeya del pueblo mexicano* at the Palacio Nacional which progresses from north to south across the central staircase in three sections: *El antiguo mundo indígena*, *México de la Conquista a 1930* and *México de hoy y mañana*. The countless historical actors crowding this vast pictorial field form a dense human tapestry that Rivera himself likened to 'un organismo vivo' [a living organism].[22] Echoing the ambitious claims of Porfirian visual historians such as Riva Palacio, who subtitled his historical encyclopedia 'Historia general y completa del desenvolvimiento social, politico, religioso, militar, científico y artístico y literario de México desde la antigüedad más remota hasta la época actual' [A general and complete history of the social, political, religious, military, scientific, artistic and literary development of Mexico from the most remote past to the present day], Rivera hailed the triptych as 'el único intento, en toda la historia del arte, para representar en un solo lienzo continuo de pared la historia de todo un pueblo desde su pasado hasta su futuro predecible' [the only attempt in the history of art to represent the history of an entire nation from its past to its foreseeable future on a single and continuous wall canvas].[23] In line with the didactic aims of contemporary official history, which sought 'mostrar al alumno la sociedad tal cual es y cómo ha sido y cómo se pretende que sea' [to show the student exactly how society is, how it has been and how it hopes to be], the muralist echoed his predecessor's positivist teleological conception of history by situating the Revolution within a broader narrative of social evolution.[24]

While the chronological sweep of Rivera's mural is reminiscent of Riva Palacio's illustrated historical survey, its scale and spatial presentation are modelled on the totalising historical art form par excellence of the nineteenth century: the panorama. Popularised in revolutionary and post-revolutionary France, these vast circular canvases produced a sense of visual mastery by enabling viewers to absorb complex historical scenes at a single glance. As a public spectacle, the panorama served as both a form of popular entertainment and a propagandistic tool by presenting audiences with a historical narrative that was accessible but also highly suggestive. Adapting this format to his post-revolutionary context, Rivera's composition offers an all-encompassing view of the nation's past, from its indigenous origins through the Independence and revolutionary movements and towards an imagined industrialised utopian future. Again taking its cue from the format of the panorama, Rivera's vast historical fresco sought to promote a sense of historical unity, not only through its visual projection of a shared past, but also by fostering, to borrow Maurice Samuels's phrasing, 'imaginary bonds' between viewers as they engaged in a public act of collective remembering.[25] As any contemporary visitor to the triptych will attest, the open architectural layout of the interlinked stairways and upper balcony successfully elicits this form of mass reception, encouraging interactions and conversations between observers as they occupy the shared spaces. Discussing these ritual aspects of the mural, Leonard

Folgarait describes how the central stairway guides the viewer to the elevated and distanced vantage point of the first floor landing where a complete view of all three panels can be achieved.[26] From this position, the viewer experiences the sense of visual and spatial mastery associated with the panorama and can best access Rivera's imagery of the Revolution, identified as a defining moment in the nation's evolutionary process by its location in the central lunette.

Painted between 1929 and 1931, the central panel narrates two of the nation's most formative historical experiences, as scenes of the Conquest surge up from its base to merge with episodes of revolutionary history in the upper arch. Recalling the strategies of de Certeau's nineteenth-century historian, who must selectively edit the past to guarantee its coherence and intelligibility, Rivera employs a cast of easily identifiable historical personalities within the confined space of the lunette (Fig. 1.1) to visually summarise the complex ideological conception and development of the Revolution. Following the representational model of the Porfirian liberal pantheon, the figures comprising this tightly knit group belong to various phases of Mexico's recent political history, from the Independence movement of 1810–1821 through to the Constitution of 1857 and the Revolution of 1910–1920. At the centre of this crowd, Miguel Hidalgo (1753–1811), the father of Mexican Independence, stands alongside fellow revolutionary priest José María Teclo Morelos y Pavón (1765–1815). To their left, Vicente Guerrero (1782–1831) and Agustín de Iturbide (1783–1824), the architect of the Plan de Iguala (1821), are located below the post-revolutionary presidents and Rivera's patrons Plutarco Elías Calles (1877–1945) and Álvaro Obregón (1880–1928). In the uppermost part of the arch, Emiliano Zapata (1879–1919), complete with signature moustache, is positioned alongside two other agrarian martyrs: the former Yucatán governor Felipe Carrillo Puerto (1874–1924) and the peasant leader José Guadalupe Rodríguez (1870–1915). The inclusion of Calles within this illustrious community is significant as it draws attention to Rivera's shifting political alliances during the period in which the triptych was executed. While the concluding panel, *México de hoy y mañana* (1934–1935) denounces the corruption and increasing authoritarianism of the Maximato, the central section *México de la Conquista a 1930* positions the president alongside historical agents of revolutionary change and aligns with his government's conciliatory view of the nation's recent political past.

The most innovative aspect of Rivera's compositional approach in this section of the mural is his manipulation of architectural space for the purposes of visual metaphor. Literalising de Certeau's notion of historiography as an act of entombment, Rivera suppresses the factionalised origins of the Revolution by configuring these political heroes in the form of a unitary corporeal monument. The narrow vertical dimensions of this upper section and the curvature of the lunette create the impression of a dome-topped structure. The mass of political personalities inhabiting this imaginary cupola is buttressed by the pillar-like figures of anonymous *campesinos* positioned below, who embody the peasant foundations of the agrarian movement. Rivera's composition of this revolutionary unit prefigures the structure of the real Monumento a la Revolución, designed by Carlos Obregón

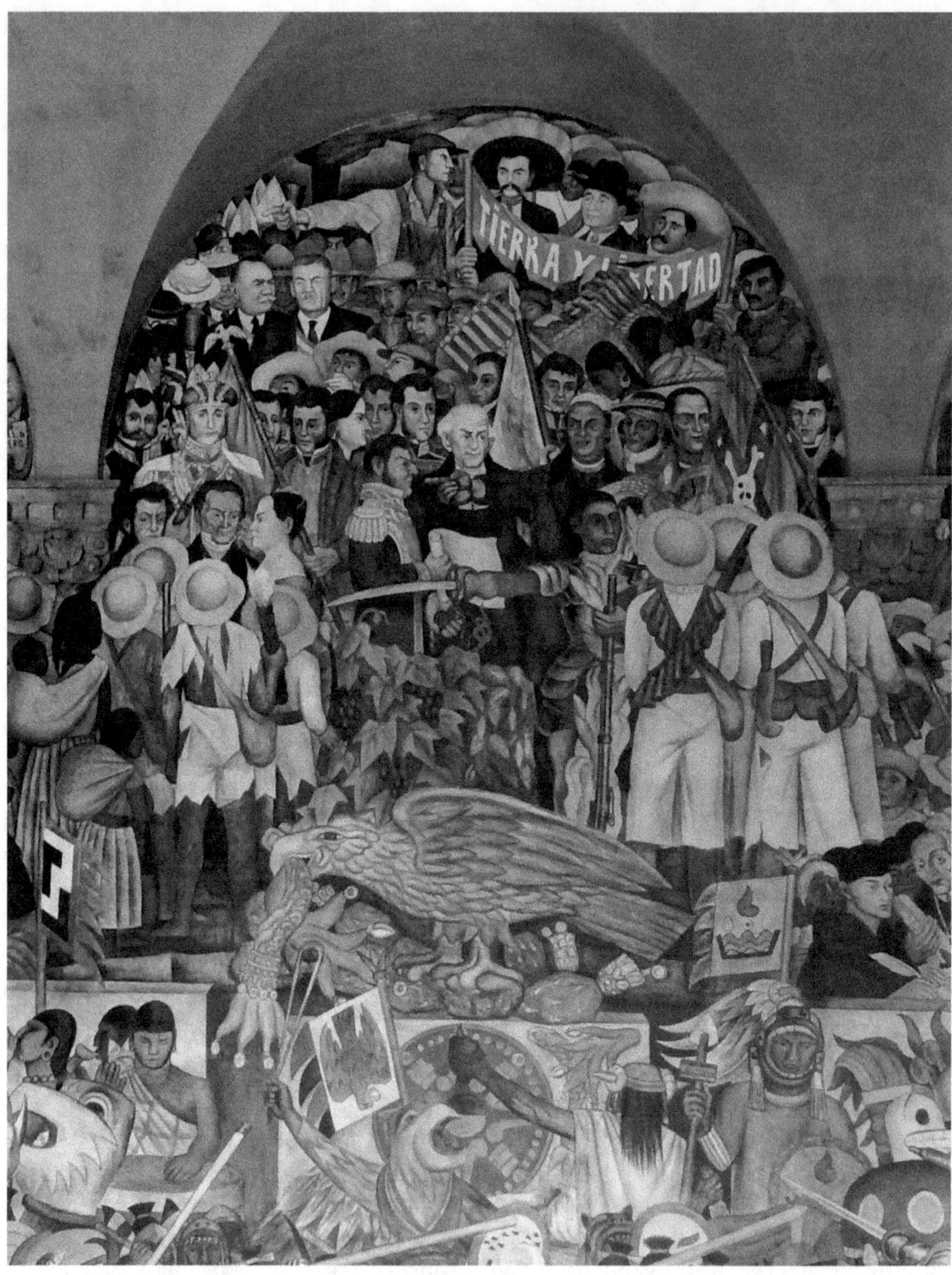

Fig. 1.1. Diego Rivera, Central lunette of *De la Conquista a 1930* (1929–1930), Palacio Nacional © Banco de México Diego Rivera Frida Kahlo Museums Trust, Mexico, D.F. / DACS 2021

Santacilia, and constructed in Mexico City between 1933 and 1938. As Rivera and Obregón Santacilia collaborated on the architectural and decorative schemes for the Secretaría de Salud (1929) and the Hotel del Prado (1933–1946) it is possible that the concept and composition of the muralist's image served as a source of inspiration for the architect's commemorative project. For the structural basis of the monument, which is composed as a hemispheric dome supported by four arches adorned with sculptures of peasants and workers, Obregón Santacilia employed the iron skeleton of the unfinished Palacio Legislativo, an administrative building designed for the Díaz government. Although Obregón Santacilia's proposal to integrate a revolutionary Panteón de los Hombres Ilustres was never formally approved, the idea gradually materialised as the mortal remains of Carranza (1942), Madero (1960), Calles (1969), Cárdenas (1970) and Villa (1976) were deposited in the different piers of the monument. Just as Rivera cast his revolutionary narrative within a distinctly nineteenth-century representational scheme, Obregón Santacilia's use of the Palacio Legislativo as the structural foundation for his monument reflects the manner in which state-sponsored memorialisation of the Revolution paradoxically relied on Porfirian frameworks, both conceptual and literal, into the 1930s.

In line with de Certeau's notion of the past as a legible body or a 'cipher that awaits deciphering', Rivera maintains the Porfirian link between visuality and historical knowledge in the revolutionary segment of the central wall by engaging the viewer in an optical exercise of 'reading' these emblematic bodies to configure a particular narrative of the nation's political past.[27] This segment of the triptych is presented as a veritable portrait gallery and Rivera later explained that he had selected the most recognisable historical figures to ensure the panel achieved its desired social effect. He depicted the personalities he considered 'más representativos y mejor conocidos porque [...] la ideología del tema tenía que ser suficientemente sencilla y escoger hechos suficientemente claros y conocidos por los mexicanos para llenar la función social que quiere que tenga la pintura' [most representative and famous because ... the ideology of the subject needed to be sufficiently simple and the events chosen needed to be sufficiently clear and familiar to Mexicans in order to fulfil the painting's desired social function].[28] Rivera's didactic use of the body for the purposes of historical narrativisation can be productively compared with Henri Gervex's and Alfred Stevens's historical panorama *Histoire du siècle* (1889), which includes almost a thousand of France's most notable political, intellectual and artistic figures from the period of the Revolution through to the following century. In her brief analysis of the work's composition Beatriz González-Stephan explains how:

> Thanks to the careful reproduction of portraits, the public was challenged to identify each individual represented. Here the exhibitionary complex was put to the test, as was the dexterity of sight, for knowing how to read the images was also knowing how to recognise identities. It was also an exercise in selective memory that fixed some canonical faces while erasing others.[29]

The revolutionary section of Rivera's triptych demands a similar visual acuity, engaging the viewer in an optical exercise of identifying and memorising particular bodies and their position within the pantheon while subtly effacing others. A logical sense of interconnectivity governs this crowd of political figures, each of whom, as Rivera himself explained, is 'dialécticamente conectado con sus vecinos, de acuerdo con su papel en la historia' [dialectically connected with his neighbours according to his role in history]. Referring to the details of the mural, Rivera affirmed 'nada era solitario, todo era relevante' [nothing was isolated, everything was relevant].[30] The panel thus functions as a visual history lesson that invites the observer to identify and decode certain clues and details in order to identify the historical function of each individual and his political relationship to the adjacent bodies. This didactic aspect of the triptych, notably described by Rivera as a 'poema épico plástico' [plastic epic poem], reflected his belief that painted murals should replace historical texts in their pedagogical function: 'escribir en enormes murales públicos la historia de la gente iletrada que no puede leerla en libros' [to write on enormous public murals the history of the illiterate people who are unable to read it in books].[31] While Rivera sought to render Mexico's history more accessible to the wider public in the Palacio Nacional, the philosopher Samuel Ramos later noted that in comparison to his other works: 'el texto (es) mucho más cerrado [...] no ofrece ningún resquicio para dar vuelo a la fantasía' [the text (is) much more closed... it offers no opportunity to give flight to the imagination].[32]

In the revolutionary section of the central wall, the relatively rigid nature of Rivera's interpretative scheme is indicated by his inclusion of visual cues and textual fragments that guide the viewer to certain conclusions. Positioned at the very centre of the group, Hidalgo clasps a broken chain in one hand, an obvious symbol of liberation, while the other holds forth the flag bearing the image of the Virgin of Guadalupe that he famously brandished upon proclaiming independence. Elsewhere, banners play an equally important role in clarifying the ideological positions of certain figures. Guerrero triumphantly holds aloft the *bandera trigarante*, symbolising the promise of independence, while in the opposite corner, the insurgent flag, known as *El doliente de Hidalgo*, identifies its bearer as the Spanish insurgent Francisco Javier Mina (1789–1817). The role of these props in enhancing the legibility of specific bodies is even more literal in the case of Zapata, Carrillo Puerto and Guadalupe Rodríguez, who are enveloped in the banner emblazoned with the agrarian slogan 'Tierra y libertad'. Political affiliations are further suggested by smaller visual details such as the modern suits and presidential sashes worn by Calles and Obregón, setting them apart as representatives of the institutionalised Revolution. By positioning these contemporary politicians alongside the ideological architects of the Revolution and the anonymous *campesinos* located in the lower section of the arch, Rivera stresses the historical continuity of the Revolution through its official conversion into government. A notable absence from this central section narrativising the official institutionalisation of the Revolution is Francisco 'Pancho' Villa, who can be found in a neighbouring lunette on the central wall alongside several other figures associated with the Porfiriato and the early stages of the Revolution. As Villa's revolutionary credentials were not fully recognised by the state until the 1960s, Rivera's strategic grouping of historical bodies subtly engages viewers in the process of selective remembering and forgetting described by de Certeau.

While the various symbols and textual elements inserted in this section of the mural highlight the specific political roles of individual figures, the most striking aspect of its composition is its elision of difference. Although the inclusion of recently assassinated revolutionaries such as Obregón and Rodríguez hints at the Revolution's fractured origins, Rivera's collective configuration of these bodies eschews all traces of internal disharmony and political rivalry. Surveyed from the opposite-facing balcony, *México de la Conquista a 1930* corporeally narrates the nation's trajectory from political upheaval to harmonious unity. While the colonial confrontation is marked by a sea of erratic human movements in the lower section, this bodily chaos dissipates as we move up to the independence and revolutionary phases, where the spatial restrictions of the lunette compresses the figures into an orderly mass. In contrast to the lower section of the mural, where we are granted a full-length view of the bodies in a range of dynamic poses, the restricted composition of the upper section fixes the figures in rigidly frontal postures and renders them visible only from the shoulders up, creating a strikingly similar effect to the bust style portraits used to depict the heroes of the Porfirian liberal pantheon. The dense overlapping of figures in this section of the mural creates an effect of visual ellipsis that enables them to achieve form only as a unit, illustrating the indissolubility of the Revolution across political generations and social classes.

Alternative Voices: Revisionist Historiography and the Question of Historical Truth

In the opening sequence of Emilio Fernández's *Río Escondido* (1947), a landmark film of the so-called 'Golden Age' of nationalist cinema that spanned roughly from the mid-1930s to the late 1950s, the patriotic schoolteacher Rosaura Salazar, played by María Félix, arrives at the Palacio Nacional for a personal interview with President Miguel Alemán. As she ascends the central stairway, a disembodied voice guides Rosaura through key sections of Rivera's mural, providing a condensed history lesson that will prepare her for her role in the government's transformative social project. Although the film testifies to the enduring cultural presence of Rivera's historical vision towards the middle of the century, the model of historical representation enshrined in this epic panorama and its unitary pantheon of revolutionaries would soon face intellectual scrutiny.

With the decline of the state's revolutionary ideals during the Alemán era, the monolithic accounts that had been constructed during the initial post-revolution era gradually gave way to historiographical reassessments of Mexico's recent political past and philosophical debates regarding the question of historical truth. Although the revisionist phase of revolutionary historiography would not flourish until the 1960s, critical reassessment of recent political developments had already been initiated by the previously mentioned essays of Cosío Villegas, Colín, Iturriaga and Silva Herzog during the late 1940s and early 1950s. Matute contends that from 1955 onwards scholarly examinations of the Revolution increasingly exposed 'su falta de unidad, sus paradojas internas y las crisis por las que atravesó en diferentes momentos' [its lack of unity, its internal paradoxes and the crises it suffered at different stages].[33] He adds that:

> Ya no se trataba de recrear el esencialismo revolucionario, sino de investigar, sacar a la luz nuevos conocimientos en torno al proceso histórico de la Revolución, a partir de preguntas que ponían en crisis todo aquello que se tenía como esencial y, por lo tanto, inamovible. La Revolución se convirtió en un asunto que había que revisar.[34]
>
> [It was no longer a matter of reproducing revolutionary essentialism, but of investigating, of bringing to light, new knowledge of the historical process of the Revolution, starting with questions that plunged everything that was believed to be essential, and therefore fixed, into crisis. The Revolution became a topic that needed to be revised.]

Moving away from the totalising historical models of the previous decades, Pérez Montfort asserts that historical research 'dio pasos en favor de la problematización de los fenómenos históricos, tratando de dejar atrás, sin lograrlo siempre, las definiciones de índole autoritaria y absoluta' [took steps towards problematising historical phenomenon, looking to leave behind, not always successfully, definitions of an authoritarian and absolute nature].[35] In this regard, post-revolutionary developments were in keeping with the broader mid-century shift in historiographical attitudes outlined by Hayden White in *Metahistory* (1973). White notes that while 'historical knowledge' was considered 'an autonomous domain in the spectrum of human and physical sciences' during the nineteenth century, by the middle of the twentieth century, questions surrounding what it meant to 'think historically' were 'undertaken in a somewhat less confident mood and in the face of an apprehension that definitive answers to them may not be possible'.[36]

In Mexico, such historical scepticism was fostered by contemporary philosophical discussions related to the notions of perspectivism and historical relativism that had been introduced into mainstream debate during the 1940s by exiled Spanish intellectuals fleeing the Spanish Civil War such as José Gaos, a disciple of José Ortega y Gasset. The most influential aspect of Orteguian philosophy introduced by these thinkers was the notion of perspectivism, which proposed that reality was composed of 'infinitas perspectivas, todas ellas igualmente verídicas y auténticas' [an infinite number of perspectives, each one equally true and authentic].[37] Writing in 1952, Patrick Romanell argued that the concept had become 'the greatest single intellectual force in the nationalization of the Mexican mind'.[38] During a 1945 roundtable entitled 'Sobre el problema de la verdad histórica', Alfonso Caso highlighted the philosophical roots of contemporary historiographical debates:

> Es indudable que el problema de la verdad en materia histórica, no es un problema histórico, sino filosófico, es cuestión epistemológica, que queda comprendida dentro de la gran interrogación: ¿Qué es la verdad?[39]
>
> [Undoubtedly, the problem of the truth in relation to history is not a historical, but rather a philosophical problem, it is an epistemological issue that falls within the greater question: 'What is the truth?']

A mutually influential relationship between historiography and literary production can be identified during these decades. Moving away from the sweeping historical narratives of the muralists, from the late 1940s onwards writers began eroding the state's monolithic accounts of the past by exploring the alternative microhistories it had previously denied. Building on earlier works such as Nellie Campobello's testimonial-style novel *Cartucho* (1931), more localised and marginalised perspectives on the Revolution came to the fore in mid-century novels such as Agustín Yáñez's *Al filo del agua* (1947), Rulfo's *Pedro Páramo* and later in Garro's *Los recuerdos del porvenir* (1963). These rather grim literary portraits of provincial communities foreshadowed the turn towards more regionally focused historical research heralded by historian Luis González y González's *Pueblo en vilo: Microhistoria de San José de Gracia* (1968). Just as Teja Zabre had drawn influence from Rivera's murals during the 1930s, González acknowledged his indebtedness to the fictional works of Yáñez, Arreola and Rulfo in developing this groundbreaking account of national events from the perspective of a small town in Michoacán.[40] The privileging of personal recollections of the Revolution and the accommodation of multiple perspectives in the works of Rulfo, Garro and Fuentes suggests links with other contemporary methodological innovations. In 1954 the Instituto Nacional de Estudios Históricos de la Revolución Mexicana (INEHRM) created the Archivo Sonoro, a pioneering initiative in the domain of oral history that was followed by the founding of the official Archivo Sonoro de la Revolución Mexicana by historian Wigberto Jiménez Moreno in 1959.[41] By compiling the recorded first-person testimonies of participants and witnesses of the armed conflict in various regions, these initiatives sought to establish an 'archivo fónico de la Revolución' [phonic archive of the Revolution].[42]

As his literary career developed in the 1940s and 50s, Rulfo maintained a deep personal interest in historical research. Víctor Jiménez recalls how 'Rulfo declaró de manera repetida que su verdadera vocación era la historia de México, antes aún que la literatura' [Rulfo repeatedly declared that his true vocation was the history of Mexico, even before literature], adding that, 'la aproximación de Juan Rulfo a ciertos periodos de la historia de México [...] permite imaginar al historiador que pudo ser: uno muy crítico sin duda' [Rulfo's approach to certain periods of Mexican history... allows us to imagine the kind of historian he could have been: undoubtedly a very critical one].[43] It was this critical approach that later motivated Rulfo to revise a number of school textbooks circulating in Jalisco and Guadalajara that he claimed were 'falseando la verdad' [bending the truth] in relation to regional history:

> Entre los textos que tomé como fuentes, fueron esos, los textos que enseñan en las escuelas primarias y que desde entonces empiezan a llenar la mente de estos jóvenes con datos falsos. Tomé en cuenta todo lo mal que se decía en esos textos, todo lo mal hecho, pero tampoco encontré la solución.[44]
>
> [Among the texts that I used as sources were the texts that are taught in primary schools and from that point onwards start to fill young people's minds with false information. I took into account all of the errors in those texts and everything that had been done incorrectly, but I didn't reach a solution either.]

The writer hastily qualified his proposed revisions to these texts by noting: 'Tampoco lo que yo juzgo verdadero, no lo tomen al pie de la letra; simplemente son divagaciones, más bien hipótesis' [But whatever I judge to be true, don't take that literally either, these are simply ramblings, or rather hypotheses].[45] Although Rulfo was dissatisfied with the inaccuracies of official history, he was also profoundly aware of the difficulty of achieving historical truth in any absolute sense. This historical scepticism pervades his literary universe where the past occupies a central yet precarious position. Recalling a series of misfortunes that has befallen his family due to a recent flood, the narrator of 'Es que somos muy pobres' prefaces each of his recollections with the phase 'tal vez' [perhaps], while attempts to reconstruct past events by the amnesiac narrators of 'El hombre' and 'Macario' are similarly obstructed by a series of inexplicable memory lapses. Rulfo explores the fragility of human memory most comprehensively in *Pedro Páramo*, a multi-voiced text that offers the clearest literary reflection of mid-century historiographical developments and anxieties regarding the limitations of historical knowledge.[46] In keeping with the gradual shift towards oral testimony and paving the way for regional studies such as González's, the novel examines revolutionary experience through the microhistory of Comala, a post-revolutionary ghost town whose fractured past is partially reconstructed through the voiced recollections of its deceased inhabitants.

Although its narrated events appear to unfold in a temporally unmoored rural dreamscape, Rulfo's novel is anchored in a concrete historical moment. Based on a few scattered temporal markers, Boldy estimates that the narrative spans from the Porfiriato in the 1880s through to the 1910 Revolution and the Cristero Rebellion of 1926, up until the 1940s.[47] Yet despite being set during this period of political transformation, the novel intentionally de-monumentalises the Revolution by offering only fleeting glimpses of it, such as the brief dialogue between the *cacique* [local boss] and a group of rebels which satirically exposes its ideological incoherence (284–85). Composed of a series of chronologically disordered narrative segments, Rulfo's brief novel formally dismantles the totalising model of official history enshrined in Rivera's panoramic triptych and its assumptions of interpretative mastery.

The Body as Crisis of Historical Representation in *Pedro Páramo*

The first section of Rulfo's novel is narrated by Juan Preciado, who travels to the desolate village of Comala at the request of his dying mother to locate his estranged father Pedro Páramo. As he proceeds through the village, Preciado is assailed by a swarm of unidentified voices emanating from different historical moments spanning from the late nineteenth to the mid-twentieth century. It is only about halfway through the novel that we learn that Preciado, and indeed all of Comala's inhabitants, are dead and that their voices are emanating from different tombs in the village graveyard. Initially framed as a search for personal origins, the novel soon evolves into an investigation into the collective identity of Comala as Preciado, and by extension the reader, assumes the role of the historian who must weave together these disparate oral testimonies to reconstruct the village's past. However, the protagonist's investigative task is repeatedly frustrated by the competing accounts of the villagers which interrupt, contradict or misinterpret one another.

This fundamental irreducibility of the past, powerfully communicated through the trope of spectrality, establishes a parallel between historical and corporeal opacity in the novel. On his arrival to the town, Preciado catches sight of a woman wearing a shawl who swiftly disappears and soon afterwards encounters Doña Eduviges, his first female guide in Comala, whose bloodless face appears transparent before him: 'su cara se transparentaba como si no tuviera sangre, y sus manos estaban marchitas; marchitas y apretadas de arrugas. No se le veían los ojos' [her face was transparent as if it were drained of blood and her hands were withered; withered and shrivelled with wrinkles. Her eyes could not be seen].[48] The translucent and shrunken figure of Eduviges alerts the reader at an early stage to the precarious position of the body in Comala, where, as Rulfo explained, 'la gente no tiene cara, las figuras humanas no se definen' [people have no faces, human figures are undefined].[49] There is of course a spectrum of spectrality in the novel. While it is clear that certain characters such as Doña Eduviges and the incestuous siblings residing in Los Confines are in some way visible to Preciado, they are described as elusive and physiologically unstable entities whose perceived physical presence could in fact be the product of his visual hallucinations: 'veo cosas y gente donde quizás ustedes no vean nada' [I see things and people where perhaps you see nothing] (243). The correlation between the obscurity of the villagers' bodies and that of their past is established in the only explicit reference to ghostliness in the novel, when we learn that the nostalgic Páramo fears nightfall when he must 'encerrarse con sus fantasmas' [shut himself away with his ghosts] (311). In the closing description of the *cacique*'s death, recollection is again directly linked to a process of obfuscation as his mind is flooded by memories that blur (*desdibujar*) the present (311).

Through these linkages, the figure of the spectre in *Pedro Páramo* emerges as a figurative body of history, a corpus of knowledge about the past that eludes total intelligibility. De Certeau's conceptualisation of historiography as a *heterology*, a discourse of the 'other', that at times resists the grasp of the historian and threatens our sense of knowledge, aligns with Colin Davis's identification of spectrality as a metaphor for historiographical scepticism. Following Levinas's description of scepticism as a ghostly shadow that haunts reason, Davis claims that it speaks for:

> non-coincidence and fractured temporalities rather than a stable, unified plane of intelligibility in which everything can be reduced. It is like a ghost because it comes from a domain which reason cannot entirely capture or dominate. It is disturbing, disruptive, ungraspable.[50]

De Certeau's and Davis's identification of the ghostly with an interrogative and ethically-oriented mode of historiography that accepts the irrecuperability of certain aspects of the past illuminates Rulfo's use of spectrality as an expression of historical scepticism. Like the Revolution itself, the bodies of Comala's villagers are figured as a fleeting presence in the novel's pages, obliquely glimpsed as distorted silhouettes or spectral forms that abruptly dissolve into shadows (205, 213, 91). In these images, Rulfo amplifies the inherent spectrality of the textual body which, as Hillman and

Maude note, has no immediate means of conveying its concrete materiality on the written page.[51] Echoing Ellmann's description of writing as 'an art of discarnation', they assert that there are in fact 'no bodies in literature [...] there would seem on the face of it to be an apparent mutual exclusivity of the body and language —the one all brute facticity, the other supposing precisely the absence of matter'.[52] If, as Davis suggests, the phantasmatic body speaks to a profound historiographical crisis, Rulfo evokes this through a form of textual experimentation that plays on the limits of both literary and historical representation.

This correlation suggests that the writing of literature and history were closely interlinked for Rulfo. Pointing to the fundamental parallels between historical and fictional discourse, White highlights how the inherently discursive and interpretive nature of historical writing inevitably results in its incorporation of literary conventions such as narrative structures and rhetorical devices.[53] However, as Linda Hutcheon has demonstrated in relation to postmodern literature, texts can also destabilise totalising master narratives and create alternative histories by rendering literary form fragmented and discontinuous.[54] The non-linear and fractured form of *Pedro Páramo*, with its multiple gaps and inconclusive narrative strands, suggests that Rulfo's literary engagement with the past was influenced by his anxieties as a historian. Although the writer felt compelled to revise misleading official historical accounts, he remained acutely aware of the impossibility of achieving an objective description of the past. 'Todo es hipotético, todo es un supuesto' [Everything is hypothetical, it is all conjecture], he insisted, 'nada nos acerca a la verdadera realidad' [nothing brings us close to true reality].[55]

By problematising the legibility of the past through the spectral body (from the Latin *specere*: to look at), Rulfo's novel challenges the epistemological assumptions underpinning the aesthetic historiographical model that surfaces in Rivera's work and the visual forms of knowledge on which it is founded. Karen Jacobs explains how the de-valorisation of vision in the early twentieth century manifested itself in the works of Anglo-American modernist writers who reacted against nineteenth-century realism and naturalism and their positivist faith in a 'universal and accessible visual language' by undermining the reliability of human sight.[56] Preciado's inability to locate Eduviges's eyes as he contemplates her transparent face points to a similar crisis of vision that affects many of the novel's characters. Preciado claims that he has brought Dolores's eyes to see Comala, but it becomes apparent that this inherited vision is impaired as she loses sight of him, leaving him to grope his way through the village unguided.[57] Throughout the novel, human sight is repeatedly described as limited or partially obstructed, with characters often perceiving their surroundings through half-opened eyes (213, 279, 305) or glimpsing others from the corner of their eyes (248, 300). Like Dorotea, whose eyes are 'tan sin mirada' [so deprived of sight] (253), Fausta admits that she too is blind (298). Susana complains of blurred vision (265) and her grotesque description of her eyeballs melting away (301) can be situated alongside other references to ocular damage in the novel. Páramo's father Lucas dies with a mangled eye while an anonymous man claims to have been left cross-eyed following an altercation with the *cacique* (267).

This sustained assault on visual perception is also registered on the level of reader reception. Overturning the principles of visual control and dexterity that shaped Rivera's historiographical model, *Pedro Páramo* plunges the reader into an imagined environment so obscure that Patrick Dove compares the reader's navigation of the text to 'undergoing an experience of blindness'.[58] Such a devaluation of sight logically results in a heightened sensitivity to sound which is revealed in the profoundly phonic quality of Rulfo's literary language. In a text that relies heavily on alliteration, onomatopoeia and other sound devices, this primacy of the auditory over the visual is appropriately captured in the sonorous description of a lamp extinguishing in Eduviges's house: 'la lámpara que ardía en un rincón comenzó a languidecer; luego parpadeó y terminó apagándose' [the lamp that was burning in a corner began to languish; then it flickered and went out] (221).

The novel's acoustic innovations were noted by early commentators such as Francisco Zendejas, who identified *Pedro Páramo* as 'el primer caso de "sentido de oído" que yo he visto en la literatura Mexicana' [the first example of "hearing" that I have seen in Mexican literature].[59] The most powerful aural presence in *Pedro Páramo* is of course the human voice, which provides the only means of retrieving information about the past. Interspersed with exhausted laughter, sighs and screams, the voices of the townsfolk offer fragmentary personal recollections ranging from the mundane to the euphoric and the tragic. Indeed, Dolores's description of Comala as 'una alcancía donde hemos guardado nuestros recuerdos' [a collection box where we have kept our memories] (246), echoing Eduviges's earlier remark that she is storing the trinkets of departed villagers in her home (199), encourages us to conceptualise the sepulchral village as a kind of polyvocal archive of collective memories —a literary *archivo fónico* of the nation's past. Through this chaotic intermingling of voices, *Pedro Páramo* stages, to recall de Certeau, the return of those marginalised perspectives previously denied by official history.

In literary theoretical terms, the multi-voicedness of *Pedro Páramo* can be aligned with Bakhtin's concept of polyphonic narration whereby 'several consciousnesses meet as equals and engage in dialogue that is in principle unfinalizable'.[60] Building on the experimental narrative strategies of Campobello and Yáñez, Rulfo's novel utilises this polyphonic effect to problematise the process of historical narrativisation and the possibility of historical consensus. Unlike the monologic novel in which 'all confirmed ideas are merged in the unity of the author's seeing and representing consciousness', the polyphonic text privileges no single point of view and is instead comprised of 'a plurality of independent and unmerged voices and consciousnesses, a genuine polyphony of fully valid voices'.[61] The link between polyphony and what Bakhtin describes as 'unfinalisability', that is, the impossibility of integrating individual points of view within a single field of vision, provides a literary counterpart to the Orteguian perspectivist assumption that reality is shattered into 'facetas innumerables' [innumerable facets].[62]

While it places a thematic emphasis on disembodiment, the distinct vocal texture of Rulfo's novel encourages particularly embodied forms of reading. We have already been alerted to the multisensory quality of *Pedro Páramo* by Dove's equation of reading the text to a sensation of blindness. This effect is evident in the first-person description of Preciado tentatively groping his way through the crepuscular corridors of Eduviges's house:

> En cuanto me acostumbré a la oscuridad y al delgado hilo de luz que nos seguía, vi crecer sombras a ambos lados y sentí que íbamos caminando a través de un angosto pasillo abierto entre bultos (199).
>
> [As soon as I became accustomed to the darkness and the thin thread of light that was following us, I saw shadows grow on both sides and felt that we were moving along a narrow passage between different objects.]

Vivid literary descriptions such as these encourage what Vittorio Gallese has defined within the field of neuroaesthetics as 'embodied simulation', a process through which mirror mechanisms in the brain enable us to virtually participate in the real or imagined movements and sensations of others. In the context of literary reception, the impression of a shared phenomenological or physiological state blurs the distinction between the body of the reader and that of the fictional character.[63] The reader of *Pedro Páramo* not only vicariously experiences Preciado's obscured vision and physical disorientation, but also his aural hallucinations. The proliferation of verbs such as *murmurar* [to murmur], *susurrar* [to whisper] and *suspirar* [to sigh] throughout the novel transforms Comala into a chaotic soundscape of indistinct vocalisations; Dolores's disembodied maternal voice, which launches Preciado's journey is 'secreta, casi apagada, como si hablara consigo mismo' [secret, almost muffled, as is she were talking to herself] (194) and his mind is subsequently inundated by 'secret' muttering voices (247). Here, as elsewhere in Rulfo's fictional world, speech is conceptualised as a fundamentally interior phenomenon that offers access to the closed-off mental spaces of characters rather than facilitating communication between them. In keeping with the prevalence of what Perus refers to as 'monodialogues' in earlier stories such as 'Macario' and 'El hombre', Rulfo's novel (originally entitled *Los murmullos*) places an emphasis on private or intimate forms of speech such as murmuring and whispering.[64] Steven Connor's description of these interiorised forms of speech as 'closet speech' or 'speaking within', recalls the isolated tombs from which the townsfolk tirelessly rehearse their recollections.[65] Unlike Rivera's unifying mausoleum, these solitary sepulchral dwellings, which are inhabited by only one (such as Susana, who delivers her monologues from a 'black coffin') or two villagers (as in the case of Preciado and Dorotea), function as self-contained echo chambers.

The most striking instance of interior vocal activity in the novel is Preciado's involuntary internalisation of the villagers' voices which soon become inescapable.[66] Through its emphasis on interiorised speech, Rulfo's novel is intimately attuned to what Connor describes as the 'inner sonority' of silent reading, that is, the internal sound effects generated by the reader's mental enunciation of the text.[67] As the eye scans symbols on the page, subtle nerve impulses travel from the brain to the larynx and tongue, producing an internal voicing of the text perceptible only to the inner ear of the reader. The previously cited quote from Zendejas, who identifies Rulfo's prose as the first example of literary sound he has ever *seen* in Mexican literature, highlights how Rulfo's text exploits literature's ability to 'auditise the field of the visible', as Connor puts it.[68] Recent inquiries into the phenomenological nature of silent reading have demonstrated that these subvocalisations possess identities that are distinct from the hearer and can assume diverse auditory properties including volume, pitch, and tone.[69] Reading can thus be understood as a kind of ghostly auditory hallucination, the internal perception of incessant yet unlocatable disembodied voices. These processes of inner speech and hearing are particularly effective in the case of Rulfo's polyphonic novel as they convert the mind of the reader, like that of Preciado, into what Connor terms 'an auditorium or *arena of internal articulations*' or a 'complex space of inner resounding'.[70] Just as Preciado's head is inundated by the disembodied voices of the villagers, the act of reading conjures a steady and inescapable murmur at the back of the reader's mind. This phenomenological aspect of the reading process brings into focus the unique demands made on the body by literature and muralism on the level of aesthetic reception and their significance in relation to collective memory. While the public dimensions of Rivera's mural art both visually and spatially engage viewers in a process of collective remembering, the interiorised forms of speech promoted by Rulfo's text evoke the solipsistic discourse of Comala's townsfolk who fail to establish any collective framework for interpreting the past.

In both their thematic content and aesthetic form, Rivera's epic visual narrative and Rulfo's literary microhistory constitute two very different *tombeaux* of revolutionary memory that both responded and contributed to historiographical developments from the 1920s to the 1950s. By tracing the transformation of Rivera's unified revolutionary pantheon into the chattering cemetery of Comala, my analysis has shed light on the evolution of post-revolutionary commemorative and historiographical practices, as well as the close links that developed between political, intellectual and artistic activity during these decades. Read comparatively, these works reflect Blanco and Peeren's conception of historiography as both 'a haunted (and haunting) practice'.[71] By resurrecting and silencing the revolutionary dead in the Palacio Nacional, Rivera suppresses a factionalised past that returns to haunt the reader of *Pedro Páramo*. Rulfo's configuration of Comala's graveyard as a chaotic polyvocal archive dramatises the resurgence of these previously marginalised perspectives which, to recall de Certeau, 'continue to speak in the text/tomb that erudition erects in their place'.[72] As visual and literary historians, Rivera's and Rulfo's works illustrate a broader transition in post-revolutionary historiographical practices, from the nineteenth-century modes of historical narrativisation that persisted into the 1920s to a mid-twentieth century awareness of the limitations of such interpretative and representational frameworks. Following de Certeau's corporeal metaphors of the historiographical process, this shift can be perceived through both artists' figuration of literal and figurative bodies as receptacles for historical knowledge. Unsettling the epistemological assumptions underpinning Rivera's legible corporeal narrative of the Revolution in the Palacio Nacional, the elusive spectres of Comala problematise the process of reading history as a visible *corpus* or 'body' of knowledge by opening up an inconclusive and ungraspable collective past.

Part II: Encounters with the 'Other': Evolving Visual Discourses of *Indigenismo*

While revolutionary memory was manipulated to secure public faith in the state's political agenda, illusions of historical unity were also crafted by intellectuals to satisfy the cultural exigencies of the period. This narrative of cultural unity and continuity was provided by *indigenismo*, a complex and contradictory state-sponsored discourse that forged collective memory around the notion of a shared indigenous past and aesthetically celebrated these roots as the basis for an authentic post-revolutionary cultural identity. These aspects of the *indigenista* project achieve poetic expression in Alfonso Reyes's profoundly visual essay 'Visión de Anáhuac' (1917), which recreates the first impressions of the Spanish chroniclers upon reaching the Valley of Mexico in 1519. Through the eyes of the conquistadores, the narrator perceives indigenous figures amidst the lush vegetation whose smiling faces encourage him to advance.[73] In the closing lines, Reyes identifies an emotional response to the landscape as evidence of a telluric bond linking twentieth-century Mexicans to their indigenous ancestors:

> Nos une con la raza de ayer, sin hablar de sangres [...] la emoción cotidiana ante el mismo objeto natural [...] engendra un alma común.[74]
>
> [We are bound to the race of yesterday, without entering into the question of blood... the everyday emotion inspired by the same natural object... engenders a common soul.]

Reyes's description of a 'common soul' uniting modern Mexicans with their indigenous forebears exemplifies the 'intimate' tone of early twentieth-century *indigenista* discourse which, as Estelle Tarica has demonstrated, employed a 'language of spirit and sentiment' to foster a sense of 'shared communication and experience rather than an external, objective position vis-à-vis Indians'.[75] While Reyes's emotive prose clearly looks to evoke such an 'intimate affinity with Indians', his projection of this 'vision' from the perspective of the Spanish invaders illuminates the neocolonial ideas underpinning the movement's discursive and aesthetic revalorisation of the indigenous. Post-revolutionary *indigenismo* was intertwined with Vasconcelos's utopian vision of *mestizaje*, which identified the formation of a hybrid *mestizo* race composed of both European and indigenous racial elements as the foundation for a unified and progressive collective identity. During the early decades of the twentieth century, the imagined figures of the *indio* and the *mestizo* were established as key protagonists in the cultural narrative of post-revolutionary collective unity and advancement, respectively embodying Mexico's historical indigenous heritage and contemporary mixed-race population.[76] *Indigenismo* served the purposes of *mestizaje* by advocating the cultural and racial assimilation of native communities into the mainstream *mestizo* body politic, while also asserting Mexico's cultural singularity by pursuing a rediscovery of its primitive origins in the indigenous body. In contrast to traditional colonial paradigms, in which the difference between coloniser and colonised is easily asserted due to geographical and cultural distance, post-revolutionary nation-builders were forced to reckon with the *indio* as an 'other' residing within the boundaries of the national community.

As an internal colonial discourse, *indigenismo* constructed a relationship between *mestizo* and *indio* based on identification and intimacy, while also maintaining the inferiority of the country's indigenous population.

The contradictory set of relations that formed the basis of post-revolutionary *indigenismo* was deconstructed by Luis Villoro in his landmark study *Los grandes momentos del indigenismo* (1950). Mapping changing constructions of indigeneity within the national consciousness from the sixteenth century to the contemporary moment, Villoro explains how the post-revolutionary period witnesses a shift in attitudes towards *lo indígena*. In contrast to the Porfiriato, when the indigenous was confined to a distant pre-Columbian past, he claims that after the Revolution, as vividly dramatised in Reyes's text, there begins 'un nuevo movimiento de acercamiento de lo indígena [...] no habrá peligro alguno en aproximarlo; su misma positividad nos incita a ello' [a new movement towards the indigenous... there is no danger in approaching it, its positive value encourages us to do so].[77] Adopting a metaphor of visualisation, Villoro argues that this interaction with the *indio* facilitates a process of self-realisation for the *mestizo*: 'Al mirar al indio, se reconoce el mestizo como impulso hacia la unidad' [Looking at the Indian, the *mestizo* recognises himself as an impulse towards unity].[78] Despite its unifying impulse, Villoro underlines how the unidirectionality of this gaze relegates the indigenous other to a position that is 'siempre revelada y nunca revelante' [always revealed and never revealing].[79] Villoro concludes, however, by pointing to the potentially constructive capacity of *indigenismo* to destabilise national identity and trigger a moment of self-reflection in which the *mestizo* 'vuelve la mirada sobre sí mismo para conocerse y descubre en su interior la inestabilidad y la contradicción' [turns the gaze back upon himself to understand himself and discovers his inner instability and contradictions].[80] Maintaining the metaphor of the gaze, Villoro suggests that this could lead to a more equal relationship between *mestizo* and *indio* based on mutual recognition: 'Vendrá el momento en que no haya jerarquías en las razas ni dominio de una sobre la otra; en que todas las que ahora se diversifican se reconozcan recíprocamente' [The time will come when there will be no racial hierarchies or domination of one race over the other; when all of the races which are now distinguished from one another will recognise each other reciprocally].[81]

Exploring for the first time the intersections between intellectual and visual discourses of post-revolutionary *indigenismo*, the second section of this chapter examines how Rivera's and Rulfo's plastic and photographic depictions of the indigenous body align with the two possible models of *mestizo*-indigenous relations outlined by Villoro. By engaging in a historically and culturally contextualised reading of specific mural panels and photographs produced by both artists from the mid-1920s to the mid-1950s, I consider how these works reflect a fundamental shift in intellectual and artistic interpretations of the relationship between the *mestizo* and the *indio* by moving from an immersive aesthetic model to one founded on critical distance and self-reflexivity. Beginning with Rivera's indigenous imagery in the Palacio Nacional and the SEP, I explore how these representations reflect the contradictory impulses of *indigenismo* by aesthetically reproducing the intimate but unequal encounter between the *mestizo* and indigenous other described by Villoro. Analysing *El antiguo mundo indígena* (1929) at the Palacio Nacional in relation to the aesthetic philosophies of the Ateneo de la Juventud, I examine how this panel aesthetically stages *indigenista* efforts to overcome the *mestizo*'s fundamental exteriority to the indigenous other by using immersive strategies that draw the viewer into the imagined space of the mural. While these devices create an illusion of proximity between observer and subject, the panel upholds the unidirectional power relations of post-revolutionary *indigenismo* by figuring the native body as an object of contemplation. Situating Rulfo's mid-century photographs of Oaxaca within a broader contemporary shift in visual and intellectual discourses surrounding indigeneity, I consider how the gaze serves a different function in these works. Focusing on one of his previously unexamined photographs of a female Mixe performer, I examine how the returned indigenous gaze disrupts the viewer's immersion in the image, signalling a shift towards the more self-reflexive model of *indigenismo* anticipated by Villoro.

Indigenismo: Incorporating the Indigenous into National Culture

During the early decades of the twentieth century, the *indigenista* movement was spearheaded by the anthropologist Manuel Gamio, who crusaded for 'la redención de la clase indígena' [the redemption of the indigenous class] by stressing the validity of indigenous culture and aesthetics.[82] In *Forjando patria* (1916) and *La población del valle de Teotihuacán* (1922), Gamio identified the nation's autochthonous culture as the bedrock of contemporary *mexicanidad* and advocated the integration of Mexico's indigenous populations into mainstream national culture as a means of establishing a racially, culturally and linguistically homogenous national identity.[83] Gamio attributed a crucial function to aesthetics in bringing the *indio* to the forefront of the national consciousness.[84] In the visual domain, this cultural revalorisation of the *indio* was carried out through positive pictorial representations of indigenous figures and spaces by artists such as Dr. Atl, Roberto Montenegro, Fernando Leal and Fermín Revueltas, and regional dance performances choreographed by the artist-intellectual Adolfo Best-Maugard. As Guillermo Bonfil-Batalla notes, during this visually-saturated campaign, 'México profundo mostró por un momento su presencia real y no fue posible cerrar los ojos ante él' [deep Mexico momentarily revealed its real presence and it was impossible to close one's eyes to it].[85] The powerful visual dimension to the *indigenista* project encapsulated the fundamental contradictions of a movement that sought to enhance the visibility of the indigenous body in the cultural sphere, while simultaneously advocating its gradual erasure through assimilation.

Like Gamio, who hoped that positive expressions of indigeneity would enable Mexicans to 'forjarse —ya sea temporalmente —un alma indígena' [forge — albeit temporarily —an indigenous soul], the muralists viewed art as a means of resurrecting an indigenous spirit that had been lying dormant within the national consciousness.[86] In their 1923 manifesto, they stressed the *mestizo*'s racial and spiritual bond with the *indio*:

> No solamente todo lo que es trabajo noble, todo lo que es virtud, es don de nuestro pueblo (de nuestros indios muy particularmente), sino la manifestación más pequeña de la existencia física y espiritual de nuestra raza como fuerza étnica brota de él.[87]
>
> [Not only are all forms of noble work and virtue gifts of our people (especially of our Indians), but also the smallest manifestation of the physical and spiritual existence of our race as an ethnic force that springs from them.]

As self-elected spokespersons of the nation's downtrodden, the muralists adopted the indigenous body as a core component of their pictorial vocabulary. The formal dimensions of their art form secured it a privileged position within the *indigenista* cultural campaign. Inspired by pre-Hispanic artistic traditions, muralism provided a sense of cultural continuity with the nation's autochthonous past while also harnessing what Rivera identified as the profoundly emotion-centred quality of indigenous artistic expression.[88] Although Rivera amassed an extensive collection of ethnographic photographs, he notably never experimented with the medium to depict indigenous subjects. Rivera's aesthetic preferences appear to have been consistent with those of contemporary Andean *indigenistas* who, as Deborah Poole explains, celebrated the 'sentimental realism' of painting over photography in its ability to capture 'el sentimiento andino' [the Andean sentiment].[89] According to Poole, these artists 'could translate this sentiment into the painterly art of color, emotion, and personal —as opposed to mechanical —sensibility'.[90] In Mexico, this perceived superiority of painting was reflected in the pictorial style adopted by folkloricist photographers during the early decades of the twentieth century, who sought to conceal the indexical nature of their medium by using the camera 'as a nineteenth century paintbrush', to portray indigenous bodies and landscapes.[91]

Interacting with the *indio*: Aesthetic Immersion in *El antiguo mundo indígena* (1929)

In 1921 Rivera had returned from Paris to Mexico, where the heady cultural climate of the early nation-building period encouraged his engagement with pre-Columbian artistic forms. Eager to cultivate his interest in national themes, Vasconcelos invited Rivera to visit the Yucatán Peninsula in 1921 and the Isthmus of Tehuantepec in Oaxaca the following year. These experiences proved formative for the artist, who accumulated an extensive archive of sketches and mental images from which he would draw throughout his career. Although Rivera had already included indigenous figures in several of his early murals, the Palacio Nacional commission represented his most significant engagement with this theme to date. Saturated in warm colour and distinguished by its open spatial configuration, *El antiguo mundo indígena,* which occupies the entire north wall, immediately attracts the viewer's eye from the vantage point of the upper balcony. To the centre of the panel, a group of votaries kneel in devotion around the Mesoamerican deity Quetzalcoatl, adorned with an elaborate headdress. The centre-left of the panel revolves thematically around indigenous artistic expression, depicting figures engaged in sculpting, weaving, dancing and ceramic and gold production. Beneath a line of overlapping labouring bodies positioned to the centre left of the image, a fierce battle between warring communities unfolds in the bottom left-hand corner. Set apart from the more crowded central and south walls, the compositional simplicity of the north panel and its narration of events through clearly defined groupings of bodies forms an almost pictographic visual language reminiscent of the Mesoamerican codices. More recent historical influences can also be detected. The epic nature of Rivera's pictorial homage recalls Porfirian projects to commemorate Mexico's pre-Hispanic heritage which, as Tenorio-Trillo explains, synthesised national history in 'visual, monumental form'.[92]

While the panel can be surveyed from a range of perspectives, the spatial cues of the main staircase invite us to engage with it from the closer vantage point of the steps ascending alongside the north wall. Viewed from this angle, the mural can be seen to stage an encounter between the implicitly *mestizo* viewer and indigenous subject that closely aligns with the early post-revolutionary model of *indigenismo* described by Villoro. The racial and class assumptions on which this model of viewer engagement is predicated are consistent with the realities of mural reception in the late 1920s. Despite their revolutionary claims to democratise art, the location of the muralists' works in public buildings in Mexico City rendered them largely inaccessible to those sections of the population they claimed to elevate, such as indigenous communities and peasants. As Coffey points out, prior to 1934, 'the frescos intended for a broad public were actually limited to a mostly cosmopolitan and urban audience' composed of middle-class students and civil servants.[93] Speaking at the American Artists' Congress (ACC) in 1936, Siqueiros reflected on this fundamental contradiction:

> We gave little thought to questions of revolutionary strategy in the placing of our works. We were at this time Utopians in our conception of revolutionary art with little direct contact with the masses [...] Our murals were in places more or less inaccessible to the masses.[94]

While photographic reproductions of the murals were included in magazines and SEP publications distributed in rural areas, the opportunity to both visually and spatially experience these works was reserved for a relatively small number of educated observers living in the predominantly *mestizo* capital.

Approaching *El antiguo mundo indígena* with this audience in mind enables us to better understand how Rivera exploits architectural and visual aspects of his medium to aesthetically stage the moment of 'communion' or 'communication' with the *indio* described by post-revolutionary intellectuals such as Héctor Pérez Martínez and Agustín Yáñez.[95] In this sense, I develop an earlier observation by Folgarait by exploring exactly how and why Rivera looks to transform the viewer into a 'co-participant with the painted historical characters'.[96] In its attempt to transport the viewer to an imagined pre-Columbian reality, Rivera's vivid imagery provides a striking pictorial analogue to Reyes's poetic vision of Anáhuac. Reyes's highly sensuous prose vividly reconstructs the Valley of Mexico, drawing the contemporary reader into contact with the nation's pre-Columbian ancestors. In addition to its rich visual texture, underlined by Paz's description of the essay as a 'vasto fresco en prosa' [vast fresco in prose], the melodic language of the local inhabitants, perceived as 'una canturía gustosa' [joyful singing], adds an acoustic dimension to the text, resulting in a 'mareo de los sentidos' [dizzying sensory experience].[97]

Reyes's multi-sensorial evocation of the indigenous world was consistent with the aesthetic theories of the Ateneo, of which both he and Rivera were members. Railing against Porfirian positivism, the Ateneo embraced the theories of Henri Bergson, privileging sensory perception and emotional intuition as the most effective means of comprehending reality. Vasconcelos identified this form of intuition as the most appropriate for the 'raza emotiva' [emotional race] of Latin America and underlined the persuasive power of artworks with sensory appeal, claiming that 'los hombres son más impresionables cuando se les aborda por el conducto de los sentidos como acontece cuando alguien contempla hermosas formas y figuras o escucha hermosos ritmos y melodías' [men are more impressionable when approached through their senses, as happens when one contemplates beautiful forms and figures or listens to beautiful rhythms and melodies].[98] Like Antonio Caso, Vasconcelos asserted that the immediate perception of beauty could produce a response of 'emotional empathy' through which the perceiver would become 'fused' with the work of art.[99] As Tirres notes, this empathetic merging of subject and object through the contemplation of a work of art provided Vasconcelos with an aesthetic counterpart to the process of cultural and racial fusion enacted through *mestizaje*.[100]

Rivera's *El antiguo mundo indígena* can be understood as an attempt to generate the experience of aesthetic empathy outlined by his fellow Ateneístas by activating the immersive qualities of muralism. Discussing the evolution of all-embracing image-spaces from antiquity to the present day, Oliver Grau explains how artworks lacking the concrete boundary imposed by the frame aim 'to appeal not only to the eyes but to all other senses so that the impression arises of being completely in an artificial world'.[101] In line with the aesthetic objectives of the Ateneo, this illusionistic form of visual representation produces a model of viewer engagement that is 'characterised by diminished critical distance to what is shown and increasing emotional involvement in what is happening'.[102] In the Palacio Nacional, Rivera maximises this immersive potential by integrating optical illusions that extend the action of the composition beyond the pictorial plane. The tense musculature of the bare-chested warriors in the foreground injects the battle scenes with a sense of physical immediacy, creating such a powerful illusion of three-dimensionality that their stretched limbs and raised spears appear to jut out of the wall. A similar optical effect can be discerned in the far right-hand side of the wall where a young woman, positioned near eye-level, sits weaving. The rope connected to her loom appears to be attached to the concrete wall of the palace, dissolving the boundary between the mural and the external architectural space. Directly above this figure in the upper right-hand side of the composition a percussionist leans forward, as if adapting her body to the curve of the exterior wall framing the mural.

These details demonstrate Rivera's application of 'plastic integration', a theory developed by the muralists to promote the harmonious interrelation of the artwork with its architectural setting. This principle informs Rivera's exploitation of specific architectural elements along the north stairway to engage the viewer physically and sensorially and thus create the impression of a co-extensive aesthetic environment. Photographs taken while work on the north wall was still underway show that a lightbulb was originally suspended from the ceiling directly level with the blazing sun located at the top of the composition above Quetzalcoatl. Transitioning from the less illuminated area of the central stairway towards the north stairs, this electric source would have created the impression of light radiating out from the mural onto the spectators gathered before it. The illusion of a shared aesthetic environment is enhanced by the perceiver's physical navigation of this architectural space. As the viewer ascends the stairs to follow the visual narrative, her movement infuses the entire scene with vitality, creating a sense of kinetic unity with the animated indigenous figures inhabiting its painted interior. Rivera's reliance on a mobile viewer to activate the composition in this way anticipates Siqueiros's theories of polyangular composition: 'Quiero que cuando entre aquí el espectador, y camine, todo entre en movimiento: las formas y los volúmenes, el piso, los muros' [When the viewer enters this space, I want everything to start moving: the forms and volumes, the floor, the walls].[103] The physical movements of the spectator along the north stairway also generate sound effects that further destabilise the boundaries separating the inner pictorial space of the mural and external reality. Lending visual form to the 'beautiful forms' and 'beautiful melodies' described by Vasconcelos, the graceful bodies of the dancers in the upper right-hand corner of the wall move to the rhythm dictated by the accompanying musicians. This acoustic image again offers something of a pictorial equivalent to Reyes's interpretation of synaesthesia as a form of 'audición colorida' [coloured hearing], however Rivera further enhances its sensory appeal by again dynamically incorporating the viewer into the scene.[104] The shuffle and echo of footsteps on the stone steps creates the impression of sound emanating from the dancers' percussion instruments, producing a kind of rhythmic identification between the bodies moving alongside the mural and those inhabiting its interior.

Rivera's *Indigenista* Optics

Villoro identifies this sense of communion with the imagined figure of the *indio* as a defining aspect of post-revolutionary *indigenismo*. Through the metaphor of the gaze, however, he also underlines how, despite these illusions of intimacy and unity, *indigenismo* deprives the indigenous other of knowledge and agency: 'el indígena es comprendido y juzgado ("revelado") por el no indígena' [the Indian is understood and judged ('revealed') by the non-Indian].[105] As Mario Teodoro Ramírez asserts, in this encounter, 'la reciprocidad de las miradas, del reconocimiento, está excluída' [the reciprocity of gazes, of recognition, is ruled out].[106] The visual metaphors used by Villoro to explain *indigenismo*'s internal colonial project foreshadow Edward Said's discussion of orientalism as a power network and set of imaginative or aesthetic practices in *Orientalism* (1978). In this seminal work, Said illustrates how the West has discursively and visually constructed the Orient to validate Western dominance in colonial power relationships. While *indigenismo* differed fundamentally from the Anglo-French colonial paradigm through its focus on an internal other, Villoro's study prefigures many of Said's arguments by demonstrating how the imagined figure of the *indio* has served to consolidate notions of *mestizo* identity and authority. In light of these parallels, the conceptual framework of orientalism and its strategies of representation are useful for understanding how Rivera's mural visually reproduces the colonial narrative perspective framing Reyes's essay.

As in the revolutionary segment of the central panel analysed in the first part of this chapter, Rivera here confers considerable control to the viewing eye. In keeping with the conventions of orientalist visual representation, the *indigenista* project of 'rediscovering' the *indio* is registered on a corporeal level in his panel through the 'uncovering', or 'laying bare' of the indigenous body. In contrast to the more compacted scenes in the upper sections of the central and south walls, where the layering of bodies renders individuals only partially visible, the relative spaciousness of the northern section grants the observer a complete view of the bare and semi-clothed indigenous figures inhabiting its interior. The muralist notably positions the more exposed bodies in the lower foreground of the mural where they are immediately visible to the spectator. Although Rivera repudiated Porfirian easel painting, his treatment of the indigenous body in this regard is consistent with historical paintings produced by the artists of the Academia de San Carlos, his alma mater, during the late nineteenth century. The works of academic painters such as Leandro Izaguirre, José Jara, Joaquín Ramírez and Félix Parra, which contributed to the Porfirian project of national reconciliation by fashioning a glorious pre-Hispanic past, placed a strong emphasis on the sculpted physicality of the heroic native body. Although more robust and active than these earlier neo-classical models, Rivera's indigenous subjects display a similarly statuesque muscularity that invites a sustained gaze. Like his Porfirian predecessors, Rivera monumentalises the indigenous body while also presenting it as a source of visual pleasure. Foucault's identification of seeing as the basis for knowledge and thus power, illustrated by the etymological linking of *voir*, *savoir* and *pouvoir*, is helpful for understanding the implications of these visual practices within the context of the *indigenista* project. Like the previously discussed revolutionary-themed section of the triptych, Rivera's imagery here reveals a concern with visual mastery; in this case, a desire to know and gain visual control over the indigenous body. The positioning of exposed muscular bodies in the lower sections, which are closer to eye level, establishes an unbalanced viewing power dynamic that is further enforced by his use of the rear-view pose. Several of the prominent male figures located in the lower left-hand section of the panel are turned away, encouraging the viewer's full immersion in this impressive anatomical display.

These optical dynamics acquire a more overtly voyeuristic dimension in Rivera's imagery of indigenous female bathers in the SEP, which adheres to the orientalist convention of depicting women in more intimate settings. Stepping into the enclosed space of the elevator vestibule on the ground floor of the Patio del Trabajo, the viewer enters a timeless scene of Tehuana women bathing in the cenotes of Yucatán (1924) (Fig. 1.2). Rivera's decision to set the scene in this recessive area, which is set apart from the open and naturally illuminated patio, is indicative of a recurring link between the nude female body and contained architectural spaces in his muralism that I return to in Chapter 3. After the Revolution, the figure of the Tehuana was upheld as the embodiment of an authentic and uncorrupted national essence and became the focal point for *indigenista* iconography. Although distinguished by her distinctive regional dress, the much-discussed sexually liberated attitude of the Tehuana validated artistic portrayals of her exposed body. This aesthetic celebration of the Tehuana and initiatives such as the India Bonita pageant of 1921 were part of a broader effort to validate indigenous beauty by directing the *mestizo* male gaze towards the native female body. Rivera's panel pursues this eroticisation of the indigenous female by taking inspiration from the painterly genre of the bathing scene, a long-standing pictorial theme that was rejuvenated by European primitivist painters and adopted by numerous Mexican artists to depict the indigenous female body in the early twentieth century. In the panel located on the left-hand side of the alcove, a group of indigenous women bearing baskets and water jugs stand amidst the tropical foliage on the elevated part of the riverbank. Below, at the water's edge, four naked and semi-clothed indigenous women lean into the rock pools to wash themselves and their white sheets, their dark skin seamlessly merging with their untamed natural surroundings.

As in the Palacio Nacional, Rivera again positions the more exposed bodies in the immediately visible lower section of the panel and presents them from a rear angle to suggest their obliviousness to the viewer's gaze. In this way the panel recreates Rivera's personal impressions of the native women of Oaxaca who, according to Marnham, enthralled him with their 'combination of sensuality and innocence' and 'were scarcely aware of his presence'.[107] During the 1920s, the motif of the bathing Tehuana was repeatedly used to play out this scopophilic fantasy of a unidirectional gaze cast on the naïve and unsuspecting indigenous female. In early works by Rufino Tamayo, Fermín Revueltas and Miguel Covarrubias, as well as several of Rivera's easel portraits, the undressed Tehuana is depicted with her face turned away or obscured to facilitate the viewer's voyeuristic contemplation of her exposed body. By exploiting the unique architectural dimensions of the dimly lit alcove, Rivera extends this voyeuristic experience to a spatial level by creating the impression that the viewer is physically inhabiting this private scene. Margaret A. Majumdar's observations on the function of the unreciprocated gaze in orientalist visual art again illuminate the colonial power dynamics underpinning these images. Echoing Villoro's description of *indigenismo* as an encounter in which the *indio* is 'judged and 'revealed' by the *mestizo*, she explains how 'in the orientalist gaze, the possibility of judgement is always there, but it is a one-sided judgment, that of the voyeur'.[108]

In his analysis of artistic expressions of *indigenismo*, Villoro describes the resurrection of the *indio* as an event that is produced and controlled by the *mestizo*

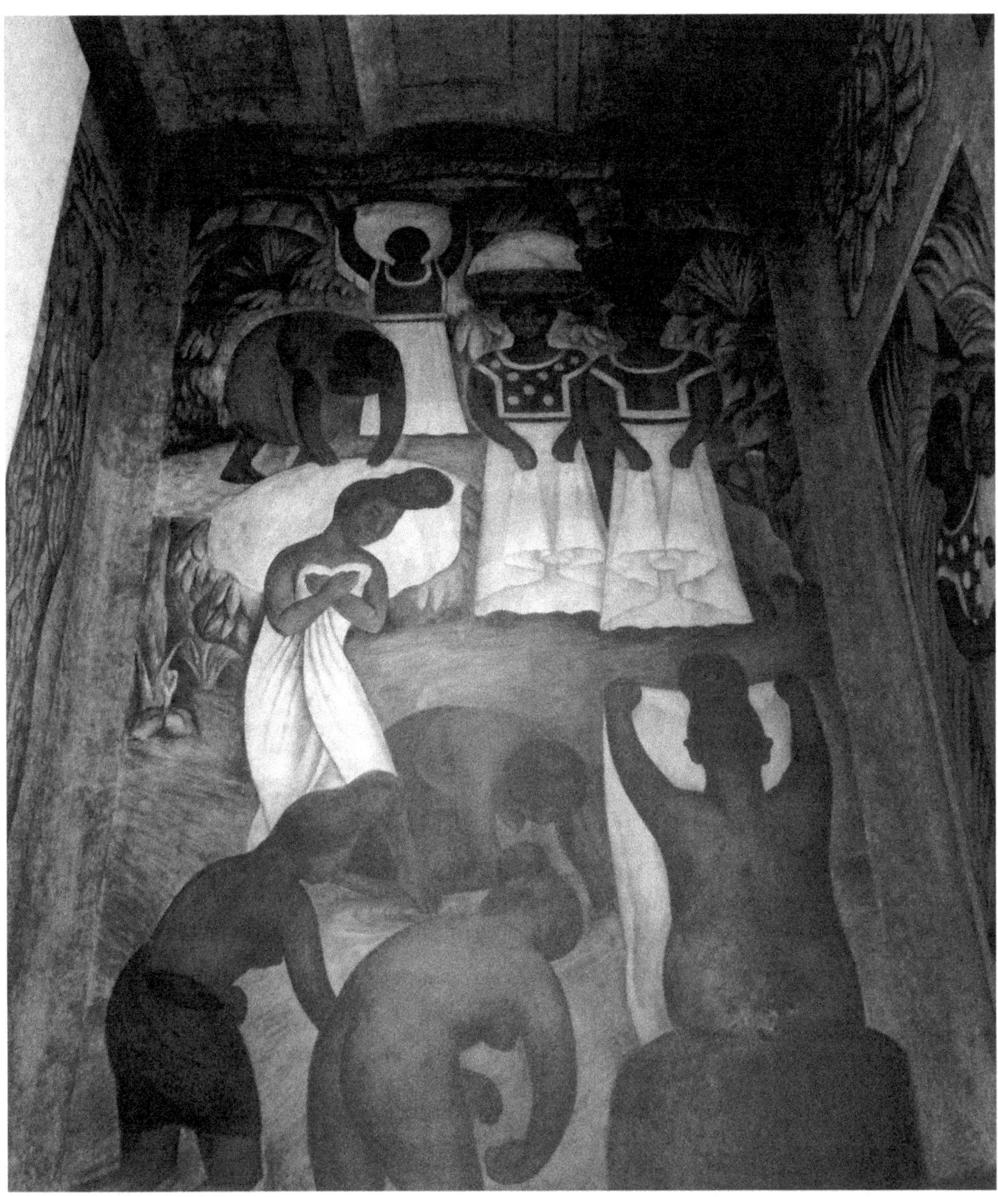

Fig. 1.2. Diego Rivera, Mural in elevator vestibule of the Patio del Trabajo (1924), Ministry of Public Education © Banco de México Diego Rivera Frida Kahlo Museums Trust, Mexico, D.F. / DACS 2021

imagination, citing Rivera's muralism as a key pictorial example of this project.[109] Villoro's study anticipated a broader shift in attitudes towards *indigenismo*. From the mid-1960s the paternalistic and racist aspects of *indigenista* anthropology became the focus of increasing scrutiny, as did the efficacy of incorporationist and acculturation strategies, which at the start of the following decade were denounced as a form of internal colonialism.[110] In the realm of visual culture, this more critical perspective found a parallel in photographic practices that subtly problematised the conventional representational dynamics associated with *indigenista* aesthetics. Erica Segre writes that 'from the mid-1950s, photography in Mexico becomes increasingly self-reflexive, especially in its relation to indigenous culture, in response to the institutionalisation and discursive ubiquity of national anthropology'.[111] She identifies the period from the 1920s to the 1950s as a particularly formative phase for Mexican photographers who became 'jointly exercised by the conceptual and the political problem of visual identity and intrigued by the production of visuality itself'.[112] This more interrogative approach originates with key visual practitioners of the 1920s and 30s such as Manuel Álvarez Bravo, Tina Modotti and Edward Weston whose works experimented with more thought-provoking ways of seeing that unsettled picturesque representational paradigms. The photographs of Álvarez Bravo were particularly emblematic of this turn, interweaving symbolism, surrealism and visual ambiguity to create an anti-exotic aesthetic that demanded a critical rather than sentimental response from the viewer. Echoing Villoro's assertion that *indigenismo* protects the *mestizo* from the judgment of the indigenous gaze, the photojournalist Nacho López, a prominent disciple of Álvarez Bravo during the 1950s, underlined the power imbalances implicated in the act of looking and considered how photography might invert these dynamics:

> Poner el ojo en el visor fotográfico, encuadrar al sujeto y oprimir el botón es fácil si se piensa que lo folclórico es el motivo principal. Ellos están tras las rejas, nosotros fuera. Si invertimos la imagen, los cautivos somos nosotros.[113]
>
> [Putting your eye in the viewfinder, framing the subject and pressing the button is easy if you are looking to achieve a folkloric aesthetic. They are behind bars while we remain outside. If we invert the image, we are the captives.]

Reversing the Gaze: Self-Reflexivity and Distance in Rulfo's Photographs

It was during this dynamic period of photographic activity in Mexico from the 1930s to the 1950s that Rulfo experimented with his own Leica and Rolleiflex cameras and developed into a skilled practitioner. A particularly productive phase in his photographic activity coincided with his work as a researcher for the Comisión del Papaloapan between 1955 and 1957, an experience that laid the foundations for his subsequent career in anthropology. Rulfo joined the publications department of the INI in 1962 and remained there until his death in 1986. A closer examination of Rulfo's anthropological and photographic activity during the mid-1950s brings to light his ambivalent stance on the indigenous question. Established by President Alemán in 1947, the Comisión del Papaloapan carried out an infrastructural modernisation project involving the construction of the hydroelectric Miguel Alemán Dam in the predominantly indigenous-populated Papaloapan river basin in Oaxaca. The Commission worked closely with anthropologists from the INI which had been established in 1948. Conceived as a long-term solution to sporadic flooding in the basin, the construction of the dam also provided the government with an opportunity to further its integrationist and developmentalist objectives in the region. Writing in 1955, the INI anthropologist Alfonso Villa Rojas explained that the main objective of the Commission in the area was 'elevar el nivel de vida de sus pobladores así como incorporar a la economía nacional la vasta riqueza potencial que encierran sus múltiples recursos naturales' [to elevate the standard of living of its inhabitants and incorporate the vast potential wealth held in its multiple natural resources into the national economy].[114] Contrary to Villa Rojas's progressive vision, the Papaloapan project was a catastrophic failure in social, environmental, economic and health terms.[115] Schwartz notes that anthropologists played a contradictory role in the process, promoting the modernisation and acculturation of local communities while also seeking to preserve their uniquely indigenous cultural qualities.[116]

These contradictory objectives formed the basis for Rulfo's activities for the Commission during the mid-1950s. Working as a researcher alongside anthropologists from the INI, Rulfo assisted with the challenging task of relocating diverse indigenous groups that had been displaced from the Papaloapan river basin, a project paternalistically hailed by Villa Rojas as 'un proceso de cambio de la vida tribal a la vida de nuestro tiempo' [a process of transition from tribal life to the life of our times].[117] During this two-year period, Rulfo produced a series of unpublished texts and approximately three hundred and fifty photographs of the Oaxacan landscape. Many these photographs were taken in Tlahuitoltepec and Zacatepec between February and June of 1955 while Rulfo was working as a scriptwriter and photographer alongside the photojournalist Walter Reuter on a short documentary entitled *Danzas mixes*. Sponsored by the Commission, this short film focusing on the traditional dances of the Mixe community would have served the preservationist objectives of the organisation.

Despite his active role in implementing the modernising and integrationist objectives of the Commission, Rulfo expressed a scepticism towards contemporary discourses of national unity that manifests in his photographic production. Rulfo insisted on Mexico's insurmountable heterogeneity, stating: 'No hay una cosa determinada que pueda permitirnos decir: Así es México [...] Es uno de tantos Méxicos' [There is no single thing about which we can say: that is Mexico... it is one of many Mexicos.][118] Describing the devastating impact of the Conquest on Anáhuac's inhabitants in a piece published in 1986, Rulfo claimed that *mestizaje* had replicated oppressive colonial systems, describing it 'una estrategia criolla para unificar lo disperso, afirmar su dominio, llenar el vacío de poder dejado por los españoles' [a creole strategy to unify the dispersed, to affirm their domination, to fill the power vacuum left by the Spanish].[119] In light of these statements and Rulfo's metaphorical critique of the continuity of colonial power structures through the theme of *caciquismo* in *Pedro Páramo*, it seems unlikely that the perpetuation of such dynamics through post-revolutionary integrationist projects would have escaped him.

Despite his lengthy anthropological career and complex stance on race relations in Mexico, Rulfo's extensive photographic engagement with indigenous subject matter has received limited scholarly attention. This can in part be attributed to the critical tendency to read these works as visual extensions of his literary images, as evidenced by the description of the collection *Inframundo* (1984) as a 'photographic companion to *El Llano en llamas*', or the editorial decision to present his photographs alongside excerpts from his literature in *Juan Rulfo's Mexico* (2002).[120] One of the few scholars to look beyond such superficial comparisons and consider the common political aspects of Rulfo's textual and visual corpora is Amit Thakkar, who questions whether his 'photographs of indigenous peoples in dances, festivals and processions are exotic and sentimental or ironic and challenging'.[121] The first interpretative approach proposed by Thakkar is entirely plausible when we consider not only Rulfo's aforementioned anthropological activities, but also the distribution and publication history of his photographs. Following the appearance of his first photographs in the magazine *América* in 1949, his works featured in tourist travel guides such as the tyre manufacturer Goodrich Euzkadi's *Caminos de México* in 1950 and 1958 and *Mapa: Revista de Automovilismo y Turismo*, the official magazine of the Mexican Automobile Association, in 1952. While promoting the modernising impulse of an expanding automotive industry, Jennifer Jolly explains how the picturesque photographs illustrating guides like *Mapa* also encouraged 'the quest for an indigenous past in the modern present'.[122] Echoing contemporary rhetoric of national unity, these publications invited motorists to establish contact with unknown worlds located within the national territory: 'Salgamos de nuestro mundo para ponerlo en comunicación con esos otros mundos que, aunque diversos, se integran a la unidad de la Patria' [Let us leave our modern world and bring it into contact with other worlds, which, although different, also form part of the Homeland].[123]

While Rulfo's Oaxacan photographs could be seen to uphold the image of a romantic and accessible indigenous Mexico, such a reading is complicated by certain aspects of these works. A more recent essay by Thakkar has attempted to open up this line of inquiry, drawing on the photographic theories of Roland Barthes and Susan Sontag to illustrate how a particular photograph taken by Rulfo of the indigenous inhabitants of Janitzio cuts against assumptions of rural folkloricism.[124] Taking up Thakkar's invitation for further investigation into this subject, I turn to Rulfo's lesser-studied Oaxacan photographs to explore how the returned gaze challenges conventional *indigenista* representational strategies by dramatising a fundamental disconnect between viewer and indigenous subject. While there is no concrete evidence that Rulfo read Villoro during the early 1950s it seems highly likely, given his increasing professional engagement with anthropology during the decade and voracious appetite for reading, that he was aware of his landmark study.[125] Situating his photography for the first time in the context of changing mid-century intellectual and artistic perspectives on indigenism, I demonstrate how the estranging and subtly surrealist aspects of Rulfo's depiction of the indigenous body indicate a shift towards the more self-reflexive mode of *indigenismo* anticipated by the Hiperión thinker.

While I do not intend to follow previous critics in cataloguing parallels between the content of Rulfo's photographic images and specific passages of his literary texts, his brief depiction of an indigenous community in *Pedro Páramo* provides a useful starting point for an analysis of his photographs. Although early commentators of the novel believed the villagers of Comala to be indigenous, Rulfo later clarified that 'en la novela no hay ningún indio. Sólo una vez cuando bajan de Apango' [there are no Indians in the novel. Only on one occasion when they come down from Apango].[126] Subsequent comments by Rulfo suggest that his reluctance to include indigenous characters derived from profound anxieties about the problem of representing Mexico's internal 'other'. Echoing the Peruvian critic Antonio Cornejo Polar's discussion of the 'perspectiva exterior' [external perspective] of the *indigenista* writer, Rulfo argued in 1981 that it was impossible for the non-indigenous writer to access indigenous reality:[127]

> Resulta difícil, cuando no imposible, adentrarse en su mentalidad [...] Esto lo digo con conocimiento de causa, ya que, a pesar de ser Jefe del Departamento de Publicaciones del Instituto Nacional Indigenista, y habiendo publicado más de 80 obras de Antropología Social, todavía desconozco cómo y por qué motivos actúa la mente indígena.[128]
>
> [It is difficult, if not impossible, to penetrate their mindset... I say this with first-hand experience because, despite being Head of the Department of Publications at the National Indigenous Institute, and having published more than eighty works on social anthropology, I still do not know how the indigenous mind works, nor what motivates it.]

Despite the conspicuous absence of indigenous characters from Rulfo's fiction, their fleeting appearance in the forty-eighth fragment of his novel is revealing. Although the singularity and brevity of this passage within the novel can in itself be interpreted as an indirect critique of post-revolutionary integrationist efforts, I want to briefly highlight the specific role of the indigenous gaze in conveying the disjuncture between the imagined worlds of the *mestizo* and the *indio*. In this episode, Susana's maid Justina Díaz visits the market to buy rosemary from the indigenous vendors who have travelled from Apango during a torrential downpour. While the merchants converse amongst themselves, Justina's internal monologue is voiced separately to the reader, reducing her interaction with the *indios* to a wordless interplay of gazes:

> Entró en el portal. Los indios voltearon a verla. Vio la mirada de todos como si la escudriñaran. Se detuvo en el primer puesto, compró diez centavos de hojas de romero, y regresó, seguida por las miradas en hilera de aquel montón de indios (274).
>
> [She came in through the gate. The Indians turned to look at her. She saw all of them staring as if they were scrutinising her. She stopped at the first stall, bought ten cents worth of rosemary and left, followed by the line of gazes of that bunch of Indians.]

Here the scrutinising gazes of the indigenous sellers immediately mark Justina as an outsider and appear to almost drive her out of the marketplace. In Rulfo's photographic portraits of the native communities of Oaxaca, taken the same year that *Pedro Páramo* was published, the gaze performs a similar function in conveying a profound disconnection between *mestizo* and indigenous worlds. While José Carlos González Boixo has claimed that Rulfo 'rehúye que los personajes miren a la cámara (el espectador siente que esta mirada se dirige a él, lo cual remarca el propio acto fotográfico, algo que Rulfo quiere esconder)' [avoids having his subjects look at the camera (the spectator feels that this gaze is directed to him, which draws attention to the very act of photography, something that Rulfo wants to conceal)], his Oaxacan portfolio includes numerous photographs of indigenous performers, onlookers and church-goers whose wary or at times openly hostile glances alert us to our external position as observers.[129] These reactions highlight the uniquely invasive nature of photographic representation. Unlike painting (with the obvious exception of portraiture involving live sitters), the creator of the photograph is assumed to be physically present at the scene depicted, inhabiting the same space as his or her subjects at the time of the image's production. Although in this sense, Rulfo's photographs enact in real terms the spatial interaction between the *mestizo* and *indio* simulated by Rivera's mural, it produces the opposite effect, creating a sense of distance between viewer and subject. While Rivera's medium was seen to affirm an enduring cultural bond among the nation's races due to its pre-Hispanic origins, the intrusive presence of Rulfo's camera brings into sharp focus a profound cultural disjuncture between representer and represented. The returned gaze not only accentuates a position of exteriority to the *indio* that *indigenismo* strived to overcome, but also overturns the power dynamics inscribed in its conventional modes of visualisation. As photography theorist Margaret Olin explains, 'the returned gaze [...] rescues the beheld's sense of self. If you look back you cannot be possessed by the gaze of the other'.[130] Olin's assertion that the reciprocated gaze initiates 'some kind of dialogism, in which a totalistic, hegemonic gaze is replaced by the mutual gaze of equality' indicates the potential for photography to produce a more egalitarian visual aesthetic of *indigenismo* in which, as Villoro suggests, *mestizo* and *indio* 'se reconozcan recíprocamente' [recognise one another reciprocally].[131]

This destabilising effect of the returned gaze is most striking in a photograph taken by Rulfo in 1955 of two Mixe performers in Zacatepec (Fig. 1.3). While at first glance this image adheres to the representational conventions of the native performance as spectacle, the indigenous gaze unsettles these assumptions by exposing the power relations implicated in the act of looking. The photograph depicts a man and a woman dressed in the costumes traditionally worn for the 'danza de moros y cristianos', a popular ritual dramatising the act of Conquest that was imported to Latin America by the Spanish during the sixteenth century. Hellier-Tinoco has demonstrated the centrality of traditional performances to touristic and nationalistic constructions of a folkloric indigeneity during the post-revolution period, yet Rulfo's photographs cannot be easily located within this representational model.[132] In contrast to many of the images of indigenous musicians and dancers published in contemporary magazines and reports focusing

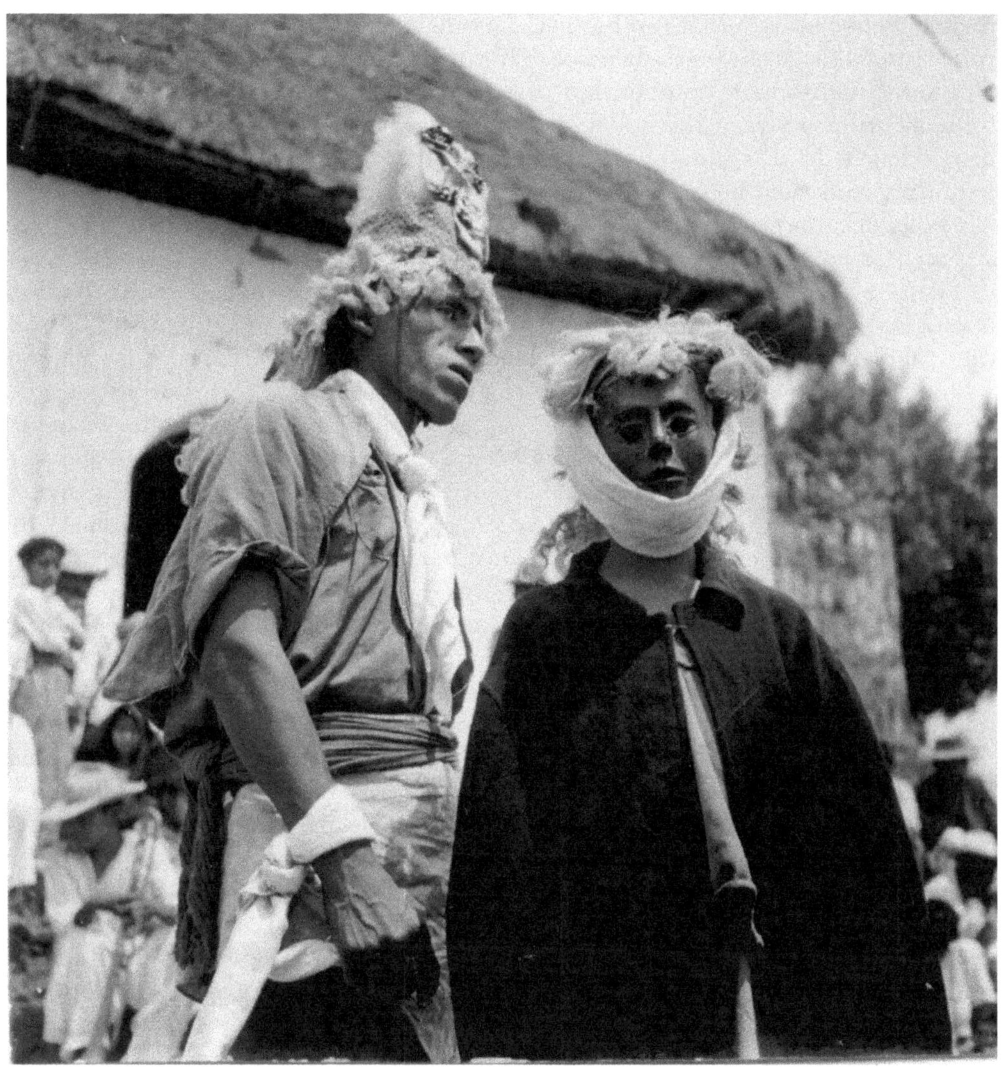

Fig. 1.3. Juan Rulfo, Mixe dancers in Zacatepec, Oaxaca (1955)
© Herederos de Juan Rulfo

on the inhabitants of the Papaloapan region, this photograph, like most of Rulfo's portraits of indigenous performers, is paradoxically devoid of movement. The sensuous immediacy and sonority of Rivera's vibrant imagery is here replaced by a muted stillness that unsettles picturesque notions of indigenous performance.

A folkloric reading of the photograph is further obstructed by the female figure positioned to the centre-right of the frame who poses a number of optical difficulties for the viewer. Much like the literary spectres of Comala, this particular body resists immediate legibility. The woman, who appears in at least one other photograph, is dressed in a modern coat and wig, but unlike her male companion her face is obscured by an expressionless black mask. A scarf wrapped around her head conceals the gap between the mask and her neck, momentarily creating the impression that this artificial surface is in fact her face. This unsettling visual ambiguity is enhanced by the monochromatic composition of the photograph which provides little tonal differentiation between the colour of the mask and her exposed skin. While the man's clenched fist is slightly raised to reveal the protruding veins of his forearm, her arms, concealed beneath her oversized coat, hang limply by her side, lending her body an almost doll-like appearance that is accentuated by the synthetic wig and stylised countenance of the mask.

These features and her slightly tilted posture recall another of Rulfo's photographs from the same period depicting a female mannequin in traditional dress and headscarf positioned at a road-side stall, suggesting a surrealist fascination with the uncanny doubling of animate and inanimate human forms. In his limited writings on photography, Rulfo praised the challenging ethnographic styles of Henri Cartier-Bresson and particularly Nacho López, who himself was an admirer of Rulfo's work. The subtle resemblance between Rulfo's two photographs invites comparisons with the surrealist-inflected depictions of mannequins produced by these visual practitioners during the 1930s and 50s. López's photography, which Rulfo credited with revealing Mexico's 'más profunda realidad' [most profound reality], explored the hidden realities lying beneath the surface of the familiar and experimented with unusual ocular motifs to expose the artifice of image production and the mechanics of voyeurism.[133] In this photograph, Rulfo relies on similarly self-reflexive visual strategies by employing the mask as an estranging device that plays on the surrealist tension between appearance and reality. One of the few critics to perceive surrealist elements in Rulfo's photography is André Stoll, who argues that his haunting portrayals of natural and architectural spaces reveal a history of colonial violence. Stoll asserts that although Rulfo's collection of photographs of Oaxaca 'podría prometer auténticos paraísos del exotismo' [could promise authentic paradises of exoticism], it in fact opens up 'una amplia variedad de perspectivas que inquietan al observador y le incitan a la reflexión sobre lo representado' [a wide range of perspectives that unsettle the observer and prompt him or her to reflect on what is represented].[134] While Stoll focuses exclusively on Rulfo's landscape imagery, his surrealistic treatment of the indigenous body here serves a similar purpose in prompting reflection on the politics of representation in the context of Mexico's colonial history.

Like Thakkar, I find Barthes's concepts of *studium* and *punctum* particularly useful tools for challenging a folkloric reading of Rulfo's photography. Specifically, these concepts illuminate the role of the mask in inverting the conventional visual power dynamics of *indigenista* representation in the photograph under analysis. While Barthes uses the term *studium* to refer connotatively to the immediately decodable meaning of the image and the cultural context in which it is interpreted, he identifies the *punctum* as that destabilising detail that disrupts reception and 'pricks' the viewer. Although the *studium*-based aspects of Rulfo's photograph encourage an interpretation grounded in picturesque indigenism, these assumptions are disrupted by its *punctum*: the two black eye holes literally puncturing the mask's surface.

In this particular photograph the *punctum* enacts López's strategy of reversing the power dynamics of folkloric photography. Overturning the conventions of *indigenista* visual representation, whereby the passive native body is revealed by the gaze of an anonymous voyeur, the observer here becomes the object of an unanswerable indigenous gaze. This transformation of the indigenous subject from spectacle to spectator is of course particularly significant from a gender perspective as it overturns the scopophilic strategies of earlier *indigenista* representations of the indigenous female body. In this way, Rulfo's use of the mask foreshadows Graciela Iturbide's surrealist portraits of Zapotec and Mixtec women in which veils, costumes, headdresses and masks frequently destabilise conventional models of viewership in relation to indigenous performance.

Exemplifying what Segre perceives as the increasingly self-reflexive quality of mid-century photography, the mimeticism of the mask in Rulfo's photograph further disrupts the viewer's immersion in the photograph by drawing attention to the very process of image construction.[135] As Shields asserts, in photography, masking conventionally 'emphasises the processes of making and interpreting images while, at the same time, it calls attention to and even questions the act of representation'.[136] The tension between visibility and concealment encapsulated by the mask establishes a direct link between the representational dynamics of Rulfo's photograph and the popular spectacle it documents. The popular 'danza de moros y cristianos', which re-enacts the defeat of the Moors at the hands of the Spanish Christians, is considered the archetypal dance of conquest. Although these dances were originally introduced by the colonisers as a means of encouraging native communities to perform their own subordination, Max Harris has demonstrated how over time indigenous participants appropriated and reconfigured these theatrical narratives by working off a 'hidden transcript' of dissent and resistance to subtly critique these regimes.[137] Harris identifies the dancers' masks as an apt metaphor for this disjuncture between the outward visible purpose of the performances and their subversive hidden agenda: 'masks, which are ordinarily thought to conceal, in this instance reveal resistance'.[138] The mask fulfils a similar symbolic function in Rulfo's photograph, pointing to two alternative readings generated by the *studium*-based surface appearance of the image or the subversive subtext revealed by its *punctum*.

The strategies employed by Rivera and Rulfo to visualise the indigenous body are indicative of broader changes in how the relationship between the *mestizo* and the *indio* was intellectually and artistically negotiated from the 1920s to the 1950s. Exploiting the immersive qualities of his medium, Rivera aesthetically evoked *indigenismo*'s 'impulse towards unity' in his murals by creating an embodied viewing experience that dramatically reduced the perceived distance between viewer and indigenous subject. As I have demonstrated, despite this unifying intent, the muralist's works replicate the unidirectional *mestizo* gaze described by Villoro by framing the indigenous body as an object of visual pleasure. The gaze operates to contrary effect in Rulfo's mid-century photography, where it forges a distance between spectator and indigenous subject and unsettles the colonising visual strategies employed by *indigenista* visual artists. Evaluating Rulfo's photography within the context of the more interrogatory intellectual climate that evolved from the late 1930s into the 1950s, my analysis has shed light on the critically overlooked political dimensions of his visual corpus. This comparative reading has also drawn attention to the complex and contradictory positions of both artists in relation to the indigenous question. While Rivera's representational strategies undermine the language of communion and communication that surrounded *indigenismo* by establishing unequal viewing relations between viewer and indigenous subject, the use of estranging devices in Rulfo's photographs reveal a more complex stance on issues of indigenous autonomy than his role as an agent of the government's national integration project would initially suggest.

As a myth of ethnic solidarity, *indigenismo* complemented the master narratives of revolutionary unity being forged from the political centre in the immediate aftermath of the revolution's military phase. Through a comparative analysis of their plastic, literary and photographic works, the chapter as a whole has explored how the corporeal images produced by Rivera and Rulfo from the 1920s to the middle of the century express certain anxieties regarding the nation's political and cultural foundations. Rivera's murals at the Palacio Nacional and the SEP manipulate collective memory for the purposes of national unification by configuring the Revolution as a singular heroic pantheon and creating a sense of proximity between the viewer and the indigenous 'other'. As I have shown, however, these myths of political and ethnic cohesion are subtly unsettled in Rulfo's mid-century literary and photographic works. As in Comala, where the villagers struggle to establish any meaningful form of communication that might lead to a collective understanding of the past, his photographs convey a fundamental disconnect between *mestizo* and indigenous communities. Like the spectral bodies of *Pedro Páramo*, which speak to an unintelligible collective past, Rulfo's portrait of the female Mixe dancer calls into question the link between visuality, knowledge and power established in Rivera's murals by foregrounding an elusive indigenous subject that resists complete visualisation.

Notes to Chapter 1

1. Reprinted in *La crítica de arte en México en el siglo XIX: Estudios y documentos III (1879–1902)*, ed. by Rodríguez Prampolini (Mexico City: UNAM, Instituto de Investigaciones Estéticas, 1997), pp. 245–46 (p. 246). The newspaper *El Partido Liberal* was subsidised by the Porfirian administration.
2. Alan Knight, *The Mexican Revolution Vol.2: Counter-Revolution and Reconstruction* (Cambridge: Cambridge University Press, 1986), p. 2.
3. Michel de Certeau, *The Writing of History*, trans. by Tom Conley (New York: Columbia University Press, 1998), p. 2.
4. Ibid., p. 2; p. 4.
5. Ibid., p. 3.
6. Ibid., p. 3.
7. Michel de Certeau, *Heterologies: Discourse on the Other*, trans. by Brian Massumi (Manchester: Manchester University Press, 1986), p. 8.
8. While the Revolution itself is rarely explicitly mentioned in *Pedro Páramo*, the estimated chronological scope of the novel, which covers the period spanning from the late nineteenth century to the mid-twentieth century, coincides with the critical transitional phase leading from the Porfiriato to the institutionalised Revolution. Boldy, p. 113.

9. María del Pilar Blanco and Esther Peeren, 'Haunted Historiographies/ Introduction', in *The Spectralities Reader: Ghosts and Haunting in Contemporary Cultural Theory*, ed. by María del Pilar Blanco and Esther Peeren (New York: Bloomsbury Academic, 2013), pp. 481–87 (p. 482).
10. Alan Knight, 'Interpreting the Mexican Revolution', in *Texas Papers on Mexico* (Austin: Institute of Latin American Studies, 1988), paper no. 88–02, p. 8; Alan Knight, 'The Peculiarities of Mexican History: Mexico Compared to Latin America, 1821-1992', *Journal of Latin American Studies*, 24 (1992), 99-144 (p. 140).
11. Plutarco Elías Calles, quoted in José María Muriá, *Historia de Jalisco* (Jalisco: Gobierno de Jalisco, Secretaría General, Unidad Editorial, 1982), p. 535.
12. Tenorio-Trillo, p. 68.
13. Thomas Benjamin, 'Mexico's Monument to the Revolution', in *Latin American Popular Culture: An Introduction*, ed. by William H. Beezley (Wilmington: SR Books, 2000), pp. 169–79 (p. 172).
14. Emilio Portes Gil, *En memoria de Zapata. Un balance social político del momento actual en México* (Mexico City: IR, Biblioteca de Cultura Social y Política, 1936), p. 264.
15. Enrique Florescano, *Historia de las historias de la nación mexicana* (Mexico City: Taurus, 2002), p. 379.
16. Martínez Rodríguez, p. 334.
17. Maurice Samuels, *The Spectacular Past: Popular History and the Novel in Nineteenth-century France* (Ithaca: Cornell University Press, 2004), p. 57.
18. Michael J. Gonzales, 'Imagining Mexico in 1910: Visions of the Patria in the Centennial Celebration in Mexico City', *Journal of Latin American Studies*, 39 (2007): 495–533.
19. Fernando Benítez, 'Diego Rivera y su visión de la historia de México', in *Diego Rivera y los escritores mexicanos: Antología tributaria*, pp. 25–37 (p. 25).
20. Wolfe, p. 263.
21. Martínez Rodríguez, p. 335.
22. Diego Rivera, Unpublished interview, interviewed by Rafael Heliodoro Valle, Archivo Frida Kahlo y Diego Rivera, Museo Frida Kahlo, 23 May 1938.
23. Diego Rivera, quoted in Raquel Tibol, 'Palacio Nacional en el torrente muralista riveriano', in *Los murales del Palacio Nacional*, ed. by Raquel Tibol (Mexico City: INBA, 1997), pp. 27–38 (p. 35).
24. Josefina Zoraida Vázquez, *Nacionalismo y educación en México* (Mexico City: Colegio de México, 1970), p. 188.
25. Samuels, p. 57.
26. Leonard Folgarait, 'Revolution as Ritual: Diego Rivera's National Palace Mural', *Oxford Art Journal*, 14 (1991), 18–33 (p. 18).
27. De Certeau, *The Writing of History*, p. 3.
28. Diego Rivera, quoted in Alicia Azuela, *Arte y poder: Renacimiento artístico y revolución social: México, 1910–1945* (Mexico City: Fondo de Cultura Económica, 2005), p. 168.
29. Beatriz González-Stephan, 'Forms of Historic Imagination: Visual Culture, Historiography, and the Tropes of War in Nineteenth-Century Venezuela', in *Building Nineteenth-Century Latin America: Re-rooted Cultures, Identities, and Nations*, ed. by Juan Carlos González Espitia and William G. Acree (Nashville: Vanderbilt University Press, 2009), pp. 101–32 (p. 128).
30. Diego Rivera, *Mi arte, mi vida. Una autobiografía hecha con la colaboración de Gladys March* (Mexico City: Herrero, 1963), p. 131.
31. Diego Rivera, quoted in Carlos Monsiváis, 'Diego Rivera: Creador de públicos', *Historias*, April–June 1986, p. 119; Diego Rivera, quoted in Guadalupe Rivera Marín, *Encuentros con Diego Rivera* (Mexico City: BNCI, 1993), p. 338.
32. Ramos, 'Diego Rivera', p. 68.
33. Álvaro Matute, 'Orígenes del revisionismo historiográfico de la revolución mexicana', *Signos Históricos*, 1 (2000), 29–48 (p. 44).
34. Ibid., p. 45.
35. Ricardo Pérez Montfort, 'Representación e historiografía en México 1930–1950: "Lo mexicano" ante la propia mirada y la extranjera', *Historia Mexicana*, 62 (2013), 1651–94 (p. 1655).
36. Hayden White, *Metahistory: The Historical Imagination in Nineteenth-Century Europe* (London: Johns Hopkins University Press, 1975), p. 1.

37. José Ortega y Gasset, 'La doctrina del punto de vista', in *El tema de nuestro tiempo: El ocaso de las revoluciones: El sentido histórico de la teoría de Einstein* (Madrid: Revista de Occidente, 1966), pp. 188–201 (p. 199).
38. Patrick Romanell, *The Making of the Mexican Mind: A Study in Recent Mexican Thought* (Lincoln: University of Nebraska Press, 1952), p. 184.
39. Edmundo O'Gorman and others, 'Sobre el problema de la verdad histórica (1945)', in *La teoría de la historia en México 1940–1973*, ed. by Álvaro Matute (Mexico City: SEP,1974), pp. 32–65 (p. 43).
40. Luis González y González, *Pueblo en vilo: Microhistoria de San José de Gracia* (Mexico City: El Colegio de México, 1968), p. 19.
41. Patricia Galeana, 'Origen y actualidad del Instituto Nacional de Estudios Históricos de las Revoluciones de México', in *60 años: Historia del Instituto Nacional de Estudios Históricos de las Revoluciones de México*, ed. by Patricia Galeana (Mexico City: INHERM, 2013), pp. 15–24 (p. 19).
42. Enrique Liekens, 'Archivo fónico de la Revolución: grabaciones históricas', *El legionario órgano de la legión de honor mexicana*, 28 February 1959, p. 77–78.
43. Víctor Jiménez, 'Introduction', in *Nuevos indicios sobre Juan Rulfo: Genealogía, estudios, testimonios*, ed. by Jorge Zepeda (Mexico City: Fundación Juan Rulfo: Juan Pablos Editor, 2010), pp. 1–5 (p. 1).
44. Juan Rulfo, 'Donde quedó nuestra historia', in *Toda la obra*, pp. 421–28 (p. 421).
45. Ibid., p. 421.
46. Despite insisting that 'el escritor debe ser el menos intelectual de todos los pensadores' [the writer must be the least intellectual of all thinkers], Rulfo was clearly interested in philosophical developments. As noted in the introduction, during his earlier years in the capital he attended lectures delivered at the UNAM by Alfonso Caso and Eduardo García Máynez, a Hiperión thinker who went on to apply Orteguian perspectivism to the field of legal studies. Rulfo, 'El desafío de la creación', in *Toda la obra*, pp. 388–91 (p. 385).
47. Boldy, p. 113.
48. Juan Rulfo, *El Llano en llamas, Pedro Páramo, Castillo de Teayo* (Barcelona: RM Verlag, 2011), p. 198; p. 206. Further references to this edition are provided after quotations in the text.
49. Juan Rulfo, quoted in Vital, *Noticias sobre Juan Rulfo*, p. 205.
50. Colin Davis, 'The Skeptical Ghost: Alejandro Amenábar's *The Others* and the Return of the Dead', in *Popular Ghosts: The Haunted Spaces of Everyday Culture*, ed. by María del Pilar Blanco and Esther Peeren (London: Continuum, 2010), pp. 64–74 (p. 66).
51. Hillman and Maude, p. 4.
52. Maud Ellmann, *The Hunger Artists: Starving, Writing, and Imprisonment* (London: Virago, 1993), p. 4; Hillman and Maude, p. 4.
53. White, p. 1–43.
54. Linda Hutcheon, *The Politics of Postmodernism* (London: Routledge, 2001), p. 63.
55. Rulfo, 'Donde quedó nuestra historia', p. 421.
56. Karen Jacobs, *The Eye's Mind: Literary Modernism and Visual Culture* (Ithaca: Cornell University Press, 2001), p. 9. While Rulfo's novel casts a sceptical eye on state-endorsed narratives of national progress, scholars such as Deborah Cohn have suggested that his experimentation with Anglo-American modernist stylistics also dovetailed with the internationalising and modernising interests of the government by linking the local and the universal. The intersection between Rulfo's creative activity and the state's modernising agenda comes into focus again in his photographic contributions to documentary projects funded by the Comisión de Papaloapan and Ferrocarriles Nacionales de México, which I discuss in the second section of this chapter and in Chapter 2, respectively. Deborah Cohn, 'The Mexican Intelligentsia, 1950–1968: Cosmopolitanism, National Identity, and the State', *Mexican Studies/Estudios Mexicanos*, 21 (2005), 141–82.
57. Dolores tells him: 'No, hijo, no te veo' [No son, I can't see you] (245)
58. Patrick Dove, *The Catastrophe of Modernity: Tragedy and the Nation in Latin American Literature* (Lewisburg: Bucknell University Press, 2004), p. 112.
59. Francisco Zendejas, 'Carta a los intelectuales de México: Deberes de la inteligencia en esta hora y ante los problemas del país', *Revista de América*, August 1955, p. 12.

60. Gary Saul Morson, *Mikhail Bakhtin: Creation of a Prosaic* (California: Stanford University Press, 1990), p. 239.
61. Mikhail Bakhtin, *Problems of Dostoevsky's Poetics*, ed. and trans. by Caryl Emerson (Minneapolis: University of Minnesota Press, 1984), p. 82; p. 8.
62. José Ortega y Gasset, 'Verdad y perspectiva', in *Obras completas de José Ortega y Gasset*, vol.2 (Madrid: Alianza, 1983), pp. 15–21 (p. 19).
63. Vittorio Gallese, 'Embodied Simulation: From Neurons to Phenomenal Experience', *Phenomenology and the Cognitive Sciences*, 4 (2005), 23–48.
64. Françoise Perus, *Juan Rulfo: El arte de narrar*, intro. by José Pascual Buxó (Mexico City: RM–UNAM, 2012), p. 147.
65. Steven Connor, *Beyond Words: Sobs, Hums, Stutters and Other Vocalizations* (London: Reaktion Books, 2014), p. 50.
66. 'Mi cabeza venía llena de ruidos y de voces' [My head was filling with sounds and voices] (198); 'seguí por mitad de la calle; pero las oía igual, igual que si vinieran conmigo' [I continued halfway down the street, but I could hear them just the same, as if they were coming with me] (247).
67. Steven Connor, *Beckett, Modernism and the Material Imagination* (Cambridge: Cambridge University Press, 2014), p. 106
68. Ibid., 113.
69. Ruvanee P. Vilhauer, 'Inner reading voices: An Overlooked Form of Inner Speech', *Psychosis: Psychological, Social and Integrative Approaches*, 8 (2016), 37–47.
70. Connor, *Beckett, Modernism and the Material Imagination*, p. 107; p. 109.
71. Blanco and Peeren, p. 483.
72. De Certeau, *Heterologies*, p. 8.
73. Alfonso Reyes, 'Visión de Anáhuac', in *Última Tule y otros ensayos* (Caracas: Biblioteca Ayacucho, 1991), pp. 3–17 (p. 6).
74. Ibid., p. 16.
75. Estelle Tarica, *The Inner Life of Mestizo Nationalism* (Minneapolis: University of Minnesota Press, 2008), p. xxii–xxiii.
76. I employ the term *indio* throughout this section to reflect its common usage in debates relating to *indigenismo* during this period. For the same reason, I also translate indio directly as 'Indian', rather than 'Indigenous person'.
77. Luis Villoro, *Los grandes momentos del indigenismo* (Mexico City: Ediciones de la casa chata, 1979), p. 236.
78. Ibid., p. 183.
79. Ibid., p. 240.
80. Ibid., p. 227.
81. Ibid., p. 229.
82. Manuel Gamio, *Forjando patria* (Mexico City: Librería de Hermanos Porrúa, 1916), p. 31.
83. Ibid., p. 14.
84. Ibid., p. 67.
85. Guillermo Bonfil Batalla, *México profundo: Una civilización negada* (Mexico City: Grijalbo, 1989), p. 167.
86. Gamio, p. 40.
87. David Alfaro Siqueiros, 'Manifiesto del Sindicato de Obreros, Técnicos, Pintores y Escultores', in *Palabras de Siqueiros*, ed. by Raquel Tibol (Mexico City: Fondo de Cultura Económica, 1996), pp. 23–26 (p. 24).
88. Rivera, *Mi arte, mi vida*, p. 43.
89. Deborah Poole, *Vision, Race, and Modernity: A Visual Economy of the Andean Image World* (Princeton: Princeton University Press, 1997), p. 194.
90. Ibid., p. 194.
91. John Mraz, *Looking for Mexico: Modern Visual Culture and National Identity* (Durham: Duke University Press, 2009), p. 77.
92. Tenorio-Trillo, p. 66.

93. Coffey, *How a Revolutionary Art Became Official Culture*, p. 22.
94. David Alfaro Siqueiros, 'The Mexican Experience in Art', in *Artists Against War and Fascism: Papers of the First American Artists Congress*, ed. by Matthew Baigell and Julia Williams (New Brunswick, N.J.: Rutgers University Press, 1985), pp. 208–12 (p. 210).
95. Villoro cites these phrases as evidence of the language of solidarity and sentimentality associated with *indigenismo*. Villoro, p. 197.
96. Folgarait, 'Revolution as Ritual', p. 18.
97. Octavio Paz, *Las peras del olmo* (Mexico City: Imprenta Universitaria, 1957), p. 20; Reyes, 'Visión de Anáhuac', p. 6.
98. José Vasconcelos, *Indología: El pensamiento latinoamericano* (Mexico City: Editorial Limusa, 1958), p. 1224; José Vasconcelos, *Pitágoras: Una teoría del ritmo* (La Habana: Imprenta, 1916), p. 13.
99. Roberto S. Goizueta, *Caminemos con* Jesús: *Towards a Hispanic/Latino Theology of Accompaniment* (New York: Orbis Books, 1995), p. 97–98; Arthur Berndtson, 'Mexican Philosophy: The Aesthetics of Antonio Caso', *The Journal of Aesthetics and Art Criticism*, 9 (1951), 323–29 (p. 326–27).
100. Christopher D. Tirres, *The Aesthetics and Ethics of Faith: A Dialogue Between Liberationist and Pragmatic Thought* (New York: Oxford University Press, 2014), p. 70.
101. Oliver Grau, *Virtual Art: From Illusion to Immersion* (Cambridge, Mass: MIT Press, 2003), p. 14.
102. Ibid., p. 13.
103. David Alfaro Siqueiros, *Cómo se pinta un mural* (Mexico City: Ediciones La Rana, 1998), p. 23.
104. Alfonso Reyes, *Tres puntos de exegética literaria* (Mexico City: El Colegio de México, 1945), p. 63.
105. Villoro, p. 11.
106. Mario Teodoro Ramírez, 'Estadios de la otredad en la reflexión filosófica de Luis Villoro', *Diánoia*, 52 (2007), 143–75 (p. 157).
107. Patrick Marnham, *Dreaming with His Eyes Open: A Life of Diego Rivera* (London: Bloomsbury, 1998), p. 167.
108. Margaret A. Majumdar, 'Orientalism and the Problematic of Vision: A Contemporary Perspective', in *Eastern Voyages, Western Visions: French Writing and Painting of the Orient*, ed. by Margaret Topping (New York: Peter Lang, 2004), pp. 347–66 (p. 348).
109. Villoro, p. 223.
110. Arturo Warman and others, *De eso que llaman antropología mexicana* (Mexico City: Editorial Nuestro Tiempo, 1970)
111. Segre, *Intersected Identities,* p. 173.
112. Ibid., p. 158.
113. Nacho López, *Los pueblos de la bruma y el sol* (Mexico City: INI: FONAPAS, 1981), p. 89.
114. Alfonso Villa Rojas, *Los Mazatecos y el problema indígena de la cuenca del Papaloapan* (Mexico City, Ediciones del Instituto Nacional Indigenista, 1955), p. 37.
115. William L. Partridge and David B. Halmo, *Resettling Displaced Communities: Applying the International Standard for Involuntary Resettlement* (Lanham: Lexington Books, 2020), pp. 35–39.
116. Diana Lynn Schwartz, 'Displacement, Development and the Creation of a Modern *Indígena* in the Papaloapan, 1940s–1970s', in *Beyond Alterity: Destabilizing the Indigenous Other in Mexico*, ed. by Paula López Caballero and Ariadna Acevedo-Rodrigo (Tucson: University of Arizona Press, 2018), pp. 222–43 (p. 222–23).
117. Villa Rojas, p. 133.
118. Juan Rulfo, 'No puedo escribir sobre lo que veo', interviewed by Juan Cruz, *El País,* 19 August, 1979, p. iv.
119. Juan Rulfo, 'México y los mexicanos', in *Toda la obra,* pp. 443–45 (p. 443).
120. Howard M. Fraser, '"*Inframundo*": Juan Rulfo's Photographic Companion to *El Llano En llamas*', *Chasqui*, 17 (1988), 56–74; Juan Rulfo, *Juan Rulfo's Mexico,* trans. by Margaret Sayers Peden (Washington, D.C.: Smithsonian Institution Press, 2002).
121. Thakkar, p. 163.
122. Jennifer Jolly, *Creating Pátzcuaro, Creating Mexico: Art, Tourism, and Nation Building under Lázaro Cárdenas* (Austin: University of Texas Press, 2018), p. 38.
123. *Caminos de México: Guía Goodrich-Euzkadi* (Mexico City: Goodrich-Euzkadi, 1958), p. 10.

124. Amit Thakkar, 'Studium and Punctum in Juan Rulfo's "Puerta del cementerio de Janitizio"', in *Rethinking Juan Rulfo's Creative World*, ed. by Nuala Finnegan and Dylan Brennan (Abingdon: Routledge, 2016), pp. 82–101.
125. Rulfo claimed to be 'un lector casi patológico' [an almost pathological reader]. Juan Rulfo, quoted in García Bonilla, p. 89.
126. Juan Rulfo, quoted in José Carlos González Boixo, 'Aclaraciones de Juan Rulfo a su novela *Pedro Páramo*', in *Pedro Páramo* (Madrid: Cátedra, 2000), pp. 247–51 (p. 247).
127. Antonio Cornejo Polar, 'La novela indigenista: Un género contradictorio', in *Texto Crítico*, 14 (1979), 58–70 (p. 61).
128. Juan Rulfo, 'Notas sobre la literatura indígena en México', in *Toda la obra*, pp. 412–16 (p. 414).
129. José Carlos González Boixo, 'Juan Rulfo, fotógrafo', in *Territorios de la Mancha: Versiones y subversiones cervantinas en la literatura hispanoamericana: Actas del VI Congreso Internacional de la Asociación Española de Estudios Literarios Hispanoamericános*, ed. by Matías Barchino Pérez (Cuenca: Ediciones de la Universidad de Castilla–La Mancha, 2007), pp. 365–72 (p. 366).
130. Margaret Olin, 'Gaze', in *Critical Terms for Art History*, ed. by Robert S. Nelson and Richard Shiff (Chicago: University of Chicago Press, 2003), pp. 208–19 (p. 217).
131. Ibid., p. 216; Villoro, p. 229.
132. Ruth Hellier-Tinoco, *Embodying Mexico: Tourism, Nationalism and Performance* (Oxford: Oxford University Press, 2011).
133. Juan Rulfo, 'Fotografías de Nacho López: De cuántas amarguras está hecha la dura vida', in *Toda la obra*, pp. 435–36 (p. 435); Erica Segre, 'The Complicit Eye: Directorial and Ocular Paradigms in Luis Buñuel's Mexican Films and Interdisciplinary Visuality', in *A Companion to Luis Buñuel*, ed. by Rob Stone and Julián Daniel Gutiérrez-Albilla (Oxford: Wiley-Blackwell, 2013), pp. 205–25 (p. 212).
134. André Stoll, 'Iniciación fotográfica en la mexicanidad: Los desconcertantes mundos surrealistas de Juan Rulfo', *Los murmullos: Boletín de la Fundación Juan Rulfo*, 1 (1999), 54–65 (p. 55; p. 62).
135. Masks and costumes carry a particular symbolic weight in mid-century debates on national identity in Mexico. Paz dedicated a chapter of *El laberinto de la soledad* to the analysis of 'máscaras mexicanas' [Mexican masks] while Villoro described *indigenismo* as 'una historia real pero disfrazada' [a real but disguised history]. Villoro, p. 10.
136. Kathryn M. Shields, 'Masking', in *Encyclopedia of Twentieth-Century Photography*, vol. 3, ed. by Lynne Warren (London: Routledge, 2006), pp. 1014–16 (p. 1015).
137. Max Harris, *Aztecs, Moors, and Christians: Festivals of Reconquest in Mexico and Spain* (Austin: University of Texas Press, 2010), p. 25.
138. Ibid., p. 23.

CHAPTER 2

Architectural Anatomies: Stable Bodies and the Built Environment

> 'Dio un golpe seco contra la tierra y se fue desmoronando como si fuera un montón de piedras.'
>
> [He fell to the ground with a thud and started crumbling as if he were a pile of stones.]
> — Juan Rulfo, *Pedro Páramo* (1955)

> 'Diego [...] es fundamentalmente constructor, investigador y sobre todo, arquitecto. Es arquitecto en su pintura, en su proceso de pensar y en el deseo apasionado de estructurar una sociedad armónica, funcional y sólida.'
>
> [Diego... is fundamentally a builder, a researcher and above all, an architect. He is an architect in his painting, his way of thinking and in his passionate desire to configure a harmonious, functional and stable society.]
> — Frida Kahlo, 'Retrato de Diego' (1949)

In the closing lines of *Pedro Páramo*, the eponymous tyrant is attacked by his inebriated son Abundio and collapses like 'a pile of stones' (311). The *cacique*'s reduction to rubble metaphorically reveals the inorganic composition of his body, as already suggested by the etymological link between his first name and the word *piedra* [stone] and highlights a form of corporeal fragmentation that is endemic in Comala. The same process of bodily disintegration is enacted by the feverish Susana San Juan, whose thoughts appear to rupture her body from within (282). Her reveries reveal this to be a phenomenon she has experienced since infancy, recalling how as a child she screamed so violently when her mother died 'que mis manos tenían que haberse hecho pedazos estrujando su desesperación' [that my hands must have fallen to pieces from so much desperate wringing] (264) and that her nurse Justina held her so tightly that 'la hubiera apachurrado y hecho pedazos' [she could have crushed her to pieces] (276). From his own juvenile memories, Páramo similarly remembers how the roof beams caused his mother's shadow to shatter into fragments (205). He later recalls the 'cara despedazada' [shattered face] of his dead father (255) and we learn that the body of his son Miguel has been crushed after a fatal fall from his horse. Like his steed, described as 'despedazado y carcomido por dentro' [splintered and decayed inside] (212), Miguel's fractured face is concealed from the community at his wake.

Through these sustained references to bodily decomposition, Rulfo's novel brings to mind the fragmentary forms of analytical cubist painting. This earlier deconstructive phase of cubism, which lasted from approximately 1909 to 1912, involved splintering objects into a series of individual facets using a restricted monochromatic palette across the entire composition. While *Pedro Páramo* verbally recreates several analytical cubist features such as spatio-temporal dislocation, multiple perspectives and the use of a similarly limited range of expressive tools (as indicated by the repetition of *pedazo* and *despedazado* in the previous quotations), it most directly replicates its formal qualities through its architectural deconstruction of the body. As works such as Picasso's *Portrait of Daniel-Henry Kahnweiler* (1910) illustrate, the intermingling ochre tones of analytical composition formed an ambiguous visual environment in which the disintegrating objects at the centre of the painting appeared to break away into the surrounding space. According to Rosenblum, this lack of tonal or structural differentiation between object and space meant that 'no fact of vision remained absolute [...] a sharp, firm outline could abruptly dissolve into a vibrant texture, a plane that defined the remoteness of the background could be perceived simultaneously in the immediate foreground'.[1] Rosenblum's description of the comingling of object and space recalls the fictional world of Comala where characters appear in focus only to dissolve into a land that is 'baldía y como en ruinas' [barren and in ruins] (268). As this interplay continues throughout the novel, the post-revolutionary village of Comala emerges as a site of ruination where the built landscape and its inhabitants are bound together in an ongoing process of decomposition. I argue that, through this sustained imagery of anatomical and architectural decay, Rulfo's novel dramatises the gradual unbuilding of a utopian post-revolutionary society that was constructed in the euphoric decades of the 1920s and 30s.

Although the Revolution was hailed as a moment of rupture from the Díaz regime, the positivist motto of 'Order and Progress' continued to haunt revolutionary rhetoric after 1920. Chapters 2 and 3 explore how ideal Mexican bodies, both metaphorical and material, were configured according to these Porfirian principles in the decades following the armed conflict. Before examining the models of progressive (re)productive citizenship that were promoted through the state's national development programme in Chapter 3, this chapter explores how the concepts of collective societal order and stability were projected onto real bodies and built spaces during the 1920s and 1930s. During the reconstruction phase that immediately followed the armed conflict, intellectuals sought to consolidate claims of national stability by promoting the ideal of a robust and physiologically standardised post-revolutionary body. As a state-endorsed social engineering programme converged with a disciplinary functionalist model of public architecture in the 1930s, an increasingly intimate bond developed between the ideal rational bodies of post-revolutionary citizens and the built spaces they were to inhabit. However, as fissures began to appear in the image of a socially cohesive and egalitarian body politic in the 1940s and 1950s, artists and intellectuals began to analyse and disassemble the symbolic and real social structures that had been erected during the initial reconstruction period. At mid-century, this crisis assumed philosophical dimensions as thinkers dismantled existing models of national identity. Following Ramos's *El perfil del hombre y la cultura en México* (1934), a number of thinkers engaged in a more self-reflexive analysis of national questions to promote collective self-awareness and change.[2] Looking beyond the confines of cultural nationalism, Hiperión thinkers Uranga, Zea and Villoro, and other intellectuals such as Paz, engaged in a self-critical examination of national identity that would enable Mexicans to take account of their present circumstances. Although Paz did not directly collaborate with the Hiperión, he was aware of the group's activity and maintained close links with Uranga during the 1950s.[3] Paz's *El laberinto de la soledad* (1950) reflected on the nation's struggle with isolation and alienation while Uranga's *Análisis del ser del mexicano* (1952), countered Vasconcelos's discourses of *mestizo* invincibility by exploring the Mexican condition in terms of fragility, instability and insubstantiality.

Contextualising Rivera's and Rulfo's works within this evolving intellectual landscape from the 1920s to the mid-1950s, this chapter explores how both artists conceptualise the physical contours and boundaries of post-revolutionary society in contrasting ways by examining how the relationship between bodies and built spaces is configured in their works. Frida Kahlo's assertion, quoted in my second epigraph, that her husband was fundamentally an architect in his painting, thought processes and desire to forge a functional Mexican society, sheds light on an aspect of Rivera's pictorial production that has eluded scholarly attention to date. The present chapter redresses this omission by demonstrating how concepts of building design were integral to his visual aesthetic. After examining how Rivera's early state-commissioned murals uphold the biopolitical dimensions of the state's reconstruction project through their rationalised architectonic configuration of the human body, I shift my focus to the disciplinary spatial dimensions of his mural *The Making of a Fresco Showing the Building of a City* (1931). Re-examining this understudied work in light of Rivera's relationship with the architect Juan O'Gorman and his contribution to post-revolutionary architectural debates, I demonstrate how it adopts functionalist principles to establish a parallel between spatial and bodily order.

The second part of the chapter considers how this dynamic between bodies and built spaces is unsettled in Rulfo's mid-century novel and photographs of Mexico City. Drawing from Benjamin's theoretical discussion of the ruin, I explore how the indeterminate disintegrating bodies and buildings depicted in *Pedro Páramo* share the fragmentary text's potential for renovation and reconstruction. Turning to Rulfo's photographs of the capital's soon-to-be-demolished railway lines, I discuss how the elusive urban subjects of these works disturb the vision of a disciplined urban landscape and populace projected by the mid-century functionalist architect Mario Pani, by drawing attention to an elusive community that lingers in the city's interstices. Destabilising the equation between revolution and architectural-bodily order presented in Rivera's murals, Rulfo's decomposing bodies and migratory urban subjects suggest the possibility of constructing alternative narratives beyond the established parameters of post-revolutionary society.

Part I: The Post-Revolutionary Return to Order: Disciplined Bodies, Disciplined Spaces

Reassembling the pieces of Rulfo's fragmented bodies necessarily leads us back to the 1920s when, as Jean Meyer asserts, the words 'revolution' and 'reconstruction' were synonymous.[4] In an effort to consolidate political order and legitimise the state's claims of societal transformation, Obregón set about implementing an economic reconstruction programme and a new social infrastructure in the early 1920s. While the president pursued this project of socio-economic rehabilitation, state-associated intellectuals sought to rebuild the body politic by discursively constructing a new national subject. Despite their vehement rejection of positivism, these thinkers reinvigorated the biological analogies of the Científicos by metaphorically envisioning Mexico as a collective organism. Among the key intellectual architects of this post-revolutionary national body were Gamio and Vasconcelos, whose theoretical writings employed a language of construction to imagine an ideal subject characterised by specific racial, physiological and mental traits. In *Forjando patria*, Gamio outlined the necessary form the population must assume 'para que ésta constituya y encarne una Patria poderosa y una nacionalidad coherente y definida' [so that it constitutes and embodies a powerful Homeland and a coherent and defined nationality].[5] Fusing imagery of engineering and metallurgy, Gamio uses the metaphor of a metallic statue to describe historical efforts to construct a stable, racially hybrid body politic. He recalls how the heroes of Latin American independence worked like metalsmiths to construct 'una estatua hecha de todos los metales, que serían todas las razas de América' [a statue made of all of the metals that would be all the races of America], but notes that this structure was 'inconsistente y frágil' [weak and fragile] and fell several times due to the lack of a solid indigenous foundation.[6] Gamio calls on contemporary revolutionaries to rectify this structural weakness by building a new national body fortified by this racial component:

> Toca hoy a los revolucionarios de México empuñar el mazo y ceñir el mandil forjador para hacer que surja del yunque milagroso la nueva patria hecha de hierro y de bronce confundidos. Ahí está el hierro [...] Ahí está el bronce [...] ¡Batid hermanos![7]
>
> [Today it falls to Mexico's revolutionaries to grasp the mallet and keep the forger's apron close and from the miraculous anvil make the new homeland out of iron blended with bronze. There is the iron... there is the bronze... Hammer, brothers!]

Focusing on the example of racial mixing in Yucatán, Gamio directly links racial uniformity with collective stability, claiming that 'esta homogeneidad racial, esta unificación del tipo físico, esta avanzada y feliz fusión de razas, constituye la primera y más sólida base del nacionalismo' [this racial homogeneity, this unification of physical type, this progressive and fortunate fusion of races, constitutes the first and most solid foundation of nationalism].[8] Integral to this post-revolutionary drive for collective corporeal order and regularisation was the concept of *mestizaje*, which, as Ana María Alonso explains, provided 'the only way to create homogeneity out of heterogeneity, unity out of fragmentation' after the conflict.[9] Like Gamio, Vasconcelos equated the process of 'forging the nation' with that of forging a new *mestizo* body. In his major treatise on racial miscegenation, *La raza cósmica* (1925), Vasconcelos declares that Mexico must 'ir creando, como si dijéramos, el tejido celular que ha de servir de carne y sostén a la nueva aparición biológica' [start creating the cellular tissue, as it were, needed to provide the flesh and structure of the new biological entity].[10] In a subsequent lecture, he exhorts his fellow countrymen to act as 'builders of entirely new concepts of life', pointing, like Gamio, to the possibility of creating a more stable collective self:

> We are unstable, and this I believe can be easily understood by the biologist, as we are a new product, a new breed, not yet entirely shaped. I believe such weakness can be overcome by obtaining a clear definition of our aim and by devoting ourselves to a definite and a great task.[11]

The organicist metaphors employed by Vasconcelos and Gamio found parallels in official public health programmes centring on the material bodies of Mexican citizens. As Elsa Muñiz asserts:

> En México durante las primeras décadas del siglo, la perfección corporal estaba relacionada fundamentalmente con dos necesidades urgentes vinculadas al proceso de reconstrucción: la de una población sana y la de una sociedad civilizada a la altura de las más modernas del mundo, ambas con el afán de crear al nuevo mexicano.[12]
>
> [In Mexico, during the first decades of the century, bodily perfection was fundamentally related to two urgent needs linked to the reconstruction process: a healthy population and a civilised society on a par with the most modern in the world. Both reflected the desire to create a new Mexican.]

The strategies of bodily regularisation through which this ideal 'new Mexican' was to be configured after the Revolution constitute what in Foucauldian terms could be defined as the biopolitical agenda of the post-revolutionary state. In his lecture series *Society Must Be Defended* (1976), Foucault describes the emergence of disciplinary and regulatory technologies in the eighteenth century that sought to manage and regularise the vital characteristics of both individuals and entire populations.[13] In Mexico, these objectives were pursued through the social engineering and public health initiatives of the 1920s and 30s. Through the promotion of hygiene, physical education and behavioural reform relating to alcoholism and religious fanaticism, successive administrations, with a notable intensification of efforts during the Calles era, sought to construct rational and responsible citizens that would embody the order and stability of the post-revolutionary body politic. Following the establishment of the Sección de Educación Higiénica y Propaganda (1922) and the Departamento de Psicopedagogía e Higiene (1925), public health initiatives evolved into a more coherent eugenics programme in the 1930s that advocated 'la procreación de una nueva generación en la que los degenerados, enfermos y débiles sean eliminados' [the procreation of a new generation from which the degenerate, the sick and the weak will be eliminated].[14] As Nancy Leys Stepan has illustrated, Mexican anxieties regarding racial fitness and uniformity were part of a broader phenomenon during the inter-war period in Latin America, where eugenics campaigns sought to liberate populations from colonial myths of racial inferiority and forge homogenous national communities.[15] While in Mexico such initiatives aimed to engineer a radically new citizen-subject for the post-revolutionary era, they paradoxically recycled the hygienist discourses of Porfirian-era reformers, who viewed the physiological improvement of individual bodies as material evidence of collective societal order.

Diego Rivera: Visual Architect of a New Citizenry

Efforts to economically, socially and physiologically rebuild post-revolutionary society were matched by the construction of a new artistic national identity under the supervision of Vasconcelos. Through its adoption of a simplified artistic language, post-revolutionary muralism followed a similar path to post-war artistic developments in Europe, where the restoration of socio-political order was articulated through a highly structured pictorial style. In 1925, German art historian Franz Roh noted how:

> The latest painting wants to offer us the image of something totally finished and complete, minutely formed, opposing it to our eternally fragmented and ragged lives as an archetype of integral structuring, down to the smallest details. Someday man too will be able to recreate himself in the perfection of this idea.[16]

This move towards more coherent visual forms was foreshadowed by the evolution of cubism, which progressed from its early 'analytical' stage toward a later 'synthetic' phase. While analytical cubism was characterised by splintered and disconnected forms, synthetic cubism sought to reintegrate these fragments into unified objects and spaces. This impulse for order formed the basis of the purist movement led by Le Corbusier and Amédée Ozenfant. As Stanislaus von Moos explains, the aim of these artists was to create an artistic language compatible with 'social order, scientific logic and technological progress' by searching for the geometric simplicity and purity of objects.[17] Their 1918 manifesto, 'After Cubism', asserted that 'the highest delectation of the human mind is the perception of order and the greatest human satisfaction is the feeling of collaboration or participation in this order'.[18] Central to the post-bellum artistic return to order was the symbolic restoration of a war-ravaged body that ultimately culminated in Le Corbusier's Modulor, a mathematically rationalised figure that drew inspiration from Leonardo da Vinci's *Vitruvian Man*.

This same emphasis on formal simplicity and stability characterised the visual language of post-revolutionary muralism. As Minister of Public Education, Vasconcelos encouraged the muralists to produce revolutionary narratives in an accessible visual language that would also reflect Mexico's new-found societal stability. Integrating classical, futurist and pre-Columbian iconographic elements, the muralists' unique brand of social realism was undeniably modern yet rooted in familiar visual forms. While the densely populated works of all three artists expressed Mexico's collective experience in distinctly physical terms, it was Rivera's consistent choice of common workers and peasants as his revolutionary protagonists that established him as the principal visual architect of the nation's new citizenry. In keeping with the contemporary post-revolutionary culture of renovation, the muralist combined the constructive techniques of proto-cubism with an emphasis on geometric stability to configure a visually concrete body at the centre of these post-revolutionary narratives.

Rivera's engagement with official discourses of physiological and racial regularisation is reflected in his first state-sponsored mural, *Creación* (1922), located in the Anfiteatro Bolívar of the Escuela Nacional Preparatoria. This encaustic fresco depicting the dawning of a new racial order in Mexico reflects his close ideological ties to Vasconcelos during this earlier stage of his career as a muralist. To the fore of the mural, on opposite sides, are seated a *mestizo* couple resembling Adam and Eve around whom are positioned various allegorical figures representing the arts, the four cardinal virtues and the three theological virtues. The elongated forms and classical posture of these bodies endow them with a monumentality that is accentuated by their exaggerated size. These esoteric figures frame a central concave space where a *mestizo* surrounded by the flora and fauna of the Tehuantepec region emerges from the tree of life. Positioned below a blue semi-circle from which energy emanates from three points, the figure stands with arms outspread in a posture, which as Coffey has also noted, is strikingly reminiscent of da Vinci's *Vitruvian Man* (1487).[19] Da Vinci's diagram, which portrays a male figure inscribed within a circle and a square, presents the mathematically proportioned human body as a model for architectural construction. Like da Vinci, who described this human form as a 'cosmography of the microcosm', that is, the expression of external cosmological balance, Rivera projects the *mestizo* as the embodiment of post-revolutionary societal order and stability. Da Vinci based his precisely proportioned figure on the description of the human body provided by Roman engineer Marcus Vitruvius Pollio. Vitruvius analysed the body as a system of mathematical ratios and drew a direct parallel between the components of a building and those of the human anatomy: 'As in the human body, from cubit, foot, palm, inch and other small parts comes the symmetric quality of eurhythmy, so is it in the completed building'.[20] Vitruvius concludes this analogy by arguing that both the human body and built structures should combine the three fundamental qualities of *firmitas* [strength], *utilitas* [functionality] and *venustas* [beauty].

As Rivera was classically trained in Mexico and had recently returned from a visit to Italy in 1921, where he had immersed himself in classically-inspired Renaissance works, it is highly likely that he was aware of these metaphorical connotations at the time of painting *Creación*. Although subtle, Rivera's evocation of da Vinci's and Vitruvius's scientifically ideal bodies is significant in the context of the health campaigns that started taking shape during this decade. Discussing the post-war bodily imagery of artists like Le Corbusier and Oskar Schlemmer, Tom Slevin argues that 'the modernist redeployment of the Vitruvian man is part of a phantasmic recuperation of the traumatised body according to the fantasised aesthetics of a mathematically objective and universal order'.[21] By invoking Western art's definitive model of corporeal normativity and its connotations of architectural discipline, Rivera's Vitruvian *mestizo* embodies the 'universal order' urgently needed to restore a damaged post-revolutionary Mexican body politic.

Rivera's employment of the Vitruvian model reveals a concern with the geometrical stability of forms that he maintained throughout his career. From 1898 to 1906, before he moved to Paris, Rivera attended advanced courses in mathematics and geometry at the Academia de San Carlos, acquiring a mathematical appreciation of pictorial composition and proportion that prepared him for the geometric principles of cubism. According to Oles, Rivera was drawn to the scientific exactitude of cubism, rejecting 'Picasso's intuitive approach, instead taking a highly rational and mathematical path shaped by arcane discussions of the fourth dimension'.[22] The course of Rivera's artistic development from the end of his time in Paris to his return to Mexico reveals how this scientific constructive approach formed the basis of his post-revolutionary aesthetic vision. During his Parisian cubist period, Rivera gradually moved away from the analytical mode towards the synthetic style that evolved after 1912. Referring to the works of Picasso and Georges Braque, David Cottington summarises this transition in cubist figuration as:

> The sequence of changes in their painting styles from about 1908 through which, in an initial phase, the objects, figures and landscapes they depicted were dismantled by means of juxtaposed views, broken contours, geometricization, *passage* and so on, in a process of painterly 'analysis'; and in the second phase of which the flat interpenetrating planes that resulted from such 'analysis' were the starting-points for a process of 'synthesis' which reconstituted those subjects anew.[23]

Rivera followed European artists such as Juan Gris and Fernand Léger, who by 1914 had moved away from the fragmentary abstractions of analytical cubism towards a constructivist synthetic approach that strived for 'the rehabilitation of the object in its integral form'.[24] As Mexican art historian Justino Fernández notes, this later cubist idiom was fundamentally 'concerned with structures', proposing that 'painting be the expression of an essential geometrical structure derived from objects, vision reduced to an ideal scheme'.[25] This transition in Rivera's style is exemplified by works such as *El matemático* (1918), which reveal his embrace of the more integrated and cohesive pictorial approach mastered by Paul Cézanne.

This new artistic vision harmonised with the environment Rivera discovered on his return to Mexico, where 'las formas y los colores existían en absoluta pureza' [forms and colours existed in absolute purity] and ancient designs revealed 'la verdadera armadura de las cosas' [the true structure of things].[26] Over the subsequent decades, Rivera harnessed this sense of formal purity and cohesion to construct a visually concrete post-revolutionary community in his murals. As noted in the previous chapter, Rivera promoted the concept of plastic integration, a method of fusing diverse aesthetic forms such as painting and architecture within a single artwork. In a statement in 1921, Siqueiros extended this interdisciplinary link by encouraging artists to embrace a fundamentally architectural understanding of visual production:

> La base de la obra de arte, es la magnífica estructura geometral de la forma con la concepción, engranaje y materialización arquitectural de los volúmenes.[27]
>
> [The foundation of the work of art is the magnificent geometric structure of form, along with the concept, inner workings and architectural materialisation of its volumes.]

The muralists' emphasis on the architectonic solidity of forms aligned their monumental works even more closely with the nation-building discourses of the 1920s. Rivera, who consistently described fresco creation as a form of physical labour, reinforced Siqueiros's architectural comparison by asserting that building design required the same fundamental skills as painting and sculpting: 'manejar útil y lógicamente formas, volúmenes y colores' [productively and logically managing forms, volumes and colours].[28]

Rivera's architectonic construction of human forms manifests itself most clearly in the murals he painted for his first major fresco cycle at the SEP headquarters between 1923 and 1928. In *La raza cósmica*, Vasconcelos upholds the building as the concrete embodiment of his cosmic hybrid race through its combination of Spanish colonial architecture and pre-Columbian inspired mural decoration.[29] Delivering his inaugural speech at the Ministry in 1922, Vasconcelos described how its visionaries had aimed to 'construir con amplitud, construir con solidez' [construct with amplitude, construct with solidity] and praised the building as 'un edificio símbolo' [a symbolic building] whose noble and solid proportions embodied 'la conciencia de la revolución madura' [the consciousness of the mature Revolution].[30] The building's solidity and concrete stability, which for Vasconcelos represented the ideological function of the Ministry as a beacon of moral fortitude, was reflected in the painted bodies adorning its walls.[31] Across the 235 panels of the cycle, which depict a range of regional industries and festivities, Rivera projects a vision of Mexico's social life that he believed would reveal the possibilities of the nation's future to the masses.[32] By densely populating these panels with the bodies of ordinary Mexicans, Rivera articulated this aspirational societal vision through a fundamentally corporeal visual language. Repeatedly photographed in overalls and perched on scaffolds as he painted his stone canvases, Rivera cultivated a workman-like public image that emphasised his links with the contemporary culture of reconstruction. In the often overlooked panel *El pintor, el escultor y el arquitecto*, located on the building's third floor, the artist explicitly alludes to his role as the nation's post-revolutionary visual architect by depicting himself with a floor plan, rather than a paintbrush, in hand.

While the works of the Patio de las Fiestas (1928) on the third floor reflect Rivera's later shift towards the more defined muscular physiques typical of Soviet socialist realism, the simplified and solid bodily forms found in the earlier panels on the ground floor of the Patio del Trabajo (1923–1924) illustrate the influence of post-impressionist figuration on his post-cubist works. As the subsequent paintings of artists such as Julio Castellanos and Agustín Lazo attest, the model of robust corporeality developed by Rivera during this period exerted a lasting influence on post-revolutionary artists during the following decades. Echoing Cézanne, who held that the artist should render nature with 'the cylinder, the sphere and the cone', Rivera declared that 'toda forma viva puede incluirse en el cilindro, el cono y la esfera y sus combinaciones' [all living forms can be created using the cylinder, the cone and the sphere and a combination of these elements]. Unsurprisingly, Rivera highlighted the corporeal significance of this artistic method, noting that these forms also provide the structural basis for the human eye and photoreceptors (cones and rods) contained in the retina.[33] This Cézannesque architectonic approach is evident in panels such as *La quema de los Judas* (1923) in the Patio de las Fiestas, where bodies are presented as a composite of simplified geometric shapes. In this scene depicting the popular Mexican festival, three effigies of Judas lurch over a crowd of onlookers that disperses in an explosion of movement. While the bodies occupying the background remain obscured by the crowd, those to the fore are clearly defined by their physical solidity and vibrant attire. Rivera's emphasis on the visual stability of the body is exemplified by the male figure to the centre-right of the composition who shields his head as he is swept backwards. This particular body is clearly composed of separate elements: a blocky rectangular torso, tubular limbs and disc-like hat, which together form a stable architectonic whole.

Drawing from synthetic cubist techniques, Rivera also exploited colour to reinforce the visual autonomy of these separate forms. While analytic cubism relied on a monochrome palette that blurred the distinction between object and space, synthetic artists employed vibrant colours to create greater formal definition. This strategy drew from Cézanne's proto-cubist 'architectural plan' which used 'oppositions of shape and colour to build up, and, as it were, recreate form from within'.[34] In *La quema,* as in most of the ground floor panels, the use of strong contrasting colours serves to solidify individual bodies and clearly distinguish them from their equally concrete visual environment. The efficacy of tonal differentiation as an anatomical structuring device is again evident in the central figure, whose contrasting orange shirt, pale green trousers and brown hat accentuate the body's contours, providing it with a visually coherent structure. This early panel again reveals Rivera's indebtedness to Cézanne's highly structured pictorial style which, as the French painters Albert Gleizes and Jean Metzinger noted, achieved the 'profoundest reality' through its incorporation of 'primordial volumes'.[35] These qualities served the nativist aesthetic of the muralist, who claimed that the use of three-dimensional geometric shapes and a bold palette to pictorially configure the human body captured the 'elemental purity' of precolonial artistic expression.[36] Rivera's integration of the simplified volumetric forms of post-impressionism to accentuate the weightiness of his figures reflected Gamio's emphasis on the robustness of Mexico's indigenous population.[37] Aside from accentuating corporeal solidity, Rivera's use of these reductive forms further reinforced his *indigenista* credentials by recalling the simplified figuration of pre-Conquest Aztec texts such as the Codex Mendoza.[38] Rivera's turn to neo-primitivism and formal purism in the corporeal imagery of these earlier panels suggest parallels with the post-war works of his former Parisian acquaintance Léger, whose 'tubist' works employed shading to configure human body parts like three-dimensional cylindrical shapes.

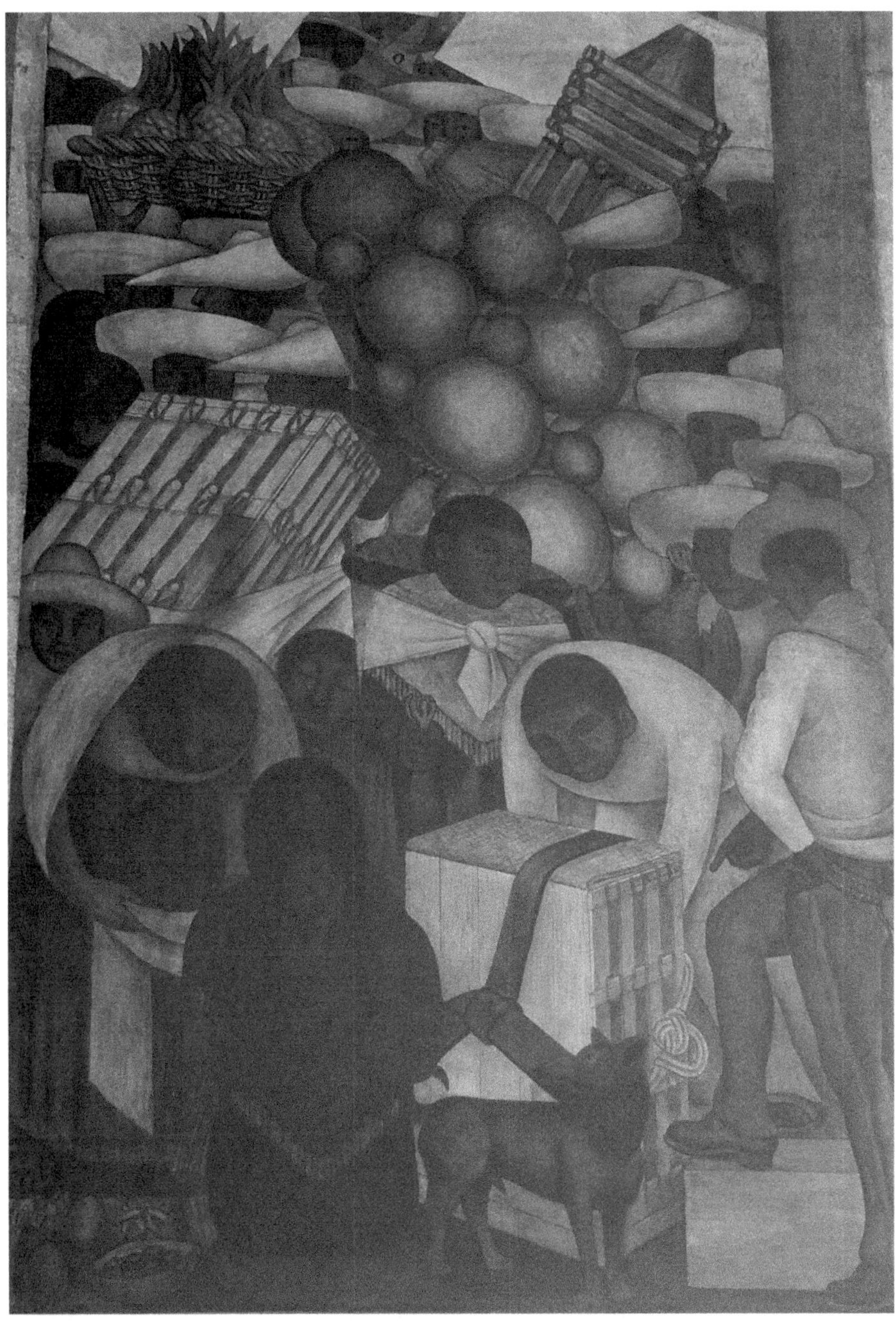

Fig. 2.1. Diego Rivera, Detail from *El tianguis* (1923–1924), Ministry of Public Education © Banco de México Diego Rivera Frida Kahlo Museums Trust, Mexico, D.F. / DACS 2021

Justifying his shift away from cubist figuration, the French artist later explained: 'I had broken down the human body, so I set about putting it together again'.[39]

Léger's technique of architecturally assembling visual objects out of different structural components was not new to Rivera. At the Academia de San Carlos, Santiago Rebull had also encouraged the young artist to use 'formas puras, permanentes e imperecederas; es decir las figuras que trazan y construyen los arquitectos: el cilindro, el cono y la esfera' [permanent and enduring forms, that is to say, the figures sketched and constructed by architects: the cylinder, the cone and the sphere].[40] Although Rivera never pursued these principles to the same extent as Léger, a similar process of architectonic anatomical construction can be detected in panels such as *La quema* and *El tianguis* (1923–1924), also located on the first floor of the Patio de las Fiestas. In contrast to many of the more serene scenes on the ground floor, the agoraphobic quality of this larger, tightly packed panel prefigures Rivera's epic triptych at the Palacio Nacional. Following a similar composition to *La quema*, the background of *El tianguis* is formed by a chaotic sea of white tarpaulins, *sombreros* and woven baskets. If we focus on the section to the far right of the mural (Fig. 2.1), it is only at the very fore of the composition that the bulky bodies and oval faces of the indigenous sellers come into focus. An indigenous woman wearing a traditional *rebozo* is positioned to the centre of this section with two female figures crouching to her right and a man lifting a large wooden crate to her left. Adopting a similar strategy to Léger, Rivera once again stresses the three-dimensionality and structural integrity of her body by presenting it as a fusion of simplified geometric shapes. Over her *rebozo*, which is configured as a kind of inverted pentagon, another shawl is composed from two triangular shapes that merge to form a spherical knot mirroring the rounded form of her head. Exploiting the packed environment of the market, Rivera reinforces the fixity and concreteness of the body by encouraging the viewer to draw a direct formal comparison between the bulbous heads and thick torsos of the market-goers with the spherical and cuboidal objects surrounding them.

Rivera's Functionalism: The Spatial Politics of *The Making of a Fresco* (1931)

As I have shown, the corporeal forms of *La quema* and *El tianguis* reflected Rivera's belief that all living forms can be artistically reproduced using three-dimensional geometric shapes as the basic units of construction. Notably, the same descriptive language surfaces in an architectural review he wrote for the magazine *Mexican Folkways* in 1926. Discussing a group of utilitarian houses designed by Obregón Santacilia and fellow architect José Villagrán, Rivera's description lingers on the 'ágiles tuberías y estáticos cilindros de los tinacos, los cubos y paralelogramos, sencillos y puros de las habitaciones' [agile pipes and static cylinders of the water tanks, the pure and simple cubes and parallelograms of the rooms], establishing a direct link between its architectural structure and the geometric composition of his painted bodies.[41] Rivera goes on to praise the economical design of this 'vecindad de habitaciones baratas, higiénicas y con belleza (donde) todo dispendio de material fue evitado: utilizáronse como factores de belleza la economía de material y su máxima utilidad' [neighbourhood of cheap, hygienic and beautiful living spaces, in which waste of any kind was avoided: the economy of their materials and their maximum utility were used as features of beauty].[42] These qualities of spatial efficiency, hygiene and structural order formed the basis of a functionalist model of architecture that would contribute to the state's biopolitical mission to shape healthy and orderly citizens in the 1930s. As I will go on to discuss, during that decade Rivera developed an interest in this disciplinary model of architecture that would manifest itself in the spatial dimensions of his murals.

As the steady population growth of Mexico City led to a housing and sanitation crisis in the 1920s and 30s, the demand for economical and hygienic architectural designs like those proposed by Obregón Santacilia and Villagrán grew increasingly urgent. In an effort to impose order on the urban landscape and promote Mexico's international image as a socially and industrially progressive nation, a systematic planning programme started to take shape in the early 1930s. Although post-revolutionary intellectuals often criticised the Eurocentrism of the Porfiriato, and its imitation of French cultural models in particular, Mexican urban visionaries of this decade turned to the French tradition in search of architectural theories, this time those of the Swiss-French artist and architect Le Corbusier. In keeping with his purist doctrine, Le Corbusier's architectural manifesto 'Towards a New Architecture' (1923) addressed 'the necessity for order' in post-war European society by positing a functionalist architectural paradigm for the industrial age that was founded on the principles of strict geometric logic, hygiene and spatial efficiency.[43] Articulating his urban vision in anatomical terms, Le Corbusier conceptualised the city as a disciplined living organism, configuring a 'plan that arranges organs in order' according to their specific function.[44] Linking the formal austerity of his designs with their intended social function, the theorist argued that the regulating line provided a 'guarantee against wilfulness'.[45]

This capacity of built spaces to maintain social order, a notion Le Corbusier expressed through the dictum 'Architecture or Revolution', paradoxically came to define post-revolutionary public architecture in Mexico from the 1930s into the 60s, as the state continued to legitimise itself through its rhetorical commitment to the social ideals of the Revolution.[46] In line with the discourses of physiological improvement dominating the contemporary public health programme, urban theorists conceptualised the city as a sprawling and disproportioned body that, through strict spatial management, could be transformed into a disciplined and functional organism. Adopting Le Corbusier's medicalising language, Carlos Contreras, founder of the Asociación Nacional para la Planificación de la República Mexicana and editor of the journal *Planificación*, argued that:

> (La ciudad) no ha evolucionado como un organismo mediante la expansión correlativa de todas sus partes; de idéntica manera que el niño crece hasta la virilidad, no engordando simplemente, sino logrando que sus miembros, su cerebro y todos sus órganos se desarrollen en proporción para constituir un conjunto armonioso y racional.[47]

> [(The city) has not evolved as an organism according to the corresponding growth of all of its parts; in the same way that a child grows into manhood not simply by gaining weight, but by the manner in which his limbs, brain and all of his organs develop in proportion to construct a harmonious and rational whole.]

Contreras's corporeal metaphors reflected the distinctly physiological dimensions of the post-revolutionary architectural 'return to order'. As the desire to rationalise and cleanse the urban landscape gained momentum in the 1930s, public architecture became increasingly interlinked with the state's biopolitical objectives. During this decade, functionalism, which stressed the transformative capacity of the built environment to promote social order and shape healthy, disciplined bodies, emerged as the dominant architectural paradigm. The first significant interpreter of functionalism in Mexico was Juan O'Gorman, who drew heavily from Le Corbusier's theories to devise an architectural model based on cost efficiency, hygiene and spatial order as a solution to the urban crisis. In a speech delivered to the Sociedad de Arquitectos Mexicanos in 1933, O'Gorman reminded his colleagues that 'los hombres sólo son animales racionales, y que proceder por cualquier sistema que no sea el máximo rendimiento con el mínimo esfuerzo, es no actuar racionalmente' [men are rational animals and to follow any system that does not guarantee maximum efficiency for minimum effort is not rational behaviour].[48] O'Gorman's direct linking of rational building construction with rational human behaviour highlights a parallel between spatial and bodily discipline that lay at the heart of his functionalist philosophy. Despite abandoning his medical studies to pursue architecture, O'Gorman devoted his early career to converting Mexico's built spaces into tools for physiological improvement. Echoing the Porfirian belief that 'the construction of public works would transform the city into a health-giving environment', O'Gorman prioritised hygiene, natural light and ventilation in his designs to promote 'higiene del cuerpo y de la inteligencia' [hygiene of the body and the mind].[49]

O'Gorman's cost-effective and socially-minded designs appealed to a government seeking to accelerate economic reconstruction while maintaining a veneer of revolutionary progress. In 1931, Rivera introduced O'Gorman to the Minister of Public Education Narciso Bassols (1931–1934) who commissioned the architect to construct a series of primary schools in the capital. Building on his earlier designs for cellular high-rise housing complexes such as his Proyecto de Habitaciones Colectivas Para Obreros (1928), O'Gorman replicated Le Corbusier's grid-based compositions to impose a strict spatial order on the schools, allocating precisely one square metre per child inside the buildings and five square metres in the playgrounds.[50] Rather than waste resources on superfluous decoration, O'Gorman intentionally exposed the structural components of the buildings as evidence of their structural 'honesty': 'no se quiso disfrazar la construcción [...] sino que al revés, la muestra con toda sinceridad, orgullosa de ella' [there was no intention to conceal its construction... but on the contrary to display it proudly and with total honesty].[51]

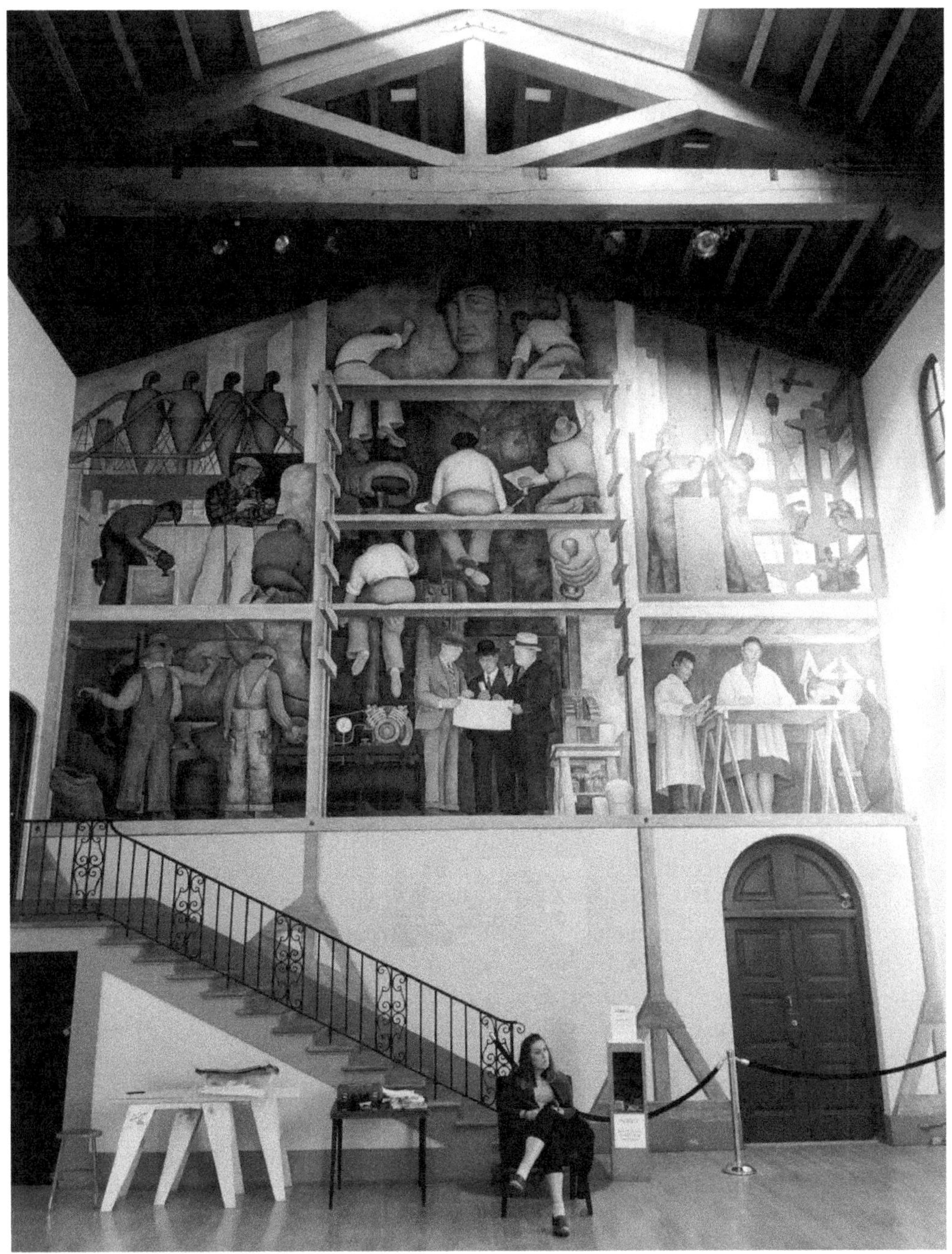

Fig. 2.2. Diego Rivera, *The Making of a Fresco Showing the Building of a City* (1931), San Francisco Art Institute © Banco de México Diego Rivera Frida Kahlo Museums Trust, Mexico, D.F. / DACS 2021

A childhood friend of Kahlo's, O'Gorman became acquainted with Rivera while he was painting *Creación* (1922) and a strong friendship developed between the two that in turn fostered Rivera's interest in rationalist design. Rivera's admiration of Obregón Santacilia's utilitarian building in the aforementioned review underscores a concern with aesthetic utility that was fundamental to his conception of proletarian art. Rivera's functionalist artistic ethic manifested itself not only in the socially committed thematic content of his murals but also in his utilitarian approach to pictorial space. Mirroring the spatial efficiency of O'Gorman's architectural designs, Rivera ensured that every inch of his epic compositions was meticulously structured and charged with narrative significance. Although this highly controlled approach to space underlies all of Rivera's post-revolutionary works, it manifests itself most clearly in his utopian vision of an industrial proletarian society in *The Making of a Fresco Showing the Building of a City* (Fig.2.2), which he painted at the San Francisco Art Institute in 1931. In this rendering of a utopian worker-centred industrial society, Rivera draws on functionalist architectural principles to establish a parallel between the order and discipline of built spaces and the bodies inhabiting them.

Upon his arrival in the United States in 1930, Rivera departed from the more historically themed content of his domestic murals to embrace a new industrial aesthetic inspired by the cityscapes of San Francisco, Detroit and New York. His visit to the US coincided with several major construction projects across the northern country and *The Making of a Fresco* captures his enthusiasm at man's creative capacity. In this piece, Rivera intertwines industrial progress and societal harmony by depicting the construction of a steel and concrete landscape through a system of productive human cooperation. Although executed in San Francisco, Alicia Azuela notes how 'the actual location is undefined, the workers could be at any site; the urban landscape could belong to any country, any social system'.[52] This relative lack of geographical referents in comparison to his other US work, enables the viewer to read *The Making of a Fresco* as a more generalised representation of how Rivera envisioned the ideal modern proletarian society.

The mural's full title establishes a central comparison between the process of fresco production and the construction of a city, which is allegorised as a giant industrial worker in denim overalls, positioned at the centre of the composition. In front of this enormous figure, who is operating two giant levers, a large scaffold imposes a rigid structure across the visual field, dividing it into eight individual cells. The compartments to the centre and left of the lower section of the mural depict the conceptual stages of the city's design as donors and architects pour over sketches and blueprints, while the bottom left and upper cells show these plans being realised by groups of artists and manual workers. Two teams of sculptors are positioned in the lower and middle cells on the left-hand side, while Rivera and his assistants occupy the central section where they paint the mural of the giant worker. The artist summarised the mural's composition as follows:

> El andamio subdivide al muro en compartimentos o celdas. Como sabemos el andamio es la preconstrucción indispensable de todo edificio. El andamio

no es solamente visible, sino que constituye el marco mismo de la obra e indica la sencillez estructural y honradez plástica de la composición. Estos varios compartimentos contienen todos los elementos de la construcción arquitectónica.[53]

[The scaffold divides the wall into compartments or cells. As we know, the scaffold is an essential part of the pre-construction phase for any building. The scaffold is not just visible but constitutes the very framework of the construction and shows the structural simplicity and plastic honesty of the composition. These different compartments contain all of the elements of architectural construction.]

The most striking aspect of Rivera's commentary is his use of functionalist terminology. He highlights the visibility of the scaffold, which functionally divides the composition into distinct 'cells' or zones of activity. Recalling O'Gorman's description of the structural sincerity of his buildings, which proudly displayed rather than concealed evidence of their own construction, he explains how the exposed scaffold attests to the 'structural simplicity and plastic honesty' of the finished work.

Rivera's use of functionalist language is significant in light of the unique composition of this particular mural, which stands out in his oeuvre due to its distinctly house-like appearance. Unlike many of his Mexican murals, which wrap around the interiors of entire buildings, *The Making of a Fresco* occupies a relatively confined physical space. Although the president of the San Francisco Art Commission, William Gerstle, originally offered Rivera a smaller section of wall, measuring just one hundred and twenty feet, the artist opted for the larger but rather unusually shaped interior north wall of the Institute's exhibition hall. While commentators have tended to focus solely on the mural's visual field, a more holistic view incorporating the entire north wall and its distinctive architectural features, provides a better understanding of the visual effects Rivera was trying to achieve. An analytical approach encompassing these visual and structural elements is all the more necessary when we consider Rivera's promotion of plastic integration.[54] The slanting ceiling of the gallery causes the upper part of the mural to taper in like a roof, creating a dolls' house effect that is enhanced by the scaffold's vertical and horizontal division of the composition into separate compartments or 'rooms', and by the presence of a real door positioned below. Although the mural's title refers to the process of building a city, Rivera's subsequent claim that he intended to portray a scene of 'técnicos, proyectistas y artistas trabajando juntos para hacer un edificio moderno' [surveyors, draftsman and artists working together to construct a modern building] clarifies that this aspect of the fresco's appearance was intentional.[55]

Rivera's configuration of the mural as a distinctly house-like functionalist building is relevant given the period in which it was executed. In 1929 the artist had commissioned O'Gorman to construct a functionalist house-studio for himself and Kahlo in Avenida Altavista, San Ángel. Construction for the studio, widely regarded as 'a triumph of functionalist principles', began that year and was completed in 1931, coinciding exactly with the beginning of Rivera's mural project in San Francisco.[56]

Taking inspiration from the Paris studio designed by Le Corbusier for the artist Amédée Ozenfant in 1923, O'Gorman composed the complex as two conjoined cubic buildings, painted red and blue to indicate their function as separate living spaces for Rivera and Kahlo, respectively. Toyo Ito's claim that the dominant red building and its leaner blue counterpart resemble the rotund Rivera resting his hand on the shoulder of the svelte Frida again highlights the link in O'Gorman's functionalism between the architectural form of his buildings and the bodies, real or imagined, of their inhabitants.[57]

Rivera's configuration of the mural as a distinctly house-like functionalist building encourages a comparative reading with O'Gorman's contemporaneous architectural project in Mexico that brings to light a number of compositional and theoretical similarities. The scaffold used to rigidly compartmentalise the mural space replicates the rigid cubic dimensions of the buildings whose 'interiors were expressed as distinct, separate elements'.[58] The painted vertical wooden beams of the scaffold extend below the painted space to the floor of the gallery, creating the illusion of pilotis, while a set of steps to the right of the mural recall the external stairs leading to Kahlo's elevated quarters. These structural parallels are compounded by a chromatic correlation between the dark blues, reds and yellows used to decorate the exterior and interior walls of O'Gorman's cubic buildings and the predominance of these primary colours in Rivera's mural.

Rivera's pictorial interpretation of functionalist theories is most clearly revealed in his spatial arrangement of human bodies. By configuring the mural space as a functionalist house, *The Making of a Fresco* provides a striking visual metaphor for the rigid spatial architecture that characterised Rivera's post-revolutionary murals. As Anna Indych-López demonstrates, Rivera achieved this sense of compositional structure by integrating the conceptual grid system used in cubist painting.[59] Composed of intersecting vertical and horizontal lines, this concealed architectural device facilitated the harmonious distribution and integration of objects within the pictorial field. While Indych-López provides a compelling commentary of how the conceptual grid functions as an organising principle in Rivera's works, she overlooks the impact of this device on the bodies contained within them. The panel *Los tejedores* (1923–1924), located on the first floor of the SEP, illustrates how Rivera used the cubist scaffolding system to spatially control figures within the visual field. In this portrait of three weavers working at a loom, the grid manifests itself in the intersecting lines of the threads and the wooden frames to which they are connected. This network of converging lines fixes the figures in space, rooting them respectively within the foreground, middle-ground and background of the composition. Rivera employed the cubist grid as a device for restraining human figures in the majority of his murals; however, it manifests itself most clearly in his utopian projection of an industrial proletarian society at the San Francisco Art Institute. While the conceptual grid is subtly interwoven into the fabric of *Los tejedores*, this device is intentionally revealed in *The Making of a Fresco*, where it is metaphorised by the large *trompe-l'oeil* wooden scaffold that divides the visual field into self-contained zones of activity.

While *The Making of a Fresco* (alternatively entitled *Workers in Control of Production*) ostensibly projects the empowerment of the worker within a modern industrial society, the grid scheme highlights the disciplinary spatial technologies at work within the mural. By making the grid an integral part of his utopian societal vision, Rivera establishes a parallel between architectural and collective social order that visually articulates Le Corbusier's belief that 'where order reigns, wellbeing reigns'.[60] More specifically, his use of the cellular grid in this particular mural can be aligned with the biopolitical dimensions of O'Gorman's functionalism in its equation of spatial and bodily discipline. In his 1976 lecture, Foucault employs the orthogonal grid design as a pertinent architecture metaphor for disciplinary networks, noting how it structurally articulates, 'in a sort of perpendicular way, the disciplinary mechanisms that controlled the body' by facilitating 'spontaneous policing or control'.[61] Dreyfus and Rabinow elaborate on Foucault's identification of the grid as the definitive architectural metaphor for disciplinary technologies:

> In disciplinary technology the internal organisation of space depends on the principle of elementary partitioning into regular units. This space is based on a principle of presences and absences. In such a simple coding, each slot in the grid is assigned a value. These slots facilitate the application of techniques of discipline to the body. Once the grid is established, the principle reads, 'Each individual has a place and each place has its individual'.[62]

In *The Making of a Fresco*, the architectural frame of the scaffold fulfils this disciplinary purpose by systematically grouping bodies in sections of the grid according to their specific role in the construction process. Foucault's assertion that the grid achieves its regulatory effect by facilitating complete surveillance allows us to understand how this compositional approach fits within Rivera's broader artistic preference for totalising forms of vision. Here the scaffold renders clearly visible the human activities being carried out in each section. This technique of distribution also functionally compartmentalises the bodies to maximise their efficiency while uniting them within a single system of production. The correlation between architectural and bodily discipline suggested by this system is illuminated by comments made by Rivera in 1934. Reiterating O'Gorman's earlier statements in more explicitly physiological terms, the artist claimed that:

> El día de mañana, la arquitectura, madre de todas las artes plásticas, será racionalizada; arrojará las escamas leprosas de la ornamentación tradicional [...] para sustituirlos por habitats racionales cuyas brillantes paredes lucirán espléndidamente iluminadas por grandes espacios de cristal y luz que serán el habitat adecuado al funcionamiento cerebral del hombre civilizado.[63]
>
> [Tomorrow, architecture, the mother of all plastic arts, will be rationalised; it will slough off the leprous scales of traditional ornamentation... and replace them with rationalised dwellings whose bright walls will be splendidly illuminated by great expanses of glass and light — a dwelling suitable for the cerebral functioning of the civilised man]

Rivera's belief that the rationalisation of architecture would produce rational new subjects is further reflected in the relationship between architectural and anatomical forms within the mural, which, as in O'Gorman's studio-house design, is conceptualised in highly fluid terms. The clearest example of this is the central visual metaphor of the mural, which equates the creation of a fresco depicting the body of a worker with the construction of a modern building. This comparison is reinforced by the correlation between the composition lines being sketched on the wall beside the worker's head and the steel cables being used to erect the skyscraper in the upper right-hand compartment of the mural. This intermingling of human and industrial elements again manifests itself in the distinctly anthropomorphic ventilators in the upper left-hand cell, composed of cylindrical trunks and tubular limbs, and the block of stone being chiselled by the sculptors below, which resembles the side profile of a human face. These subtle parallels are confirmed by the anatomical language employed by Rivera in his commentary. The muralist's description of the sculptors giving 'formas vivientes' [living forms] to the stone while the metal workers raise the building's 'esqueleto de acero' [steel skeleton] again reflects the central logic of O'Gorman's functionalism, in which the properties of architectural structures and the bodies inhabiting them become interchangeable.

Over the following decades, the social value of functionalism faced increasing scrutiny. Disillusioned with its failure to improve living conditions for the working classes, O'Gorman abandoned architecture in 1938 and dedicated himself to easel painting and mural production. O'Gorman's break from functionalism, which by the late 1930s had been established as the official architectural mode of the post-revolutionary state, was motivated by recent economic and political developments. As Camacho and subsequent presidents adopted a stronger developmentalist ethos, applications of functionalism in public architecture reflected the changing priorities of a government that increasingly measured national progress in economic and industrial, rather than social terms. O'Gorman bitterly lamented this shift, arguing that the maxim of 'maximum efficiency for minimum cost', had been distorted by the ruling classes to maximise profit and control the working class population.[64] During the 1940s and early 1950s Rivera published equally harsh reassessments of Le Corbusier's projects in the magazine *Espacios* and contributed as a set designer to José Revueltas's *El cuadrante de la soledad* (1950), a play that explored the psychologically damaging impact of overcrowding on the capital's marginalised lower middle-classes. Like O'Gorman, Rivera's turn away from the utilitarian aesthetics of functionalism stemmed from his disappointment with the disintegration of the Revolution's social ideals. Discussing the dominance of functionalism in an article published in 1952, he asserted that:

> Ahora entra el país en el periodo de la consolidación burguesa, fruto de la revolución que, con el sacrificio de más de dos millones de campesinos, obreros y soldados, el suelo fecundado con su sangre, empieza a recoger su cosecha la nueva burguesía.[65]
>
> [The country is now entering a period of bourgeois consolidation. This is the result of a Revolution in which more than two million peasants, workers and soldiers sacrificed themselves and fertilised the soil with their blood so that the new bourgeoisie could reap its fruits.]

During this period, both men embraced the organic style of the American architect Frank Lloyd Wright who held that architecture should serve a therapeutic and spiritually elevating purpose rather than merely satisfying basic human needs. Reconfiguring his earlier corporeal analogies, Rivera equated the body's need for aesthetic nourishment with its nutritional requirements: 'una arquitectura, como destinada que está a seres humanos, no es realmente funcional si no provee a las necesidades del aparato endocrinosimpático de ellos, tan importantes como las del aparato digestivo' [architecture, as it is designed for human beings, is not truly functional if it does not satisfy the needs of the endocrine-sympathetic system, which are as important as those of the digestive system].[66] In a similar vein, O'Gorman's writings of this period draw from digestive metaphors to explain the need for aesthetic fulfilment, comparing extreme architectural rationalism to a kind of nutritional supplement which, despite its utilitarian efficiency, is so unpalatable it is rejected by the stomach: 'malograda su eficiencia alimenticia lo desecharíamos, porque vomitaríamos si lo comiéramos, no obstante su "máximo de eficiencia alimenticia por el mínimo de esfuerzo en costo"' [despite its nutritional efficiency we would throw it away because we would vomit if we ate it, regardless of its 'maximum nutritional efficiency for the minimum cost'].[67] The similarities between these physiological metaphors reveal how O'Gorman's and Rivera's architectural philosophies remained remarkably compatible even after they distanced themselves from functionalism.

O'Gorman's move towards a more organic visual aesthetic is reflected in the haunting ruinscapes he produced following his turn to easel painting in the 1940s. In works such as *Los mitos* (1944) and *De unas ruinas nacen otras ruinas* (1949), architectural structures melt away and merge with roots and other matter. O'Gorman's turn to the seemingly functionless ruin in his rejection of disciplinary functionalist architecture strikingly foreshadows Rulfo's artistic treatment of built spaces in the 1950s. As I discuss in the next section, in his mid-century novel and photographs of Mexico City, human bodies mirror the structural instability of their architectural environment and embrace the residual spaces of the ruin and the urban interstice.

Part II: Human and Architectural Indeterminacies: Ruins and Urban Interstices

Páramo's final glimpse of 'la tierra en ruinas' [the land in ruins] (311) as he crumbles in the closing passage of *Pedro Páramo* directly links the anatomical decomposition of the townsfolk to the physical disintegration of their surroundings. As Preciado proceeds through Comala, our attention is repeatedly drawn to the architectural decay of the village (197, 200, 135, 242). In their overlapping commentaries, Preciado and Páramo point to fissures in the walls of Comala that are infiltrated by nostalgic voices and drops of water (247, 213). After abandoning Doña Eduviges's dilapidated home, Preciado stumbles upon an incestuous couple living in 'una casa con la mitad del techo caída' [a house where half the roof had fallen in] (235).

His descriptions of the building's cracked walls and broken roof point to a state of architectural collapse that is subsequently mirrored in the decomposing body of the sister: 'el cuerpo de aquella mujer hecho de tierra, envuelto en costras de tierra, se desbarataba' [that woman's body which was made of earth, layered in crusts of earth, was crumbling] (245). This description of bodily fragmentation fits within a broader poetics of undoing in the novel, where a proliferation of verbs bearing the prefix *des-*, such as *desmoronarse* [to collapse], *desgajarse* [to break off], *despedazar* [to break into pieces] and *deshacerse* [to fall apart] are descriptively applied to the human anatomy. Rulfo's literary depictions of structural and corporeal decay are echoed in his writings on Mexican architecture, where ruinous churches are compared to 'esqueletos mutilados' [mutilated skeletons], and again in his photographs of anthropomorphic ruins and eroding Mayan statues.[68]

In his analysis, Lanin A. Gyurko argues that fragmentation 'defines the basic themes of the novel: disintegration of the universe, loss of an integral self, and the hopelessness of redemption'.[69] Patricia Reagan supports this view, stating that in Comala 'hopelessness is all that is left for the future'.[70] While many critics have identified the novel's use of fragmentation as evidence of a crushingly pessimistic societal vision, the potentially constructive dimensions of ruination in Rulfo's work merit consideration, particularly in light of the previously discussed transition towards a more self-reflexive attitude regarding national issues by mid-century thinkers. One intellectual to challenge 'the old order, the official narrative, the post-revolutionary nationalist epistemology' was the Hiperión philosopher Emilio Uranga, who expressed admiration of Rulfo's literature.[71] While Vasconcelos looked to Mexico's *mestizo* identity as the basis for national unity and progress, Uranga identified the fusion of indigenous and European racial elements as a source of ontological instability for the Mexican. In his *Análisis del ser del mexicano* (1952), the philosopher developed the Nahuatl concept of *nepantla* to describe the condition of the Mexican as one of instability, indeterminacy and in-betweenness.[72] While Uranga's emphasis on these and other traits such as insufficiency and melancholy would appear to uphold an essentialising interpretation of Mexicanness, he understood such characteristics as the product of specific and constantly evolving historical circumstances, and thus evidence of a dynamic rather than static mode of identity that is constantly transforming.

Intellectual efforts to deconstruct established models of post-revolutionary nationhood reverberated in the artistic domain. In the field of literature, the interpretations of national identity presented in the narratives of Yáñez, Revueltas and theatrical works such as Rodolfo Usigli's *El gesticulador* (1938) reflected a mid-century reappraisal of the Revolution's legacy and the state's commitment to its social ideals. For Fuentes, this move from a didactic stance towards a more interrogatory tone constituted a defining feature of the modern Latin American novel. Underlining the innovative and constructive nature of this critical approach, he asserts that 'la nueva novela hispanoamericana actual no se resigna a ser solo documento de protesta sino que aspira a constituir una verdadera creación' [the new Hispanic American novel does not resign itself to being solely a document of protest but aspires to being a true creation].[73] Situating Rulfo within this period of significant intellectual and artistic transition encourages us to look beyond the apparent hopelessness of his literary vision and consider how his corporeal fragments and ruins may function as tools for constructive self-reflection and criticism.

The constructive dimensions of Rulfo's fragmentary aesthetic can be better understood in light of Walter Benjamin's discussion of the ruin in *The Origin of German Tragic Drama* (1928). In this seminal work, Benjamin describes the act of allegorical interpretation as a redemptive process that can lead to creative action in the present. Diverging from the romantic tendency to project the ruin as an external referent for the author's melancholia, Benjamin interprets it, along with the fragmentary baroque corpse, as evidence of the politically progressive force of allegory in its capacity to destroy the symbol's 'false illusion of totality'.[74] As an emblem of an absent wholeness, allegorical contemplation initiates a constructive act of deconstruction through which fragments of the past can be used to build new structures. In asserting that 'allegories are, in the realm of thoughts, what ruins are in the realm of things', Benjamin politicises the ruin by conceptualising it as an allegory for the very process of thinking.[75] Following a similar line of argumentation, Julia Hell and Andreas Schönle have more recently identified an 'unstable semantic potential' in the ruin's architectural incompletion that 'signals the impending breakdown of meaning and therefore fosters intensive compensatory discursive activity'.[76]

In formal terms, this productive capacity of the incomplete structure is exemplified by the fragmentary nature of Rulfo's novel, which requires the reader to creatively intervene and reconstruct the narrative's events. Although scholars have since illuminated the complex structure of *Pedro Páramo* and its intricate network of recurring motifs and images, its apparent lack of narrative scaffolding constituted a key point of contention for early commentators such as Archibaldo Burns, who lamented that 'les falta estructuración (a los personajes) como arquitectura al relato' [the characters lack structuring and the story lacks architecture].[77] Rubén Salazar Mallén was equally unforgiving in his review of the 'poorly constructed' novel, concluding that Rulfo had failed to fulfil the fundamental task of the writer: 'organizar sus materiales, esto es, construir con ellos su obra' [to organise his or her materials, that is, to use them to construct the work].[78] While these critics pointed to the novel's seeming lack of narrative framework as its most serious defect, Benjamin's reading of the ruin as a symbol of intellectual productivity allows us to consider how the ruinous textual landscape of *Pedro Páramo* is not hopeless but rather charged with creative potential. Rulfo opted to work with textual fragments rather than conventionally structured chapters and removed large portions of the text prior to publication: 'Quité ciento cincuenta páginas a *Pedro Páramo*: había divagaciones, elucubraciones mías, intromisiones, explicaciones' [I removed one hundred and fifty pages from *Pedro Páramo*: there were digressions, ramblings of mine, interventions and explanations].[79] This act of textual decomposition was an intentional strategy to engage readers in a process of semantic construction by filling the novel's gaps and silences:

> La intención fue [...] quitarle las explicaciones. Era un libro un poco didáctico, casi pedagógico: daba clases de moral y no sé cuántas cosas y todo eso tuve que eliminarlo porque no soy muy moralista [...] fui dejando algunos hilos, aquellos hilos colgando para que el lector me [...] pues, cooperara con el autor en la lectura. Entonces, es un libro de cooperación. Si el lector no coopera, no lo entiende; él tiene que añadirle lo que le falta.[80]
>
> [The intention was... to remove the explanations. It was a somewhat didactic book, almost pedagogical: it gave morality lessons and I don't know how many other things and I had to get rid of all of that because I am not very moralistic... I started leaving some threads, loose threads so that the reader would... cooperate with the author through reading. So, it is a book of cooperation. If the reader does not cooperate, they will not understand it; they need to add what it is missing.]

Rulfo's comments align the novel with Barthes's notion of the *texte scriptible*. Unlike the closed *texte lisible*, which communicates its pre-determined meaning through a legible format, Barthes describes how the unconventional 'writerly' text is characterised by an unsettling sense of loss that encourages the reader to actively generate its meaning in a more self-reflective manner. In *Pedro Páramo*, narrative fragmentation thus functions as a political strategy which, in contrast to Rivera's didactic aesthetic model, requires the reader to become what Julio Cortázar terms a 'lector cómplice' [reader-accomplice] by actively participating in the act of narrative construction and the production of the text's meaning.[81]

For Benjamin, the allegorical destruction of the organic whole is powerfully embodied by the corpse whose corporeal remnants fall 'away from the body piece by piece'.[82] The potential of these bodily fragments to generate new and evolving forms of meaning, like Barthes' incomplete text, is revealed to Benjamin through the regenerative nature of the corpse, which exists in a transitional state of ongoing decay.[83] This sense of potentiality is encapsulated in the ruinous Rulfian body, which is engaged in a continuous process of decomposition. Despite the apparent abruptness of his collapse in the novel's closing lines, we learn that in fact Páramo 'estaba acostumbrado a ver morir cada uno de sus pedazos' [was used to seeing each piece of him die] (310). In conversation with his daughter Susana, Bartolomé San Juan also highlights the gradual nature of the villagers' bodily decomposition when he describes how the world weighs down upon them, 'deshaciéndonos en pedazos' [breaking us into pieces] (272). As in the novel's closing lines, where we are told that Páramo 'se fue desmoronando' [started crumbling] (311), Bartolomé's use of the gerund form of the verb *deshacerse* [to fall apart] highlights how these bodies are engaged in a dynamic process of physiological transformation that is still ongoing. In contrast to Rivera's static architectonic figures, this recurring use of the present-continuous tense endows Rulfo's deteriorating bodies with a changeable quality which, as Bruce Dean Willis asserts, is more readily expressed through literary rather than pictorial means. In contrast to the fixity of the painted image, he notes that, due to the temporal properties of literature 'the aging of a character's body, for instance, can be depicted after the appropriate narrative exigencies to suggest the passage of time, or the bodily effects of an illness, operation or accident can be relayed in ways that allow for a comparison of before and after'.[84] Embracing this intrinsic mutability of the literary body, Rulfo's metaphors of corporeal ruination express a capacity for ongoing transformation that is denied to the monolithic *mestizos* populating Rivera's murals.

For Svetlana Boym, the fertile potentiality of the ruin derives from its spatio-temporal interstitiality. Caught between past and present, absence and presence, the ruin's indeterminacy prompts reflection about a 'past that could have been and a future that never took place'.[85] Her assertion that ruins invite us into 'a labyrinth of ambivalent language — no longer, not yet, nevertheless, albeit' resonates in the dreamlike Comala, where phrases such as *tal vez* and *quizás* [perhaps] and imperfect subjunctive *como si* [as if] clauses abound and the villagers repeatedly conjecture about hypothetical situations.[86] Evoking the notion of the aperture, a Rulfian motif I return to later in this discussion, Lucy Bell suggests that in Rulfo's short stories 'the subjunctive mood constitutes an opening that renders the text inexhaustible'.[87] Much like the literal gaps that separate the novel's fragments, these ambiguities open up undefined narrative spaces that invite speculation and intervention on the part of the reader. Situated betwixt and between different structural and temporal states, Rulfo's ruinous village, where a sense of expectation hangs in the air, speaks to Victor Turner's interpretation of liminal space as 'a storehouse of possibilities [...] striving after new forms and structures'.[88] Indeed, the verb *esperar*, which captures this sense of anticipation and futurity in its possible meanings of 'to wait' and 'to hope', appears fifty two times within the novel's sixty-nine fragments. Theoretical interpretations of the liminal ruin as a metaphor for intellectual inquiry and creativity allow us to read Rulfo's ruinous textual and corporeal structures as constructive sites that provoke reassessments of the past while also fostering creative speculation about alternative configurations for the future.

This concept of liminality, derived from the Latin *limen,* meaning threshold, draws attention to another prominent architectural motif in *Pedro Páramo*. In a youthful recollection of his mother, Páramo recalls the figure of 'aquella mujer, de pie en el umbral; su cuerpo impidiendo la llegada del día' [that woman standing in the doorway, her body obstructing the arrival of day] (214) and later describes her contorted silhouette in the doorway as she weeps (255). On various occasions, Páramo, Bartolomé San Juan and Padre Rentería all observe Susana San Juan from the threshold of her bedroom (301, 288, 279). The motif of the doorway highlights the restlessness of Comala's inhabitants who appear fleetingly only to dissolve away again into the landscape. Their constant movement is facilitated by the porosity of Comala's built environment which is suggested by recurring references to other architectural openings in Preciado's descriptions and the memories of the other villagers (197, 200, 213, 264). Like his father, who appears at the window of a local woman named Margarita, Miguel Páramo climbs through the bedroom window of Ana Rentería, Padre Rentería's niece, when he visits her after nightfall. This liminal positioning of the body is visually reproduced in several of Rulfo's rural photographs depicting townspeople in the doorways and windows of dilapidated buildings. While Rulfo's deployment of the threshold as a visual framing device in the novel reveals his compositional sensibilities as a photographer, it more importantly highlights the liminality of a restless Rulfian body that lingers in the ambiguous zones between past and present, life and death, memory and reality.

While many scholars have described Comala as 'static and unchangeable', these architectural openings draw attention to the permeable nature of its built landscape and the mobility of its inhabitants.[89] The notions of indeterminacy and transition evoked by the threshold motif reflect the purgatorial status of Comala. Although the village has often been interpreted by critics as an infernal space, its inhabitants are described as 'ánimas', a term applied to souls in purgatory whose eternal fate has yet to be decided. Moreover, Hell is described as a place that is geographically distinct from Comala. Early in the novel Abundio remarks that many of the villagers who die 'al llegar al infierno regresan por su cobija' [come back for their quilt once they reach Hell] (196). That the fate of the villagers remains unresolved is further suggested by the existence of multiple intersecting pathways leading into and out of Comala. Before entering the village, Juan encounters Abundio at Los Encuentros where we are told, 'se cruzaban varios caminos' [several paths intersected] (195). Later, at a crucial point in the novel, when Preciado asks the incestuous sister how he can leave Comala she affirms that there is a 'multitud de caminos' [multitude of ways], including a vertical route through the broken roof of their house: 'me señaló con sus dedos el hueco del tejado, allí donde el techo estaba roto' [she pointed to a hole in the roof where the ceiling was broken] (239). The porous physical and architectural composition of Comala, where *caminos* and openings out lead to unknown destinations, establishes an affinity with the textual composition of the novel. Fabienne Bradu's assertion that 'los blancos que separan los fragmentos son esto: puertas abiertas' [the blank spaces separating the fragments are this: open doors] highlights the sense of potential implied by both the architectural apertures and pathways running through Comala and the novel's textual interstices.[90]

Rulfo's Urban Photographs: Interstitial Bodies and the Fragmentation of Built Space

A concern with the body's 'in-betweenness' establishes a link between Rulfo's contemporary literary and visual corpora. While architectural frames emerge as a recurring motif in Rulfo's portraits of indigenous rural communities, his photographs of Mexico City repeatedly capture bodies inhabiting interstices in the built environment. Taken in 1956 at the height of mid-century *desarrollismo* [developmentalism], photographs of the capital visually document the old railyards to the north of the capital shortly before they were demolished to make way for a functionalist housing unit designed by the architect Mario Pani and replaced by the new Terminal del Valle de México in Tlalnepantla. Rulfo's photographs, first published together in the collection *En los ferrocarriles* (2014), were the product of a collaborative project with director Roberto Gavaldón, who invited Rulfo to work as a photographer on a documentary commissioned by the state-owned railway company Ferrocarriles Nacionales de México.[91] This short piece of government propaganda entitled *Terminal del Valle de México* (1956) was to document the success of the urban renewal project by contrasting the degenerating old railway lines and the surrounding working-class districts with the pristine new installations in the suburbs. Just as the Papaloapan project, discussed in Chapter 1, sought to impose the government's vision of progress on an indigenous rural space, the urban regeneration programme aimed to bring efficiency and order to the landscape of the industrialising capital.

As in the case of his work for the Comisión del Papaloapan on *Danzas mixes*, a tension emerges here between the professional context of Rulfo's photographic production and the content of these works. Analysing these contemporaneous bodies of work side by side reveals how Rulfo challenged the ideals of national cohesion and progress he was employed to promote through his photographic practice. Of the one hundred and forty photographs Rulfo produced while working on *Terminal del Valle de México*, a distinction can be detected between the images that uphold the aims of the documentary, such as his helicopter views of the city and the new railway terminal, and those more intimate scenes of urban life to which his lens appears to have been drawn. Deviating from the intentions of Gavaldón's film, Rulfo's photographic imagery challenges Pani's functionalist vision of a disciplined and totalised urban landscape and population by revealing a mobile urban citizenry that slips between the cracks and crevices of the built environment. Offering a visual urban counterpoint to his literary texts of the same period, which present a neglected post-revolutionary rural *campesinado*, these photographs undermine contemporary rhetoric of national progress by depicting a disenfranchised urban community on the margins of the state's modernisation project. As I will attempt to demonstrate, by drawing attention to these elusive, ill-defined bodies and the indeterminate spaces they inhabit, Rulfo's works unsettle the principles of visibility and socio-spatial discipline that defined Pani's functionalist plans for an orderly urban landscape and population.

By the middle of the century, the urban housing crisis previously addressed by Rivera and O'Gorman during the 1930s had intensified due to increasing immigration. During the phase of economic growth known as the 'Mexican Miracle', rural migrants and rail workers gravitated towards the peripheral working-class *vecindades* [neighbourhoods] that had evolved around the railroads during the Porfiriato, leading to chronic overcrowding and sanitation problems. As conditions worsened in the 1940s and 50s, functionalism was adopted as state policy and the disciplinary dimensions of public architecture became increasingly pronounced. Pani, who replaced O'Gorman as one of the main proponents of functionalism in Mexico, responded to the housing crisis by proposing high-rise residential units known as *multifamiliares* as a hygienic and spatially efficient alternative to the slums and sprawling make-shift settlements to the north of the city. Employing Le Corbusien biological analogies, Pani identified the city's informal areas as sites of disease and moral corruption within the urban organism. In an article that employs an explicit medical metaphor, 'Penicilina para la ciudad' (1950), the architect states that building the *patria* involves 'purificando la podredumbre y construyendo sobre el terreno lavado y redimido nuevos hogares' [purifying the putrefaction and constructing new homes on clean and redeemed terrain]. He goes on to describe this process of urban spatial cleansing in disturbingly violent terms: 'el problema es tremendo, pero hay que proceder con energía. Meter dinamita, como ya dije, y regar petróleo' [the problem is tremendous but we must proceed energetically. Plant dynamite, as I have said, and spray petrol].[92] With the support of government commissions, Pani carried out a number of functionalist social-housing projects such as the Multifamiliar Miguel Alemán (1949) and the Multifamiliar Presidente Juárez (1952). These self-contained complexes followed a spatially restrictive cellular grid-based design that led inhabitants to compare the density of the 1949 complex to a concentration camp and, as O'Gorman later pointed out, earned it the nickname of 'la penitenciaría' [the penitenciary].[93]

The Conjunto Urbano Nonoalco Tlatelolco was Pani's most ambitious residential project to date, consisting of one hundred and one apartment buildings as well as clinics, recreational areas and schools for its ten thousand residents. While Pani's monumental unit appeared to uphold the social ideals of the Revolution by providing affordable housing for multiple families, its design was rooted in the Le Corbusien principles of discipline, efficiency and surveillance. Reaffirming his faith in architecture as a strategy of behavioural reform, Pani believed that transferring working-class families from sprawling *vecindades* to the 'células urbanas' [urban cells] of his new concrete residential blocks would contribute to the healthy development of the city and transform these 'individuos fracasados' [failed individuals] into civilised citizens.[94] This socially disciplining function of the complex was underlined by President Adolfo López Mateos at its inauguration in 1964 when, echoing the Le Corbusien dictum of 'architecture or revolution', he reminded the public that 'una revolución pacífica evita una revolución violenta' [a peaceful revolution prevents a violent revolution].[95]

In Rulfo's photographs, however, Pani's vision of urban spatial order and human containment is unsettled by the manner in which bodies negotiate the built environment. By combining aerial and ground level shots, the photographs juxtapose panoramic views of the city's modernising landscape with glimpses of its poorest inhabitants living precariously in the environs of the old rail yards. The distinction between these alternative perspectives of urban reality is illuminated by de Certeau in his essay 'Walking in the City' (1980). Using the dualistic framework of the 'concept' city and the 'migrational' city, de Certeau contrasts the orderliness of the urban landscape surveyed from a height, with the movements of city dwellers on the ground who complicate its legibility.[96] Surveying Manhattan from the top of the World Trade Centre, he describes how this elevated position provides him with a sense of panoptic mastery and accentuates the structural definition of the territory below by reducing the city's streets and buildings to a rigid and highly legible 'text' or 'texturology'.[97] De Certeau explains how this meticulously ordered view of the city, which he identifies with the gaze of the all-seeing urban planner or architect, is challenged by spatial strategies of resistance enacted by the improvised movements of the everyday pedestrian on the ground.

For the purposes of the documentary project, Rulfo and Gavaldón were granted access to a helicopter in order to view the new installations from a height. By

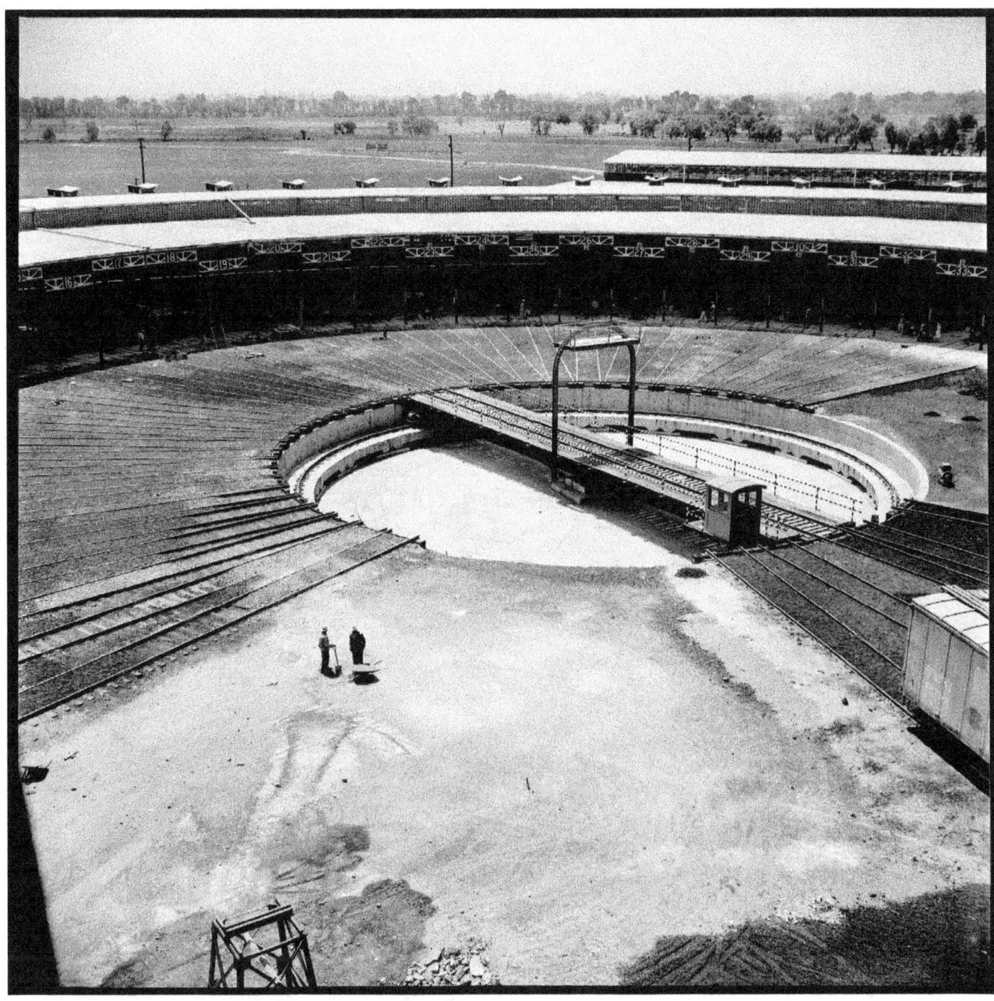

Fig. 2.3. Juan Rulfo, Helicopter view of the Terminal del Valle de México (1956)
© Herederos de Juan Rulfo 2020

integrating aerial perspectives, Gavaldón's film not only showcased the success of contemporary urban modernisation but also the technologically sophisticated forms of urban cartography available at the time. Advances in cartographic technology resulting from Mexico's participation in World War II during the Camacho administration enabled aerial photography companies to offer planners more precise and comprehensive methods of visualising urban territories. Rulfo captures this totalising perception of the city in photographs of the new installations in the Terminal del Valle de México (Fig. 2.3) and other bird's eye shots of buildings such as the Lotería Nacional skyscraper, where urban spaces are reduced to a legible design of interlocking geometric forms. Siegfried Kracauer's assertion that in aerial images 'all spatial configurations are incorporated into the central archive

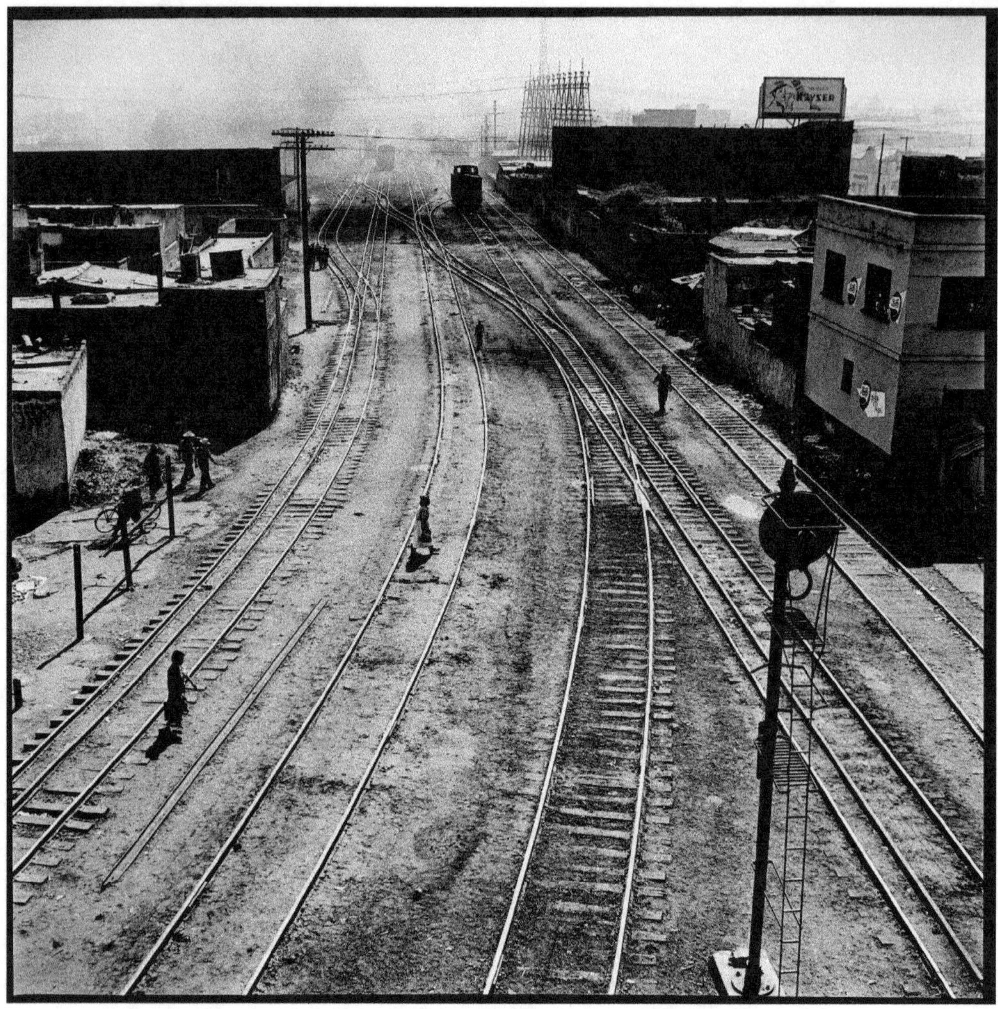

FIG. 2.4. Juan Rulfo, Corridor of the Nonoalco Railyard (1956)
© Herederos de Juan Rulfo 2020

in unusual combinations which distance them from human proximity' is reflected in the dramatic reduction or total elimination of human presence from these photographs.[98]

In Rulfo's ground-level shots, however, this geometric stability is unsettled by human agitation. Like de Certeau's 'spatial practitioners', Rulfo's subjects on the ground trouble the structural integrity of the 'conceptual city' devised by post-revolutionary planners through their constant and unregulated movement.[99] Resisting the biopolitics of spatial control at the heart of Pani's modernist project, these urban bodies display a fluid approach to spatiality. In one of the most striking photographs of the collection, four indistinct figures cross a derelict railway line in Nonoalco (Fig. 2.4). Like the spectral villagers of Comala, these blurred forms

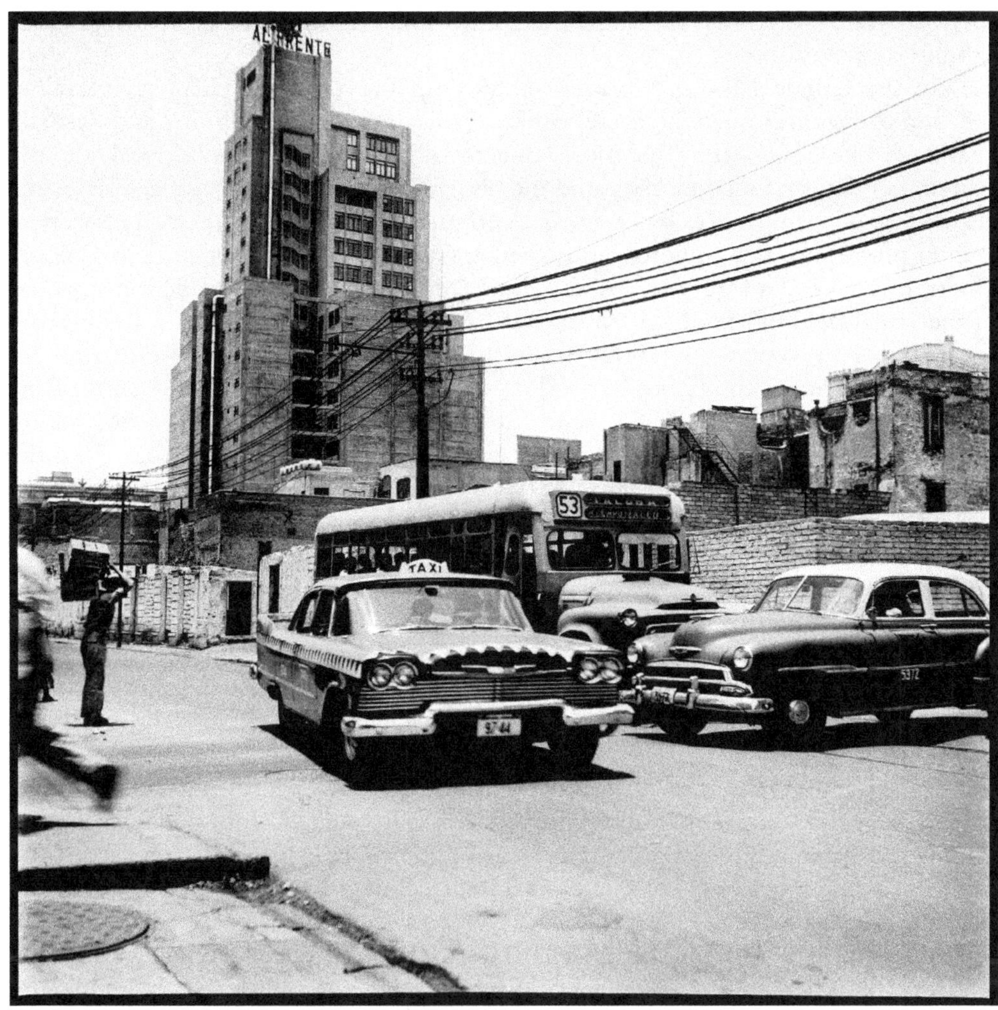

Fig. 2.5. Juan Rulfo, Calle de la Santa Veracruz in Colonia Guerrero (1956)

flit ghost-like across the unsheltered landscape at different points and in different directions, as if seeking refuge in the shadowy ruins on the far side. A similar emphasis on human movement is evident in photographs of pedestrians hastily traversing the railway lines at the Calzada de Nonoalco and women crossing the tracks in front of a freight train at the Tacuba Station. In most of these photographs, human activity is concentrated around the railway tracks, constituting a point of confluence for the intersecting paths of local pedestrians. Indeed, an entire section of the published collection entitled '*Crucero*-Crossing' is dedicated specifically to photographs documenting this ebb and flow of human movement at the intersections between the railway and the adjoining roads. The range of angles displayed in these photographs suggest that Rulfo was as restless as the city-dwellers he photographed; constantly clambering onto static carriages or crouching on the ground by the rail lines.

Like the female Mixe performer analysed in the previous chapter, several of the bodies foregrounded in these works resist immediate legibility and visually challenge the spectator. Technical aspects of these photographs, such as the blurring effect produced by the rapid movement of the pedestrians, accentuates the elusiveness of these figures by obscuring certain body parts. This motion blur effect is most pronounced in a photograph taken at Calle de la Santa Veracruz in Colonia Guerrero where the figure of a man who has just run across the junction slips out of the visual field of the image on the left hand side (Fig. 2.5). Dramatically blurred by his rapid movement, his body resists both visual definition and containment within the frame of the photograph. The vague forms and fluid movements of the bodies captured in these images recall the spectral figures of Comala who, we are told, 'andan sueltas por la calle' [wander freely through the streets] (204). Like the phantasmal nomads of *Pedro Páramo* or the wandering *campesinos* of his stories, these shrouded figures are ever in transit, slipping between the tracks and other gaps in the built environment.[100]

This interstitial positioning of the body is significant in the context of Pani's plans for a structurally totalised urban landscape. As Dreyfus and Rabinow note, if the panoptic strategies of control outlined by Foucault are to function, space 'must be ordered; there should be no waste, no gaps, no free margins; nothing should escape'.[101] In Rulfo's photographs, however, it is precisely these gaps in the built environment that his subjects appear to seek out.[102] In the previously examined photographs of human activity around the railway crossings, for example, figures appear to insert themselves in the gaps between the individual steel rails. Rulfo also detects interstitial activity within the more concealed crevices of the built environment. In a photograph at Tacuba, a man and a woman move along the confined passageway between a line of tank cars and a dilapidated adjacent building (Fig. 2.6). Hemmed in by the train barriers on one side and a crumbling wall on the other, they navigate their way between the piles of rubble and wire obstructing their path. In another at Tacuba station, a man walks towards the camera between an illuminated box car and the gloomy wall of the station building (Fig.2.7), a compositional structure that is replicated in several other photographs of rail workers and children standing between halted carriages and derelict station buildings. Due to Rulfo's careful framing and manipulation of light, his human subjects not only slip between built spaces but also between darkness and light, at times becoming almost entirely consumed by the shadows.

While Rulfo's panoramic images of the new terminal and the city's skyline are bathed in a sterile white light that stresses the formal rigidity and cleanliness of the urban landscape, these ground level shots dwell on the crepuscular spaces and bodies located at the margins of the tracks.[103] In its preoccupation with the shadowy recesses of the rail yards, Rulfo's photographic aesthetic opposes the principles of luminosity and visibility that defined functionalist design. As light-deficiency and poor ventilation had been identified as contributors to poor health in the capital,

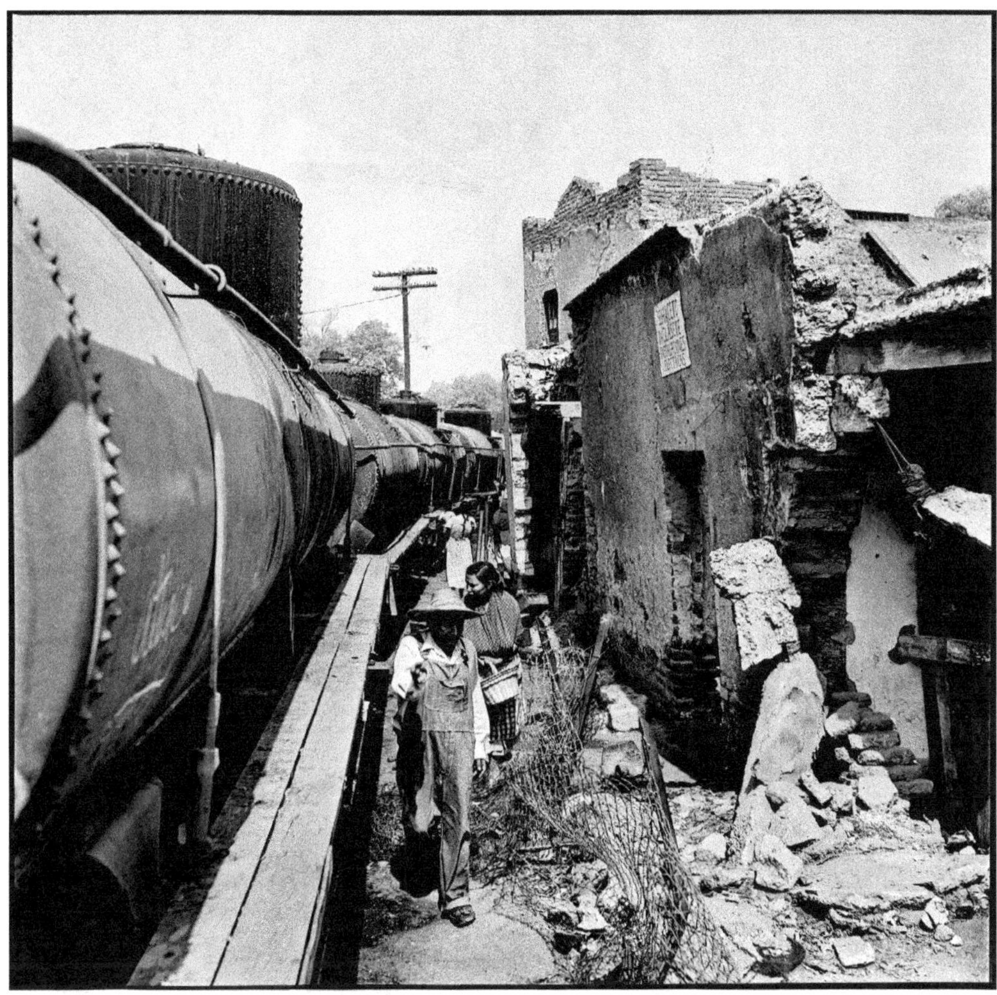

Fig. 2.6. Juan Rulfo, Man and woman at Tacuba station (1956)

Pani stressed the importance of natural illumination as an essential component of public architecture. By replicating Le Corbusier's grid format for the Conjunto Urbano, Pani exploited the hygienic and morally cleansing connotations of natural light, but also utilised transparency as a strategy for behavioural reform by including expanses of window that enhanced the external visibility of its inhabitants. Pani's article, which is accompanied by black-and-white photographs of indistinct figures inhabiting shanty huts and dank tenements, conveys a profound phobia of barely visible bodies lurking in the unchartered corners of the capital. Pani refers to Plaza de Romita in Colonia Roma as a 'nidero de ladrones, de borrachines' [a nest of thieves and drunkards] and warns that the existing low-rent housing blocks are 'oscuros, estrechos, reinos del chisme y del pleito' [dark, narrow, realms of scandal and conflict].[104]

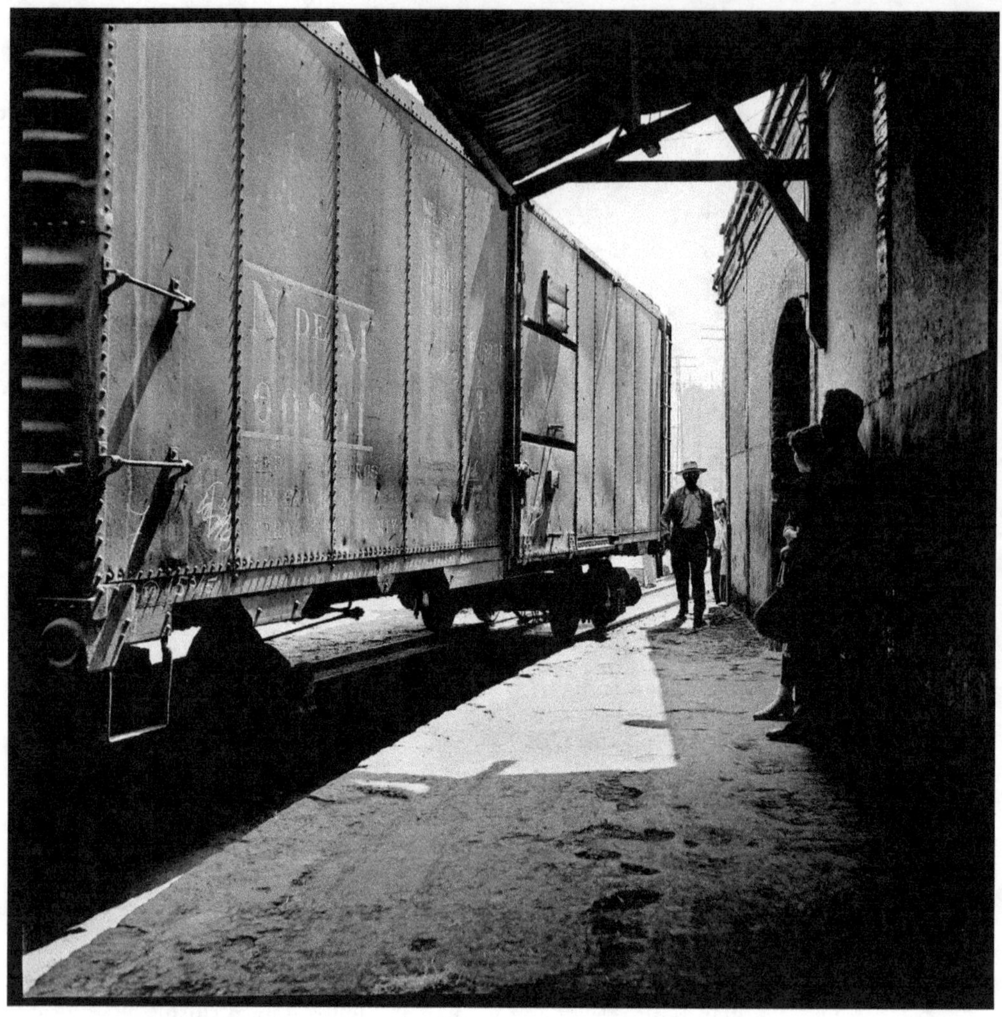

FIG. 2.7. Juan Rulfo, Tacuba station (1956) © Herederos de Juan Rulfo 2020

Several of Rulfo's photographs seem to intentionally play on this anxiety surrounding the visibility of urban spaces and bodies by exploring human activity in the concealed enclaves of the rail yards and their environs. A photograph taken in Colonia Guerrero depicts two women standing at the foot of a stairway in the dimly lit courtyard of a tenement basement (Fig. 2.8). Clothes hanging loosely from an overhead washing line provide a phantasmal correlative to the photograph's human subjects. While our gaze is initially drawn to these two figures positioned to the centre of the patio, previously undetected bodies gradually materialise from the surrounding space if we continue to strain our eyes. A third female figure, partially obscured by the clothes, can be seen descending the stairs and the outline of a fourth can just about be glimpsed behind the woman standing by the sink. Behind the two girls seated to the right of the stairway, the nebulous figures of two other children

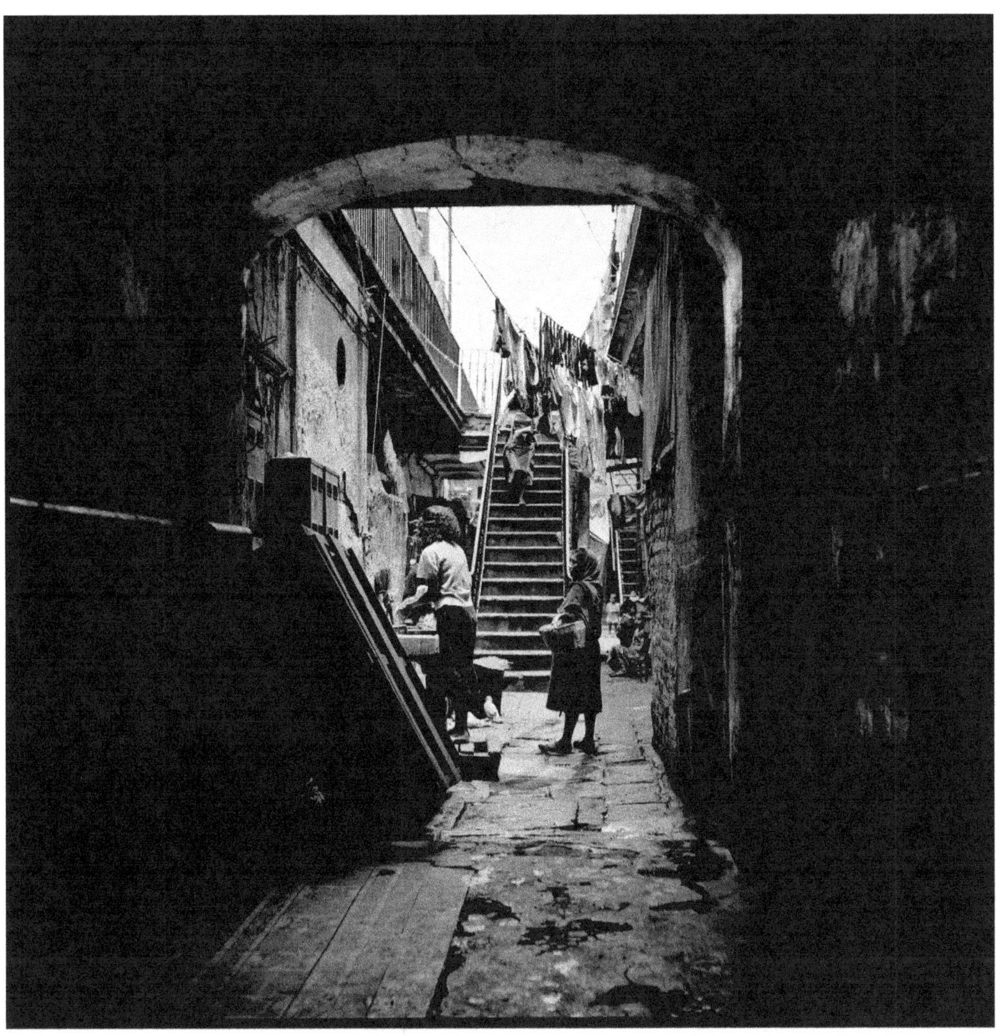

Fig. 2.8. Juan Rulfo, Basement patio in Colonia Guerrero (1956)

can also be discerned further along the patio. Unsettling Pani's panoptic strategies of control, the timing and angle of this photograph accentuate the ambiguity of urban bodies and spaces that stubbornly resist total visualisation.

Rulfo's concern with the indeterminate is further suggested by his sustained focus on the informal spaces inhabited by these figures. In photographs of women and children huddled beside makeshift dwellings at the margins of the Tlatelolco tracks and of children sitting amidst shanty huts in the Tacuba rail yard, Rulfo directs our gaze to the everyday human narratives unfolding in the irregular spaces Pani deemed a threat to the spatial order of the city. By 1955 the Departamento del Distrito Federal had demanded the abolition of all irregular settlements and the systematic eviction of squatters to maximise spatial efficiency. Commonly referred to as 'wastelands', 'dead zones' and 'urban voids', derelict urban interstices such as alleys, underpasses and abandoned railway yards have historically been considered evidence of the failure of urban development as they obstruct the structural totality and utility of the modern city.[105] More recently, however, urban theorists such as Andrea Mubi Brighenti have pointed to the politically active nature of these seemingly functionless non-spaces by suggesting that 'interstitial territorialities can only be appreciated by taking into account the dynamics of power and resistance, of fluidity and boundedness, of mobilities and moorings, of smoothness and striatedness that occur in the contemporary city'.[106]

Brighenti's understanding of interstices as porous or 'loose' zones in the urban environment suggests links with the medical term interstitium, referring to the fluid-filled gaps located between the functional parts of a tissue or organ that facilitate the transit of proteins and nutrients. Considered in the context of the biological analogies popularised by urban theorists like Le Corbusier, urban interstices can thus be understood as unfixed zones connecting the city's 'functional' components. Recalling the porous architectural environment of Comala, which presents Preciado with a 'multitude of paths', Brighenti identifies the interstice's unfixity as the source of its potentiality, asserting that 'understanding interstitiality as porosity — literally, "possibility of ways" — may therefore suggest an approach to the city that stresses the many spatial modes in which a plurality of social differences associate'.[107] By lingering on these ambiguous zones in the built landscape, Rulfo's photographic vision destabilises the functionalist anatomical analogy of the tightly regulated organism and instead evokes the biological concept of the interstitium as a flexible space of movement and fluid exchange within the urban body. While the forms of urban navigation explored in these photographs serve little purpose as real political strategies for their ultimately disenfranchised subjects, they open up spaces in the functionalist landscape where a productive critique of these disciplinary urban practices can take place.

Rulfo's visual documentation of the capital during this phase of mid-century urban restructuring reflects his broader artistic and academic interest in Mexico's built landscape. Alongside his literary descriptions of ruins in *Pedro Páramo* and stories like 'Luvina' and 'El día del derrumbe', Rulfo composed approximately four hundred texts of varying length on Mexican buildings and archaeological sites and photographically traced the evolution of the country's architecture from its Mayan pyramids and sixteenth-century buildings to the sky-scrapers of the Paseo de la Reforma.[108] Like his written commentaries, which according to González Boixo, 'ratifican su interés por relacionar los edificios con el proceso histórico' [confirm his interest in connecting buildings with the historical process], Víctor Jiménez asserts that:

> Hay en sus fotos sobre la arquitectura mexicana una relación, igualmente, con la que fue una de sus pasiones: la historia de México; es decir el conocimiento de su gente, su territorio y aquellos testimonios que la actividad de los hombres ha dejado en nuestro suelo a lo largo de los siglos.[109]

> [His photographs of Mexican architecture are connected to another of his passions: the history of Mexico, that is, the knowledge of its people, its territory and the testimonies that man's activity has left on our land over the centuries.]

As suggested by the recurring focus on precolonial and colonial ruins in both his textual and photographic documentation of Mexican architecture, Rulfo viewed Mexico's history as an ongoing cycle of oppression:

> Yo creo que si hay un constante en la historia de México, esa constante, a partir de la Conquista, está caracterizada por una lucha de los pocos contra los muchos, por una guerra contra el pueblo. De aquí la espantosa desigualdad que no ha podido ser resuelta.[110]
>
> [I believe that if there is one constant in the history of Mexico, that constant, from the period of the Conquest, is the struggle of the few against the many, a war against the people. This is the root of the terrible inequality that it has not been possible to resolve.]

In his photographs of the soon-to-be demolished rail yards, Rulfo again looks to the ruin to reflect on Mexico's more recent historical trajectory during a phase of increasing state authoritarianism. The industrial aesthetic of Pani's Conjunto Urbano and its spatially restrictive design encapsulated the shifting values of the post-revolutionary state as it resurrected the Porfirian ideals of 'Order and Progress'. The derelict spaces it would replace had once functioned as key industrial centres during the Díaz era, when the locomotive was established as the symbol par excellence of material progress. In the late nineteenth century, the new railway lines became the veins and arteries of the 'vasto organismo federal' [vast federal organism], bringing cohesion and industrial connectivity to the capital.[111] In his photographs, taken during the industrialising years of the 'Miracle', Rulfo's camera gaze resembles that of Benjamin's angel of history, who looks back upon the ruinous landscape as it is swept away by the storm of progress.[112] Rather than foreground the terminal and the capital's other new concrete monuments to progress, his lens lingers on these remnants of Porfirian modernity in a way that provokes critical reflection on Mexico's relentless quest for national renovation.

Alongside his splintered narratives and literary imagery of architectural and human rubble, Rulfo's photographic fascination with the urban ruin fits within a broader aesthetic impulse towards fragmentation. Anthropologist Néstor García Canclini identifies the fragmentary form of photography as the ideal medium for documenting urban modernity in Latin America:

> Las fotografías, con su captación de instantes aislados, con los enormes espacios virtuales que dejan entre una imagen y otra, parecen representar mejor que el cine las percepciones y los saberes fragmentados que se obtienen de una gran ciudad. Hay una correspondencia entre las operaciones de recorte y encuadre que hacen las fotos y el conjunto de experiencias desarticuladas que se obtienen en una megaciudad.[113]
>
> [In their ability to capture isolated moments and in the enormous virtual spaces they leave between one image and the next, photographs seem to represent

> better than cinema the fragmented forms of perception and knowledge that are acquired in a large city. There is a correlation between the techniques of cropping and framing used in photography and the disjointed experiences of the megacity.]

In highlighting the disjointed quality of photographic representation, García Canclini echoes Sontag's assertion that, 'through photographs the world becomes a series of unrelated freestanding particles [...] it is a view of the world which denies interconnectedness, continuity'.[114] Rulfo alludes to this fragmentary quality of the photographic image in one of the most memorable opening images of the novel, in which Juan contemplates the disintegrating portrait of his mother Dolores (196). This ekphrastic moment which launches Preciado's fragmented narrative journey in *Pedro Páramo* points to a broader concern with the decomposed or fragmented aesthetic object that defines Rulfo's artistic corpus.

Rulfo's literary and visual fragments and Rivera's monumental concrete murals provide potent artistic metaphors for the intellectual climates of their respective periods. Through their treatment of bodies and built spaces, the works of these two artists can be seen to aesthetically map the erection and deconstruction of the social architecture that defined Mexico in the formative decades following the Revolution. Writing in 1925, at the height of the state's nation-building initiatives, Rivera stated that his painterly aim was to express the 'sentido arquitectónico y constructivo' [architectural and constructive meaning] that he perceived at the heart of all creative activity.[115] The architectonic bodies and regimented visual spaces he configured in the 1920s and 30s reflect the real efforts of the state's social engineering and public architectural projects to construct a stable and rational post-revolutionary society. Forged during the more interrogative intellectual climate of the 1950s, Rulfo's literary and photographic works propose an alternative post-revolutionary aesthetic defined by ruination and fragmentation. The instability of the ruinous body and the proliferation of textual and architectural apertures in *Pedro Páramo* underscore the fundamental inconclusiveness of a narrative that demands the creative intervention of a constructive reader. The urban nomads of Rulfo's photographs and the anti-utilitarian interstices they inhabit similarly open up potentially productive spaces for rethinking the rigid functionalist model of the city. Rather than signal an irrevocably hopeless societal vision, bodily and architectural unbuilding in Rulfo can be read as a constructive processes that unsettle the structural boundaries of the imagined post-revolutionary community envisioned by Rivera and others and stimulate speculation about its potential renovation.

Notes to Chapter 2

1. Robert Rosenblum, *Cubism and Twentieth-Century Art* (New York: Harry N. Abrams, 2001), p. 9.
2. Doremus, p. 156.
3. Enrico Mario Santí, 'Introduction', in Octavio Paz, *El laberinto de la soledad*, ed. by Enrico Mario Santí (Madrid: Cátedra, 1993), pp. 11–137 (p. 54).
4. Jean Meyer, 'Revolution and Reconstruction in the 1920s', in *Mexico since Independence*, ed. by Leslie Bethell (Cambridge: Cambridge University Press, 1991), pp. 201–40 (p. 204).

5. Gamio, p. 325.
6. Ibid., p. 6.
7. Ibid., p. 6.
8. Ibid., p. 13.
9. Ana María Alonso, 'Conforming Disconformity: "Mestizaje", Hybridity, and the Aesthetics of Mexican Nationalism', *Cultural Anthropology*, 19 (2004), 459–90 (p. 462).
10. José Vasconcelos, *La raza cósmica: Misión de la raza iberoamericana: Notas de viajes a la América del Sur* (Barcelona: Agencia Mundial de Librería, 1928), p. 18.
11. José Vasconcelos, 'The Race Problem in Latin America', in *Aspects of Mexican Civilization: Lectures on the Harris Foundation*, ed.by José Vasconcelos and Manuel Gamio (Chicago: University of Chicago, 1926), pp. 75–102 (p. 95).
12. Elsa Muñiz, *Cuerpo, representación y poder: México en los albores de la reconstrucción nacional, 1920–1934* (Mexico City: Universidad Autónoma Metropolitana, 2002), p. 103.
13. Michel Foucault, *Society Must Be Defended: Lectures at the Collège de France, 1975–76*, trans. by David Macey (London: The Penguin Press, 2003), p. 249.
14. 'El departamento de Salubridad Pública hace una obra educativa acerca de los problemas de higiene racial, el certificado prenupcial y el futuro en el hogar', *Eugenesia, higiene y cultura física para el mejoramiento de la raza*, 3 (1935), 33–34 (p. 33).
15. Nancy Leys Stepan, *The Hour of Eugenics: Race, Gender and Nation in Latin America* (London: Cornell University Press, 1991).
16. Franz Roh, 'Magic Realism, Post-impressionism', in *Magical Realism: Theory, History, Community*, ed. by Lois Parkinson Zamora and Wendy B. Faris, trans. by Wendy B. Faris (London: Duke University Press, 1995), pp. 15–30 (p. 30).
17. Stanislaus von Moos, *Le Corbusier: Elements of a Synthesis* (Cambridge, Mass: MIT Press, 1979), p. 56.
18. Amédée Ozenfant and Charles-Edouard Jeanneret, 'After Cubism', in *L'Esprit Nouveau: Purism in Paris, 1918–1925*, ed. by Carol Eliel (Los Angeles: Los Angeles County Museum of Art, 2001), pp. 134–39 (p. 134).
19. Mary K. Coffey, 'The "Mexican Problem": Nation and "Native", in Mexican Muralism and Cultural Discourse', in *The Social and the Real: Political Art of the 1930s in the Western Hemisphere*, ed. by Alejandro Anreus and others (University Park: Pennsylvania State University Press, 2006), pp. 43–70 (p. 50).
20. Vitruvius, *On Architecture*, vol. I, trans. by Frank Granger (London: W. Heinemann, 1931), p. 27.
21. Tom Slevin, *Visions of the Human: Art, World War I and The Modernist Subject* (London: Tauris, 2005), p. 189.
22. James Oles, *Diego Rivera, David Alfaro Siqueiros, José Clemente Orozco: The Mexican Muralists* (New York: Moma Artist Series, 2011), p. 8.
23. David Cottington, *Cubism and its Histories* (Manchester: Manchester University Press, 2004), 167.
24. Von Moos, p. 56.
25. Justino Fernández, *A Guide to Mexican Art: From its Beginnings to the Present*, trans. by Joshua C. Taylor (Chicago: University of Chicago Press, 1969), p. 154.
26. Diego Rivera, 'Volver a nacer', p. 367; Diego Rivera, 'De la libreta de apuntes de un pintor mexicano', in *Textos de Arte*, ed. by Xavier Moyssén Echeverría (Mexico City: UNAM, 1986), pp. 71–77 (p. 73).
27. David Alfaro Siqueiros, 'Tres llamamientos de orientación actual a los pintores y escultores de la nueva generación americana', *Vida Americana: Revista norte centro y sudamericana de vanguardia*, May 1921, p. 3
28. Diego Rivera, 'The New Mexican Architecture: A House by Carlos Obregón /La nueva arquitectura mexicana: Una casa de Carlos Obregón', *Mexican Folkways*, 2 (1926), 19–29 (p. 27).
29. Vasoncelos, *La raza cósmica*, p. 40.
30. José Vasconcelos 'Discurso inaugural del edificio de la SEP', in *Obras completas*, vol.2 (Mexico City: Libreros Mexicanos Unidos, 1957), pp. 796–92 (p. 797; p. 800).
31. Ibid., p. 797.
32. Antonio Rodríguez, *Guía de los murales de Diego Rivera en la Secretaría de Educación Pública* (Mexico City: SEP Cultura, 1984), p. 12.

33. Paul Cézanne, *Conversations with Cézanne,* ed. by Michael Doran, trans. by Julie Lawrence (Berkeley: University of California Press, 2001), p. 121; Diego Rivera, quoted in Loló de la Torriente, *Memoria y razón de Diego Rivera* (Mexico City: Renacimiento, 1959), p. 23.
34. Roger Fry, 'The Post-Impressionists-II', in *Post-Impressionists in England,* ed. by J. B. Bullen (London: Routledge, 1988), pp. 130–31 (p. 130).
35. Albert Gleizes and Jean Metzinger, 'Cubism', in *Art in Theory, 1900–1990: An Anthology of Changing Ideas,* ed. by Charles Harrison and Paul Wood (Oxford: Blackwell, 1992), pp. 187–96 (p. 189).
36. Diego Rivera, quoted in de la Torriente, p. 25.
37. Gamio, p. 32.
38. Craven, *Art and Revolution in Latin America,* p. 40.
39. Fernand Léger, quoted in José María Faerna, *Léger,* trans. by Alberto Curotto (New York: Abrams, 1996), p. 30.
40. Diego Rivera, 'Las formas puras', in *Palabras ilustres,* pp. 155–56 (p. 155).
41. Rivera, 'The New Mexican Architecture/ La nueva arquitectura mexicana', p. 26.
42. Ibid., p. 22.
43. Le Corbusier, *Towards a New Architecture,* trans. by Frederick Etchells (London: Rodker, 1931), p. 67.
44. Le Corbusier, *The Four Routes* (London: D. Dobson, 1947), p. 2.
45. Le Corbusier, *Towards a New Architecture,* p. 67.
46. Ibid., p. 280.
47. Carlos Contreras, 'Editorial (Respecto a la necesidad de un plano regulador para la ciudad y Valle de México)', in *Planificación y urbanismo visionarios de Carlos Contreras: Escritos de 1925 a 1938,* ed. by Rafael López Rangel (Mexico City: UNAM, 2003), pp. 75–78 (p. 75).
48. Juan O'Gorman, 'Conferencia en la Sociedad de Arquitectos Mexicanos', in *La palabra de Juan O'Gorman: selección de textos,* ed. by Ida Rodríguez Prampolini (Mexico City: UNAM, 1983), pp. 108–12, (p. 109).
49. Agostini, p. xii; O'Gorman, 'Conferencia en la Sociedad de Arquitectos Mexicanos', p. 111.
50. Valerie Fraser, *Building the New World: Studies in the Modern Architecture of Latin America, 1930–1960* (London: Verso, 2000), p. 47–48.
51. Juan O'Gorman, 'Escuelas Nuevas', *Imagen,* 1 (1933), n.p.
52. Alicia Azuela, 'Rivera and the Concept of Proletarian Art', in *Diego Rivera: A Retrospective,* ed. by Stanton L. Catlin (Detroit: Detroit Institute of the Arts, 1986), pp. 125–29 (p. 126).
53. Diego Rivera, 'Retrato de América', in *Textos de arte,* pp. 213–17 (p. 214).
54. Rivera also stressed the need for artists to have a strong grounding in architectural theory and attempted to introduce an architectural element into the curriculum at the Escuela Central de Artes Plásticas during his brief time as director in 1929. Rafael López Rangel, *Diego Rivera y la arquitectura Mexicana* (Mexico City: SEP, Dirección General de Publicaciones y Medios, 1986), pp. 24–26.
55. Diego Rivera, quoted in Laura Cortés Gutiérrez, *Diego Rivera* (Mexico City: SEP, Dirección General de Publicaciones y Medios, 1988), p. 151.
56. Robert Buffington, 'Architecture', in *Mexico: An Encyclopedia of Contemporary Culture and History,* ed. by Don M. Coerver and others (Santa Barbara: ABC-CLIO, 2004), pp. 21–26 (p. 24).
57. Toyo Ito, 'El prodigio de la vanguardia y la pureza: Las casas de Diego Rivera y Frida Kahlo y la casa del arquitecto Juan O'Gorman', in *Casa O'Gorman 1929,* ed. by Xavier Guzmán Urbiola and others (Mexico City: Editorial RM, 2015), pp. 79–85 (p. 80).
58. Edward Burian, 'The Architecture of Juan O'Gorman: Dichotomy and Drift', in *Modernity and the Architecture of Mexico,* ed. by Edward Burian (Austin: University of Texas Press, 1997), pp. 127–50 (p. 138).
59. Anna Indych-López, 'An Abstract Courbet: The Cubist Spaces of Rivera's Murals', in *Diego Rivera: The Cubist Portraits 1913–1917,* ed. by Sylvia Navarrete (London: Philip Wilson Publishers, 2009), pp. 150–54 (p. 151).
60. Le Corbusier, *Towards a New Architecture,* p. 54.
61. Foucault, *Society Must be Defended,* p. 251.

62. Hubert L. Dreyfus and Paul Rabinow, *Michel Foucault: Beyond Structuralism and Hermeneutics* (Chicago: University of Chicago Press, 1983), p. 155.
63. Diego Rivera, 'Retrato de América', p. 206.
64. Juan O'Gorman, 'Abstracción y realismo en la arquitectura de hoy en México', in *Juan O'Gorman: autobiografía, antología, juicios críticos y documentación exhaustiva sobre su obra*, ed. by Antonio Luna Arroyo (Mexico City: Cuadernos Populares de Pintura Mexicana Moderna, 1973), pp. 275–85 (p. 279).
65. Diego Rivera, 'Un pintor opina', in *Diego Rivera y la arquitectura mexicana*, pp. 116–19 (p. 118).
66. Diego Rivera, 'Diego Rivera opina', in *Diego Rivera y la arquitectura mexicana*, pp. 123–24 (p. 123).
67. Juan O'Gorman, 'Más allá del funcionalismo (II)', in *Juan O'Gorman, arquitecto y pintor*, ed. by Ida Rodríguez Prampolini (Mexico City: UNAM, 1982), pp. 107–10 (p. 108).
68. Juan Rulfo, 'Tutotepec', in *Juan Rulfo: Letras e imágenes*, ed. by Víctor Jiménez (Mexico City: Editorial RM, 2002), p. 34.
69. Lanin A. Gyurko, 'Twentieth Century Fiction', in *Mexican Literature: A History*, ed. by David William Foster (Austin: University of Texas Press, 1994), pp. 243–304 (p. 263).
70. Patricia Reagan, *Deconstructing Paradise: Inverted Religious Symbolism in Twentieth-Century Latin American Literature* (Lanham: Lexington Books, 2016), p. 9.
71. Carlos Alberto Sánchez, '20th Century Mexican Philosophy: Features, Themes, Tasks', *Inter-American Journal of Philosophy*, 7 (2016), 1–25 (p. 16); Armando Gómez Villalpando, 'Presentación', in Emilio Uranga, *Ensayos* (Mexico City: Gobierno del Estado de Guanajuato, 1991), pp. 7–14 (p. 12).
72. Uranga and Sánchez, p. 80–82.
73. Fuentes, *La nueva novela hispanoamericana*, p. 13.
74. Walter Benjamin, *The Origin of German Tragic Drama*, trans. by John Osborne (London: Verso, 1998), p. 176.
75. Ibid., p. 178.
76. Julia Hell and Andreas Schönle, 'Introduction', in *Ruins of Modernity*, ed. by Julia Hell and Andreas Schönle (London: Duke University Press, 2010), pp. 1–14 (p. 6).
77. Archibaldo Burns, '*Pedro Páramo* o la unción y la gallina', *México en la cultura, novedades*, 15 May 1955, p. 3.
78. Salazar Mallén, p. 3.
79. Rulfo, 'La literatura es una mentira que dice la verdad', p. 466.
80. Rulfo, 'Juan Rulfo examina su narrativa', p. 453.
81. Julio Cortázar, *Rayuela*, ed. by Julio Ortega and Saúl Yurkiévich (Madrid: C.S.I.C, 1991), p. 326.
82. Benjamin, *The Origin of German Tragic Drama*, p. 218.
83. Ibid., p. 218.
84. Bruce Dean Willis, *Corporeality in Early Twentieth-Century Latin American Literature: Body Articulations* (Basingstoke: Palgrave Macmillan, 2013), p. 8.
85. Svetlana Boym, 'Ruins of the Avant Garde, From Tatlin's Tower to Paper Architecture', in *Ruins of Modernity*, ed. by Julia Hell and Andreas Schönle (London: Duke University Press, 2010), pp. 58–85 (p. 58).
86. Ibid., p. 58.
87. Lucy Bell, *The Latin American Short Story at its Limits: Fragmentation, Hybridity and Intermediality* (London: Routledge, 2017), p. 41.
88. Preciado remarks that 'Todo parecía estar como en espera de algo' [everything seemed to be waiting for something] (195). Victor W. Turner, 'Are there Universals of Performance in Myth, Ritual, and Drama?', in *By Means of Performance*, ed. by Richard Schechner and Willa Appel (Cambridge, Cambridge University Press, 1990), pp. 8–18 (p. 12).
89. Arthur Ramírez 'Spatial Form and Cinema Techniques in Rulfo's *Pedro Páramo*', *Revista de Estudios Hispánicos*, 15 (1981) 233–49 (p. 245).
90. Fabienne Bradu, *Ecos de Páramo* (Mexico City: Fondo de Cultura Económica, 1989), p. 56.
91. Juan Rulfo, *En los ferrocarriles: Juan Rulfo: Fotografías*, ed. by Víctor Jiménez (Mexico City: UNAM, Editorial RM, 2014).
92. Mario Pani, 'Penicilina para la ciudad', *Arquitectura/México*, 30 (1950), 309–12 (p. 312).

93. Antonio Acevedo Escobedo, 'La vida en el multifamiliar', *Arquitectura*, 33 (1952), 181–84 (p. 181); Juan O'Gorman, 'Notas sobre arquitectura', in *La Palabra de Juan O'Gorman: Selección de textos*, ed. by Ida Rodríguez Prampolini (Mexico City: UNAM, Instituto de Investigaciones Estéticas, 1983), pp. 132–40 (p. 138).
94. Pani, p. 312.
95. Adolfo López Mateos, quoted in *Conjunto urbano "Presidente López Mateos" (Nonoalco-Tlatelolco): Una realización del Presidente Adolfo López Mateos* (Mexico City: Banco Nacional Hipotecario Urbano y de Obras Públicas, 1963), p. 7.
96. Michel de Certeau, 'Walking in the City', in *The Cultural Studies Reader*, ed. by Simon During (London: Routledge, 1999), pp. 126–33 (p. 128).
97. Ibid., p. 127.
98. Siegfried Kracauer, *The Mass Ornament: Weimar Essays*, ed. and trans. by Thomas Y. Levin (London: Harvard University Press, 1995), p. 62.
99. De Certeau, 'Walking in the City', p. 128.
100. Rulfo's work as a migration officer in both Mexico City and Guadalajara in the 1940s and later as a travelling salesman for Goodrich Euzkadi sheds some light on his literary and photographic interest in the theme of human migration. He also recalled that in 1940 'anduve en la vagancia recorriendo el país' [I went roaming around the country]. Juan Rulfo, quoted in Vital, *Noticias sobre Juan Rulfo*, p. 59.
101. Dreyfus and Rabinow, p. 154.
102. Erica Segre also notes this focus on the 'interstice' in Rulfo's urban photography. Segre, *Intersected Identities*, p. 135.
103. Millán asserts that Rulfo took his photographs of the new installations at noon to ensure maximum luminosity. Paulina Millán, 'Juan Rulfo entre vías y trenes', in Juan Rulfo, *En los ferrocarriles: Juan Rulfo: Fotografías*, pp. 29–34 (p. 32).
104. Pani, pp. 311–12.
105. Gil M. Doron, 'The Dead Zone and the Architecture of Transgression', *City*, 4 (2000), 247–63 (p. 247).
106. Andrea Mubi Brighenti, 'Introduction', in *Urban Interstices: The Aesthetics and the Politics of the In-Between*, ed. by Andrea Mubi Brighenti (Farnham: Ashgate Publishing, 2013), pp. xv–xxiv (p. xvi).
107. Ibid., p. xix.
108. Víctor Jiménez, 'Juan Rulfo: Literatura, fotografía e historia', in *Juan Rulfo: Letras e imágenes*, pp. 22–19 (p. 22).
109. José Carlos González Boixo, 'Esteticismo y clasicismo', in *Tríptico para Juan Rulfo: Poesía, fotografía, crítica*, ed. by Víctor Jiménez and others (Mexico City: Editorial RM, 2006), pp. 249–85 (p. 277); Víctor Jiménez, 'Introduction', in Juan Rulfo, *Arquitectura de México: Fotografías de Juan Rulfo* (Mexico City: Consejo Nacional para la Cultura y las Artes, 1994), p. 1.
110. Juan Rulfo, 'Juan Rulfo y Fernando Benítez hablan sobre los indios', interviewed by Fernando Benítez, *México Indígena* (December, 1978): pp. 259–60 (p. 260).
111. Justo Sierra, 'Respuesta del presidente del congreso, Lic. Justo Sierra', in *Informes y manifiestos de los poderes ejecutivo y legislativo de 1821 a 1904*, ed. by José A. Castillón (Mexico: Imprenta del Gobierno Federal, 1905), pp. 479–80 (p. 479).
112. Walter Benjamin, 'Theses on the Philosophy of History', in *Illuminations*, ed. by Hannah Arendt, trans. by Harry Zorn (London: Cape, 1970), pp. 255–66 (p. 259–60).
113. Néstor García Canclini, *La ciudad de los viajeros: Travesías e imaginarios urbanos, México, 1940–2000* (Mexico City: Universidad Autónoma Metropolitana,1996), p. 109.
114. Susan Sontag, *On Photography* (Harmondsworth: Penguin, 1979), p. 23.
115. Rivera, 'De la libreta de apuntes de un pintor mexicano', 73.

CHAPTER 3

Body Articulations of Progress: (Re)productive Citizenship and National Development

Located in the stairway of the Pacific Stock Exchange Luncheon Club in San Francisco, Rivera's *Allegory of California* (1931) projects the monumental glowing body of the American tennis champion Helen Wills Moody against a densely packed industrial factoryscape. This female figure embodying California's natural abundance is populated by industrious male engineers and inventors wielding emblems of scientific and technological innovation. With one hand the personified state holds forth her ripened fruits, while the other reveals her subsoil to labouring miners who extract its natural resources using a phallic mechanical drill. By enforcing the long-standing gendered oppositions linking man with culture and chronological progress, and woman with nature and space, the mural offers a foundational visual narrative for a prosperous capitalist society. Although executed in the United States, Rivera's vision of a technologised worker productively penetrating the fertile feminised landscape metaphorically articulates the models of productive citizenship that were assigned to male and female bodies as part of the post-revolutionary Mexican state's programme of national development during the 1920s and 30s.

As I outlined in Chapter Two, in the decades immediately following the armed conflict, the Mexican state posited a revolutionary societal vision that paradoxically reinforced the Porfirian principles of 'Order and Progress'. Following on from this discussion of the corporeal dimensions of the post-revolutionary 'return to order', the present chapter explores how the ideals of progress and productivity were projected onto both real and imaginary post-revolutionary bodies during the same period. In the aftermath of the Revolution, government efforts to promote economic and industrial progress became intertwined with a parallel campaign of collective corporeal development that sought to maximise the economic utility of citizens' bodies. Although *desarrollismo* did not start to gain momentum until the Cárdenas administration, the previous decade saw the implementation of a gendered framework of (re)productive citizenship that sought to transform men into efficient industrial workers and women into prolific mothers. The conventional gendered dichotomy established in *Allegory of California* which aligns man with chronological progress and woman with space provides a general framework for my readings of the (re)productive male and female bodies presented in Rivera's and Rulfo's works. The second section of this chapter will turn to both artists' spatial configuration of the female body in the context of the restrictive reproductive models of female citizenship that were promoted by the post-revolutionary state and its affiliated intellectuals to secure the nation's future prosperity during the 1920s. Before moving on to this analysis, the first section examines selected murals by Rivera at the SEP (1923–1928) and the Detroit Institute of Arts (1932–1933) alongside Rulfo's mid-century short stories 'Macario' and 'El hombre' and his novel to chart the gradual breakdown of the technologised male body as an articulation of national progress.

Art historian Hal Foster argues that twentieth-century modernist figurations of the machine can be mapped according to 'the double logic of prosthesis', which implies a 'paradoxical view of technology as both extension and constriction of the body'.[1] Foster explains that, while techno-enthusiast groups such as the Soviet constructivists interpreted the machine within 'a communist system of relations, as an *extension* of the body', this was rejected by the surrealist and dadaist movements, which respectively associated the mechanical with psychic regression and portrayed the technologised subject as a kind of 'broken automaton'.[2] These distinct models are useful for understanding Rivera's and Rulfo's visual and textual machine aesthetics, which reflect shifting perspectives on the post-revolutionary drive for industrialisation by respectively conceptualising the technologised male body in terms of corporeal enhancement or cognitive and perceptual impairment. From the 1920s to the 1950s, the initial enthusiasm for industrial and technological progress among artists and thinkers gradually gave way to reassessment of the cost of capitalist development as the realities of industrialisation began to be felt. Moving from Rivera's constructivist-inspired images of an enhanceable labouring subject to Rulfo's use of visual technologies to articulate a state of perceptual crisis, I explore how the body functions as a site for articulating contemporary aspirations or anxieties regarding the societal and human implications of industrialisation. Before beginning my analysis of these works, I briefly outline how the ideal of an efficient labouring body for the industrial age was culturally constructed during the 1920s and early 30s.

Part I: Attuning the Male Body to the Rhythms of Industrial Modernity

The discourses of bodily *desarrollismo* that evolved in Mexico during this initial post-conflict period can again be illuminated by Foucault's theorisation of anatomo-politics as a disciplinary technology that conceptualises 'the body as a machine' and concentrates on 'the optimization of its capabilities, the extortion of its forces, the parallel increase of its usefulness and its docility, its integration into systems of efficient and economic controls'.[3] This fantasy of corporeal improvement was integral to Vasconcelos's vision of the implicitly male *mestizo* as a bridge to Mexico's glorious future. Although he rejected positivism, Vasconcelos believed in the redemptive capacity of technology and *La raza cósmica* can be seen as an attempt to reconcile science and metaphysics in his theorisation of racial improvement, while maintaining the primacy of the latter.[4] The link between racial and technological progress in this utopian text is made explicit through his futuristic description of Universópolis, the imaginary capital city of the continent's cosmic fifth race. In line with what Foucault would theorise as the docile body, an entity that is 'pliable', capable of being 'manipulated, shaped, trained', Vasconcelos stresses the *mestizo*'s capacity for constant adaptation and improvement due to his 'maleabilidad, comprensión rápida y emoción fácil' [malleability, rapid comprehension and easy emotion].[5] Although here Vasconcelos is again projecting the mixed-race subject as the imagined embodiment of the post-revolutionary nation, his emphasis on the *mestizo*'s capacity for constant development can be directly linked to real, state-led initiatives starting in the 1920s and 30s that sought to enhance the economic utility of Mexican citizens by attuning their bodies and behaviours to the rhythms of industrial modernity.

A key aspect of this campaign of corporeal *desarrollismo* was the introduction of a nationwide physical education programme that would enable citizens to fulfil a productive role within a system of capitalist production. As Dafne Cruz Porchini writes:

> La frase *mens sana in corpore sano* aludía al hombre nuevo y vigoroso encargado de conducir a la sociedad hacia un futuro ideal [...] Si el nuevo hombre-ciudadano tenía un buen desempeño físico, su potencial laboral-productivo aumentaría en forma notable, fuera en un contexto urbano o rural.[6]
>
> [The phrase *mens sana in corpore sano* referred to the strong, new man who was entrusted with propelling society towards an ideal future... if the new male citizen was able to perform well physically, his potential productivity as a labourer would increase significantly, be it in an urban or rural context.]

This emerging post-revolutionary physical culture was showcased through choreographed athletics and gymnastics displays at the Estadio Nacional in the capital and the Xalapa stadium in Veracruz in the 1920s. Smaller-scale precision drills were integrated into physical education programmes in schools, which promoted productivity as a key civic virtue through the implementation of task-based pedagogical strategies during the same decade.[7] Such demonstrations of collective agility were in keeping with evolving public health discourses during the 1920s and 30s that linked individual efficiency and productivity to that of the wider body politic. Writing in the medical journal *Medicina* in 1926, Dr José Zozaya, future Director of the Instituto de Higiene, stresses that 'la eficiencia de una nación, depende de la eficiencia de cada uno de los individuos que forman parte de ella' [the efficiency of a nation depends on the efficiency of every one of the individuals that form part of it].[8] This idea is echoed in an editorial published in 1930 in *Salubridad*, official journal of the Departamento de Salubridad Pública, where the labouring body is explicitly identified as a machine on which the nation's future progress and prosperity depends.[9]

Economic growth and industrialisation were part of a drive for national development during the Cárdenas administration that the president situated within a broader narrative of revolutionary progress:

> La Revolución no quiere que se pierda el tiempo esperando que los niños de hoy crezcan con una nueva orientación, sino que la Revolución quiere que los hombres de hoy cambien de criterio para que con un nuevo sentido de su responsabilidad vengan a participar en el movimiento económico que la República busca a favor de sí misma.[10]
>
> [The Revolution does not want us to waste time waiting for today's children to grow up with a new orientation, but rather that the men of today change their mind so that, with a new awareness of their responsibility, they will participate in the economic movement that the Republic pursues for its own benefit.]

This sense of urgency was reflected in the implementation of a new national calendar during his presidency which established clear divisions between work and leisure to maximise productivity and minimise fatigue. Leticia González del Rivero's observation that such frameworks operated 'bajo la premisa de que sin disciplinar el tiempo no se podía tener la insistente energía del hombre industrial' [under the premise that without disciplining time it would not be possible to sustain the energy of the industrial man], indicates the extent to which, by the mid-1930s, the government had come to view the worker's body as a mechanical unit in need of regulation to achieve optimum efficiency.[11]

Technological and Corporeal Progress in Rivera's SEP and Detroit Cycles

Although industrialisation advanced slowly during the 1920s, artists embraced the machine as an emblem of national progress.[12] In 1921 Siqueiros called for the creation of a new industrialised visual aesthetic, urging artists of the Americas to celebrate the modern machine and the novel emotional responses it provoked.[13] In Mexico, his call was most enthusiastically answered by the literary and visual practitioners of the futurist-inspired Estridentista movement, led by Manuel Maples Arce, whose avant-garde aesthetic coupled an enthusiasm for the sensory dynamism of industrial urbanity with a Bolshevik concept of revolution. Rivera was attracted to the techno-enthusiasm of the Estridentistas and contributed illustrations and calligrams to their magazines *Horizonte* and *Irradiador* in the early 1920s. Although Siqueiros was the first to call for a technologically inspired mode of artistic production, it was Rivera who most comprehensively explored the machine's utopian possibilities, producing murals that interlinked technological advancement with societal and physiological progress. The notion of malleability, common to Foucault's conception of the docile machine-body and Vasconcelos's definition of the *mestizo,* can shed light on the evolution of Rivera's corporeal imagery in the SEP and Detroit Institute fresco cycles, which illustrate the increasing mobility, dynamism and functional precision of the body as it adapts to the rhythms of mechanised labour.

The SEP cycle represents an important departure in Rivera's early mural production as it includes the first works to incorporate the motifs of labour and technology — themes that would come to define his visual aesthetic during the 1930s. While the content of several of these panels thematically takes its cue from nineteenth-century works such as Juan Cordero's positivist-inspired allegorical mural *El triunfo de la ciencia y el trabajo sobre la envidia y la ignorancia* (1874), Rivera stresses the corporeal dimensions of his subject matter by mobilising both the painted bodies inhabiting these compositions and the physical body of the observer. *La mecanización del campo* (1926), an extended fresco that sweeps up the main stairway of the SEP, provides a stunning visual manifesto of his early technological utopianism and demonstrates the physically engaging nature of his muralism. By ascending the steep staircase, the viewer sets in motion a visual narrative depicting the gradual electrification of the Mexican landscape, achieving, according to the artist, 'una visión simbólica del progreso del hombre' [a symbolic vision of man's progress].[14] This vision of human development is communicated in fundamentally corporeal terms in Rivera's visual eulogy to labour in the Patio del Trabajo on the first floor, where he diverges from the hieratic allegorical figures of *Creación* to introduce a range of dynamic new postures through the labouring body. In *El trapiche* (1923), the stirring motion of the sugar mill workers synchronises with the circular movement of the waterwheel positioned in the background, while the elongated dancerly figures of the foundry workers sway back and forth in a steady pendular motion in *La fundición* (1924). This shift in Rivera's imagery towards themes of industrial labour coincided with his increasing engagement with the PCM in the early 1920s and was central to the flowering of a specifically masculine proletarian art in the sphere of visual culture in the 1920s. As Lear notes, the male-centered images of *El Machete,* the official organ of the PCM, in the early 1920s reflect the general marginalisation of women within the labour movement and the domain of revolutionary politics more broadly during these years.[15] While Rivera's SEP panels bear iconographic similarities to the illustrations of *El Machete* and representations of the male worker by contemporary artists such as Agustín Lazo and Ramón Alva de la Canal, the spatial dynamism of his works marks a profound innovation by extending these corporeal ideals to the material bodies of the spectators interacting with them. As suggested by the composition of *La mecanización del campo*, the experience of viewing the SEP cycle in its entirety is a physically demanding one. The architectural distribution of the mural programme, which requires us to traverse the lengthy patio and upper corridors, scale steep staircases and constantly reposition ourselves around pillars, reveals that Rivera designed the cycle with a mobile and able-bodied viewing subject in mind.

The industrial images of the SEP offer the first outlines of a malleable labouring body that Rivera would further develop in his later frescoes in the Garden Court of the Detroit Institute of Arts. Rivera's proposal for the Detroit programme was approved in 1931 by Edsel B. Ford, Chair of the city's Arts Commission and he moved there with Kahlo the following year. Located in the Institute's naturally illuminated interior courtyard, the cycle offers an exhaustive visual account of Detroit's recent scientific and technological developments. Smaller panels depicting advancements in the areas of pharmaceuticals, aeronautics and chemistry frame the two principal murals portraying the construction process for the Ford V-8 model. Through a series of interconnected episodes, the central panels on the north and south walls respectively depict the manufacturing of the engine and the assembly of the car's body. Fusing the labour-centred imagery of the Patio del Trabajo panels and *The Making of a Fresco* with a more sophisticated industrial visual vocabulary, these monumental scenes of activity within the Ford River Rouge Plant offer a utopian vision of the combined power of human and mechanical labour. The lack of a singular point of focus in these compositions provokes a restlessness in the observing eye that animates the figures across the entire pictorial field.

The remarkable human vitality of Rivera's scenes was, however, dramatically at odds with the grim contemporary reality of the factory. While both frescoes accentuate the collective energy of the city's robust labour force, he and Kahlo had in fact arrived at the peak of the Great Depression and just weeks after a communist-organised hunger strike of three thousand Rouge Plant workers. As Gallo notes, the muralist based his sketches on photographs taken by W. J. Stettler but dramatically increased the number of bodies in his painted reproductions, erasing all trace of the city's rising unemployment rates.[16] The scene's emphasis on interracial harmony is equally deceptive, eliding the deportation crisis that had devastated vast numbers of Mexican workers in Detroit towards the end of the 1920s. Rivera had reaffirmed his commitment to communism in 1932 and, as Anthony Lee convincingly suggests, the muralist's emphasis on the imagined collective might of the workforce may have been an attempt to sidestep the obvious ideological contradictions of his apparent homage to capitalist industry.[17]

Despite this compensatory strategy, Rivera's collaboration with one of America's most powerful capitalists, and his remarkably inaccurate interpretation of conditions in the Rouge Plant, inevitably provoked accusations of ideological inconsistency from PCM-affiliated artists. In his damning article 'Rivera's Counter-Revolutionary Road' (1934), Siqueiros criticised Rivera's 'ideologically obscure' Detroit cycle for its failure to address injustices against the proletariat.[18] The politically precarious position in which Rivera found himself in the early 1930s is reflected in his works of this period. While the portable panels produced for his MoMA exhibition such as *Frozen Assets* (1931–32) and the mural *Portrait of America* (1933) criticise capitalist corruption, the Detroit cycle, like *The Making of a Fresco*, projects an unmistakably optimistic vision of industrial progress. These oscillations reflect Rivera's struggle to reconcile his admiration of the scale and sophistication of US industrial production with his status as a revolutionary artist. In Detroit, the body of the male worker embodies these conflicting political agendas, articulating both the fantasy of a dynamic proletarian subject and the Taylorist ideal of a regulated working body.

The ideological tensions at the heart of Rivera's utopian vision of the Rouge Plant can be traced back to his earlier engagement with the techno-enthusiast artists of the Russian constructivist movement. Rivera had travelled to the USSR in 1927 to mark the tenth anniversary of the Russian Revolution. The following year he joined the October Group, a visual arts collective formed of several former constructivist artists including El Lissitzky, Alexandr Rodchenko and Aleksei Gan. Like Mexico, the Soviet Union was, as Foster puts it, 'more advanced in the representation of industry than its implementation' in the early twentieth century.[19] Despite lagging productivity in the early years of the Soviet Union, Tim Harte describes how these artists, embracing the cult of speed celebrated by the Italian futurists, looked to technology as the basis for 'a faster, more receptive human mind and body; a proletarian, Marxist consciousness for the new era; and a more efficient society'.[20] This corporeal utilitarianism was partly inspired by the theories of scientific management that had been devised by Frederick Winslow Taylor at the beginning of the century. Modelling human functionality on that of the machine, Taylorism sought to maximise efficiency along the assembly line by assigning specific tasks to individual workers and streamlining their movements to eliminate all superfluous gestures. Fascinated by the capacity of the technologised environment to forge a more dynamic and efficient labouring body, the constructivists looked to the factory as a 'university for the new Socialist man'.[21] With the implementation of Stalin's first Five-Year Plan in 1928, the constructivists' avant-garde abstractionism was gradually replaced with a more robust visual idiom. While official propaganda maintained the dynamic angles and accelerated movements of constructivist iconography, it also increasingly emphasised the vigour and muscularity of the hero-worker.

Although Rivera only remained in Moscow for eight months, this Soviet fantasy of an enhanced industrialised corporeality exerted a significant influence on his mural imagery of the early 1930s. While the artist's murals and writings would address the more sinister political applications of the machine during the same decade, his description of the Detroit programme clearly aligns with the constructivists' interpretation of technology as a liberating force for the proletarian worker:[22]

> Mi pasión juvenil por los juguetes mecánicos se ha transformado en deleite ante la maquinaria por la maquinaria en sí y por lo que significa para el hombre: su superación y liberación del trabajo degradante y de la pobreza. Por eso he colocado al héroe colectivo, hombre-máquina, en el lugar superior al de los héroes tradicionales del arte y la leyenda.[23]
>
> [My childhood passion for mechanical toys has turned into a delight in machinery for its own sake and for what it means for man: his overcoming of, and liberation from, degrading work and poverty. That is why I have placed the collective hero, the machine-man, above the traditional heroes of art and legend.]

In Detroit, Rivera lends visual form to this heroic 'machine-man' by combining the technophilic imagery of the constructivists with the robust corporeality of socialist realism. The constructivists' interpretation of the machine as a prosthetic augmentation of the body is conveyed in highly literal terms on the south (Fig. 3.1) and north (Fig. 3.2) walls of the Detroit cycle, where the bodies of the workers are extended through their engagement with the surrounding machinery. To the very centre of the south wall, a worker in beige overalls leans forward with his back heel slightly raised off the ground in a posture reminiscent of early constructivist configurations of the industrial body such as Lissitzky's *New Man* (1923). In Rivera's image, it is the worker's physical contact with the piston cylinder and the overhead

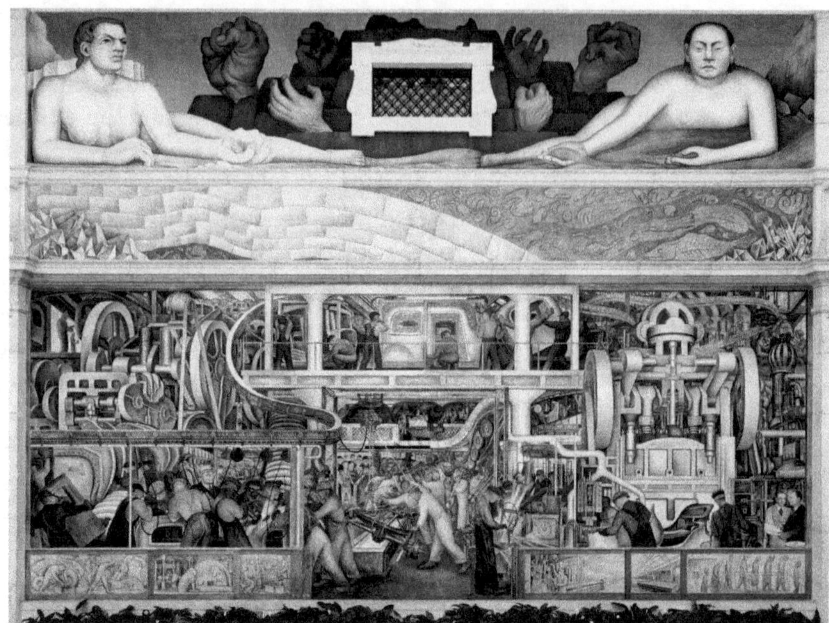

FIG. 3.1. Diego Rivera, Detroit Industry, South Wall (1932–1933), Detroit Institute of Arts, Gift of Edsel B. Ford

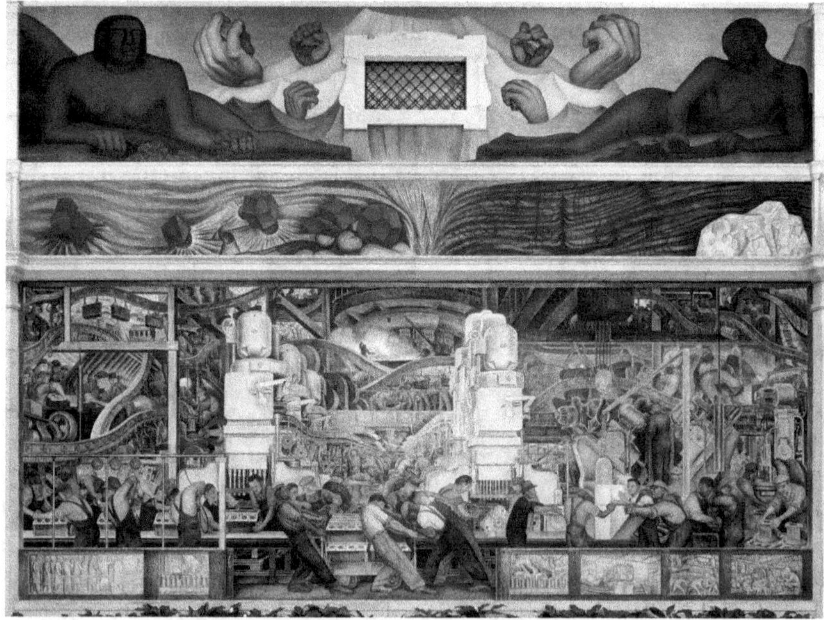

FIG. 3.2. Diego Rivera, Detroit Industry, North Wall (1932–1933), Detroit Institute of Arts, Gift of Edsel B. Ford

wire that elongates his body, pulling it forward into space.[24] This capacity of technology to literally extend the human body is again illustrated to the right of this figure where a worker dressed in dark overalls wields an electric saw. Here the beams of light generated by the saw radiate directly from the body in a manner reminiscent of the 'force lines' developed by the Italian futurists to represent 'an invisible extension of the essence of objects, projected beyond their material finitude'.[25] By positioning this mechanical apparatus over the worker's groin, Rivera reinforces the concept of the machine as a bodily appendage while also emphasising the virility of the male industrial worker. Images such as these from Detroit were instrumental in the shift towards a coherent machine-body aesthetic in state-sponsored visual culture in Mexico which, in contrast to Soviet visual discourses of the industrial worker, remained exclusively masculine.[26]

Taylorist organisation strategies had been in operation in the Detroit plant since 1913 and the disciplinary aspects of these theories come into sharper focus on the north wall, where Rivera aligns the body's movements to the repetitive rhythms of the factory. The artist recalled how his visit to Detroit had rekindled a childhood interest in the interrelation between human and mechanical mobility:

> Más que todo me gustaban las máquinas, las armas, los animales y, por supuesto, todos los juguetes mecánicos [...] los hacía funcionar y los desarmaba para ver cómo trabajaban. Después trataba de volverlos a armar [...] Entre los tres y los cinco años me inquietaba la necesidad de saber cómo se mueven los seres humanos y los animales.[27]
>
> [More than anything I liked machines, weapons, animals, and of course, all kinds of mechanical toys... I would make them function and then take them apart to see how they worked. Then I would try and put them back together again... Between three and five years old I was obsessed with understanding how humans and animals moved.]

Rivera's long-standing fascination with the dynamics of human motion is revealed on the north wall, where he draws inspiration from the serial motion studies developed by Étienne-Jules Marey during the late nineteenth century to analyse the dynamics of human locomotion. These chronophotographic sequences, which represented an intermediary stage in the transition from still photography to cinematography, provided the theoretical foundations for Taylorism's reduction of the labouring body to a series of discrete repetitive movements in order to maximise its efficiency. Paintings such as Marcel Duchamp's *Nude Descending a Staircase (No. 1)* (1911) and Giacomo Balla's *Girl Running on Balcony* (1912) demonstrate how early twentieth-century artists recreated the impression of multiple superimposed exposures to render visible successive phases of bodily movement. By employing the same time-lapse visual effect in the context of the Rouge plant, Rivera articulates Taylorism's use of repetition to enhance human efficiency in pictorial terms. In the receding lines of identical workers located at various points across the north wall, the use of repeated, overlapping forms reproduces the chronophotographic impression of a single figure moving rapidly through space. This recycling of almost identical human forms across the mural pictorially aligns with Taylorist principles of motion economy. As in *The Making of a Fresco*, Rivera distributes the workers according to their respective tasks, but here the movement of the labouring bodies is more meticulously choreographed, with specific gestures assigned to each group. The complementary poses and counter-poses of the workers leaning over a trolleycart to the centre-fore of the mural, and those assembling engine blocks along the assembly line to the left foreground are drawn from the limited repertoire of postures devised by the Italian futurists, who modelled human movement on 'the swing of a pendulum' and the 'in and out motion of a piston inside a cylinder'.[28] Through this regulation and standardisation of human movement, Rivera visually communicates the Taylorist ideal of an anonymous mass-produced man, efficient and interchangeable.

The chronophotographic images from which Rivera drew inspiration in Detroit exemplify the capacity of modern visual technologies to open up what Walter Benjamin describes as the realm of the 'optical unconscious'. In his essay, 'The Work of Art in the Age of Mechanical Reproduction' (1936), Benjamin explains how through its 'interruptions and isolations, its extensions and accelerations, its enlargements and reductions', technologised forms of vision have penetrated dimensions of reality inaccessible to the naked human eye.[29] Rivera's interest in technology's role in enhancing human vision is further suggested by his inclusion of optical devices pertaining to the field of medical science such as X-ray apparatuses and microscopes in the grisaille panels of the SEP and later works such as *Man at the Crossroads* (1933) and the *La historia de la cardiología* (1943–1944). Considered in this context, Rivera's reluctance to engage with modern visual media such as photography and cinematography is, as noted by Gallo, particularly curious. Despite the numerous allusions to technologised forms of vision in his murals and his celebration of the machine's capacity to enhance human capabilities, Rivera himself never adopted the camera as a prosthetic extension of the eye. Reflecting on this apparent contradiction, Gallo concludes that Rivera was 'unaware that machines and mechanical processes could have a more profound effect on his work beyond appearing as subjects of representation'[30]. However, it is inconceivable, given his links to prominent photographers and cineastes including Tina Modotti, Edward Weston and Sergei Eisenstein, that the muralist never considered the aesthetic possibilities presented by such media. It seems more likely that Rivera was looking to preserve muralism's status as a manual form of artistic labour that was potentially under threat from technological advancements. The tactility of the hand is central to Benjamin's understanding of changes in the conditions of production and human experience with the transition to technological modernity. With the shift from pre-industrial artisan labour or *handwerk* to the mechanised labour of the assembly line, the role of the hand in the production process is severely diminished, giving way to a new form of experience in which soul, eye and hand are disconnected. Benjamin discusses these alternative models of experience in 'On Some Motifs in Baudelaire' (1939), where he traces this atrophy of experience as a shift from *Erfahrung*, in which perception, bodily experience and memory are fully integrated, to a disconnected and fragmentary mode of experience defined as *Erlebnis.* This latter model originates in the isolated 'shock' experiences of the industrial worker along the assembly line and achieves formal expression in photographic and cinematic media.[31] The skill and dexterity of the painter's hand is replaced by a single snap of the camera button and a seeing eye that functions only in conjunction with the machinery of the lens.[32] As Esther Leslie puts it, with this transition to mechanical forms of artistic reproduction, 'culture's co-ordination with the body has transformed'.[33]

Notions of pre-industrial craftsmanship were integral to Rivera's conception of revolutionary art as a form of 'labor plástica' [plastic labour] carried out by the skilled artisan.[34] The artist's desire to maintain the primacy of the human hand in the artistic process is reflected not only in his reluctance to exchange the paintbrush for the camera, or indeed the prominence of the hand as a pictorial motif in his work, but also in his particular approach to mural production. While Siqueiros accelerated this process by using industrial spray guns, photographic projectors and other electric tools, Rivera remained faithful to the more traditional pigment-and-plaster techniques of fresco painting. Moreover, it seems likely that Rivera was conscious of preserving what Benjamin describes as the 'auratic' quality of pre-industrial artwork, that is, the particular aesthetic experience generated by 'its unique existence at the place where it happens to be'.[35] Linking the concept of aura with *Erfahrung*, Hansen notes that its root '*fahren* (to ride, to travel) [...] conveys a sense of mobility, of journeying, wandering, cruising', that calls to mind the viewer's navigation of the mural's architectural setting.[36] A closer examination of Rivera's thematic and formal engagement with the machine in his muralism thus brings to light certain limitations to his technological enthusiasm. While the muralist embraced technology as an instrument for societal and corporeal advancement, he was less willing to adopt mechanical forms of production that might diminish what he understood as the embodied dimensions of artistic labour and consumption.

In a subtle self-portrait in the upper left-hand side of the north wall mural, Rivera appears amidst the throng of toiling bodies, surveying the harmonious display of human and mechanical movement unfolding before him. Towards the end of the 1940s, Rulfo would develop an alternative impression of the assembly-line process while occupying a similar vantage point on a factory floor in Mexico City. The writer moved to the capital in 1935 and held a number of positions before securing a job as a factory supervisor with the tyre manufacturers Goodrich Euzkadi in 1947, just as the *alemanista* drive for industrialisation was gaining momentum. In private letters written to his wife Clara Aparicio during this period, the factory emerges as a dystopian world of mechanised capitalist production where 'el hombre es una máquina y la máquina está considerada como hombre' [man is a machine and the machine is considered a man].[37]

By the 1940s in Mexico, Rivera's American vision of industrialisation was steadily materialising, with the automobile industry emerging as a key catalyst for economic growth.[38] The Camacho administration (1940–1946) was firmly committed to an industrial capitalist model that increased the presence of textile, automotive and cement factories in major cities.[39] The initial phase of the 'Miracle' witnessed the transformation not only of Mexico's urban spaces but also its media landscapes, with the continued expansion of the mass media in the form of print, radio, television and cinema. While economic growth brought undeniable prosperity, the stagnation of the countryside and harsh working conditions exposed the Revolution's failure to bring lasting socio-political change. The dehumanising impact of industrialisation became a focal point in philosophical discussions towards the middle of the century. In his 1938 article 'La mecanización de la vida humana' and subsequent book *Hacia un nuevo humanismo* (1940) Ramos warned that, rather than liberate man from the drudgery of physical labour, technology would reduce him to a deindividualised, machine-like state.[40] This perspective was echoed by Paz in *El laberinto de la soledad*, where he criticised the alienating conditions of the industrial system where 'el obrero pierde, bruscamente y por razón misma de su estado social, toda relación humana y concreta con el mundo' [as a result of his social status, the worker suddenly loses all human and concrete contact with the world].[41] Paz envisions that, adhering to the rhythms of the capitalist machinery, 'la sociedad marcharía con eficacia, pero sin rumbo. Y la repetición del mismo gesto, distintiva de la máquina, llevaría a una forma desconocida de la inmovilidad: la del mecanismo que avanza de ninguna parte hacía ningún lado' [society would march efficiently but without direction. And the repetition of the same movement which is so characteristic of the machine would lead to an unknown kind of paralysis: that of the mechanism that advances from nowhere towards nowhere].[42]

Already in the 1930s, Rivera's fellow muralists had countered his optimistic industrial vision by exploring the more menacing aspects of the machine. Although Siqueiros increasingly turned to technologically inspired methods such as photomontage and cinematic perspective in an effort to reinvigorate muralism, works such as *Retrato de la burguesía* (1939–1940) recall Orozco's earlier imagery of mechanised human destruction in *Catarsis* (1934) by depicting pylons and industrial chimneys surging up behind a machine that spews out blood and gold coins. Within the domain of literary production it was Juan José Arreola, a close friend of Rulfo's during his early years in the capital, who most actively interrogated cultural narratives of technological progress. Offering a sceptical antidote to the earlier techno-optimism of the Estridentista writers, Arreola experimented with a satirical mode of science fiction writing in stories such as 'Baby H.P' (1952), which imagines a mechanical device capable of harnessing a child's energy to power electrical appliances.

Textual Technologies: Rulfo's Assembly-Line Poetics

Similar concerns regarding the human cost of technological progress surface in Rulfo's letters to Clara, written in Mexico City between 1944 and 1950. Rulfo secured his position as a foreman with Goodrich through his uncle Edmundo Phelan, but almost immediately requested to be transferred to the advertising department, where he worked as a travelling salesman and publicist until 1952. Rulfo's correspondences indicate that this swift departure was primarily motivated by the dehumanising conditions of the factory. According to his biographer Juan Ascencio, Rulfo was particularly distressed by the mechanical automatisation of the workers' movements:

> Contaba que había una máquina llamada 'La Bámbury', que era controlada por un obrero fortachón que sujetaba una especie de manubrio siempre en sacudimiento. Un día hubo apagón. El obrero siguió en sacudidas de sus fuertes brazos como si la máquina no se hubiese detenido. El hombre-máquina hería la sensibilidad de Juan.[43]
>
> [He talked about a machine called 'The Banbury' which was operated by a burly worker who held on to a kind of handle that was constantly shaking. One day there was a power cut and the worker's strong arms continued to shake as if the machine had never stopped. Juan found the machine-man disturbing.]

Here, the 'machine-man' so heroically portrayed in Detroit has evolved into a tragic figure for whom the internalisation of technological rhythms has resulted in a loss of lived sensation. Echoing the Estridentistas's glorification of technology's capacity to amplify the senses, the muralist described the internal workings of the factory as 'una orquesta mecánica (que producía) una maravillosa sinfonía' [a mechanical orchestra (that produced) a marvellous symphony].[44] In a letter written to Clara in 1949, however, Rulfo stresses the brutalising and disorienting effect of this environment:

> Lo que quiero es liberarme de esta debilidad de voluntad que se ha hecho cargo de mí desde que comencé a trabajar en esa dichosa fábrica. Créeme, antes sabía a dónde iba, sabía pensar y desarrollar alguna idea [...] Ahora me parece que ando volando. Que tengo los ojos cerrados y que camino a ciegas por todas partes y casi necesito que me lleven de la mano.[45]
>
> [I want to free myself from the weakness of will that has taken over me since I began working in this damned factory. Believe me, before I knew where I was going, I knew how to think and to develop an idea... Now it seems like I'm wandering about, like I'm walking around blindly with my eyes closed and almost need someone to guide me by the hand.]

Rulfo's personal account again recalls elements of Benjamin's 1939 essay, where he looks to the 'shock' experiences of the industrial worker along the conveyor belt as evidence of technology's transformation of the human sensorium. Delving into the neurological foundations of Benjamin's concept of shock, Susan Buck-Morss links this disintegration of the individual's capacity for experience to the notion of neurasthenia, a nervous disorder originally attributed to the accelerated pace of industrialised urban life during the nineteenth century. Understood as a mechanical failure of the nervous system, neurasthenia was linked to various symptoms of psychic and physiological dysfunction. Highlighting its links with Benjamin's notions of shock and *Erlebnis*, she explains how the condition was metaphorically evoked through descriptions of '"shattered" nerves, nervous "breakdown", "going to pieces", "fragmentation" of the psyche'.[46] The link is significant in light of Rulfo's personal experience of the capital during the early years of the 'Miracle'. Writing to Clara in 1946, he recounts that the doctor has prescribed him medication because he was 'muy neurasténico y todo enfermo del hígado' [very neurasthenic and suffering from liver problems].[47] Further references to anxiety, depleted energy, digestive problems and depression in these letters, alongside other biographical details, lend substance to his diagnosis.[48] Amat claims that Rulfo struggled consistently with nervous disorders after moving to the capital while Antonio Alatorre, who worked alongside Rulfo as a civil servant, recalls that he was often absent due to 'choque nervioso' [nervous shock].[49]

Despite his aversion to the industrialised environment, Rulfo was an avid user of technology. Unlike Rivera, who never learned to drive, Rulfo drove across Mexico as a tyre salesman for Goodrich between 1947 and 1952. During this time he used his Rolleiflex 6x6 camera to visually document Mexico's diverse landscapes and resigned when the management refused to install a radio in his company car.[50] The following year, he spent a significant portion of his CME grant on a new Model 17 Remington Rand typewriter. Scattered allusions to mechanical devices in Rulfo's literary works suggest that these narratives are not entirely disconnected from modern technological developments. Alongside references to a gramophone in 'Paso del Norte' (141) and a telegraph in a fragment of *Pedro Páramo* relating to Páramo's youth (210), an early description in the novel centres on the photograph of Dolores that Preciado has brought to Comala (194). As Dan Russek has pointed out, this crucial passage not only links the fictional space of the novel to forces of 'urban progress and technological modernity' but also 'a new economy of representations'.[51] The reference to photographic production is all the more significant when we consider, as Russek notes, the total absence of pre-industrial visual media such as painting or engraving in Comala. Russek's observation is significant as it encourages us to consider the relationship between visual technologies and literary technique in Rulfo's work, specifically in relation to the camera. As noted in the previous chapter, Rulfo was a prolific photographer, amassing a collection of over seven thousand negatives, and developed a keen interest in cinematography. He worked as a film censor during the 1950s and later delved into the world of script writing, earning credits on films including *El despojo* (1960), *Paloma herida* (1963) and *La fórmula secreta* (1965). These biographical details complicate the conventional view of Rulfo as a fundamentally rural writer whose literary vision is at odds with contemporary processes of modernisation. While Rulfo's literary works are often seen as depicting 'un mundo premoderno, prehistórico' [a premodern, prehistoric world], their aesthetic form is closely bound to the context of industrialisation and mass technologisation in which they were produced.[52] One of the few scholars to bridge the gap between Rulfo's literary and visual production is Lucy Bell, who examines how 'photographic presentation is linked with phenomenological purity and present-ness' in his short stories.[53] Drawing attention to the intermedial connections that interlink his visual and textual production, in what follows I explore how Rulfo's literature integrates mechanised modes of perception to evoke certain transformations in the nature of human perception, cognition and experience brought about by the transition to technological and industrial modernity. Drawing from Benjamin's and Buck-Morss's linking of the camera with *Erlebnis* and the 'shock' experience of modernity, I explore how Rivera's image of a technologised male subject attuned to the rhythms of industrial modernity is reconceptualised in Rulfo's literature where the perceptual frameworks of photography and cinema are used to articulate sensory crisis and corporeal alienation.

In the short story 'Macario', first published in the magazine *Pan* in 1945, Rulfo reproduces the automatic and unmediated nature of photographic registration to convey the perceptual and cognitive limitations of his narrator. While the simplistic language and syntax of the story's opening lines initially suggest the narrative voice of a child, Macario's references to the sexual nature of his relationship with his nurse Felipa suggest he is in fact a young man with some form of learning disability.[54] In contrast to the perspectival plurality that characterises much of Rulfo's literature, the fictional environment of 'Macario' is perceived through the singular lens of the story's eponymous first-person narrator. As the story opens, Macario is positioned motionless beside the gutter waiting for the frogs to emerge so he can strike them with a wooden plank (89). This opening passage, which portrays Macario as a kind of static surveillance apparatus, evokes Rulfo's description of photography as an act of aiming and firing to capture the fleeting image. Playing on the dual meanings of the verb *disparar* [to shoot a gun, to take a photograph], he claimed: 'Yo tenía ojo, cuando veía la foto disparaba. Tenía buena puntería' [I had a good eye, when I saw the photo I would shoot. I had good aim].[55] Rulfo's metaphor of photography as rapid-fire and the description of Macario poised to strike the frogs recall Benjamin's identification of the sudden 'snapping' action of the photographer as one of the most powerful instances of 'shock'.[56] This photographic analogy is reflected in the early part of Macario's monologue, which is formed of a quick succession of vivid but disjointed images of the toads, his godmother's eyes and the hibiscus flower he associates with Felipa's breast milk. Rulfo's rendering of Macario's thought sequence as a series of photographic snap-shots is reinforced by the short, abrupt form of the sentences which imitate the sharp movement of a camera shutter:

> Las ranas son verdes de todo a todo, menos en la panza. Los sapos son negros. También los ojos de mi madrina son negros. Las ranas son buenas para hacer de comer con ellas (89).
>
> [The frogs are green all over, except on their bellies. The toads are black. The eyes of my godmother are also black. The frogs are good to eat.]

Following on from the descriptions of blindness in *Pedro Páramo* and the indistinct forms of his urban photography, discussed in previous chapters, Macario's unusual perspective hints again at Rulfo's aesthetic interest in limited forms of visual perception. Like the obsessive view of the camera eye, Macario perceives his surroundings through a restricted lens, fixating on specific details such as the colour of the frogs' bellies and the seemingly black eyes of his godmother (89). As these magnified and decontextualised images resist integration into a coherent or purposeful stream of thought, Macario's particular mode of vision, like that of the camera, represents an amplification but also a reduction of normal visual perception. Eliding the distinctions of time, space, cause and effect, Macario registers his reality in a dispassionate manner that is severed from conscious reflection. The narrator's heightened attention to detail and distracted, primarily image-based thought process suggests that he is affected by some form of developmental disorder. Like the fragile and clumsy boy of José Revueltas's story 'El hijo tonto' (1944) who is dismissed as 'tan tonto, tan inútil' [so stupid, so useless], Rulfo's inclusion of a developmentally disabled protagonist is particularly significant in the context of the state's ongoing efforts to produce a progressive and industrious populace.[57] Although a grown man, in the eyes of the modernising state, Macario exemplifies the *niño problema* [problem child], a term broadly applied by eugenicists to mentally or physically 'defective' children who posed an obstacle to national development.[58]

Buck-Morss's contention that the 'motor responses of switching, snapping, the jolt in movement of a machine have their psychic counterpart in the "sectioning of time" into a sequence of repetitive moments without development' establishes a link between the automated reflexes of the assembly-line worker and the automatic exposures of the camera.[59] Buck-Morss's description of these mechanical actions as a 'sequence of repetitive moments without development' can be applied to Macario's monologue, where repetition, integral to the mechanically streamlined Taylorist body, negates narrative progress. Macario states that Felipa's milk 'es dulce como las flores del obelisco' [is sweet like hibiscus flowers] (90) only to reiterate the same idea: 'muchas veces he comido flores de obelisco para entretener el hambre. Y la leche era de ese sabor' [I've eaten hibiscus flowers many times to keep my hunger at bay. And the milk tasted the same] (91). Repetition again results in linguistic inefficiency when he states that 'lo de lavar los trastes a mí me toca. Lo de acarrear leña para prender el fogón también a mí me toca' [it's my turn to wash the dishes. It's also my turn to collect the wood to light the stove] (89). While repetition is a common feature of Rulfo's prose, Macario's monologue moves at a markedly swift pace, creating a monotonous narrative rhythm that is paralleled by the constant thud of his head against various surfaces in the house. A further correlation between bodily and narrative movement can be detected in the link between the text's paralytic form and the arrested cognitive development and physical immobility of its protagonist, who remains perfectly still throughout his monologue. Echoing his opening statement, Macario affirms in the closing lines that he is still waiting beside the gutter (94), revealing a circular narrative structure that negates all possibility of textual development.

Technologised perception and sensory crisis are again intertwined in *Pedro Páramo* and 'El hombre', where Rulfo draws from the perceptual schema of cinema. In his 1936 essay, Benjamin explains the corporeal implications of the shift from traditional forms of visual representation to a new cinematic visual grammar composed of rapid cuts, close-ups and montage by establishing a parallel between the painter and the magician on one hand, and the photographer and the surgeon on the other. While the painter, like the magician, heals the body through a 'laying on of hands', the cinematographer shares the surgeon's capacity to violate corporeal integrity, dissecting the image into 'multiple fragments that are assembled under a new law'.[60] Susan McCabe explains how this anatomizing impulse of the cinematic lens was harnessed by modernist poets to explore 'cultural tropes of the fragmented, dissociated corporeality, most notably, the hysteric mechanical body, newly fabricated in modernity'.[61] In *Pedro Páramo* and 'El hombre', Rulfo similarly exploits this dissective capacity of the camera to convey a mode of perception that is severed from lived experience. In the novel, perceptual-motor dissociation is conveyed through close-up images of Preciado's hands striving to relinquish themselves from his mother's dying grip (65) and of his hand floating in front of Eduviges's door: 'mi mano se sacudió en el aire como si el aire la hubiera abierto' [my hand shook in the air as if the air had already opened it] (198). The state of corporeal alienation suggested by this depersonalising camera-eye effect is confirmed by the protagonist's descriptions of his feet moving of their own accord (198) and his sudden awareness of the sound of his own footsteps (243). These dissociative episodes foreshadow a more serious breakdown in Preciado's bodily functioning which, alongside recurring imagery of limp, trembling and faltering bodies elsewhere in Rulfo's literature, undermines post-revolutionary ideals of corporeal progress and productivity. As he stumbles through Comala, Preciado is overwhelmed by fatigue and gradually relinquishes control over his body. Following a series of minor lapses in consciousness, the protagonist suffers a violent seizure in the house of the incestuous couple which is conveyed through verbs of erratic movement such as *zangolotear* [to shake] and *revolcarse* [to thrash around]. As in 'Macario', a correlation between bodily and narrative rhythms becomes apparent in *Pedro Páramo* as Juan's fitful movements are mirrored in the novel's spasmodic perspectival and temporal shifts.

Rulfo's use of cinematic effects to enact a Taylorist fragmentation of the body in *Pedro Páramo* can be traced back to the story 'El hombre', which lays the foundations for the novel in its experimentation with filmic devices. Presented as a tale of double-vengeance, the story traces the movements of a fugitive named José Alcancía who has recently murdered the family of a man called Urquidi. It subsequently emerges that Urquidi was previously responsible for the death of Alcancía's brother. Although the identities of the two men are initially obscured by the existence of three overlapping narrative voices, it becomes apparent that Urquidi is tracking Alcancía as he flees across the countryside. As in *Pedro Páramo*, filmic close-ups of specific body parts here evoke the body's apparently mechanical capacity to act outside the realm of conscious intention. The opening tracking description of the man's feet scrambling up the hillside recreates the restrictive view of the moving camera:

> Los pies del hombre se hundieron en la arena dejando una huella sin forma, como si fuera la pezuña de algún animal. Treparon sobre las piedras, engarruñándose al sentir la inclinación de la subida, luego caminaron hacia arriba, buscando el horizonte (61).
>
> [The man's feet sank into the sand, leaving a formless footprint, like the hoof of some animal. They climbed over the stones, digging in when they felt the slope and then continued upward, searching for the horizon.]

These decontextualising techniques of framing and close-up are sustained in the following description of Alcancia's feet as he scrambles along the mountain track: 'los pies siguieron la vereda, sin desviarse' [his feet followed the path without straying] (61). The impression that his feet are operating independently from the rest of his body is reinforced by the use of the third-person plural form of the verbs *hundirse* [to sink], *trepar* [to climb], *caminar* [to walk] and *seguir* [to follow] to describe their movements. In a flashback to the murder, other parts of Alcancía's body are fragmentarily revealed through isolated and magnified images of his hand clasping a machete and his tear-stained face (63). In these descriptions Rulfo plays on the capacity of cinematic vision to open up configurations of the unconscious that for Benjamin lie 'outside the normal spectrum of sense perceptions', providing access to an inner world of 'psychoses, hallucinations and dreams'.[62] Like Macario, who fails to fully recall his act of violence, the somnambulant Alcancía appears to have committed his crime in a state of semi-consciousness; pushing open the door to the family's home unintentionally and proceeding to kill more of them than he had originally intended in the darkness (62). In his inability to integrate these actions into conscious thought or memory, the psychotic Alcancía, much like Macario and Preciado, embodies a fragmentary and disconnected state of being that, to recall Benjamin, is 'sealed off from experience'.[63]

Rulfo's literary appropriation of mechanised forms of perception to articulate a crisis of perception and bodily integrity marks a shift from Rivera's conceptualisation of technology as a tool for corporeal augmentation and discipline in the 1920s and early 30s. While Rivera's imagery visualises the progressive potential of the machine in a revolutionary society, Rulfo's literary works of the industrialising 'Miracle' years, reflect how both human perception and aesthetic form have adapted in response to the integration of the machine into the very fabric of everyday life and labour practices. In these works, technology is not presented as a subject in or of itself, but is rather profoundly integrated into human perception. In her analysis of high modernist literature, Sara Danius suggests that the works of Marcel Proust, Thomas Mann and James Joyce reflect the increasing mechanisation of contemporary society by staging a progressive internalisation of the technological within the human body. Moving from Mann's early descriptions of the X-ray to the complete integration of technology into quotidian perception in Joyce, Danius illustrates how these works reveal a historical shift from *prosthesis* (the thematisation of the external device) to *aisthesis* (the interiorisation of technology).[64] In exploring the body's capacity to attune itself to the rhythms of industrial modernity, Rivera's and Rulfo's evolving machine aesthetics map a similar transition in the post-revolutionary context, from the external thematisation of technology to its infiltration of human cognitive and sensory processes. Moving from the muralist's prosthetic fantasy of the machine as a tool for corporeal augmentation, Rulfo's use of visual technologies to articulate perceptual crisis reflects, in a Benjaminian sense, the alternative forms of 'training' to which the human sensorium has been subjected in the fully industrialised environment.[65]

Part II: Corporeal Landscapes: Negotiating the Boundaries of Reproductive Femininity

Rivera's projection of the technologised male as an agent of societal transformation in his Detroit murals was consistent with gendered debates regarding revolutionary culture that developed in the early 1920s. Maples Arce's call for a visual culture shaped by 'el espíritu revolucionario y la energía viril' [revolutionary spirit and virile energy] found powerful expression in Rivera's pictorial language, which, according to Henríquez Ureña, exuded 'vigor masculino' [masculine vigour].[66] A journalistic polemic regarding an appropriate form of 'revolutionary' literature was couched in similarly gendered terms. In a thinly veiled attack on the 'effeminate' cosmopolitanism of contemporary avant-garde writers such as the Contemporáneos, Julio Jiménez Rueda's article 'El afeminamiento en la literatura mexicana', published in *El Universal* in 1924, lamented the lack of a sufficiently masculine literary style to narrate the nation's social transformation. Francisco Monterde responded within days, upholding the robust realist prose of Mariano Azuela as evidence that a 'virile' revolutionary literature did in fact exist.[67] As these comments make clear, the masculinisation of revolutionary culture within the fields of art and literature established the feminine as antonymous to societal transformation and excluded women and homosexual men from the national narrative. In what follows, I comparatively analyse Rivera's and Rulfo's visual, architectural and literary configurations of the female body to shed light on the gendered dimensions of their narratives of revolutionary development. I interpret the transformation of the female body from a state of containment to overflow across these works as evidence of a gradual shift away from the restrictive state-endorsed models of female citizenship that were established in the early post-revolution period.

Although the military phase of the Revolution temporarily disturbed the established gender order in Mexico, the urgent project of national economic rehabilitation demanded the return to more conservative and primarily procreative models of female citizenship. This restriction of female societal participation to the sphere of reproduction to secure societal stability and prosperity once again took its cue from late nineteenth-century interpretations of femininity which, as Oliva López Sánchez explains, identified women as 'el arsenal moralizante de la sociedad y las reproductoras de la materia humana necesaria para contribuir con el desarrollo económico de la joven nación' [society's moral armoury and the reproducers of the human matter necessary to contribute to the young nation's economic development].[68] Within the cultural sphere, this image of the self-abnegating mother as both procreator and moral custodian of Mexico's citizens was championed by Gamio and the Chilean writer Gabriela Mistral, who was recruited by Vasconcelos to contribute to the educational campaigns of the 1920s. Gamio envisaged the ideal 'feminine' Mexican woman as a chaste, healthy and fundamentally maternal figure whose societal function was to produce a resilient and 'virile' national race.[69] Mistral upheld the view that motherhood constituted the most powerful form of female patriotism in her educational text *Lecturas para mujeres* (1923) and prose pieces such as 'A la mujer mexicana' (1923), which reinforced the long-established link between female and natural generative forces by venerating the Mexican mother as a 'colaboradora de la tierra' [collaborator of the earth].[70] Defending these ideals from feminist criticism, Mistral asserted 'yo no he reducido a la mujer a la maternidad: he querido circunscribirla, directa o indirectamente, al niño en los trabajos y en las profesiones' [I have not reduced women to maternity: I have tried to circumscribe them, directly or indirectly, to children in their tasks and occupations].[71] Mistral's self-proclaimed intention to 'circumscribe' the sphere of female activity underlines how, contrary to its egalitarian rhetoric, post-revolutionary culture sought to confine women to the realm of the maternal. These cultural models were complemented by contemporary eugenics discourses. Writing in 1923, the eugenicist José Eduardo González insisted on the importance of sexual education campaigns in enabling women to accept their maternal 'destiny' as a social and moral obligation:

> Un papel muy importante desempeñaría en nuestro medio la educación sexual puesto que para la mujer es muy difícil, si no imposible, tener conciencia de su destino: la procreación, sin el conocimiento de su obligación moral y de su papel social.[72]
>
> [Sexual education will play a very important role in our field given that it is difficult, if not impossible, for women to achieve awareness of their destiny — procreation — without understanding their moral obligation and social role].

The 1930s saw the introduction of a more developed programme of what Alexandra Minna Stern terms 'maternalist eugenics', which brought the procreative and child-rearing abilities of Mexican women under scientific scrutiny and looked to 'produce a body politic untainted by dysgenic sexual unions'.[73] As Schell notes, however, by the end of that decade, Mexican eugenicists started to shift their focus away from sexual and reproductive behaviour.[74] Although the state continued to promote a primarily domestic role for women during the 1940s, as evidenced by initiatives such as the nationwide competition run by the newspaper *Excélsior* for Mexico's most prolific mother in 1941 and the unveiling of a national monument celebrating maternity in 1949, women also finally gained access to the political domain with the introduction of female suffrage in 1953. The expansion of the middle class towards the middle of the century enabled more Mexican women to engage in cultural and artistic activities outside the home and explore previously taboo themes. By the 1930s and 40s, artists such as Frida Kahlo, Isabel Villaseñor and María Izquierdo had started to lend visual expression to female sexuality and experiences of miscarriage and bodily trauma in their works. During the 1950s, a number of female writers began to break into the sphere of literary production and similarly tested the generic and thematic boundaries that had conventionally restricted women's writing.[75] Rosario Castellanos played a critical role in opening up the literary field to women writers both in Mexico and Latin America. Following on from her thesis *Sobre cultura femenina* (1950), which according to Elena Poniatowska provided the starting point for the feminist movement in Mexico, Castellanos's corpus of literary and intellectual writings challenged prevailing social norms by engaging with themes of failed motherhood and female sexual pleasure.[76]

Alongside Castellanos, the 1950s brought to the fore a number of other prominent female writers such as Poniatowska and Elena Garro, whose works further explored hitherto unexamined aspects of female corporeality.

In what follows, I consider how this renegotiation of strictly procreative models of femininity is reflected in the female corporeal landscapes mapped in Rivera's and Rulfo's works. Drawing on Plato's concept of *chôra* and its subsequent reformulations by Julia Kristeva and Elizabeth Grosz, I examine Rivera's fresco cycle at the Escuela Nacional de Agricultura (ENA) in Chapingo (1924–1927) alongside Rulfo's novel and short story 'Es que somos muy pobres', to trace a representational shift in depictions of the female body as it transitions from a state of corporeal containment to one of openness and overflow. Engaging with the often overlooked spatial dimensions of Rivera's muralism, I demonstrate how both the visual and architectural aspects of the mural programme at Chapingo align with contemporary state discourses regarding the sexual regulation and subordination of female bodies by presenting feminised space as a clearly demarcated and contained territory to be productively occupied by man. Rivera's metaphorical equation of female fertility with revolutionary potentiality through his use of the woman-as-land trope in Chapingo is complicated by Susana San Juan of *Pedro Páramo* and Tacha of 'Es que somos muy pobres', whose non-reproductive sexuality poses a threat to national progress. Turning to Rulfo's portrayal of female autoeroticism and prostitution, I explore how the contravention of state-endorsed models of femininity is figured as a transgression of corporeal boundaries for these characters whose overflowing bodily fluids merge with sea and rain water. My reading also addresses the link between gender and narrative agency, arguing that while Rivera foregrounds male agency in his visual and spatial narratives of revolution at Chapingo, Rulfo's female characters disrupt both societal and narrative order by colonising textual space or destabilising the masculine narrative architecture of his works.

Corporeal Cartographies: Controlling the Feminine Land in Chapingo (1924–1927)

Rivera executed his fresco cycle at Chapingo during a transitional moment in the history of the ENA. In 1923, under the direction of Marte R. Gómez, the school was relocated from Mexico City to the former Hacienda of Chapingo, previously owned by a close ally of Porfirio Díaz and former Mexican president, General Manuel González, and a new curriculum for its aspiring agronomists was introduced. Gómez hoped that this new architectural space would contribute to the ideological formation of the school's male students, preparing them for their role in realising the government's vision of revolutionary change in the countryside. The director entrusted Rivera with the task of artistically crafting 'un mensaje que estableciera el clima y saturara la atmósfera que nos interesaba hacer respirar a las nuevas generaciones de ingenieros agrónomos' [a message that would set the tone and infuse the atmosphere that we wanted the new generations of agronomists to breathe].[77] Taking inspiration from the school's motto, 'Aquí se enseña la explotación de la tierra, no la del hombre' [Here we teach the exploitation of the land, not that of man], the resulting cycle revolves around a gendered metaphor of agrarian renewal that foregrounds man's repossession and productive exploitation of the fertile, feminised land. The gendered dimensions of these and other murals by Rivera were of course shaped by his understanding of revolutionary culture as inherently masculine, a position also reflected in the accusations of effeminacy he levelled at artistic rivals and political enemies.[78] The 700m^2 programme at Chapingo is distributed over two architectural spaces: the former chapel, containing forty-one panels of varying dimensions, and the upper floor of the administrative building, which is decorated with four large landscape-scene murals. On entering the chapel, the observer is immediately confronted by the cycle's centrepiece *La tierra liberada con las fuerzas naturales controladas por el hombre* (1926–1927), an expansive mural depicting the reclining nude figure of Rivera's pregnant then-wife Lupe Marín configured in the form of the Yucatán Peninsula. This central 'woman-as-land' metaphor thematically links all of the panels contained within this architectural space. The nation again assumes feminine contours in the panels *La tierra oprimida*, located on the upper archway of the west wall and *La tierra dormida*, located in a lunette of the *coro alto*, where the Italian photographer Tina Modotti, with whom Rivera was also romantically involved at the time, is envisaged as the sleeping virgin earth.

In these panels, Rivera offers a post-revolutionary interpretation of a longstanding trope of Mexican nationalist iconography. The fertile woman-as-land as a symbol of national potentiality appears as a central motif in paintings of the independence period such as *Alegoría de la Patria* (1821) and again in illustrated Porfirian era works like Riva Palacio's *México a través de los siglos* (1884), where the modern mestizo nation is depicted as a fair-skinned young woman.[79] Adapting this motif to the post-revolutionary context, Rivera presents the fecund female as a metaphorical expression of national regeneration achieved through successful agrarian reform and modernisation. As in nineteenth-century applications of the trope, the muralist's imagery reflects the paradoxical position of women within traditional allegorical formulations of nationhood, whereby the female body metaphorically constitutes a national space from which the bodies of real material women are excluded. These gender dynamics were particularly marked within the domain of mural production. Artists such as Rivera and Siqueiros exploited the symbolic value of the female body in their works while protecting public muralism as an exclusively male enterprise by marginalising female practitioners such as Izquierdo.[80]

For Grosz, this feminine conception of space, which is deeply embedded in the Western philosophical tradition, can be traced back to Plato's description of *chôra* as a neutral womb-like container in *Timaeus* (c.360BC). This association with the female reproductive anatomy is illuminated by Plato's conceptualisation of *chôra* as a 'receptacle of all becoming', a site of transformation in which ideas come into material existence.[81] Kenneth Olwig also notes the cartographic dimensions of Plato's concept, highlighting the etymological linkage between *chôra* and chorography, 'the study of the enclosed, bodily shapes of the earth'.[82] Elaborating on the geographical and architectural implications of *chôra*, Grosz illustrates how this maternal analogy has provided the foundation for Western concepts of spatiality that use 'a disembodied femininity as the ground for the production of a (conceptual and social) universe'.[83] These interpretations of *chôra* as a form of maternal container but also a referent for a physical geographical territory and an abstract social space are important for understanding Rivera's use of the woman-as-land trope at Chapingo. As I will go on to discuss, in both its visual and architectural dimensions, Rivera's cycle conceptualises the female body as a symbolic national space to be productively occupied by male agents of revolutionary transformation.

While critics have tended to analyse the iconographic content of the chapel and the administrative wing separately, or indeed to entirely overlook the latter, an integrated analysis of Chapingo's entire visual programme reveals how both sets of murals play on the same metaphors of colonisation and containment in relation to the feminised landscape. In *La tierra liberada*, the prostrate feminised earth poses with her swollen stomach and full breasts exposed to the viewer, capturing the dual fantasies of 'maternal containment' and 'sexual assertion' that Annette Kolodny identifies as integral to the woman-as-land metaphor.[84] Here the fertile and sexually available female embodies a latent national potentiality waiting to be activated by the muscular *mestizo* who stands before an electric turbomachine pointed directly toward her vagina. This phallic penetration of the feminised earth, which recalls this chapter's opening description of *Allegory of California*, is reiterated in the panel *La organización del movimiento agrario*, located on the west wall, where a peasant positions a spade directly over the groin of a male worker as he sinks it into the soil, and in the adjacent *El agitador*, where miners thrust into subterranean rock with drills and shovels positioned near their lower abdomen. These sexualised metaphors depicting man's aggressive penetration of the land are implicitly maintained in the murals located on the first floor of the administrative building, such as *El buen gobierno*, where tractors, pylons and railway lines demonstrate man's industrial colonisation of the countryside. This scene of a rapidly modernising Mexican landscape recalls the detailed panoramas of Rivera's Porfirian mentor Velasco and that regime's concern with forging a scientifically stable image of the nation's territories through processes of surveying and mapmaking.[85] In Rivera's murals in the administrative building, cartographic strategies also facilitate human control of the natural environment. In *El buen gobierno* politicians and surveyors are shown using tripod-mounted telescopes and blueprints to measure the terrain, while in *El reparto de tierras*, an exclusively male crowd of peasants and government officials congregates around a map demarcating the surrounding land.

The ongoing metaphorical interplay between the landscape imagery presented in the murals of both architectural spaces brings to light a connection between the strategies of territorial demarcation depicted in the administrative wing and Rivera's painterly approach to the female body in the chapel. By transposing the geographical outline of Mexico onto Marín's body in *La tierra fecunda*, the artist establishes a direct parallel between the fixity of cartographic and corporeal borders that is reflected in his visual regulation of the female form. In modelling his allegorical figures on the classical ideal of the female nude, Rivera drew inspiration from a visual tradition that, according to Lynda Nead, has historically been concerned with the 'regulation and containment of the female sexual body'.[86] Nead's suggestion that the configuration of the female nude as a bounded entity seeks to rectify the fluctuations of the real, leaking female body is reflected in Rivera's emphasis on the corporeal boundaries of his female subjects.[87] Years after completing the cycle, the artist recalled how Marín's figure had left an permanent imprint on his imagination: 'las curvas y sombras de esa maravillosa creación dejaron una huella imborrable en mi cerebro de pintor' [the curves and shadows of that marvellous creation left an indelible impression on my painterly mind].[88] In *La tierra fecunda*, Rivera lends a sculpted definition to these bodily contours by applying *chiaroscuro* to her rounded breasts, thighs and belly. This heavy shading imposes a unbroken outline around the circumference of her body that brings her pale *mestiza* complexion into even greater relief against the dark ochre tone of the surrounding space. Prominent male Mexican art historians have stressed the muralist's mastery of line, form and proportionality in his composition of the nude elsewhere in the cycle. Discussing Rivera's portrayal of Modotti as *La tierra dormida*, another female figure who assumes the lateral supine pose typical of the classical nude, Justino Fernández praises his capacity to adjust the forms and lines of the body to create a female form that is 'tranquilo, sereno y grandioso, según el ideal clásico' [calm, serene and majestic, according to the classical ideal].[89] In a similar vein, Antonio Rodríguez commends the artist's use of regulating lines and shading in the panel *Maduración* to regulate the female form and create an overall impression of bodily integrity and proportionality:

> El dibujo respeta la sensualidad de la línea, las proporciones de las partes y la integración de éstas al todo. La luz y la sombra, al modular el cuerpo, completan la tarea del dibujo, el cual se propone aquí alcanzar, por la máxima representación de la verdad poética, el más alto ideal de la belleza.[90]
>
> [The drawing respects the sensuality of the line, the proportion of its parts and their integration into the whole. Light and shadow, by regulating the body, complete drawing's task, which in this case is to achieve the greatest representation of poetic truth, the highest ideal of beauty.]

Rivera's classical emphasis on the borders of the female nude in Chapingo is of course particularly important given its function as an expression of the national territory. This interpretation of the female form as a vast maternal container for Mexico's citizens is clearly communicated in the panels adorning the east wall such as *Germinación*, where bulb-like foetuses are suspended in a cavernous subterranean environment, and in *La sangre de los mártires revolucionarios fertilizando la tierra*, located in the chapel's vestibule, where the corpses of revolutionary leaders Otilio Montaño and Emiliano Zapata inhabit the soil beneath a glowing cornfield. Rivera's linking of revolutionary sacrifice to this particular landscape evokes the metaphorical function of the maize cycle as an expression of human death and rebirth in pre-Hispanic cultures. As Florescano explains in relation to Mesoamerican agricultural practices, the 'entrance of the seed into the heart of the earth and its prodigious rebirth in the form of a life-producing plant was a cycle that also implied sacrifice'.[91]

These opposing yet intertwined impulses are similarly embodied by the Aztec birth-death goddess Coatlicue, subsequently integrated into Rivera's Detroit cycle and *Pan American Unity* (1940), who represents the twin functions of the earth as both womb and tomb. In an essay from 1950, Paz underlines this fundamental aspect of Rivera's gendered interpretation of matter: 'la concibe como una madre, como un gran vientre, una gran boca y una gran tumba. Madre, inmensa matriz que todo lo devora y engendra [...] como todas las grandes divinidades de la fertilidad' [he conceives of it as a mother, as a great womb, a great mouth and a great tomb. Mother, the immense matrix that devours and produces everything... like all of the great fertility deities].[92] Connecting the imagery of posthumous repose presented in *La sangre de los mártires* with the recurring depictions of gestation found throughout the chapel reveals how the cycle as a whole conceptualises the maternal land as a kind of all-receiving receptacle for Mexico's deceased and future revolutionaries.

This visual metaphor of feminised space as a container for the nation's revolutionary subjects operates on a broader architectural level at Chapingo. Plato's vision of the womb-like *chôra* as a nurturing site of transformation that provides, as Grosz puts it, 'the point of entry, as it were, into material existence', suggests a link between the gendered visual and spatial metaphors operating in the chapel and administrative building which trace the evolution of the Revolution from its ideological inception to ultimate realisation.[93] Rivera's didactic objectives with the decorative programme at Chapingo, which was geared specifically towards the trainee agronomists of the ENA, were consistent with his broader commitments to 'the masses' as a revolutionary artist: 'servirles como organizador de conciencia y ayudar a su organización social' [to serve them as an organiser of consciousness and assist with their social organization].[94] Grosz's interpretation of *chôra* as 'the ground for the production of a (conceptual and social) universe' is useful for appreciating how Rivera configures the feminised architectural interior of the chapel as a ritual space that encourages the formation of a revolutionary consciousness in the observer.[95] In Chapingo, Rivera more comprehensively develops the link between the female anatomy and enclosed architectural spaces previously identified in the *tehuana*-themed vestibule of the SEP. In the confined and dimly-lit interior of the chapel, images of rest and gestation combine with a palette of predominantly warm red and earthy tones to transform the space into an intimate and distinctly womb-like environment. Rivera emphasises this impression of an enclosed uterine space by embellishing the chapel's semi-cylindrical vaulted ceiling with 'intersecting mouldings to create the appearance of a rib vault'.[96] By decoratively accentuating this aspect of the building's structure, the muralist establishes a visual connection between the vast concave space and the protruding, ribbed form of Marín's abdomen in the cycle's centrepiece. Architectural and female reproductive anatomical forms again converge in the panel *Maduración* on the east wall, where a recessed window is integrated into the composition to create the impression of a vaginal opening. Configured as a giant vulvar flower, Rodríguez describes the rounded aperture as a giant orifice.[97] While the ENA's repurposing of the Hacienda at Chapingo, formerly owned by one of the most powerful Hacendados of the Díaz era, was symbolic of the nation's revolutionary transition, the muralist's conceptualisation of the chapel interior in terms of the female body harks back to the anatomical-architectural models in vogue during that regime. According to Ageeth Sluis, during the late nineteenth and early twentieth centuries trainee architects at the Academia de San Carlos were encouraged to use the female nude as a key point of reference for building design.[98]

A similar form of Porfirian haunting can be perceived in the visual metaphors of the chapel, specifically the sustained parallel between social and organic evolution established in the two sets of panels located on either side of the central nave. Evoking the positivist analogy between history and the natural sciences, Rivera directly links the early stages of the revolutionary struggle in *La transformación social* to the botanical and biological developmental processes depicted in *La evolución natural*. The equation of the development of revolutionary ideology with that of human life suggests that the viewer should begin their journey in the womb-like space of the chapel before proceeding to the administrative building. As in the case of the SEP murals, Rivera here relies on a mobile spectator to activate the cycle's narrative. By experiencing Chapingo's visual programme in this order, the observer moves from the allegorical scenes of biological and revolutionary gestation depicted in the chapel's shadowy and muted interior to the more open and naturally illuminated space of the administrative building. Here, scenes of upright male workers and politicians actively cultivating the land demonstrate the fruition of the movement's social objectives. This implied shift from the theoretical conception of the Revolution to its realisation, mirroring the choratic transition from idea to reality, is also registered on a stylistic level as the abstract allegorical imagery of the chapel gives way to the predominantly realist visual language of the administration building.

Understanding the ritual dimensions of the chapel in terms of Plato's notion of *chôra* reveals how Rivera uses this founding concept of 'disembodied femininity' to facilitate an embodied male viewing experience. The muralist's conceptualisation of both national and architectural space as a kind of feminised receptacle enables him to foreground male agency in both pictorial and spatial terms at Chapingo. By communicating the notion of agrarian renewal through sexualised metaphors of territorial control and colonisation, the cycle addresses and empowers an implicitly male observer who mobilises its visual narrative of revolutionary progress by re-enacting these strategies of spatial occupation as he navigates the two buildings. The muralist's identification of man as an agent of both historical and narrative progress within the feminised visual and architectural spaces of Chapingo endorses a long-standing gendered dualism between time and space that carries significant societal implications. As Massey points out, this codification of 'history, progress, civilization, politics and transcendence' as masculine, and space, absence or lack as feminine is inseparable from a philosophical and societal viewpoint that associates the female with 'stasis, passivity and depoliticisation'.[99] By utilising the female form as the metaphorical basis for his image of the national territory, Rivera creates a spatial and visual narrative of revolutionary development from which real female bodies are implicitly excluded.

Renegotiating the Boundaries of Post-Revolutionary Femininity in Rulfo's Literature

The visual and architectural metaphors operating in Chapingo uphold the fundamental assumption in Western thought that 'woman is/provides a space for man, but occupies none herself'.[100] In the domain of post-revolutionary art, Rivera's vision of a spatially bounded female body was most radically deconstructed by his wife, Frida Kahlo. Railing against the epic form and heroic pictorial idiom of the muralists, Kahlo's psychoanalytic self-portraits of the mid-1930s unsettled the post-revolutionary ideals of reproductive femininity championed by her husband by foregrounding a sterile, mutilated and leaking maternal body. These divergences come into focus in the works produced by both artists during their time in Detroit. Recalling his symbolic interlinking of female and natural fecundity in Chapingo, Rivera's horizontal panel *Infant in the Bulb of a Plant* on the east wall of the Detroit Institute cycle is flanked on either side by imagery of two voluptuous female nudes holding fruits and grains as symbols of fertility. Rivera's exuberant celebration of female bodily productivity jars with contemporary works by Kahlo such as the lithograph *El aborto* (1932) and the painting *Henry Ford Hospital* (1932) which respond to a tragic miscarriage suffered by the artist during her time in the 'Motor City'.[101] In both artworks, the rupturing of biologically 'functional' forms of femininity is addressed as a breakdown of corporeal boundaries as tears and blood gush forth from the artist's eyes and vagina.

Kahlo's visceral self-portraits herald a broader shift towards an aesthetics of abjection in artistic representations of the female body from the 1930s onwards. In her oft-cited essay 'Powers of Horror' (1982), Julia Kristeva defines the abject as that which must be expelled from the self such as excrement, tears, sweat, menstrual blood and other bodily fluids conventionally associated with the feminine that threaten the physical limits of the body. Building on Mary Douglas's identification of the inseparability of bodily and socio-cultural boundaries, Kristeva illustrates, in the words of Kelly Oliver, how the abject 'threatens the unity and identity of both society and the subject' by calling into question the very 'boundaries upon which they are constructed'.[102] In post-revolutionary literary production, the abject interlinking of social and bodily transgression visualised by Kahlo re-emerges in Castellanos's poetry and prose writings of the 1950s. Echoing Kahlo, the poetic imagery of *Apuntes para una declaración de fe* (1948), *De la vigilia estéril* (1950) and later poems such as 'Kinsey Report' (1972), based on the controversial study on female sexual behaviour published in 1953, foreground a grotesque and often porous female body to explore themes such as infertility, miscarriage and female pleasure.[103] The poetics of abjection forged by Castellanos was further developed by Poniatowska and later writers such as Ángeles Mastretta whose works, as Jane Lavery notes, engage in a 're-mapping' of the female body through descriptions of female masturbation and orgasm.[104] In what follows, I position Rulfo within this broader attempt to aesthetically renegotiate earlier models of female sexual identity by illustrating how resistance to biologically functional forms of femininity is expressed through the unfixing of bodily boundaries in his works. While it is highly likely that Rulfo was familiar with Kahlo's work, given his detailed knowledge of Mexican art and friendship with fellow Jaliscan Izquierdo, Kahlo's most notable female contemporary, his links to Castellanos are more immediately evident. Both writers belonged to the same cohort of writers at the Centro Mexicano de Escritores (CME) in 1953 and would have regularly exchanged ideas at the institution's compulsory literary workshops.

While I draw parallels between Rulfo's representational approaches and those of Kahlo and Castellanos, I also acknowledge his privileged position as a male artist within the post-revolutionary cultural landscape. As Bowskill has demonstrated, the criteria for post-revolutionary literary success were largely determined by a network of influential male intellectuals working in the areas of publishing, literary criticism and literary awards who established themselves as 'custodians of literary knowledge'.[105] Several of the cultural *caudillos* singled out by Bowskill (Alí Chumacero, Emmanuel Carballo, Carlos Fuentes, Octavio Paz and Carlos Monsiváis) produced reviews and interpretations of Rulfo's work that were instrumental in cementing his legendary status. Over the course of his career, Rulfo also enjoyed support from the CME, an institution described by Hind as 'one node in a system of standard discriminatory practice', and his reputation was cemented by his receipt of prestigious awards such as the Premio Xavier Villaurrutia and the Premio Nacional de Literatura in 1955 and 1970, respectively.[106] Rulfo's gender perspective also inevitably informs the fundamentally androcentric nature of his literary vision. Hind has gone so far as to count his novel among examples of male-produced Mexican texts in which a thematic emphasis on male loneliness is combined with aggressive 'macho' language to create an impression of 'authentic masculinity'.[107] While Rulfo's predominantly male-focused narratives admittedly do not significantly deviate from the broader post-revolutionary cultural tendency to position men at the centre of the national imaginary, Hind's assessment might lead some readers to mistakenly conclude that his texts align with the 'virile' masculinist literary aesthetic advocated by Jiménez Rueda, Monterde and others during the 1920s. As we have already seen in this and earlier chapters, Rulfo's texts are populated with disoriented, stumbling and collapsing male bodies and, as I intend to demonstrate here, his depiction of female characters radically diverges from post-revolutionary cultural ideals of reproductive female sexuality in ways that subtly critique oppressive patriarchal structures.

The theme of failed maternity so poignantly explored in Kahlo's self-portraits and Castellanos's poetry recurs throughout *Pedro Páramo*, where female characters fail to fulfil a reproductive function due to their physical and mental deterioration or sexual deviancy. Building on the prevalent theme of frustrated motherhood in *El Llano en llamas*, Rulfo presents us with a cast of infertile would-be mothers in Comala.[108] Like Damiana Cisneros, who claims to have nursed him as a child (222), Eduviges asserts the status of surrogate mother to Juan (201). Driven insane by her maternal longing, Dorotea *la Cuarraca* searches feverishly for her imaginary offspring but is equally incapable of childbearing due to her visibly malnourished state (249). The implication that healthy procreation is impossible in the Rulfian universe is further suggested by recurring references to incest. Following from allusions to inappropriate sexual relations in 'En la madrugada' and 'Acuérdate', it is heavily implied in *Pedro Páramo* that Susana has been the victim of her father's sexual advances while the anonymous woman encountered by Juan in Los Confines admits that she and her brother Donis have attempted to repopulate the area.

While these allusions to sterility and incest clearly unsettle the ideal of healthy reproductive femininity promoted by the post-revolutionary state, my reading will focus specifically on Susana San Juan of *Pedro Páramo* and Tacha of the short story 'Es que somos muy pobres' as examples of two Rulfian women who pose a threat to national development due to their non-reproductive sexuality. In *Foundational Fictions* (1991), her landmark study of Latin American nation-building narratives that allegorise postbellum national consolidation through the trope of heterosexual marriage, Doris Sommer underscores the societal threat posed by unproductive female eroticism, which is deemed 'unnatural, immoral and unpatriotic'.[109] As the possibility of a consummated heterosexual union is thwarted by Susana's non-procreative sexuality and Tacha's seemingly imminent fall into prostitution, both of Rulfo's texts can be read as staunchly anti-foundational post-revolutionary narratives. Focusing on the representation of auto-eroticism and prostitution, I demonstrate how deviation from state-endorsed models of reproductive womanhood is figured as a transgression of corporeal boundaries for these female characters, whose bodies and bodily fluids symbolically merge with sea and rain water.

Building on Sommer's work, Debra A. Castillo illustrates how the transgressive capacity of so-called 'loose woman' is registered on a narrative level in Mexican literary works that position the sexually liberated female or prostitute 'at the very point at which both societal and narrative order are disrupted'.[110] Highlighting the link between bodily and vocal excess in Rulfo's works, I explore how the doubly subversive function of the 'loose woman' is performed by Susana and Tacha, who overturn socially accepted models of womanhood and disrupt narrative order by invading textual space or unsettling the masculine narrative architecture of the texts. My contention is not that these descriptions of bodily overflow signal any kind of profound emancipation for Rulfo's female characters, who meet a similarly bleak fate to their male counterparts: Susana ultimately dies after descending into madness and Tacha's future remains unclear at the story's conclusion. Rather, I am interested in how Rulfo's negation of reproductive forms of femininity and his descriptive emphasis on the borderlessness of the female body challenges state-endorsed models of post-revolutionary female citizenship and overturns the notions of passivity and corporeal containment conventionally associated with the woman-as-land metaphor.

The Non-Procreative Auto-Eroticism of Susana San Juan

The aforementioned examples of female sterility, incest and dysfunctional sexuality uphold Hugo Hernán Ramírez's assertion that, in Rulfo's literature, 'los personajes femeninos desbordan los estereotipos de virgen o madre' [the female characters exceed the stereotypes of virgin or mother].[111] Although Ramírez does not address Rulfo's female bodily imagery, his use of the verb *desbordar*, meaning 'to exceed' but also 'to overflow' and even 'to flood', hints at the corporeal implications of this transgression of culturally and socially accepted forms of womanhood. The verb also encapsulates other 'excessive' aspects of the female characters explored here, such as their ability to move beyond phallic-dominated sexual activity and fixed boundaries of language. In *Pedro Páramo*, this alternative model of femininity is most powerfully embodied by Susana San Juan, whose non-reproductive auto-eroticism challenges the ideal of self-abnegating motherhood. Although Páramo tightens his tyrannical grip on Comala by colonising its land and raping its women, Susana, the true object of his desire, eludes his possession for over thirty years. After orchestrating the death of her father, the *cacique* is finally wed to Susana but their marriage remains unconsummated as she progressively sinks into insanity and retreats to her adolescent memories of sexual awakening. The historical sequence of these events is significant. If Rulfo situates Susana's exuberant adolescent sexuality in the Porfirian period of the mid-1880s, and her mental and physical deterioration during the mid to late 1920s, as de Valdés suggests, her narrative of bodily decline directly contradicts the gendered metaphors of national regeneration formulated by Rivera during the early post-revolutionary period.[112]

A striking but overlooked aspect of Rulfo's treatment of Susana is his spatial representation of her experiences as both an object and subject of sexual desire. Throughout the novel, attempts by oppressive male figures to control Susana's body are associated with literal and figurative forms of burial. In an almost macabre reimagining of Rivera's subterranean nudes at Chapingo, Susana addresses us from the confines of her coffin following her death at the Media Luna ranch. Her real interment is foreshadowed by the description of her sickbed as a 'sepultura de sábanas' [tomb of sheets] (298) and an even earlier childhood memory, in which the incestuous Bartolomé lowers her into a mineshaft where she discovers a decomposing corpse (278). In contrast to these images of sepulchral confinement, Susana's memories of her youthful erotic experiences in the ocean are characterised by imagery of bodily and spatial openness: 'Tenía [...] los brazos abiertos, desdobladas las piernas [...] Y el mar allí enfrente, lejano' [Her... arms were open, her legs spread out... And the sea lay before her, distant] (282). In this passage, which occurs in the final third of the novel, the semi-conscious Susana recalls how her lover Florencio followed her to swim naked in the sea. Destabilising conventional tropes aligning the female body with a passive landscape, Rulfo likens Susana's exuberant sexuality to the untameable force of the sea. Although the episode has commonly been interpreted as a sex scene, Florencio's peripherality throughout the passage suggests that Susana's immersion in the sea should in fact be read as a metaphor for masturbation. Her observation that Florencio 'se sintió solo, a pesar de estar yo allí' [felt lonely despite the fact that I was there] (282) and his subsequent assertion that he prefers to make love to her beneath the sheets in the darkness (283) clearly indicate his exclusion and discomfort. He finally abandons her as she engages in an act of foreplay with the waves:

> Volví yo. Volvería siempre. El mar moja mis tobillos y se va; moja mis rodillas, mis muslos; rodea mi cintura con su brazo suave, da vuelta sobre mis senos; se

> abraza de mi cuello; aprieta mis hombros. Entonces me hundo en él, entera. Me entrego a él en su fuerte batir, en su suave poseer, sin dejar pedazo (283).
>
> [I went back. I would always go back. The sea bathes my ankles and retreats, it bathes my knees, my thighs; it puts its gentle arm around my waist, circles my breasts, embraces my neck, presses my shoulders. Then I sink into it completely. I surrender myself to its pulsing strength, to its gentle possession, holding nothing back.]

The repetition of the verb *mojar* [to dampen] alongside the sexually charged images of sea water suggest the overspilling of Susana's bodily fluids as she climaxes, while the repetition of the pronouns 'mi' and 'me' reinforce the self-focus of her sexual act. As de Valdés notes, Susana's behaviour in this episode exemplifies the Lacanian notion of feminine *jouissance*, a form of female sexual enjoyment that exceeds or 'goes beyond' the phallus and the limits of patriarchal order.[113] Kristeva's theorisation of *jouissance* represents a radical repossession of Plato's concept of *chôra* from a feminist theoretical perspective. Kristeva links this auto-erotic female pleasure back to the pre-phallic maternal sphere of *chôra*, which she compares to the sea in its all-encompassing rhythmic pulsations. In this sense, Susana's return to the ocean through memory ('I went back. I would always go back') can be interpreted as an attempt to escape a sexually oppressive male environment and turn 'back towards the auto-erotic body'.[114] This symbolic regression to the womb is further suggested by the fact that Susana dies in the foetal position: 'sintió que la cabeza se le clavaba en el vientre' [she felt her head crushing into her belly] (302).

Kristeva underlines the linguistic dimensions of *chôra* by identifying it as the source of a semiotic pre-linguistic mode of communication based on bodily drives and rhythms that precedes the phallocentric symbolic order on which social law is founded. Her assertion that the libidinal impulse of *chôra* is channelled through a poetic discourse that accentuates the corporeal elements of language such as rhyme, alliteration and onomatopoeia, sheds light on how Rulfo's novel confers a degree of narrative agency to the female body that is denied by Rivera's fresco cycle. Mirroring her bodily overflow, Susana's voice gradually invades narrative space as the novel progresses and the references to rainwater linking these narrative intrusions (275, 276, 279, 287) establish a subtle connection between her sexual and vocal empowerment. While the first part of the text is predominantly narrated by Preciado and Páramo, fragments 41–64 are dominated by Susana, whose increasingly frequent and lengthy vocal interjections compete with these male voices. Although Susana is initially confined to Páramo's adolescent fantasies, her acquisition of speech enables her to assert sexual and narrative agency. It is worth noting that Susana is not the only female character to display these forms of assertiveness. Eduviges willingly replaces Dolores on the night of her wedding to Páramo due to the latter's menstrual bleeding (207), while Donis's incestuous sister coerces Preciado into sleeping with her (245). Although Hind suggests that women are relegated to passive or ancillary roles in the novel, it is worth noting that it is Dolores's dying wish that provides the initial impetus for the narrative action and that both Eduviges and Dorotea function as critical catalysts for plot development by guiding the unstable and directionless Preciado through Comala until his narrative perspective is largely supplanted by that of Susana.[115]

Susana's rambling interjections establish her as the producer of a rhythmic and profoundly corporeal discourse that unsettles the patriarchal order of Comala by denying male ownership of her body; she refuses to acknowledge Bartolomé as her father and rejects the attempts by Padre Rentería to perform the last rites on her. When the priest instructs her to repeat the prayer, she erotically distorts his words into a grotesque image that blurs the boundaries between body and landscape: 'Tengo la boca llena de ti —de tu boca [...] Trago saliva espumosa; mastico terrones plagados de gusanos que se me anudan en la garganta y raspan la pared del paladar' [My mouth is full of you, of your mouth... I swallow foaming saliva; I chew worm-infested clods of earth that knot in my throat and scratch the roof of my mouth] (300). This description of bodily overflow captures what Kristeva identifies as the 'sonorous distinctiveness' of poetic language.[116] Recalling the earlier alliterative description of her sexual emancipation, where the repetition of 'm' sounds (*mojar, mi*) evokes her murmurs of pleasure, the repetition of 'p' sounds (*plagado, raspan, pared, paladar*) in these lines creates a forceful plosive effect, as if she were spitting the words from her dirt-filled mouth.[117]

Forms of Expulsion and Invasion in 'Es que somos muy pobres'

The association established in *Pedro Páramo* between the unbridled power of water and female sexuality is maintained in 'Es que somos muy pobres', where the developing body of the pubescent Tacha is likened to the destructive surge of a rising flood. As in the case of Susana, Tacha's disruption of patriarchal order is communicated in spatial terms, this time through interlinking bodily and natural imagery of expulsion and invasion. The story opens with Tacha's brother explaining that a sudden flood has destroyed his father's crops and swept away the cow which was intended as the dowry for his twelve-year-old sister. As the downpour persists over the following days, the water is thrust up from the riverbed, sweeping over the bridge and up the street. The narrator fears the incessant rain will break in through the roof of the family home, just as it inundated the house of a local woman called La Tambora (56). The narrator predicts that Tacha, now bereft of her dowry, will follow the path of her two older sisters, who were cast out by their father after becoming prostitutes. By anticipating Tacha's abrupt transfer from one male-dominated system of economic exchange (marriage payments) to another (prostitution), the story deftly exposes the contradictory sexual and social demands made on the female body within an oppressive patriarchal society. In this respect, the story echoes Rulfo's earlier literary portrayal of prostitution in the overlooked fragment 'Un pedazo de noche' (1940), a text that like *Pedro Páramo* opts to 'cede narrative point of view to a loose woman'.[118] The story is narrated from the first-person perspective of a sex worker who is approached by a man carrying a baby boy. In a disturbing critique of the paradigmatic mother/whore dichotomy, the female narrator finds herself expected to simultaneously perform the roles of sexual object for the male client and maternal carer for the infant who claws violently at her breasts.

Diverging from canonical Mexican narratives of prostitution such as Federico Gamboa's *Santa* (1903), a novel that illustrates the necessary expulsion of the corrupted woman from the national community, the flood does not seal Tacha's ruination, but rather mirrors a process of physiological transformation that converts her body into a strangely threatening force. The natural catastrophe that has devastated the town coincides with the pubescent development of her body, manifesting itself most clearly in her swelling breasts which inspire awe in her brother and fear in her father, who declares her a danger to the family (59). The risk to familial and social order posed by her burgeoning sexuality is suggested by the narrator's comparison of her fluctuating body to the surging flood water that threatens to destroy their home. As in the imagery of corporeal ruination examined in the previous chapter, Rulfo is concerned here with an indeterminate, processual body. With potentially incestuous desire, the narrator watches the breasts of his sobbing sister heave up and down as if the river were now swelling inside her. Like the river which has burst its banks, the girl's bodily contours dissolve as tears of filthy water stream down her face (56). The connection between natural and specifically female bodily fluids is further suggested by the narrator's subsequent comparison of Tacha's growth to a variety of pine known for producing a thick whitish resin (59).

Like Susana, Tacha's contravention of socially accepted forms of womanhood is conveyed in terms of corporeal and vocal eruption. While Tacha is sketched as a vague and mute figure in early stages of the story, the rapid growth of her body in the final paragraphs is matched by her increasing vocal presence as she begins to emit an overpowering non-human sound. These unintelligible cries, which again exemplify a semiotic privileging of bodily impulses over logic and sound over sense, are juxtaposed with the discourse of the brother-narrator, who, as Ramírez notes, comes to represent the patriarchal logic governing the community by faithfully repeating the father's judgements.[119] Although the brother speaks in an unsettlingly adult manner about the fates of Tacha and his other sisters, his narrative authority is undermined by his inability to comprehend her sudden bodily and vocal outburst, which he can only compare to the river:

> Yo la abrazo tratando de consolarla, pero ella no entiende. Llora con más ganas. De su boca sale un ruido semejante al que se arrastra por las orillas del río, que la hace temblar y sacudirse todita (59).
>
> [I try to console her by embracing her but she doesn't understand. She is crying even harder. A sound comes from her mouth like the one sweeping along the river bank, making her tremble and shake all over]

The comparison is significant as it demonstrates that, like the rising water, Tacha not only resists physical containment within her brother's embrace but also exceeds the descriptive capacities of language. The river's resistance to linguistic definition is revealed when the siblings scale the river bank to listen to the voices of the villagers watching the water, but hear no sound emerging from their open mouths. The brother's description of the river as 'la cosa aquella' [that thing] reveals, as Rowe notes, that the flood water 'cannot be contained in words, or not in the words the boy until then had at his disposal'.[120] The boy's comparison of the uncontrollable force within Tacha with that of the flood indicates that she too resists containment within the systems of signification available to him. While the brother's narrative authority is undermined by his inability to describe Tacha's transformation, other linguistic details indicate Tacha's capacity to develop into a more active narrative subject. Although the father intends to expel Tacha from the familial home, as he did her two older sisters, the verbs used to describe her influence over the men around her imply a possible reversal of this movement. Recalling the invasive movement of the water flooding the village, the narrator tells us that their father is *filled* with shame (58) when he realises that Tacha's body will *fill* the gaze of any man she meets (59).

Susana and Tacha stand alongside other abject Rulfian women whose subversive or uncontrollable sexuality is articulated as a transgression of corporeal boundaries. The adulterous Natalia of 'Talpa' weeps for days on end (77) while Macario's nurse Felipa, who engages in a sexual relationship with the learning disabled narrator, is associated with a sweet, hibiscus-flavoured milk that flows in streams from her breast (91). In *Pedro Páramo*, the incestuous sister of Donis is similarly linked to bodily fluids, sweating excessively as she sleeps beside Preciado before dissolving into a pool of mud (245). Situated alongside Kahlo's and Castellanos's visual and textual images, the bodily overflow of Rulfo's women characters signals a decisive movement away from the models of contained female corporeality that shape the visual and architectural composition of Rivera's Chapingo programme.

Through a comparative analysis of the interplay between bodily and natural forms, I have proposed that this representational shift can be mapped as a transition from fixed to fluid feminine corporeal landscapes across the works analysed. Countering the assumptions of passivity and bounded corporeality conventionally associated with the woman-as-land trope, Rulfo's equation of female sexuality with the formless and uncontrollable power of water dramatically reconceptualises woman's alliance with nature by presenting the body as an uncontainable natural force. Consistent with his broader literary use of subversive bodily imagery to critique post-revolutionary narratives of order, progress and unity, the unbounded corporeality of Susana and Tacha represents a transgression of the restrictive model of reproductive femininity on which the post-revolutionary state sought to build Mexico's economic future.

As I outlined at the beginning of this chapter, the programme of economic development pursued by the post-revolutionary state in the decades following the armed conflict evolved in conjunction with a parallel campaign of bodily *desarrollismo* that sought to fashion a male corporeal ideal in accordance with the industrial principles of efficiency and discipline and while also harnessing female reproductive labour. By analysing selected murals executed by Rivera between 1923 and 1933, I have demonstrated how the artist's corporeal imagery upholds the gendered framework of (re)productive citizenship promoted by the government by projecting man as a technologised agent of societal transformation and woman as the fertile embodiment of a post-revolutionary national potentiality. While the productive bodies populating Rivera's murals articulate the utopian impulse for a progressive collective future during the formative decades of 1920s and 30s, Rulfo's literature captures the more interrogative tone of mid-century debates surrounding the notion of 'revolutionary progress'. By figuring the mechanised male subject in terms of perceptual and corporeal breakdown and portraying non-reproductive expressions of female sexuality, his works consistently present literary bodies that challenge contemporary narratives of national development and threaten the prosperity of the post-revolutionary nation.

Notes to Chapter 3

1. Hal Foster, *Prosthetic Gods* (Cambridge, Mass: MIT Press, 2004), p. 109.
2. Ibid., p. 114.
3. Michel Foucault, *The History of Sexuality*, vol.1, trans. by Robert Hurley (New York: Vintage, 1990), p. 139.
4. Abelardo Villegas, *La filosofía de lo mexicano* (Mexico City: FCE, 1960), p. 83; Dalton, p. 35–37.
5. Michel Foucault, *Discipline and Punish: The Birth of the Prison*, trans. by Alan Sheridan (London: Allen Lane, 1995), p. 316; Vasconcelos, *La raza cósmica*, p. 37.
6. Dafne Cruz Porchini, 'Formando el cuerpo de la nación: el imaginario del deporte en el México posrevolucionario (1920–1940)', in *Formando el cuerpo de una nación: El imaginario del deporte en el México posrevolucionario (1920–1940)*, ed. by Monserrat Sánchez Soler (Mexico City: INBA, 2012), pp. 33–56 (p. 33).
7. José Manuel Puig Casauranc, 'La educación integral', *Boletín de la Secretaría de Educación Pública*, 5 (1925), 74–80 (p. 75).
8. José Zozaya, 'Higiene Mental', *Medicina, Revista Científica Mensual*, 6 (1926), p. 208.
9. 'Editorial: La Higiene, base de la Economía Nacional', *Salubridad*, 1 (1930), 9–10 (p. 9).
10. Lázaro Cárdenas, 'Discurso del candidato del PNR a la presidencia de la República', in *Palabras y documentos públicos de Lázaro Cárdenas: 1928–1970*, pp. 121–22 (p. 122).
11. Leticia González del Rivero, 'Tiempo de la iglesia versus tiempo del estado: México en la década de los treinta', in *Un Haz de reflexiones en torno al tiempo, la historia y la modernidad*, ed. by María Dolores Illescas Nájera (Mexico City: Universidad Iberoamericana, 1995), pp. 177–210 (p. 197).
12. Gallo, p. 21.
13. Siqueiros, 'Tres llamamientos de orientación', p. 2.
14. Rivera, *Mi arte, mi vida*, p. 107.
15. Lear, p. 109.
16. Gallo, p. 15.
17. Diego Rivera, 'The Revolutionary Spirit in Modern Art', *Modern Quarterly*, 6 (1932), 51–57; Anthony W. Lee, 'Workers and Painters: Social Realism and Race in Diego Rivera's Detroit Murals', in *The Social and the Real: Political Art of the 1930s in the Western Hemisphere*, ed. by Alejandro Anreus and others (University Park: Pennsylvania State University Press, 2006), pp. 201–22 (p. 206).
18. Siqueiros, 'Rivera's Counter-Revolutionary Road', p. 19.
19. Foster, p. 113.
20. Timothy Harte, *Fast Forward: The Aesthetics and Ideology of Speed in Russian Avant-Garde Culture, 1910–1930* (Madison: University of Wisconsin Press, 2010), p. 156–57.
21. El Lissitzky, *Russia: An Architecture for World Revolution*, trans. by Eric Dluhosch (Cambridge, Mass: MIT Press, 1970), p. 57–58.
22. The now destroyed *Man at the Crossroads* (1933), painted in the Rockefeller Center in New York, featured planes zooming over soldiers wearing gas masks. In 'Towards a Free Revolutionary Art' (1938), the manifesto Rivera composed with André Breton and Leon Trotsky, modern technology is identified as the weapon of 'reactionary forces'. André Breton, Diego Rivera and Leon Trotsky, 'Towards a Free Revolutionary Art', in *Theories of Modern Art: A Source Book by Artists and Critics*, ed. by Herschel Browning Chipp and Peter Selz (Berkeley, University of California Press, 1968), pp. 483–86 (p. 483).

23. Rivera, *Mi arte, mi vida*, p. 143.
24. Industrial elements are similarly visualised as an extension of the labouring male body in Estridentista Fermín Revueltas's contemporary stained glass piece *Jalando rieles* (1934).
25. Günter Berghaus, *Futurism and the Technological Imagination* (New York: Rodopi, 2009), p. 50.
26. Victoria E. Bonnell, *Iconography of Power: Soviet Political Posters Under Lenin and Stalin* (Berkeley: University of California Press, 1997), p. 75.
27. Diego Rivera, 'La obra del pintor Diego Rivera', in *Textos de arte*, pp. 118–24 (p. 118).
28. Umberto Boccioni, 'Manifesto of Futurist Sculpture', in *Futurism: An Anthology*, ed. by Lawrence S. Rainey and Christine Poggi (New Haven: Yale University Press, 2009), pp. 113–18 (p. 118).
29. Walter Benjamin, 'The Work of Art in the Age of Mechanical Reproduction', in *Illuminations*, pp. 219–54 (p. 239).
30. Gallo, p. 8.
31. Walter Benjamin, 'On Some Motifs in Baudelaire', in *Illuminations*, pp. 157–202, (p. 166, p. 177).
32. Benjamin, 'The Work of Art', p. 221–22.
33. Esther Leslie, 'Walter Benjamin: Traces of Craft', *Journal of Design History*, 11 (1998), 5–13 (p. 8).
34. Rivera, 'Los primeros murales', p. 10.
35. Benjamin, 'The Work of Art', p. 222.
36. Miriam Hansen, 'Unstable Mixtures, Dilated Spheres: Negt and Kluge's The Public Sphere and Experience, Twenty Years Later', *Public Culture*, 5 (1993), 179–212 (p. 187).
37. Juan Rulfo, *Aire de las colinas: Cartas a Clara*, ed. by Alberto Vital (Buenos Aires: Editorial Sudamericana, 2000), p. 54.
38. Stephen R. Niblo, *Mexico in the 1940s: Modernity, Politics, and Corruption* (Wilmington, Del: Scholarly Resources, 1999), p. 25.
39. Héctor Aguilar Camín and Lorenzo Meyer, *In the Shadow of the Mexican Revolution: Contemporary Mexican History, 1910–1989* (Austin: University of Texas Press, 1993), p. 163.
40. Samuel Ramos, 'La mecanización de la vida humana', *Hoy*, 20 August 1938; Samuel Ramos, *Hacia un nuevo humanismo programa de antropología filosófica* (Medellín: Canal Ramírez Antares, 1940), p. 14.
41. Paz, *El laberinto de la soledad*, p. 54.
42. Ibid., p. 54.
43. Juan Ascencio, *Un extraño en la tierra: Biografía no autorizada de Juan Rulfo* (Mexico City: Debate, 2005), p. 165.
44. Manuel Maples Arce, 'Actual No 1: Hoja de Vanguardia. Comprimido Estridentista', in *El Estridentismo: México, 1921–1927*, ed. by Luis Mario Schneider (Mexico City: UNAM, 1985), pp. 41–48 (p. 44); Diego Rivera, *Diego Rivera: Arte y revolución* (Mexico City: Consejo Nacional para la Cultura y las Artes, 1999), p. 223.
45. Rulfo, *Aire de las Colinas*, p. 284.
46. Susan Buck-Morss, 'Aesthetics and Anaesthetics: Walter Benjamin's Artwork Essay Reconsidered', in *Walter Benjamin: Critical Evaluations in Cultural Theory*, ed. by Peter Osborne (London: Routledge, 2005), pp. 291– 331 (p. 303).
47. Rulfo, *Aire de las Colinas*, p. 39.
48. Neurasthenia was still considered a valid medical condition in Mexico into the 1940s. See Samuel Ramírez Moreno, 'Concepto actual sobre la neurastenia y su patogénesis', *Medicina — Revista Mexicana*, 25 May 1940, pp. 563–80.
49. Núria Amat, *Juan Rulfo* (Barcelona: Ediciones Omega, 2003), p. 107; Antonio Alatorre, 'La persona de Juan Rulfo', *Literatura Mexicana*, 10 (1999) 225–47 (p. 231).
50. Boldy, p. 16.
51. Dan Russek, *Textual Exposures: Photography in Twentieth Century Spanish American Narrative Fiction* (Calgary: University of Calgary Press, 2015), p. 90.
52. Alberto Vital, *Palabra clave: Géneros inesperados y personajes esenciales de la literatura* (Mexico City: Taurus, 2012), p. 52.
53. Lucy Bell, 'Photography, Punctum and Shock: Re-Viewing Juan Rulfo's Short Stories', *Bulletin of Hispanic Studies*, 91 (2014), 437–52 (p. 444).

54. Felipa tickles Macario and allows him to drink her breast milk (91). Rulfo later confirmed that Macario was in his twenties. Juan Rulfo, quoted in Arthur Ramírez, 'Style and Technique in Juan Rulfo' (unpublished doctoral thesis, University of Texas at Austin, 1973), p. 117.
55. Juan Rulfo, quoted in Paulina Millán, 'A Journey Through Juan Rulfo's Photographs', in *Rethinking Juan Rulfo's Creative World*, pp. 51–65 (p. 52).
56. Benjamin, 'On Some Motifs', p. 176–77.
57. José Revueltas, 'El hijo tonto', in *Dios en la tierra* (Mexico City: Editorial Novaro, 1973), pp. 95–106 (p. 105).
58. Beatriz Urías Horcasitas, *Historias secretas del racismo en México (1920–1950)* (Mexico City: Tusquets, 2007), p. 142.
59. Buck-Morss, p. 302.
60. Benjamin, 'The Work of Art', p. 235–36.
61. Susan McCabe, *Cinematic Modernism: Modernist Poetry and Film* (Cambridge: Cambridge University Press, 2005), p. 4.
62. Benjamin, 'The Work of Art in the Age of its Technological Reproducibility', (Second Version) in *Walter Benjamin: Selected Writings, vol. 3, 1931–1938*, trans. by Rodney Livingstone, ed. by Michael W. Jennings and others (Cambridge, MA: Belknap, 2002), pp. 101–33 (p. 117).
63. Benjamin, 'On Some Motifs', p. 174.
64. Sara Danius, *The Senses of Modernism: Technology, Perception, and Aesthetics* (London: Cornell University Press, 2002), p. 3.
65. Benjamin, 'On Some Motifs', p. 177.
66. Manuel Maples Arce, *El arte mexicano moderno* (London: A. Zwemmer, 1946), p. 21; Pedro Henríquez Ureña, 'Diego Rivera', *El Mundo*, 6 July 1923, p. 3.
67. Julio Jiménez Rueda, 'El afeminamiento en la literatura mexicana', *El Universal*, 21 December 1924, n.p; Francisco Monterde, 'Existe una literatura viril', *El Universal*, 25 December 1924, n.p.
68. Oliva López Sánchez, *Enfermas, mentirosas y temperamentales: La concepción médica del cuerpo femenino durante la segunda mitad del siglo XIX en México* (Mexico City: Plaza y Valdés Editores, 1998), p. 122.
69. Gamio, p. 227–28.
70. Gabriela Mistral, *Lecturas para mujeres* (Mexico City: Porrúa, 1997); Gabriela Mistral, 'A la mujer mexicana', in *La tierra tiene la actitud de una mujer*, ed. by Pedro Pablo Zegers (Santiago de Chile: RIL Editores, 1999), pp. 129–31 (p. 129).
71. Gabriela Mistral, 'Una nueva organización del trabajo', in *La tierra tiene la actitud de una mujer*, pp. 55–58 (p. 55).
72. José Eduardo González, *Algunas consideraciones sobre eugenética* (Mexico City: Companía Editora Latino Americana, 1923), p. 94.
73. Alexandra Minna Stern, 'Responsible Mothers and Normal Children: Eugenics, Nationalism, and Welfare in Post-Revolutionary Mexico, 1920–1940', *Journal of Historical Sociology*, 12 (December 1999), 369–97 (p. 377; p. 369).
74. Patience A. Schell, 'Eugenics, Policy and Practice in Cuba, Puerto Rico, and Mexico', in *The Oxford Handbook of the History of Eugenics*, ed. by Alison Bashford and Philippa Levine (Oxford: Oxford University Press, 2010), pp. 477–92 (p. 486).
75. Ignacio Sánchez Prado, 'La destrucción de la escritura viril y el ingreso de la mujer al discurso literario: *El libro vacío y Los recuerdos del Porvenir*', *Revista de Crítica Literaria Latinoamericana*, 32 (2006), 149–67.
76. Elena Poniatowska, quoted in Consuelo Meza Márquez, *La utopía feminista: Quehacer literario de cuatro narradoras mexicanas contemporáneas* (Aguascalientes: Universidad Autónoma de Aguascalientes, 2000), p. 53.
77. Marte R. Gómez, quoted in Juan Pablo de Pina García, *Diego Rivera en los años radicales* (Chapingo: Universidad Autónoma de Chapingo, 1990), p. 42.
78. Héctor Domínguez-Ruvalcaba, *Modernity and the Nation in Mexican Representations of Masculinity: From Sensuality to Bloodshed* (New York: Palgrave Macmillan, 2007), p. 40
79. Enrique Florescano, *Imágenes de la patria a través de los siglos* (Mexico City: Santillana Ediciones Generales, 2006), p. 208. This trope features prominently in picture cards commemorating the 1910 centenary of the Independence movement.

80. In 1945 Izquierdo's contract to complete a major mural commission in the building of the Departamento del Distrito Federal was rescinded following complaints from Siqueiros and Rivera. See 'María Izquierdo vs. Los Tres Grandes', *El Nacional*, 2 October 1947.
81. Plato, *Timaeus*, trans. by Donald J. Zeyl (Indianapolis, IN: Hackett Publishing, 2000), 48e–49a.
82. Kenneth Olwig, *Landscape, Nature, and the Body Politic: From Britain's Renaissance to America's New World* (Madison: University of Wisconsin Press, 2002), p. 135.
83. Elizabeth Grosz, 'Woman, *Chora*, Dwelling', in *Gender, Space, Architecture: An Interdisciplinary Introduction*, ed. by Iain Borden and others (London: Routledge, 2002), pp. 210–22 (p. 210–11).
84. Annette Kolodny, *The Lay of the Land* (Chapel Hill: University of North Carolina Press, 1975), p. 67.
85. A noteworthy example of the use of cartography for nation-building purposes is Antonio García Cubas's *Atlas pintoresco e histórico de los Estados Unidos Mexicanos* (1885). For a detailed account of the history of cartographic practices in late nineteenth and twentieth-century Mexico, see Raymond B. Craib, *Cartographic Mexico: A History of State Fixations and Fugitive Landscapes* (Durham: Duke University Press, 2004).
86. Lynda Nead, *The Female Nude: Art, Obscenity and Sexuality* (London: Routledge, 1992), p. 6.
87. Ibid., p. 1.
88. Rivera, *Mi arte, mi vida*, p. 111.
89. Justino Fernández, *Arte moderno y contemporáneo de México* (Mexico City: UNAM, 1952), p. 328.
90. Antonio Rodríguez, *Canto a la tierra: Los murales de Diego Rivera en la capilla de Chapingo* (Chapingo: Universidad Autónoma Chapingo, 1986), p. 14.
91. Enrique Florescano, *El mito de Quetzalcoatl* (Mexico City: Fondo de Cultura Económica, 1995), p. 82.
92. Paz, 'Los muralistas a primera vista', p. 712.
93. Elizabeth Grosz, *Space, Time, and Perversion: Essays on the Politics of Bodies* (London: Routledge, 1995), p. 115.
94. Diego Rivera, quoted in Rodríguez, p. 8.
95. Grosz, 'Woman, *Chora*, Dwelling', p. 211.
96. Luis-Martín Lozano, 'Song to the Earth and Those Who Labor Thereon: Universidad Autónoma de Chapingo, Mexico, 1923–1927', in *Diego Rivera: The Complete Murals*, ed. by Luis-Martín Lozano and Juan Rafael Coronel Rivera (London: Taschen, 2008), pp. 136–45 (p. 140).
97. Rodríguez, *Canto a la tierra*, p. 14.
98. Ageeth Sluis, *Deco Body, Deco City: Female Spectacle and Modernity in Mexico City, 1900–1939* (London: University of Nebraska Press), p. 198.
99. Doreen Massey, *Space, Place and Gender* (Cambridge: Polity, 1994), p. 6.
100. Elizabeth Grosz, *Architecture from the Outside: Essays on Virtual and Real Space* (Cambridge, Mass: MIT Press, 2001), p. 159.
101. The relationship between the body aesthetics of both artists and their own corporeal experiences highlights another point of divergence. As the works mentioned here suggest, the art of the disabled Kahlo, whose injuries from a traffic accident in her youth left her unable to bear children, consistently engaged with her own physical trauma. By contrast, Rivera's Detroit murals reflect his obsession with productive, able bodies, despite the fact that he was suffering from a bout of serious ill-health and fatigue at the time of their execution.
102. Kelly Oliver, *Reading Kristeva: Unravelling the Double-bind* (Bloomington: Indiana University Press, 1993) p. 56.
103. On the grotesque in Castellanos see Nuala Finnegan, *Monstrous Projections of Femininity in the Fiction of Mexican Writer Rosario Castellanos* (Lewiston: Edwin Mellen Press, 2000).
104. Jane Lavery, 'The Physical and Textual Body in the Works of Ángeles Mastretta and Elena Poniatowska', *Romance Studies*, 19 (2001), 173–86 (p. 174).
105. Bowskill, p. 9.
106. Hind, p. 9.
107. Ibid., 81.
108. Rulfo's short stories contain multiple references to maternal and infant mortality. The mothers of Urbano in 'La noche que lo dejaron solo' and Ignacio in 'No oyes ladrar los perros' die during

childbirth while 'La vida no es muy seria en sus cosas' concludes with a pregnant woman falling down a flight of stairs. In 'Acuérdate' la Berenjena says that she has spent all her money on funerals for her children and Alcancía of 'El hombre' recalls recently burying his child.

109. Doris Sommer, *Foundational Fictions: The National Romances of Latin America* (Berkeley: University of California Press, 1991), p. 266.
110. Debra A. Castillo, *Easy Women: Sex and Gender in Modern Mexican Fiction* (Minneapolis: University of Minnesota Press, 1998), p. 16.
111. Hugo Hernán Ramírez, 'El personaje femenino en los cuentos de Juan Rulfo', *Iberoamericana: América Latina-España-Portugal*, 8 (2008), 47–63 (p. 47).
112. María Elena de Valdés, *The Shattered Mirror: Representations of Women in Mexican Literature* (Austin: University of Texas Press, 1998), p. 35.
113. De Valdés, p. 50; Megan Becker-Leckrone, *Julia Kristeva and Literary Theory* (Basingstoke: Palgrave Macmillan, 2005), p. 157.
114. Julia Kristeva, *Revolution in Poetic Language*, trans. by Margaret Waller (New York: Columbia University Press, 1974), p. 49.
115. Hind, p. 78
116. Julia Kristeva, *Desire in Language: A Semiotic Approach to Literature and Art*, ed. by Leon S. Roudiez, trans. by Thomas Gora and Alice A. Jardine (Oxford: Basil Blackwell, 1981), p. 135.
117. A similar alliterative effect is produced in Susana's recollection of caressing her own adolescent body: 'mis manos temblaban tibias al tocar mis senos' [my warm hands trembled as they touched my breasts] (p. 264).
118. Castillo, p. 63
119. Ramírez, p. 54–55.
120. William Rowe, *Rulfo, El Llano en llamas* (London: Grant & Cutler, 1987), p. 71.

CHAPTER 4

Revolutionary Redemption in the Countryside: Rural Reform and the *Campesino* Mass

One of the most progressive charters of its era, the Mexican Constitution of 1917 promised sweeping changes to rural life. Recognising the peasantry as key beneficiaries of the Revolution, Article twenty-seven affirmed the state's intention 'garantizar a la población campesina el bienestar y su participación e incorporación en el desarrollo nacional' [to guarantee the wellbeing of the rural population and its participation and inclusion in the process of national development].[1] In the 1920s, rural integration became a prominent theme in political discourse as the state, having only recently emerged from a violent civil conflict that had mobilised large sections of the peasant population, looked to establish control over the countryside. Starting in this decade, post-revolutionary national integration was pursued through a rural development programme encompassing educational and land reform that sought to bring order to the countryside, increase its productivity and nationalise its inhabitants. The Catholic Church, profoundly integrated into the social fabric of rural life, posed the largest obstacle to this project of revolutionary reform. Although the Constitution had brought the Revolution's armed phase to a close, its anti-clerical provisions reignited Mexico's longest-standing institutional conflict. In the eyes of the modernising state, Catholicism fostered fanaticism, alcoholism and other social pathologies that obstructed the nation's path to revolutionary progress. In order to establish itself as the primary arbiter of national values, the state increasingly challenged the Church for control over Mexican hearts and minds during the 1920s and 1930s. While the Obregón administration refrained from reinforcing the Constitution's more radical provisions to maintain stability during the early reconstruction years, Calles's staunchly anti-clerical stance significantly heightened Church-State tensions, ultimately culminating in the Catholic Cristero revolt of 1926.

Before examining how rural reform was implemented through the government's education and agrarian programmes of the 1920s and 1930s, it is necessary to first provide an overview of the complex and contradictory links that developed between religion and revolutionary politics during these decades. In addition to its anti-clerical policies, which dramatically restricted the Church's social and political authority, the state looked to symbolically supplant institutionalised religion by appropriating Christian rituals, rhetoric and imagery to construct a new revolutionary creed as an alternative source of national identity and cohesion. Borrowing the phrase coined by French historian Mona Ozouf, Guillermo Palacios and Adrian Bantjes argue that the post-revolutionary period witnessed a 'transfer of sacrality' which saw politicians and intellectuals adopt Catholic rites and concepts in an attempt to exploit their unifying capacity and symbolic power as constitutive elements of national identity.[2] The state's appropriation of religious frameworks to articulate its secular political agenda again highlights the continuity of Porfirian practices into the post-revolutionary period. As Acevedo and Ramírez explain, during the Díaz regime:

> Se sustituye deliberada y conscientemente el catolicismo, que había fungido como el gran cohesionador de la identidad patria, por una nueva religión, con sus figuras fundadoras y sus santos, sus rituales y liturgias y sus oficiantes: lo que Justo Sierra, usando un término de uso corriente llamaba, 'la religión de la patria'.[3]
>
> [Catholicism, which had served as the great unifier of national identity, was deliberately and consciously replaced by a new religion with its own founding figures, saints, rituals, liturgies and celebrants: what Justo Sierra, using the commonly used term, described as 'the religion of the homeland'.]

After 1920, a new revolutionary religion was forged along similar lines through the mythification of political saints and the construction of a secular moral doctrine founded on the revolutionary tenets of hard work and patriotism. The 1930s saw the implementation of a 'calendario nacionalista' [nationalist calendar] that replaced traditional saints' days with revolutionary anniversaries and the introduction of new civic rituals such as Domingos Culturales [Cultural Sundays] and Domingos Rojos [Red Sundays].[4] In the countryside, educational and agrarian propaganda drew heavily from Christian vocabularies to portray state intervention as a crusade of revolutionary redemption. Labour leader Lombardo Toledano upheld agrarian reform as the realisation of the Gospels, while government propaganda presented the state agronomist as a Christ-like arbiter of rural justice. In an attempt to challenge the Church's grip on rural education, which had been strengthened by the church-state détente during the Porfiriato, the SEP dispatched so-called 'missionary teachers' to remote rural communities to disseminate the state's secular doctrine.

Religious rhetoric appealed to revolutionary reformers looking to communicate their secular societal vision in the countryside for several reasons. As religion constituted the primary cultural framework through which much of the population understood the world, the universal intelligibility of Christian vocabularies and their affective appeal proved attractive to post-revolutionary nation-builders looking to secure popular consent.[5] Due to the cultural dominance of the Church and its longstanding influence on education, even non-believers were familiar with the basic tenets of Christianity.[6] Additionally, by recasting the Revolution within a Christian schema, official rhetoric tapped into the codes of obedience embedded in the Roman Catholic mentality and looked to redirect this unquestioning faith toward state as the sole interpreter of 'los sagrados intereses de la Revolución' [the sacred interests of the Revolution], as Obregón put it.[7] Biblical metaphors were selectively incorporated into official propaganda to project the state as the saviour of the rural masses and thus encourage an attitude of political passivity on the part of the latter.

While the post-revolutionary political appropriation of Christian rhetoric has been examined by historians such as Bantjes and Ilene O'Malley, the use of religious symbolism in artistic representations of revolutionary reform in the countryside has not yet been comprehensively explored. By analysing a range of media including murals, illustrations, literature and film, the final chapter will begin to fill this gap in scholarship by examining how Rivera and Rulfo employ biblical metaphors and religious concepts to visualise the *campesino* collective in the context of the post-revolutionary educational and agrarian projects. These readings provide a new and illuminating perspective from which to trace the state's evolving relationship with the rural peasantry. Analysing Rivera's mural *El reparto de tierras* (1924) alongside *La fórmula secreta* (1965), the experimental film on which Rulfo collaborated with the director Rubén Gámez, the second section of the chapter examines how both artists conceptualise the peasant collective as a political entity in light of the Christianised rhetoric associated with post-revolutionary agrarianism. Before undertaking this analysis, the first part of the chapter positions Rivera and Rulfo at endpoints of a spectrum of evolving visual and textual representations of the *campesino* mass and the federal teacher from the late 1920s to the early 1950s. In these readings, I explore how Rivera and Rulfo exploit biblical images to convey the peasantry's acceptance or rejection of the state's civilising intervention in the countryside. Although they have not yet been analysed in detail, these metaphors were integral to post-revolutionary discourses of educational reform. Using previously unexamined archival materials, I consider a selection of Rivera's state-commissioned illustrations from the late 1920s alongside the textual and iconographic content of the SEP's contemporary rural publications to explore how these works mobilise biblical metaphors of enlightenment and sowing to portray collective *campesino* bodies as a receptacle to be illuminated or a landscape to be cultivated by revolutionary ideology. Turning to Rulfo's fictional account of the experiences of a post-revolutionary rural educator in the short story 'Luvina', I demonstrate how the writer grotesquely reconfigures the same metaphors, using physical descriptions of the peasantry and the teacher to illustrate the failure of the state's enlightening mission.

Part I: Enlightening and Cultivating the Peasantry: The Rural Educational Crusade

As successive administrations focused on education as a crucial site for the dissemination of revolutionary ideology during the 1920s and 30s, the traditionally religious sphere of the classroom became a key battlefield in which the state waged its modernising war against the Catholic Church. Although the Revolution was hailed as a moment of profound societal transformation in its immediate aftermath, widespread illiteracy prevented Mexico from taking its place alongside the world's modern nations. For the Ateneístas, the cultural and aesthetic enlightenment of the masses constituted an integral aspect of Mexico's revolutionary, spiritual transformation. As Pedro Henríquez Ureña declared in 1924:

> Para el pueblo, en fin, la Revolución ha sido una transformación espiritual. No es sólo que se le brinden mayores oportunidades de educarse, es que el pueblo ha descubierto que posee derechos, y entre ellos el derecho de educarse [...] ha comenzado a brillar una luz de esperanza.[8]
>
> [For the people, the Revolution has, in short, been a spiritual transformation. It has not only provided them with greater opportunities to educate themselves, but the people have discovered that they have rights and that one of those is the right to be educated... A light of hope has started to shine.]

The civilising discourses of the Ateneo translated into official educational policy during Vasconcelos's term at the SEP. Drawing inspiration from the educational campaign of the People's Commissar for Enlightenment Anatoly Lunacharsky, Vasconcelos organised literary gatherings and disseminated thousands of free copies of 'classic' works by Plato, Dante and Tolstoy.[9] Vasconcelos also followed Lunacharsky in using Christian terminology to articulate his didactic vision.[10] Modelling their efforts on the civilising work of the sixteenth-century Spanish friars, the Minister hailed federal educators as 'los iniciadores de una cruzada de educación pública, los inspiradores de un entusiasmo cultural semejante al fervor que ayer ponía nuestra raza en las empresas de la religión y la conquista' [the originators of a public education crusade, who are inspiring a cultural enthusiasm similar to the zeal with which our race once dedicated itself to the enterprises of religion and conquest].[11] Following his call in 1922 for teachers to join the Ministry's 'santa cruzada contra la ignorancia' [holy crusade against ignorance], so-called 'missionary teachers' were dispatched to remote communities around the country to preach the government's modernising message.[12] Vasconcelos's emphasis on the redemptive power of public education validated state intervention in the countryside by presenting the rural school as the peasantry's only hope of liberation from a life of ignorance and poverty.

With the assistance of his Minister of Public Education, José Manuel Puig Casauranc, Calles continued to expand rural education during the mid-to-late 1920s, looking to transform peasants into functional citizens through an emphasis on secularism, scientific knowledge, hygiene, productivity and practical skills. In this emphasis on collective progress and self-improvement, post-revolutionary educational reform again drew from nineteenth-century models. Following the secular educational vision of his liberal predecessor Gabino Barreda, Porfirian Científico Justo Sierra approached education from a Spencerian evolutionary perspective, stressing its role in individual and societal development. Instrumental in shaping the outlook of socialist education during the 1930s was Narciso Bassols, Minister of Public Education between 1931 and 1934, who claimed that the rural school held as its 'finalidad más trascendente crear, multiplicar y robustecer mejores tipos humanos' [most transcendent purpose, the creation, multiplication and strengthening of improved human types].[13] Like many contemporary reformers, Bassols considered popular religion a threat to public health: religious festivals were seen to promote alcoholism, venereal disease was blamed on a lack of access to sex education and poor hygiene was attributed to the use of traditional medicines and therapies, predominantly by rural women.[14] During this period, the classroom thus became an ideological battleground in which state educators struggled against the Church, not only for the hearts and minds of rural Mexicans, but also for their bodies.

Evolving from the Vasconcelian model of the *maestro misionero*, the iconography and metaphoric language of the SEP's rural educational publications of the early 1930s portrayed federal educators as divine messengers of scientific knowledge. Among these magazines was the bimonthly *El maestro rural* (*MR*), first published in 1932 under the editorial direction of Salvador Novo, a leading member of the Contemporáneos movement. Aimed at rural teachers and peasants who had reaped the benefits of the state's literacy initiatives, *MR* looked to establish a direct channel of communication between state-affiliated intellectuals, teachers and the rural population. Alongside articles on modern farming techniques and basic lessons in hygiene and symptomatology, a number of poems and articles published in the magazine present the rural teacher as a Christ-like figure who redeems the rural masses by disseminating knowledge of modern science and technology. While poems such as 'Himno a las comunidades infantiles escolares' and 'Los apóstoles modernos' praise the work of these 'incansables sembradores de la ciencia' [tireless sowers of science] shining the light of reason upon Mexico's darkest villages, hygiene guidelines imparted by federal educators are presented as 'Los doce mandamientos de la higiene' [the Twelve Commandments of Hygiene].[15]

Visual Metaphors of Enlightenment in Rivera's Illustrations

Educational publications such as *MR* enjoyed a strong iconographic component thanks to contributions from prominent post-revolutionary visual artists such as Leopoldo Méndez, Fermín Revueltas and Ezequiel Negrete. Although somewhat eclipsed by his career as a muralist, Rivera was also a prolific illustrator, producing hundreds of images for government-funded textbooks and pamphlets and countless magazines including *MR*, *El Maestro*, *El libertador*, *El Bonete*, *El sembrador*, *Crisol*, *Revista de Revistas*, *Azulejos* and the bi-monthly *Mexican Folkways*, edited by Frances Toor. Rivera's largest, but almost completely unknown, illustration commission was to decorate the published proceedings of the conventions held by the Liga de Comunidades Agrarias y Sindicatos Campesinos in the state of Tamaulipas between 1926 and 1928. Founded in 1926 by the Governor of Tamaulipas Emilio Portes Gil and the agronomist Marte R. Gómez, the conventions assembled delegates from across the state to discuss the progress of agrarian and educational reform in their respective communities. Gómez, who had previously commissioned the Chapingo fresco cycle, invited Rivera to illustrate the convention's proceedings to make the printed text more accessible to its semi-literate rural audience.[16] Rivera attended the annual conventions between 1926 and 1928 and produced 133 images to illustrate

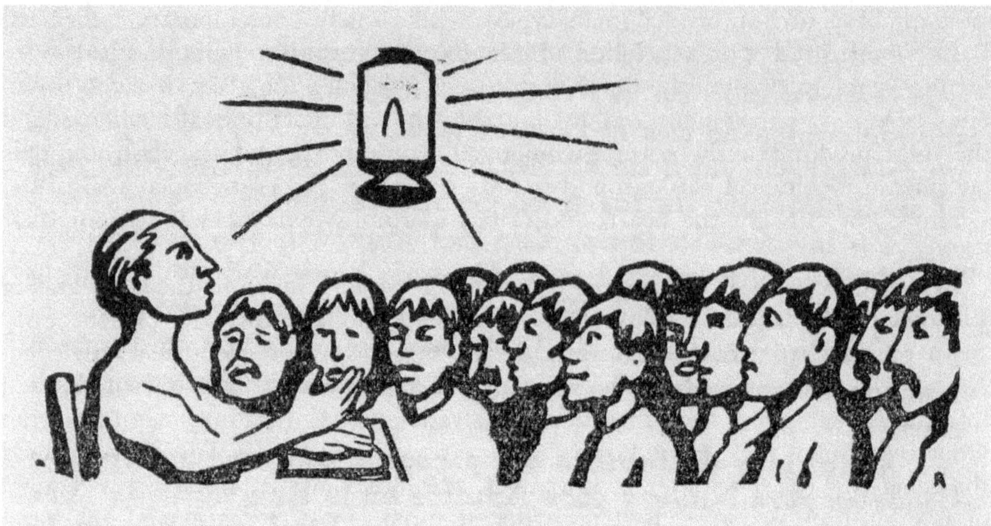

Fig. 4.1. Diego Rivera, Illustration in *Tercera convención de la Liga de Comunidades Agrarias y Sindicatos Campesinos del Estado de Tamaulipas* (1928) © Banco de México Diego Rivera Frida Kahlo Museums Trust, Mexico, D.F. / DACS 2021

the three printed volumes. Despite the apparent simplicity of their style and composition, closer examination of these early illustrations reveals how they draw from a complex network of biblical images to visually communicate the religious metaphors embedded in the text.

Although an active supporter of the government's post-revolutionary secularisation campaign, religion played a formative role in Rivera's early life. His mother, María del Pilar Barrientos, was a strict Catholic who enrolled her son in a string of Catholic schools. However, as with many of his aspects of Rivera's public persona, his faith remained ambiguous. After a prolonged period of atheism, in 1956 Rivera erased the words 'Dios no existe' [God does not exist] from his mural at the Hotel del Prado and unexpectedly declared himself Catholic. Rivera's immersion in Renaissance Christian art as a student in Italy during the early 1920s provided him with a rich source of scriptural metaphors and iconographic motifs that would continue to inform his visual language in the subsequent decades. This influence is strikingly revealed in an illustration produced by the artist for the proceedings of the League's 1928 conference (Fig. 4.1). Here, Rivera incorporates biblical metaphors of light to portray the rural teacher as a Christ-like embodiment of the 'Word' of the Revolution. The accompanying report from the delegate of San José de Santa Engracia records that:

> En el mes de febrero del presente año se fundaron las Escuelas para Niños y para Adultos en la Ranchería de 'Las Enramadas', de nuestro ejido, en un local que ha venido adaptándose con fondos de los ejidatarios de ese lugar [...] La escuela cuenta con su lámpara de gasolina y a ella están asistiendo casi todos los ejidatarios del lugar.[17]

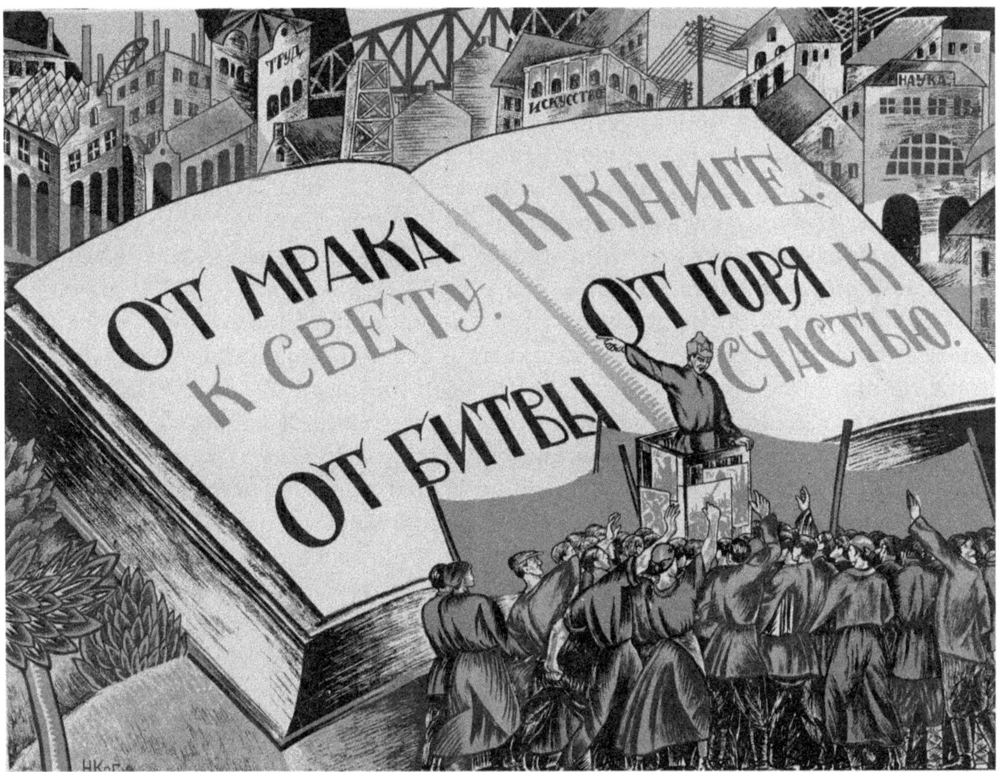

FIG. 4.2. Nikolai Kogout, *From Darkness into Light; from Battle to Books; from Misery to Happiness* (1921), Russian and Soviet posters and postcards collection, British Library

> [In February of this year the Schools for Children and Adults were founded in the settlement of 'Las Enramadas' in a premises located on our communal land that has been adapted using funds from the local land shareholders... The school has a gasoline lamp and almost all of the local land shareholders are attending.]

Although the text simply describes the installation of an electric light in the local school, Rivera's illustration converts the lamp into a divine symbol of revolutionary enlightenment. Positioned above the written report, the illustration portrays a rural teacher seated before an open book as he addresses a group of *campesinos* whose bodies are engulfed by beams of light radiating from an oversized lamp overhead. The elevated position of the teacher and his refined features, which contrast with the dishevelled and almost primitive appearance of the peasants assembled below, indicates his moral superiority and embodiment of the state's civilising values. The posture of the *maestro* is strikingly reminiscent of early Christian depictions of Christ. In such images, the codex held in Christ's left hand represents the written dogma of God, while his raised right hand denotes the spoken word of God.[18] Rivera's appropriation of this speech gesture and inclusion of the open book, a common symbol of the Bible, directly substitutes Christ as the imparter of God's wisdom with the rural teacher as the interpreter of revolutionary ideology. Given that the illustration was published a year after Rivera's first trip to Moscow, it is worth noting the similarities between these iconographic components and the visual vocabularies of Soviet socialist propaganda. In a pro-literacy poster from 1921 designed by Nikolai Kogout (Fig. 4.2), the image of a Red Army representative addressing a crowd from a pulpit against the backdrop of a giant open book conflates religious and revolutionary instruction.[19] The text imprinted on the open pages reads: 'From darkness to light, From the battle to the book', with the opening line 'От мрака к свету', recalling the well-known Russian proverb 'learning is light and ignorance is darkness'.[20]

The relationship between light, vision and enlightenment constitutes the most striking symbolic feature of Rivera's illustration. As in much religious imagery, the function of the gaze is particularly significant in this piece. While the teacher looks upward towards the lamp, indicating the divine source of his words, the eyes of the peasants remain fixed upon his face. Their slight upward gaze and the elevated position of the teacher echoes the compositional structure of proto-Renaissance and Renaissance depictions of Christ and his followers such as Giotto's and Pietro Perugino's interpretations of *The Ascension of Christ*, which portray Christ levitating above his awe-struck apostles. This interplay of gazes and the prominence of the lamp within the illustration suggests links with corporeal scriptural metaphors relating to the transmission and internalisation of divine wisdom. A powerful symbolic bond between light, sight and knowledge is established in the Gospel of John, where the ability to physically perceive light and see Jesus is equated with the perception of God's wisdom. This dualistic system based on the concepts of light and darkness, sight and blindness, provides the framework for numerous biblical images conveying Christ's power to 'enlighten the eyes' of his followers.[21] The lamp is particularly significant within this symbolic network as it represents the human eye as the point of entry for divine light into the body. This idea is expressed in 'The Sermon on the Mount' from Matthew's Gospel: 'the eye is the lamp of the body. If your eyes are healthy, your whole body will be full of light. But if your eyes are unhealthy, your whole body will be full of darkness'.[22] Here, the interlinked images of the lamp and the human eye convey the listener's receptiveness to and internalisation of God's Word. These concepts of sight, knowledge and salvation are visually intertwined in Rivera's illustration where vision is directly linked to intellectual and political illumination. The direction of the peasants' gaze towards the teacher and their illumination by the lamp's radiance suggest that their bodies have successfully absorbed the light of revolutionary ideology. The linking of visual perception and enlightenment is particularly fitting given the illustration's didactic function. Rivera's attempt to produce a pictorial language that would render the written content of the published proceedings accessible to a rural audience was consistent with his view of visual art as a powerful tool for communicating and comprehending revolutionary ideals.

Examining this illustration alongside the written entries of the League's proceedings demonstrates how it visually articulates the biblical metaphors of sight and enlightenment used by rural reformers to describe the federal education programme. Magdaleno Aguilar, the League's secretary, insists on the need to

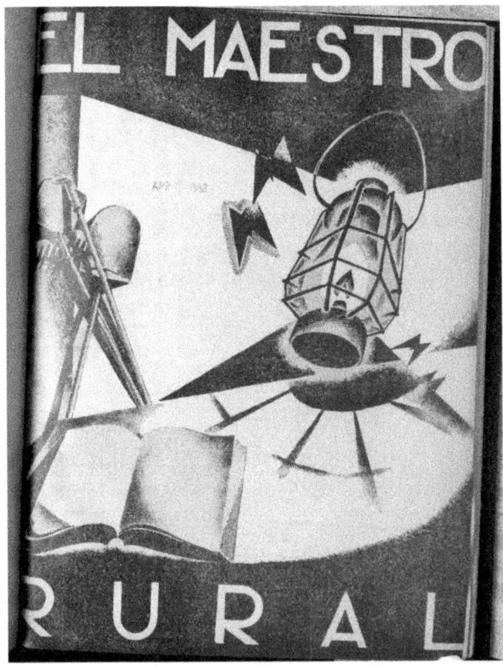

FIG. 4.3. Unknown artist, Cover illustration for *El maestro rural* (April 1933)

'llevar la luz a las conciencias' [illuminate their consciences], while its director Miguel Martínez Rojo praises federal educators for redeeming the 'obscuros campesinos' [dark peasants] by exposing them to 'la luz de la ciencia' [the light of science].[23] Textual and visual images linking revolutionary education with light also recur in editions of *MR* from the early 1930s. Recalling the cover illustration of the April 1933 edition, which depicts a lamp shining onto an open book and a collection of farming tools (Fig. 4.3), Francisco Monterde, writing in the September issue of that year, predicts that state-approved textbooks will 'alumbrar un poco las tinieblas en que han vivido sus hermanos del campo' [illuminate a little the darkness in which our rural brothers have lived].[24] Like Rivera, Argentine socialist writer Álvaro Yunque appears to draw from the imagery of Matthew in his poem 'Sé como este farol' (Fig. 4.4), featured in the May edition of 1932 alongside two images of beaming lamps:

Útil, venciendo sombras, yergue
su testa de cristal;
Y en su interior, como una idea,
Lirio hecho luz, brillando está.
¡Erguido y útil!... ¿Quién me grita
'sé como este farol?
¡'Sé un cristal límpido por fuera
Y haya una luz en tu interior'![25]

[Useful, vanquishing shadows, it holds up
its head of glass;

SE COMO ESTE FAROL . . .

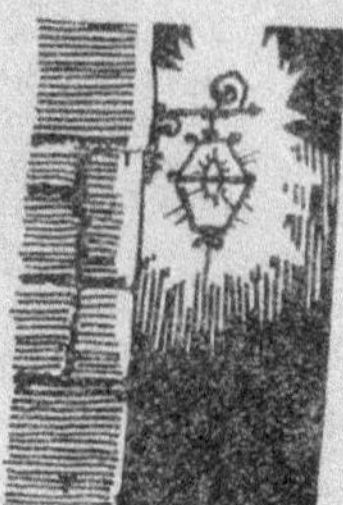

Util, venciendo sombras, yergue
su testa de cristal;
y en su interior, como una idea,
lirio hecho luz, brillando está.
¡Erguido y útil!. . . ¿Quién me grita
"sé como este farol"?
"¡Sé un cristal límpido por fuera
y haya una luz en tu interior!"

Alvaro YUNQUE.

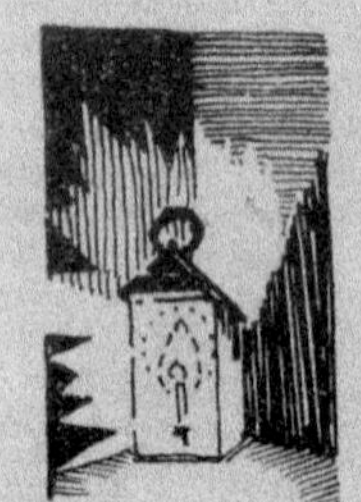

Fig. 4.4. Álvaro Yunque, 'Sé como este farol', *El maestro rural* (May 1932) Biblioteca Gregorio Torres Quintero, Universidad Pedagógica Nacional, Mexico City

And inside, like an idea,
A lily converted into light, it is shining.
Upright and useful!... Who calls to me to
'Be like this lamp'?
'Be pristine glass on the outside
And inside, let there be a light!']

The Rural Teacher as Sower: Cultivating the Peasantry

Like Rivera's illustration, these visual and poetic images draw from metaphors of divine radiance to describe the transfer of revolutionary ideology from the *maestro* to the peasant community. This idea was integral to another scriptural motif that featured prominently in educational discourses of the 1920s and 30s. The 'Parable of the Sower' (Matthew 13:1–23) describes the transmission of divine knowledge in agricultural terms by presenting Christ as a sower who plants the seed of the Word in the human heart. Like the healthy eyes described in Matthew 6:22–23, which absorb and emit divine light like a lamp, the softened heart is presented as an organ of receptiveness that provides conditions for the seed of God's wisdom to germinate.[26] Exploiting its universal accessibility to an agrarian audience, promoters of rural reform appropriated the parable to describe the successful fertilisation of peasants' hearts by revolutionary education. In the early 1920s, the pedagogical metaphor of the sower was employed by architects of the burgeoning educational program such as Vasconcelos and Mistral.[27] The parable surfaces again in the speeches delivered by Portes Gil and Aguilar at the League's 1926 convention. Portes Gil affirms that 'deseamos sembrar en cada corazón de tamaulipeco la simiente de la escuela moderna que rompe los moldes de la sociedad opresora del capitalismo' [we wish to sow in the heart of every Tamaulipan the seed of the modern school which breaks the moulds of oppressive capitalist society], while Aguilar establishes a direct parallel between the cultivation of the land and that of rural minds: 'Debemos seguir [...] dedicándonos empeñosamente al cultivo de nuestras parcelas y al cultivo de nuestras inteligencias' [We must continue... to devote ourselves resolutely to the cultivation of our plots and the cultivation of our intelligence].[28]

Rivera incorporates the parable of the sower into his illustrations for both the League's published proceedings and the children's reader *Fermín Lee*, which was published by the SEP in 1928. In the opening illustration for the third session of the 1926 convention, Rivera depicts a male figure striding across a ploughed field and scattering seeds from a satchel slung across his waist. Although the sower's face is concealed from the viewer, imbuing him with a somewhat mystical aura, his traditional peasant clothing, *sombrero* and ammunition belt clearly codify him as a rural revolutionary. The sower casts a handful of seeds that fall in an arc across the centre of the image, while another man in almost identical clothing inspects the terrain further ahead. Although Rivera provides no title for this illustration, its iconographic similarities with earlier visual representations of the parable confirm its biblical source. Consistent with the pictorial scheme adopted by nineteenth-century artists such as Vincent Van Gogh and Sir John Everett Millais, Rivera depicts the sower scattering seeds with his right hand as swooping birds threaten to intercept them.

Rivera produced a remarkably similar illustration (Fig. 4.5) for the SEP primary school textbook *Fermín Lee* (1928), written by Manuel Velázquez Andrade, a prominent pedagogue and pioneer of physical education during the late Porfirian and early post-revolutionary eras. The book was selected by the Calles administration to front its rural literacy campaign which sought to dissociate literacy from religion by promoting reading as a modern and nationalist exercise.[29] The narrative focuses on the young protagonist Fermín, who grows up during the conflict's armed phase and comes to embody the revolutionary values of hard work, patriotism and sobriety. Rivera's illustration of the sower, inserted mid-way through the book, could thus be interpreted as a visual metaphor for the text itself in its efforts to cultivate a revolutionary consciousness in young readers. Employing the same minimalist composition as the previous drawing, Rivera portrays a man dressed in traditional peasant clothing striding across a freshly ploughed field with his back to the viewer. Once again, the sower's right hand scatters the seeds, which fall in an arc over a diving bird. While Rivera's illustration is largely consistent with earlier interpretations of the parable, he diverges from the iconographic tradition by including a second man to the right of the sower who spurs two oxen with a plough. As ploughing is not an explicit image in the biblical parable, based on the notion that hearers of the Gospel are free to receive or reject the Word of God, the modification is significant. In the Old Testament, the metaphor of the plough expresses the act of softening one's own heart to receive the Word of God, as seen in Christ's plea to his listeners in Jeremiah 4:3 to 'plough up the hard ground of your hearts'. As the softened terrain of the heart will inevitably receive the seeds of divine knowledge, Rivera's inclusion of the plough predetermines a successful outcome for the parable.

Rivera's illustrations lend visual expression to a motif that remained profoundly interwoven into the iconographic and textual content of the SEP's rural publications

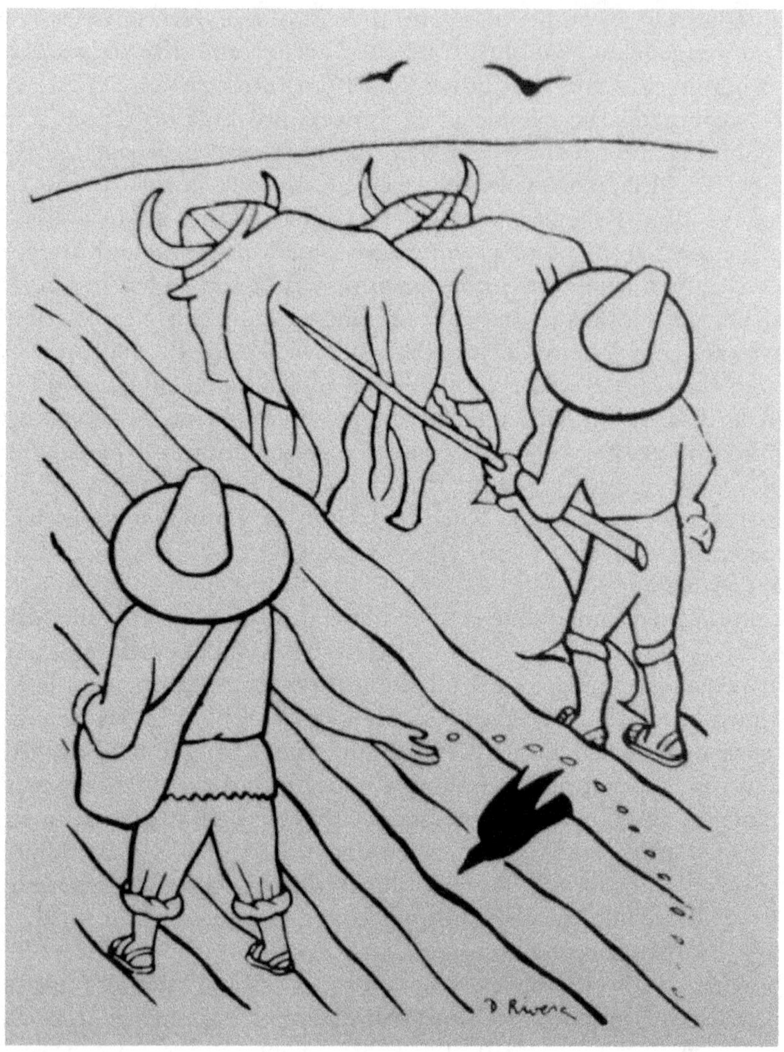

FIG. 4.5. Diego Rivera, Illustration in *Fermín Lee* by Manuel Velázquez Andrade (1928) © Banco de México Diego Rivera Frida Kahlo Museums Trust, Mexico, D.F. / DACS 2021, Memorial Library, University of Wisconsin-Madison

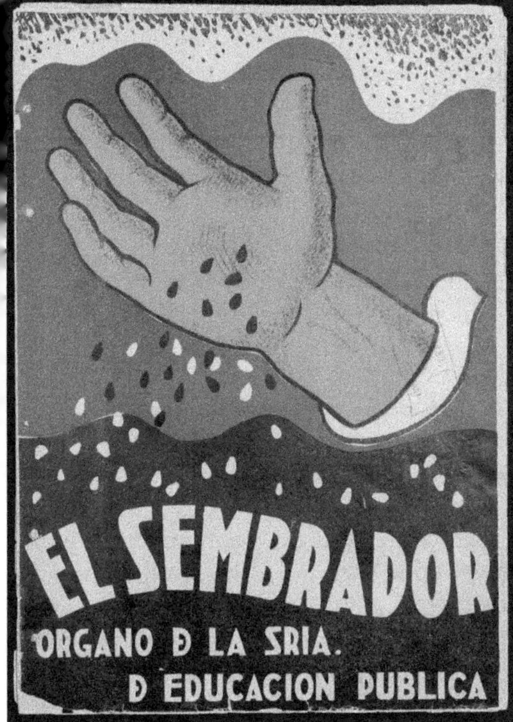

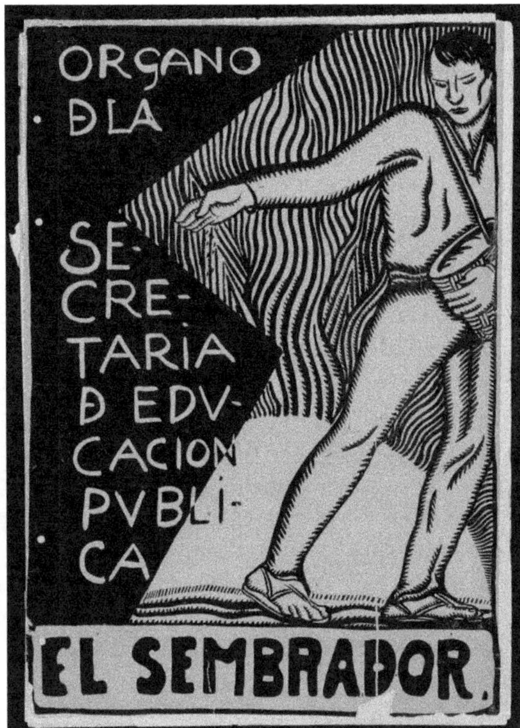

FIGS. 4.6 and 4.7. Unknown artist(s), Cover illustrations for *El sembrador* (April and May 1929), Benson Latin American Collection, LLILAS Benson Latin American Studies and Collections, The University of Texas at Austin

of the late 1920s and 1930s. This is most immediately evident in the titles of readers such as the fortnightly *El sembrador*, founded by the SEP in 1929, and the *Simiente* (1935) textbooks which were distributed as part of the Cardenista literacy campaign. The cover images for the first edition of *Simiente* and the readers published in 1939 as part of the *Serie SEP*, another series of Cárdenas-era textbooks, clarify the metaphorical significance of the motif by establishing a visual parallel between the labour of the rural teacher and that of the sower. In illustrator Julio de la Fuente's cover image for the 1935 editions of *Simiente*, children are shown listening attentively to federal educators while a figure almost identical to those depicted by Rivera sows the surrounding ploughed fields. The image of a sower or disembodied hand scattering seeds also adorns at least two covers of *El sembrador* (Fig. 4.6; Fig. 4.7), a magazine which, like *MR*, placed a strong emphasis on promoting hygiene and entrusted the rural teacher with the task of communicating such ideas to local communities.[30] As in Rivera's illustration, the identification of the right hand as the active hand in these examples from 1929 endows the sower with an air of divine authority.

The metaphor also recurs in literary contributions to *MR*, where the rural teacher is presented as a sower of scientific knowledge in the countryside. The author of 'Los apóstoles modernos', a poem included in the October 1932 edition, hails

Mexico's rural educators as 'sembradores incansables (de) todo germen de progreso' [tireless sowers of every seed of progress].[31] Such comparisons persist into the following decade. In Ángel Cifuentes's poem 'El maestro rural', published in 1940, the heroic teacher scatters grains symbolising 'La letra' [the Word] which liberate the peasants from the forces of 'negro fanatismo' [black fanaticism].[32] Elsewhere, the harvesting metaphor of the parable is used to envision the imagined fruits of the teacher's labour. One anonymous writer praises the teacher who is 'honrado y amoroso con los niños para que fructifiquen como esas tiernas y solitarias espigas' [honourable and loving with the children so that they may bear fruit like those tender and solitary sprigs of wheat], while collective peasant bodies are similarly compared to cultivated crops in the poem 'El maíz', where the pearly white teeth of the 'blessed' smiling peasants are likened to grains of corn.[33]

These poetic descriptions comparing the peasants' bodies to thriving crops draw attention to the corporeal implications of the sower parable in the context of the rural education programme. Articles published in *El sembrador* and *MR*, as well as the reports and speeches included in the proceedings of the Tamaulipas conventions, emphasise the need for rural schools to address poor nutrition and hygiene, lack of exercise and other factors that might encourage the bodily, mental and spiritual degeneration of the peasant class.[34] Considered in this context, the use of the parable to describe the work of the rural school can be linked to a network of metaphors relating to cultivation, harvesting and weeding that had been employed to explain both hereditarian and environmentalist neo-Lamarckian theories of racial improvement in Europe and the United States during the early twentieth century.[35] For example, using a remarkably similar image to those analysed in this chapter, a poster produced by the London Eugenics Society in 1930 stressed the importance of good stock by urging the public to sow 'the healthy seed'. More popular in Latin America was a Lamarckian perspective that emphasised the role of environmental factors in bringing about changes in both plants and humans.[36] A prominent proponent of this line of thought at the turn of the century was Luther Burbank, a Californian botanist who was admired by both Rivera and Kahlo and memorialised in two of their works: *Allegory of California* (1931) and *Portrait of Luther Burbank* (1930), respectively. In *The Training of the Human Plant* (1907), Burbank explained how children, like plants, could be cultivated by improving external factors such as sunshine, fresh air and improved nutrition.[37]

Following their nineteenth-century predecessors, post-revolutionary reformers acknowledged the role of both environmental and biological factors in influencing physical and mental evolution and looked to education and public health as the most effective means of eradicating sources of racial decline.[38] This continuity is reflected in the harvesting metaphors used by hygienicists during both the Porfirian and post-revolutionary periods to explain the relative importance of both the quality of the seed and the terrain in producing a healthy human crop. Writing in the late 1880s, Samuel Morales Pereira argued that: 'El hombre, como las plantas, es el producto de la semilla y de un terreno: las malas condiciones del terreno o de la semilla producen plantas enfermizas que duran poco' [Men, like plants, are the product of a seed and a plot of land: poor land or a poor seed will produce unhealthy plants that will soon perish].[39] The analogy persists in medical journals of the 1920s and 30s. Ángel Zimbrón of the *Revista Mexicana de Ciencias Médicas* insists that Mexicans of all ages represent 'campo propicio para sembrar la semilla de la higiene' [favourable land in which to sow the seed of hygiene] and as such are capable of bearing 'el fruto de la salud' [the fruit of health], while Dr Fermín Viniegra, writing in *Pasteur*, uses the same metaphor to explain the importance of infant hygiene: 'una buena semilla en terreno infecundo nace y se desarrolla mal; en cambio, hasta un mal gérmen en un buen terreno prospera y llega a adquirir las cualidades esenciales de la vida' [a good seed planted in infertile earth is born and develops badly; whereas, even a bad seed planted in good earth thrives and comes to acquire the essential qualities of life].[40] Considered alongside these analogies, the sower motif that surfaces in Rivera's illustrations and contemporary visual and textual sources relating to educational reform can be linked more specifically to the programme's hygiene concerns. While Rivera's illustrations do not directly depict the peasantry, this broader constellation of metaphors allows us to read the landscape as representative of a collective *campesino* body that through proper cultivation can be converted into a robust crop.

By the 1940s, bucolic metaphors of the peasantry flourishing under state cultivation jarred with the stark realities of the state's rural educational campaign. From the outset, the project struggled to bridge the vast cultural and ideological differences between educators and students. As most federal teachers hailed from urban backgrounds, they were often ignorant of local conditions and struggled to effectively communicate with the peasants, whom they viewed as atavistic and degenerate. They were also severely underqualified to act as modernising agents in the countryside. Although rural teachers were expected to perform the duties of educator, physician and agronomist, Engracia Loyo estimates that during the Calles administration only half had completed their primary education.[41] While regional responses varied significantly, educators were generally greeted with a suspicious or hostile response from locals who viewed schooling as a disruption to their work routines and resented government directives relating to fanaticism, recreation and hygiene. As Gillingham and Smith have noted, the implementation of state policies was not a process of unidirectional imposition, but one of negotiation and accommodation involving various conflictive social groups.[42] According to Butler, in the 1920s peasants in Michoacán often refused to attend the schools, feigned ignorance of the Revolution or intentionally flaunted their 'defiantly Catholic, "unrevolutionary" culture'.[43] The enforcement of secular education provoked significant, often armed resistance during the 1920s, fomenting a tense atmosphere that ultimately culminated in 1926 in the eruption of the Cristero War between the state and rebel Catholic groups. During this chaotic and bloody confrontation, federal repression of the rebels stirred Cristero sympathies in certain communities who retaliated by driving out SEP teachers. Rural hostility towards federal educators persisted during the 1930s in the form of assaults, kidnappings and murders.[44] Faced with strenuous popular opposition, socialist education was in retreat by the 1940s.

The *Maestro Rural* as Failed Sower in Rulfo's 'Luvina'

Growing up during the Cristero revolt in Jalisco, a focal point of the conflict, Rulfo witnessed first-hand the violent peasant response to the state's anticlerical restrictions and secular education programme. Rulfo was personally traumatised by the conflict, which claimed the lives of both his father and uncle, and as a result was highly critical of its reactionary fanatical leaders.[45] Religion also played an influential role in Rulfo's early education. Although he would subsequently reject Catholicism, the writer entered the Orfanatorio Luis Silva in 1927 and spent two years in the Seminario Conciliar del Señor San José from 1933 to 1935 at the encouragement of his grandmother, who believed he would make a good priest.[46] Following his move to the capital Rulfo also attended lectures delivered at the UNAM by Vicente Lombardo Toledano and Antonio Caso, who had engaged in a heated public polemic on the issue of socialist education in 1933. Rulfo's writings of the 1950s reflect his religious upbringing and exposure to both the violent conflicts and intellectual debates that emerged in response to the state's secular education programme. In his fictional account of the post-revolutionary educational programme in the short story 'Luvina', Rulfo reconfigures the metaphors of light and sowing in his physical descriptions of the teacher and the peasants to communicate the failure of the state's enlightening mission. While the dull and deficient eyes of Luvina's inhabitants indicate their failure to assimilate the teacher's words, parallels between their diseased bodies and the decay of the natural landscape invert the pedagogical metaphor of the sower, conveying their resistance to the state's modernising message. It is noteworthy that, like Rivera, Rulfo foregrounds a male rural teacher in this text. Given that the *maestra rural* features prominently in works by Rivera and other artists of the 1920s and 30s such as Aurora Reyes and Alfredo Zalce, and later in films like *Río Escondido* (1948), the decision of both artists to present the federal educator as male supports the view that their representations seek to evoke the figure of Christ the Sower.

'Luvina' centres around the first-person monologue of an anonymous former rural teacher who relates his harrowing experience of working in the village of San Juan Luvina to a mute interlocutor in an unidentified bar. 'Luvina' can be situated alongside other disturbing literary portraits of the rural teacher from the late 1930s onwards, such as Mauricio Magdaleno's *El resplandor* (1937), Enrique Othón Díaz's *S.F.Z.–33 Escuela* (1938), Martín Luis Guzmán's story 'Maestros rurales' (1938) and Revueltas's *Dios en la tierra* (1944). While Guzmán's fictional autobiographical account describes the difficulties of a young teacher working in the Yucatán village of Kinchil, the novels of Magdaleno and Revueltas describe the more violent fates of rural educators who are respectively poisoned and impaled by local communities. The crucifixion of the federal teacher by the local community in *Dios en la tierra* reveals a penchant for inverted biblical imagery common to both Revueltas's and Rulfo's works.

While Rulfo's *maestro* escapes from Luvina alive, his contact with the villagers results in his profound physical and spiritual deterioration: 'Allá dejé la vida [...] Fui a ese lugar con mis ilusiones cabales y volví viejo y acabado' [I left life behind there... I went to that place full of dreams and returned old and exhausted] (126). The obsessive rambling thoughts of the increasingly inebriated *maestro* create an oppressive narrative atmosphere that is only intermittently punctuated by the lyrical descriptions of the omniscient narrator. He admits that his memory is fading due to a persistent fever and his companion's unbroken silence strongly suggests that he is in fact the product of a hallucination.[47] Although the name Luvina initially conjured a heavenly image in his mind, the teacher recalls how he encountered a 'lugar endemoniado' [evil place] and subsequently concludes that 'aquello es el purgatorio' [that place is purgatory] (127, 132).[48] These terms highlight a strong biblical element to the story which, as I will argue, can be read as a grotesque rewriting of the parable of the sower. My interpretation builds on Thakkar's analysis of the story, which notes the shared recalcitrance of the landscape and the peasantry but does not identify the parabolic significance of the comparison.[49] As we have seen in the biblical parable, the fertile soil in which the seed successfully germinates represents the hearts and minds of those willing to receive the Word of God. This central metaphorical equation between human and landscape is maintained but inverted in 'Luvina', where Rulfo conflates the decaying bodies of the locals with the degenerating natural environment to illustrate their resistance to the state's modernising project.

Inspired by the messianic rhetoric of the SEP, Rulfo's teacher arrives in Luvina 'full of ideas', but discovers a human wasteland beyond all hope of revolutionary salvation. Suffocated by a deadening silence and suspended in an eternal, unmoving present, the seemingly lifeless village is inhabited by an ageing and fervently superstitious population. The townsfolk refuse to abandon their dead and the shrouded women wandering the streets in mourning embody the 'black fanaticism' alluded to in Cifuentes's poem in *MR*. While these human conditions are evidently unfavourable to state intervention, the futility of the teacher's attempts to sow the Word of the Revolution in this environment is immediately signalled in his opening description of Luvina's depleted landscape. Although the phonic qualities of the name Luvina — evoking the Spanish words 'luz', [light] 'lluvia' [rain] and 'llovizna' [drizzle] — suggest ideal conditions for natural growth, we learn that the land has been rendered sterile by a violent ash-filled wind that uproots vegetation from the hillside and casts it into darkness.[50] Sparsely populated by withering flowers and skeletal branches, these lands are, as Jiménez de Báez notes, already 'sembradas de muerte y desolación' [sown with death and desolation].[51] Composed of rocks and thorn-like mounds of earth, the infertile landscape of Luvina closely resembles the unreceptive forms of soil described in the parable. The elevated terrain of Luvina is plagued by rocks (123) and an ongoing drought has caused the parched earth to form clods that cut into human feet as if they had grown thorns (125). Although the dawn momentarily promises sunlight and dew that would moisten the earth, the droplets freeze before they reach the soil: 'en Luvina los días son tan fríos como las noches y el rocío se cuaja en el cielo antes que llegue a caer sobre la tierra' [in Luvina the days are as cold as the nights and the dew thickens in the sky before it reaches the ground] (123). The teacher's use of the verb *cuajar* here and again in the story's closing lines to describe his aborted mission in the village directly links his incapacity to educate the peasants with the impossibility of increasing the land's fertility: 'Estaba cargado de ideas [...] Pero en Luvina no cuajó eso. Hice el experimento y se deshizo' [I was full of ideas... but in Luvina they never materialised. I attempted the experiment and it fell apart] (132). The grim atmosphere and inverted biblical imagery of 'Luvina' directly prefigures those of Rulfo's novel, in which Padre Rentería notably evokes the parable to describe his failed spiritual mission in Comala: 'Yo traje aquí algunas semillas. Pocas; apenas una bolsita [...] después pensé que hubiera sido mejor dejarlas allá donde maduraran, ya que aquí las traje a morir' [I brought some seeds here. Only a few, barely a pouch... I later thought that it would have been better to leave them there where they might have matured, since I only brought them here to die] (260).

The symbolic bond between the peasants' bodies and the natural environment is strengthened by the manner in which human disease permeates Luvina's landscape. The arid terrain is likened to hardened skin, the hill on which the village sits is compared to a corpse and the sky is discoloured by a grey stain that stretches across the horizon. A clear parallel emerges between the landscape and the body as Luvina's natural decay is mirrored in the physiological deterioration of its malnourished inhabitants.[52] The teacher is haunted by the emaciated forms and toothless mouths of the villagers who swallow their own saliva to calm their hunger (131). If, as Boldy asserts, this story is set in the Cárdenas era, these lingering descriptions of the peasants' diseased bodies capture the medicalised gaze of the rural teacher during the particularly hygiene-oriented phase of socialist education in the 1930s.[53] The suggestion that, like the hardened landscape, the peasants' bodies are resistant to cultivation is confirmed in the subsequent description of their eyes. The teacher's exhortation to the villagers to move to arable lands with the assistance of the government, likely an allusion to the Cardenista *ejido* system, is greeted with blank expressions: 'Ellos me oyeron, sin parpadear, mirándome desde el fondo de sus ojos, de los que sólo se asomaba una lucecita allá muy adentro' [They listened to me unblinkingly, watching me from the depths of their eyes, where only a faint and distant light could be glimpsed] (131).[54] Like the impermeable landscape, whose perpetual sterility is indicated by the repetition of the adverbs 'nunca' [never] and 'siempre' [always], the unblinking eyes of the peasants are characterised by an impenetrable and immutable quality. Recalling those represented by the infertile soil in the parable ('though seeing, they do not see; though hearing, they do not hear or understand'), the *campesinos* of Rulfo's story hear and see the teacher but evidently fail to comprehend his words.[55] The comparison of the heart's inability to receive the seed to a state of visual impairment in the parable is significant in relation to the dull glow in the eyes of the villagers. Rulfo's literary concern with impaired or abnormal vision, previously highlighted in *Pedro Páramo* and 'Macario', resurfaces in this description. Unlike Rivera's *campesinos*, whose bodies are collectively enveloped in the glow of the lamp as they gaze up at the rural teacher, Rulfo's *maestro* detects only a distant glimmer in the eyes of the peasants staring back at him. The description recalls the metaphor of the eyes as the lamp of the body in Matthew 6:22–23 and the equation of deficient vision with resistance to God's word in the sower parable.[56] In the Matthean passage the healthy eye is perceived as a conduit for the reception and projection of divine light while the unhealthy dim eye denotes inner darkness. Interpreted within this biblical context, the dull glow emitted from the eyes of the *campesinos* indicates the failure of revolutionary teaching to illuminate their bodies. The inability of the teacher's enlightening words to penetrate their bodies is further suggested by their resistance to natural light. He describes how the bodies of the female townsfolk merge with 'el negro fondo de la noche' [the black depths of the night], while the townsfolk with whom he converses welcome the relentless gale that has prevented sunlight from reaching the village, claiming that it is God's will (131).

Returning to the present-tense scene of the bar in the story's closing lines, we discover that, as in the case of 'Macario', the intoxicated narrator-protagonist of 'Luvina' has not moved for the duration of his monologue and that the text has assumed a circular form that negates all possibility of narrative progress. The teacher gradually falls silent and cedes narrative control to the omniscient narrator who describes the babbling sounds of the river outside the bar and the gradual onset of dusk. As night begins to fall, both the body and mind of the teacher are engulfed in darkness as he slumps unconscious onto the table. Light imagery remains a significant element in this closing section. Intermittently throughout the story, the omniscient narrator refers to a gas lamp suspended above the teacher's head. Although this literary image strikingly recalls Rivera's earlier illustration of the rural teacher, the lamp is here employed for very different symbolic purposes. As the teacher delivers his monologue, termites repeatedly fly towards the light and scorch their wings, forming a pile of 'gusanitos desnudos' [naked little worms] on the table before him (132). The closing images of these mutilated insects who have been fatally attracted to the lamp's glow mirror the ravaged body of the *maestro* himself, whose seduction by the state's enlightening mission has ultimately led to his downfall.

Drawing from common biblical vocabularies, Rivera's and Rulfo's narratives of educational reform trace the imagined construction and collapse of the post-revolutionary teacher as a revolutionary redeemer of the countryside. Intellectuals and artists of the immediate post-revolution period appropriated scriptural metaphors of divine enlightenment and sowing to describe the successful transmission of revolutionary ideology from the teacher to the rural masses. However, in reality, teachers often struggled to impose the state's modern values on peasant communities and were forced to adapt to local ways of life. Discussing the work of rural educators in the 1930s, Palacios notes that 'los que trabajaban en el campo comenzaron a realizar una acción simbiótica con los objetos de su acción y a convertirse ellos mismos en seres tan miserables y necesitados del amparo del Estado Revolucionario como los propios campesinos' [those who worked in the countryside began to enter into a symbiotic relationship with the objects of their efforts and transformed into beings who were just as miserable and in as much need of protection from the post-revolutionary state as the peasants themselves].[57] The unidirectional flow of influence implied in Rivera's metaphors of enlightenment and sowing is reversed in Rulfo's story where the teacher has not only failed to disseminate the state's modernising ideology in Luvina but has become infected through his interaction with the villagers and acquired other symptoms of rural regression such as inertia and alcoholism. Rather than incorporate Luvina into the modern revolutionary nation, the corrupted body of the teacher has become assimilated into its intransigent community.

By examining Rivera's and Rulfo's works comparatively, this first section of the chapter has revealed alternative political uses of biblical imagery in artistic representations of the education reform project. A reading of Rivera's unexamined illustrations, as I have shown, demonstrates how the artist abides by the rhetoric of the state's agendas, providing visual metaphors that uphold the secular *maestro* as a rural redeemer. Moreover, they substantiate contemporary intellectual interpretations of the peasantry as inherently deficient and passive by conceptualising their minds and bodies as empty landscapes primed for ideological fertilisation or dark voids to be filled with the light of rationality. By the 1950s, the outlook on this educational agenda is starkly different. Rulfo's bleak parable — a portrayal of the peasantry's active resistance to the state's civilising crusade — represents a radical reconfiguration and dismissal of the biblical narratives presented in government propaganda.

Part II: Crowd Control: Corporatism, Land Reform and the *Campesino* Collective

Alongside education, agrarian reform constituted another key pillar of the state's post-revolutionary rural development campaign. Eager to forge an alliance with the peasantry after a protracted agrarian revolution, Obregón pursued rural reform through the *ejido* system, a communal landholding scheme incorporating all farming communities into a single state-controlled organisation. While early nation-builders hailed these efforts as the answer to Zapata's agrarian demands, the distribution was limited and regionally inconsistent. The pace of land reform remained slow under Calles, but entered an active phase during the administration of Cárdenas, whose rejuvenation of the ejido fostered the myth of Cardenismo as the dawn of a peasant utopia or 'rural arcadia'.[58]

Calles's creation of umbrella organisations for social and political groups during the early 1920s and his establishment of the PNR in 1929 provided the institutional foundations for the creation of a corporatist system under Cárdenas that sought to tie labour and peasant movements to the state. In contrast to pluralist political systems, corporatist forms of governance subordinate social groups to the state by incorporating them into a centralised and hierarchical state-controlled polity. These groups are rendered dependent on the state through the provision of protection and concessions. In the Mexican context, corporatism provided post-revolutionary governments with a framework for promoting national unification and containing rural unrest. During the 1930s, corporatist bonds between the state and the *campesinado* were strengthened through the *ejido* scheme and the creation of state-controlled organisations such as the Confederación Nacional Campesina (CNC), which rendered the peasant community economically reliant on the state and neutralised potentially subversive groups.[59] Derived from the Latin *corpus*, the corporatist model adopted by the secular Mexican state paradoxically had antecedents in organicist political metaphors employed by medieval Catholic theologians to articulate notions of hierarchy.[60] Building on Saint Augustine's comparison of the Christian community to the perfectly unified body of Christ in *De Civitate Dei* (413–426AD), Thomas Aquinas conceived society as a corporate body of hierarchically arranged social organs operating in the interest of 'the common good' (*bonum commune*). For Aquinas, human redemption could be secured through incorporation into the Body of Christ and by extension, the organic corporate whole of the Catholic church.[61] Embedded in the continent's Hispanic-Catholic heritage, corporatism remained a relatively consistent aspect of the Latin American political landscape after the colonial period and flourished in post-revolutionary Mexico following the organic and integralist, if not strictly corporatist, Porfirian regime.[62] Particularly in the context of the agrarian project, the Mexican case reflects how Latin American corporatists took inspiration from Aquinas in advocating the use of property for the benefit of society as a whole and in promoting the principles of hierarchy, order, and the pursuit of the 'common good'.[63]

Cárdenas promoted these ideas through organicist metaphors, calling on Mexicans to put aside self-interest and place their faith in the Mexican Republic which, he claimed, 'como todo organismo viviente, debe buscar en un futuro mejor la realización del interés colectivo' [like any living organism, must seek in a better future the fulfilment of the collective interest].[64] Although the corporatist state did not come into full being until the 1930s, prominent advocates of agrarian reform (known as *agraristas*) such as Lombardo Toledano and Portes Gil foreshadowed Cárdenas in using political-theological concepts to promote an attitude of cooperation and deference to the state amongst the *campesinado* during the 1920s. By adopting a Christian rhetoric of solidarity and comparing land reform to an act of divine justice, reformers encouraged peasant groups to subordinate their interests to the 'national good' and to adopt an attitude of passivity and deference in relation to the government. While Cardenista corporatism by no means created a Leviathan-like authoritarian state, it established the primary framework for political participation and the articulation of collective demands. Although organisations such as the CNC ostensibly provided the political infrastructure for addressing agrarian issues, they prevented peasant groups from evolving into a strong democratising force by binding them to the state.[65] The Camacho and Alemán administrations largely abandoned the agrarian project to pursue a developmentalist agenda and gradually withdrew political support for *campesino* movements. The emaciation of the *ejido* over the subsequent decades reversed the initial improvements achieved through land reform; by 1970, the number of landless peasants was greater than at the beginning of the Revolution.[66]

Tracing a history of aesthetic interpretations of agrarian reform from the 1920s to the mid-1960s, the second part of this chapter examines how Rivera's and Rulfo's works endorse or complicate this corporatist ideal of a docile and deferential *campesinado*. Analysing Rivera's mural *El reparto de tierras* (1924) alongside *La fórmula secreta* (1965), an experimental short film directed by Rubén Gámez and featuring a poetic monologue by Rulfo, I consider how both artists respectively borrow from Renaissance and baroque aesthetics to visualise the peasant mass as a political entity. During the Renaissance, the rejuvenation of Roman civic virtues and the influence of Thomism shaped a humanist code of civil conduct that emphasised self-sacrificing service to the greater good and the defence of state institutions.[67] The political, religious and intellectual turmoil of the seventeenth century, however, resulted in a crisis of Renaissance values and institutions that reverberated throughout the visual arts. In *Principles of Art History* (1915), art historian Heinrich Wölfflin describes this artistic transition from the closed and static order of Renaissance painting, in which individual objects are subjugated to the overall unity and integrity of the composition, to the volatile formlessness of the baroque, where figures are swept up in a swirl of dynamic motion and shadow that obscures their underlying structures.[68] While Renaissance composition is bounded by clear organisation and anchored by a central focal point, Wölfflin stresses the open and transformative nature of the baroque, which pushes outwards in radical new directions.[69]

These aesthetic models were linked to different political agendas in Mexican and Latin American artistic production more generally in the twentieth century. Although Alfonso Reyes and Pedro Henríquez Ureña both wrote on baroque aesthetics, as members of the Ateneo in the 1920s they also promoted the humanistic values of culture and education, rejuvenating the Renaissance ideal of a socially instructive mode of art. In the immediate post-revolution period, this vision was realised by the muralists and other state-sponsored artists associated with the so-called *renacimiento mexicano*, who recuperated Renaissance artistic principles to project a redemptive aesthetic vision of the Revolution and a new code of civil conduct. The most significant challenge to this cultural nationalist model during the 1920s and 30s was posed by the avant-garde Contemporáneos group who paralleled the Spanish Generation of '27 in their rejuvenation of Hispanic Golden Age poetics. As Zamora and Kaup have noted, towards the middle of the century a number of Latin American intellectuals looked again to the artistic forms that had been imported to Latin America during the Conquest as an anticolonial tool for disrupting hegemonic power structures.[70] Cuban writers such as Alejo Carpentier and Severo Sarduy creatively appropriated the seventeenth century baroque as a revolutionary aesthetic form 'que metaforiza al orden discutido, al dios juzgado, a la ley transgredida' [that metaphorises the disputed order, the god put on trial, the transgressed law].[71] A crisis of revolutionary values in Mexico during the 1950s and 60s provided the backdrop for further mobilisations of the baroque by artists reassessing established models of national identity, from Paz and Fuentes to the visual artists of the Ruptura generation.

Borrowing from Wölfflin's art historical account and Gilles Deleuze's and Félix Guattari's concepts of 'smooth' and 'striated' space, the 'fold' and 'becoming', the second section of this chapter explores how Rivera and Rulfo use Renaissance and baroque aesthetic models to political effect. Analysing both artists' portrayals of the peasant mass as a political entity, I look for the conditions that transform the *campesinado* from a meek and orderly congregation to an amorphous, animalised collective in these works. Situating *El reparto de tierras* within the ambit of contemporary Christianised *agrarista* rhetoric, I examine how Rivera draws from Giotto's approach to group portraiture to promote the notion of *bonum commune* and to portray the *campesinado* as the meek beneficiaries of state intervention. Turning to the progressively strained political climate that reached a violent turning point in the 1960s, I consider how the state-*campesino* relationship is alternatively visualised in Rulfo's monologue for *La fórmula secreta*, which evolves from an unanswered prayer for assistance to a profane litany and prophecy of apocalyptic unrest. Adopting Deleuze's interpretation of the baroque process of 'becoming' as a means of imagining alternative resistant modes of subjectivity, I explore how Rulfo's poetic imagery and the film's audio-visual elements offer an aesthetic and political alternative to the model of crowd representation presented in Rivera's mural.

Rivera's *El reparto de tierras:* The *Campesinado* and the Corporate Body Politic

Speaking in 1923, Vasconcelos affirmed that 'el verdadero artista debe trabajar para el arte y para la religión; y la religión moderna, el moderno fetiche, es el Estado socialista, organizado para el bien común' [the true artist must work for art and religion; and modern religion, the modern fetish, is the socialist State organised for the common good].[72] Conceiving their works as universally legible 'Biblias pintadas' [painted bibles], the muralists turned to Renaissance form and figuration during the early years of the movement to construct a sacralised revolutionary art founded on this collectivist ethos.[73] This link was upheld by contemporary artists and commentators such as the muralist Jean Charlot and the painter Dr. Atl, who directly compared this process of artistic renewal to developments in Renaissance Italy.[74] As a student in Italy, Rivera analysed the visual languages of Michelangelo, Gozzoli and Uccello, but was most admiring of Giotto, a critical figure in the artistic transition from the late medieval to Renaissance periods. Giotto's profound influence on the muralist's pictorial style, already seen in his Christ-like depiction of the rural teacher in the first section of this chapter, reveals itself again in his approach to configuring group scenes in *El reparto de tierras* at Chapingo. Taking inspiration from Giotto's Christian themes in the Arena Chapel fresco cycle, the mural upholds a corporatist ideal of an obedient and deferential peasantry by subordinating individual *campesino* bodies to the collective order of the composition and envisioning land distribution as an act of divine intervention on the part of the state.

Rivera's suite of murals at Chapingo provides the clearest example of his revolutionary repurposing of religious spaces and visual forms. As noted in the previous chapter, Gómez had recruited Rivera to produce imagery that would convert the chapel into a 'templo del saber' [temple of knowledge] for the school's middle-class agronomists in training.[75] Alongside the decorative scheme of the renovated chapel, which transformed it into a 'Sistine Chapel of the new age' in the eyes of one contemporary commentator, the four open-air scenes in the adjacent administrative building adhere to the simplicity and serenity of early Renaissance composition.[76] While the twin frescoes *El buen gobierno* and *El mal gobierno* (1924), situated on the east and west walls, take direct inspiration from Ambrogio Lorenzetti's *The Allegory of Good and Bad Government* (1338–39), Giotto's influence is more subtly revealed in *El reparto de tierras.* Located on the north wall of the upper floor, the mural depicts a crowd of male peasants assembled around the central figure of the state agronomist as he presides over the act of land distribution. For this particular mural, Rivera diverged from the more fluid compositional principles of plastic integration he had employed elsewhere. Reverting to Giotto's technique of structuring fresco cycles as a series of discrete narrative segments, the mural stands alone as a tightly-composed and self-contained episode on the north wall. As I will demonstrate, by adopting the strategies employed by Giotto to subordinate and restrain certain figures within his group scenes, Rivera imposes the restrictive and static order of the mural's overall composition onto the peasant mass contained within it.

Dressed in pristine white with their eyes fixed attentively on the agronomist, the overlapping forms of the peasants in *El reparto de tierras* recall the angelic congregations portrayed in Giotto's *Last Judgment* in the Arena Chapel (1304–1305) and Fra Angelico's *Christ Glorified in the Court of Heaven* (1430), where the central figure of Christ is framed by a multitude of neatly arranged angels whose gazes and tilting bodies gravitate inwards towards the saviour. The ideological implications of this visual grammar of the crowd are significant. In his analysis of crowd iconographies in Western art, Jeffrey Schnapp identifies the 'geometrically arrayed choirs that surround the Redeemer in vast tableaux of total order' in works by early Renaissance artists like Giotto and Fra Angelico as examples of what he terms an 'emblematic' mode of crowd representation. Historically used to depict disciplined followers paying reverence to the divine, the emblematic mass represents an 'orderly model of the formation of the body politic' in which 'individuals lose their contours in order to regain them within the confines of a single corporate body'.[77] Art historian Richard Offner underlines this particular emphasis on corporate unity in Giotto's approach to group portraiture:

> The composition being conceived as a system of interdependent elements, each figure is accommodated to the whole by being contoured and modelled large in order not to draw too much attention to itself by individualization or description of its physical character. To the same end its needs must be immobilised. The composition thus subjugates the individual form to a corporate order and equilibrium.[78]

Offner's emphasis on the 'corporate order' of human forms in Giotto's work supports Reiss's contention that the pictorial language of the Arena Chapel cycle is fundamentally informed by Aquinas's concept of the 'common good' as the basis of societal justice.[79] For Reiss, Giotto's murals pictorially endorse Aquinas's notion of 'civic Christianity', which stipulates that the welfare of the individual should not take precedence over that of the broader society.[80] This subordination of individual bodies to the collective order is used to strikingly similar effect in Rivera's *El reparto de tierras*, where the emblematic composition of the crowd visually upholds corporatist principles of political organisation. Here the subjugation of individual interests to the common good is reflected in the collective configuration of the peasants, whose neatly overlapping figures, uniformed attire and generic or partially erased facial features enable them to merge into a single mass. The sense of serenity emanating from this orderly arrangement of bodies is complemented by a limited palette of celestial golds and rich blue tones, again borrowed from Giotto's biblical scenes, and the harmonious interrelation of human and natural elements within the composition. Reflecting the artist's belief that agrarian reform would promote 'la armonía de los hombres con la tierra y de los hombres entre sí' [harmony between men and the land and between men], a correlation is established between the undulating forms of the peasant mass and the rolling hills on the horizon.[81]

Rivera's pictorial articulation of *bonum commune* was consistent with contemporary *agrarista* rhetoric that conflated the collectivist spirit of land reform with the Christian principles of selflessness and fraternal harmony. To the right of the composition, Gómez is shown holding a blueprint for the 'Primer Pueblo Cooperativo de la República Mexicana', an agricultural cooperative that was intended to function as an organisational model for the communities of Chapingo. A commemorative plaque located on the site aligns its communal ethos with foundational Christian values: 'No tenemos templos, nuestra oración es el trabajo. Nuestra fe, el bienestar colectivo. Nuestro dogma la cooperación' [We have no temples, work is our prayer. The collective good is our faith, cooperation our dogma].[82] Reiterating Obregón's claim that the government's programme was essentially Christian in its 'espíritu de confraternidad y de equidad' [spirit of fraternity and justice], Portes Gil claimed that the implementation of land reform in Tamaulipas had engendered a new kind of humanity founded on 'la armonía fraternal' [fraternal harmony] and 'el espíritu de cooperación' [the spirit of cooperation].[83] This moral congruency between Christian and agrarian values was also underlined by Lombardo Toledano in a pamphlet published by the Grupo Solidario del Movimiento Obrero (GSMO) in 1922, entitled 'El reparto de tierras a los pobres no se opone a las enseñanzas de nuestro señor Jesucristo y de la santa madre Iglesia'. Linked to the state-affiliated labour organisation CROM (Confederación Regional Obrera Mexicana), the GSMO had been founded by Lombardo Toledano the previous year and enjoyed the support of prominent cultural figures including Rivera, Alfonso Caso, Julio Torri and Henríquez Ureña. A vocal contributor to the agrarian debate and a prominent figure of the Mexican labour movement, Lombardo Toledano established close links with the government during the 1920s, serving as director of the Escuela Nacional Preparatoria from 1922 and as Education Secretary for the CROM. Defending land distribution from clerical detractors who deemed it a violation of the natural right to property, Lombardo Toledano presents Mexico's agrarian Revolution as 'la continuación del establecimiento del orden nacido de la doctrina de Nuestro Señor Jesucristo, que nos enseña a gobernar la Tierra por el amor de los unos a los otros y no por el egoísmo' [the continued establishment of the order originating in the doctrine of Our Lord Jesus Christ, who teaches us to govern the Earth through love for one another and not through selfishness].[84]

Land Distribution as an Act of Divine Justice

The pamphlet's eye-catching cover image, designed by Rivera, depicts a *sombrero*-clad peasant ploughing a field as he gazes up at a suspended Christ-figure whose arms are spread to display his radiant sacred heart. As suggested by their common titles, Rivera's mural at Chapingo draws thematic inspiration from this earlier illustration, particularly in its framing of land distribution as an act of divine justice. This miraculous image and the inclusion of explanatory bands of text in the upper and lower sections of the cover replicates the compositional scheme of the ex-voto, a form of popular votive offering used to express gratitude for the fulfilment of a prayer or miracle. As votive expression is inherently bound to a sense of human impotence and dependency on superior powers, Rivera's use of this popular iconographic form upholds the top-down logic of corporatist relations by conveying the peasantry's total reliance on state intervention for rural prosperity.

Rivera's depiction of the *campesinado* as the passive beneficiaries of an agrarian 'miracle' visually condenses the biblical metaphors on which Lombardo Toledano's text is based. In the pamphlet, tracts of the 1917 Constitution are positioned alongside selective citations from Aquinas on the rightful claim to private property, Pope Leo XIII's encyclical *Rerum Novarum* (1891), a text that drew heavily from Aquinas's organic-communal conception of state-societal relations, and a selectively abridged version of The Beatitudes from the 'Sermon on the Mount'.[85] As Butler explains, Lombardo Toledano's reinterpretation of the Beatitudes conflates terrestrial and celestial rewards by substituting the city on the hill with the state-controlled *ejido* and by identifying the *campesinado* as the righteous yet submissive meek who will inherit the earth.[86] This equation of the peasantry with the biblical meek is of course highly significant in the context of post-revolutionary state-societal relations, as in the Beatitudes meekness is conventionally used to refer to those who 'must look to God for help and assistance' and implies 'submission to his will; flexibleness to his Word'.[87]

These pictorial and textual metaphors were in keeping with contemporary rhetoric and visual discourses of land reform during the 1920s, which presented the *ejido* as a 'miracle' that would socially and morally elevate Mexico's humble countryfolk.[88] Palacios and Gudiño argue that the official land petition forms submitted by rural communities reflect the internalisation of these ideas, revealing:

> La representación que tienen de sí mismos (y que el discurso de los intelectuales se encarga de instituir), como los "pobres campesinos", los "desheredados", un grupo que debe 'suplicar' para que les otorguen sus tierras.[89]
>
> [The image they have of themselves (and the discourse that intellectuals are responsible for putting in place) as the 'poor peasants', the 'disinherited', a group that must 'beg' to be granted their lands.]

The government's fulfilment of these prayers is documented in official photographs depicting the federal agronomist standing alongside members of the local community. As suggested by Ignacio Gutiérrez Ruvalcaba's description, the distribution of bodies in these formulaic panoramic group portraits visually upholds the power relations previously outlined by Palacios and Gudiño:

> El ingeniero [...] aparece en las fotografías como el eje de la estructura iconográfica. Los campesinos, por su parte, tienen un papel de subordinación ya que no son el centro del arreglo formal y siempre están en términos del funcionario agrario.[90]
>
> [The agronomist... appears in the photographs as the axis of the iconographic structure. The peasants have a subordinate role as they do not occupy the centre of the formal arrangement and are always positioned in relation to the state agronomist]

Ruvalcaba links the composition of these photographs to the language of prominent *agraristas* such as Julio Cuadros Caldas, author of *Catecismo agrario* (1923), who viewed the agronomist as 'simbólicamente el que tiene en sus manos la justicia y el campesino solo es el demandante y el sujeto de justicia en el proceso' [symbolically the one who holds justice in his hands while the peasant is only the petitioner and subject of justice in the process].[91]

These power dynamics, and their biblical undertones, are clearly communicated in *El reparto de tierras*, where Rivera borrows from the gestural language of Giotto's scenes to distinguish the agronomist as the supreme arbiter of rural justice from the 'meek' peasant onlookers. As both Wölfflin and Schnapp note, Renaissance group compositions conventionally pivot around a central, often sovereign, figure.[92] This particular approach to crowd composition can be further illuminated by the concept of 'striated' space proposed by Deleuze and Guattari. In *A Thousand Plateaus* they establish a distinction between 'smooth' space, characterised as fluid, mobile and boundless and striated space, which is organised, bounded and structured around a particular focal point. For both thinkers, the principles of striated spatial organisation speak to a hierarchical 'arborescent' system of thought that is governed by centres of significance and subjectification and thus symbolically linked to the centralised power of the 'state apparatus'.[93] While *El reparto de tierras* does not adhere to strict single point perspective, the composition is clearly structured around a central focal point. The direction of the peasants' collective gaze and other visual cues such as triangulation of heads towards the centre-right of the composition guide the viewer's eye to the figure of the agronomist, establishing a hierarchy of forms which, I suggest, is reinforced by Rivera's treatment of body language.

The most likely source of inspiration for Rivera's fresco is Giotto's *The Last Judgement* (1304–1305), where the central figure of Christ, flanked by two groups of angels, determines the fate of the blessed and the damned with two distinct gestures: his upward palm signals salvation for the blessed to his right-hand side, while his downward palm seals the eternal damnation of those to his left. Like Giotto's Christ, the agronomist in Rivera's mural extends his upturned right palm to the congregation to signal their redemption. His configuration of the peasants' body language is, however, markedly different, drawing from the strategies employed by Giotto to immobilise the 'meek' figures standing at the margins of his biblical scenes. In contrast to the animated official, most of these *campesinos* stand with their hands lowered at their waist or at their side, suggesting a passive role within the visual narrative. Discussing Giotto's visual rhetoric of gesture, Moshe Barasch identifies lowered or clasped hands as a demonstration of awe that is performed by characters of lower rank to express 'humility before a sacred, mysterious event'.[94] Analysing the meek, haloed onlookers in *Lamentation* (1305), Barasch echoes Offner's earlier phrasing by describing the lowered and inactive hands of these figures as an expression of 'symbolic self-immobilisation which makes one defenceless and thus at the mercy of higher powers'.[95]

Rivera's immobilisation of the *campesino* crowd in *El reparto de tierras* marks a notable shift from his scenes of revolutionary agitation in the chapel frescoes. While scenes such as *El agitador* portray peasants as active agents of social change during the armed phase of the conflict, the murals in the adjacent agricultural school set an alternative vision for the post-revolutionary era by presenting a restrained and cooperative *campesinado*. The impression of containment created by the poses of the peasant onlookers is further enforced by Rivera's configuration of the scene as a clearly bounded panel on the north wall of the administrative building, again reflecting the capacity of striated space to restrict free movement through the imposition of fixed borders. As in previously analysed murals, architectural context here helps to shape the visual experience. The visitor first catches sight of this mural upon reaching the top of the stairs in the administrative building and turning to look across the stairwell. In contrast to the immersive aesthetic experience generated by some of Rivera's other frescoes, the framing effect in *El reparto de tierras* and its location on the far side of the stairwell activate what Deleuze and Guattari refer to as the 'long-distance vision' associated with striated space, enabling the eye to immediately grasp the composition and the figures occupying its interior. The key features of long-distance vision, which include 'constancy of orientation' and 'the constitution of a central perspective', again reflect Rivera's pictorial concern with creating an illusion of optical mastery for the viewer.[96] These elements suggest a disjunction between the aesthetic form of the work and its thematic content. Despite the mural's celebration of peasant liberation through land reform, its pictorial composition and presentation suggest a fundamental concern with the visual containment and control of *campesino* bodies.

The muralist's image of a docile and deferential peasant collective would gradually decay over the subsequent decades as the utopian aims of land reform failed to materialise. Often considered the most radical era of revolutionary reform, the Cárdenas administration entered a more conservative phase in the late 1930s that set the tone for subsequent administrations.[97] Rivera's personal disillusionment with the government during this period is reflected in his dramatic support of General Juan Andreu Almazán in his challenge to the PRM candidate Ávila Camacho in the 1940 presidential race. An anti-communist businessman who campaigned against the *ejido* system and socialist education, Almazán appealed to both counterrevolutionary groups and disenchanted revolutionaries alike. Following Camacho's victory in the 1940 election, his administration and those of Alemán and Adolfo Ruiz Cortines (1952–1958), largely neglected agrarian issues in favour of economic and industrial objectives. Discussing Lombardo Toledano's 1923 pamphlet, José Abel Ogaz Pierce highlights how the text sounds a warning note by citing the lesson from Luke 22:35–37 that 'los oprimidos recurren a la violencia ante la sordera de los opresores' [the oppressed turn to violence when faced with the deafness of their oppressors].[98] From the 1940s onwards, this biblical prophecy materialised in the form of regionally based peasant movements, most notably those led by former Zapatista Rubén Jaramillo in Morelos between 1942 and 1962.[99]

Echoing the bleak corporeal metaphors circulating in contemporary intellectual debates regarding the collapse of the revolutionary project, Lombardo Toledano claimed in 1958 that land reform 'se encuentra en estado de catalepsia: vive, pero se halla inmóvil con rigidez semejante a la de un cadáver' [finds itself in a state of catalepsy: it is alive but paralysed, displaying a rigidity similar to that of a corpse].[100] Alongside intellectuals such as Lombardo Toledano, Jesús Silva Herzog and Moisés de la Peña, Mexican writers emerged as particularly harsh critics of the agrarian programme during this decade.[101] Following from his literary portrait of failed agrarian reform in *El luto humano* (1943), Revueltas's major political essay 'Ensayo sobre un proletariado sin cabeza' (1962) criticised the state's corporatist subordination of peasant organisations and the failure of the Mexican left, particularly the PCM under Lombardo Toledano, to adequately serve the interests of the masses.[102] During the mid 1960s, Elena Garro also published a series of articles on the disintegration of the agrarian project, while Fuentes denounced a political system that 'detrás de las fachadas retóricas, aún asesina a campesinos, los despoja de tierra y les niega el derecho a trabajar' [behind the rhetorical facades, still murders peasants, deprives them of their land and denies them the right to work].[103]

Alternative Collectivities: The Baroque Pursuit of New Forms in *La fórmula secreta*

This mounting unrest over the rural question, and shifting government priorities more generally, provides the socio-historical backdrop to Rulfo's collaboration with Rubén Gámez on the experimental black-and-white film *La fórmula secreta* (1965). The opening shot of an anonymous patient receiving an intravenous transfusion of Coca-Cola makes clear the film's intentions to diagnose a crisis in the body politic in the age of globalisation and nods to the film's original title: *Coca Cola en la sangre*. This noxious formula triggers twelve hallucinatory episodes that converge to form a delirious visual commentary on contemporary Mexican identity. Although the film's disjointed and surrealist imagery defies singular interpretation, capitalist expansion, U.S cultural imperialism, Church authority and rural decline emerge as prevalent themes. A voice-over of Sabines reciting Rulfo's monologue accompanies two closely interlinked segments of the film that present a group of *campesinos* standing in a lunar wasteland.[104] Although the film has been generally neglected by Rulfo scholars, it merits consideration due to its overt social commentary and the fact that it is the only cinematic project of which he proudly acknowledged creative authorship.[105] Rulfo, who was notoriously evasive about the political content of his work, described the film as 'anti-yanqui, anti-clerical, anti-gobiernista, anti-todo... no la han dejado exhibir' [anti-American, anti-clerical, anti-government, anti-everything ... they didn't allow it to be shown].[106] However, as in the case of the photographic works discussed in chapters 1 and 2, inconsistencies emerge between the film's political agenda and Rulfo's professional activities and affiliations. While *La fórmula secreta* launches a blistering attack on *yanqui* cultural imperialism in Mexico, U.S.-funded cultural institutions played a critical role in the development of Rulfo's career.[107] The writer received substantial grants from the Rockefeller-sponsored CME in the mid-1950s and in 1964 accepted a post as a writing tutor at the centre which was supported by the CIA-funded Congress for Cultural Freedom (CCF). Patrick Iber claims that during this period the CCF was primarily concerned with protecting the centre from the influence of communist writers and viewed Rulfo as a potential counterbalance to militant left-wing literary figures such as Pablo Neruda.[108] Repeatedly employed by state agencies throughout his career, Rulfo's position could hardly be described as strictly anti-government either. Alongside Juan José Arreola, Rulfo accompanied the PRI politician Adolfo López Mateos on his presidential campaign in Jalisco and both writers edited a collection of his speeches which was published in 1963.[109] Despite lamenting government censorship of *La fórmula secreta*, Rulfo himself worked as a film censor in the 1950s alongside fellow-writer Carlos Fuentes.[110] As these examples make clear, Rulfo's professional trajectory was not unique in this regard, but rather reflective of the situation of numerous post-revolutionary intellectuals and artists who critiqued the state through their work while also depending on it for their livelihood and reputation.

Despite the increasing institutional recognition of his literature, Rulfo turned to cinema as an alternative creative outlet in the 1960s. His collaboration with Gámez was the most successful of these cinematic endeavours, earning the film first prize at the Primer Concurso de Cine Experimental in Mexico City in 1965. Unlike the generally unsuccessful screen adaptations of his works that had been produced up until this point, *La fórmula secreta* arguably provides the closest cinematic approximation to Rulfo's literary aesthetic. This can be primarily attributed to Rulfo's own creative involvement in the project, but also the fact that Gámez admitted to drawing inspiration from the writer's literature in developing his filmic aesthetic. The director's self-proclaimed desire to produce 'un cine mexicano, el mexicano de Rulfo' [a Mexican cinema, a cinema of Rulfo's Mexico] reflects the creative exchanges that began to emerge between literature and cinema in the 1960s.[111] During the previously mentioned 'Golden Age' of Mexican film production, cinema replaced muralism as the state's principal tool of visual propaganda, with directors such as Emilio 'El Indio' Fernández and the cinematographer Gabriel Figueroa transferring Rivera's monumental and folkloric graphic register to the screen. The 1960s however marked a shift away from the melodramatic style of profit-oriented studio films and heralded a wave of new experimental cinema known as the Nuevo Cine Mexicano.[112] The Grupo Nuevo Cine, which was formed by intellectuals and writers including Carlos Monsiváis, Salvador Elizondo and Jomí García Ascot advocated a more challenging and expressly political cinematic aesthetic.[113] In its 1961 manifesto and ephemeral journal of the same name, the group criticised the rigid representational conventions enforced by the domestic film industry and called for the total renovation of national cinema through the promotion of independent films and greater creative freedom for emerging directors.[114] In notably corporeal terms, Monsiváis described the 1965 competition as symbolic of this resuscitation of Mexican cinema: 'el cadáver pretendió desplazarse, el cine mexicano quiso redimirse [...] El Concurso nos reveló un fenómeno insólito entre nosotros: un cine vivo, comprometido orgánicamente con la realidad' [the corpse tried to move, Mexican cinema tried to redeem itself... the Competition revealed an unusual phenomenon amongst us: a living cinema that was organically engaged with reality].[115] The movement, which provided something of a cinematic counterpart to the contemporary literary 'Boom' in its ideological and aesthetic agenda, encouraged fluid interactions between both media. Alongside *La fórmula secreta*, which involved collaboration between Gámez, Rulfo and the poet Jaime Sabines, other films submitted to the 1965 competition displayed links to literary production. Entries to receive awards included *En este pueblo no hay ladrones* (1965), based on a short story from Gabriel García Márquez's *Los funerales de la Mamá Grande* (1962), *Amor amor amor* (1965) on which García Márquez also worked as a screenwriter and *El viento distante* (1965), based on the stories of José Emilio Pacheco. Throughout the 1960s, Fuentes and García Márquez worked on a number of other screenplays including a collaboration on *El gallo de oro* (1964), a cinematic adaptation of the eponymous short novel composed by Rulfo in the late 1950s. Literary works also provided inspiration for Luis Buñuel, who expressed an interest in adapting *Pedro Páramo* and of course Gámez who set about fashioning a more meaningful form of cinema following the literary examples of Rulfo, Garro, Paz and Fuentes.[116]

This direct link with contemporary literature in the case of Gámez's filmmaking is useful for contextualising the baroque aspects of *La fórmula secreta*. During the 1950s and 1960s, both Paz and Fuentes followed Sarduy and Carpentier in articulating political concerns through a neo-baroque aesthetic, adopting the tropes of the mirror and the labyrinth in their essayistic and literary explorations of national identity. For Ochoa, Fuentes's experimentation with a neo-baroque style is most clearly revealed in *La nueva novela hispanoamericana* (1969), which he considers a kind of literary manifesto for the Boom generation.[117] Aligning social and literary revolution, Fuentes's extended essay advocates a break from realism and the embrace of a new narrative style characterised by ambiguity and polysemy.[118] This baroque indeterminacy was also embraced by the visual artists of the counter-nationalist Ruptura and Nueva Presencia movements such as Alberto Gironella and José Luis Cuevas, both notably admired by Rulfo, whose works of the late 1950s and 1960s replaced the heroic social realist language of the muralists with unstable and distorted human forms. Echoing Wölfflin's identification of the baroque with 'the restless, the becoming', Fuentes highlighted the mobility of Cuevas's 'trans-figuras' [trans-figures] who lingered 'entre el estar y el devenir' [between being and becoming].[119] In literary and visual works such as these, the baroque emerges as a conceptual prism through which to articulate social and political unrest but also to formulate other possibilities for engaged art.

In what follows, I examine how Gámez and Rulfo similarly make use of baroque elements for political purposes in *La fórmula secreta.* The film's baroque sensibility is immediately signalled by the recurring interjections of Vivaldi's 'Gloria' and the extended footage of the interior of the *churrigueresque* church of Santa María Tonantzintla in Puebla. Jesse Lerner has also justified a neo-baroque reading of the film based on its attack on global capitalism and subversion of nationalist iconographic tropes.[120] Here I focus more specifically on the stylistic features of the film, exploring how its audio-visual components and poetic monologue harness the transformative capacity of the baroque to re-envisage the *campesinado* as a potentially subversive force. For the purpose of this discussion, I adhere to Ndalianis's understanding of the term neo-baroque as referring to a transhistorical aesthetic form that expresses the dynamism of the seventeenth-century baroque in technologically and culturally different ways.[121] Drawing from Deleuze's interpretation of the baroque processes of 'folding' and 'becoming' as both aesthetic and ontological phenomena, I consider how *La fórmula secreta* proposes an alternative to Rivera's Renaissance model of crowd representation and its underlying corporatist ideals by imagining the peasantry as a restlessly mutating organic and animal collective.

The first of the two episodes paired with Rulfo's monologue begins at approximately eight minutes into the film when Gámez cuts to a man wearing a traditional shawl standing alone in a rural wasteland. The camera slowly pans across to the right, but the man unexpectedly repositions himself to the centre of the frame to remain directly within the viewer's eyeline. As Sabines starts to recite Rulfo's text, the camera cuts to reveal several other men standing in the crevices of the landscape. The sustained visual focus on these figures as the voice-over is introduced suggests that we should interpret the disembodied voice as the poetic spokesperson for this forgotten rural community.

The opening section of the monologue poetically distils the imagery of 'Nos han dado la tierra' by describing a gradually eroding rural landscape and population.[122] Rulfo's tale of a dwindling group of peasants who trudge across a dusty plain to reach the parcel of land assigned to them through the government's repartition programme finds recurring echoes in the poetic and cinematic imagery of *La fórmula secreta.* In a subtle play on the collectivist rhetoric of agrarian reform, the poetic voice uses the verb *repartir* to state that hunger, rather than land, has been distributed amongst them.[123] The invocatory tone introduced by the refrain 'alguien tiene que oírnos' [someone has to hear us] corresponds with Gámez's alternating shots of the *campesinos* gazing upwards from the plain and the wide-eyed baroque angels peering down from the profusely ornamented church ceiling.[124] This interplay of gazes, implying that the peasants are now collectively addressing these heavenly beings, cinematically reproduces the tiered pictorial scheme of the ex-voto, which, as Jean Charlot explained, portrays man as 'a kind of deep-air animal crawling on rock bottom, his face lifted to a stratosphere where the holy beings dwell'.[125] While this spatial aspect of the sequence reproduces the hierarchical power relations underpinning Rivera's presentation of land reform as an act of divine justice, the impassive faces of the angels suggest that the prayers of these peasants will remain unanswered. The juxtaposition of the high-angle view of the *campesinos* and the upward tilting shots of the angels enforces a vertical tension between these celestial beings and the lowly peasants that is reinforced by subsequent still shots of their seemingly lifeless bodies lying crumpled on the terrain.

These spatial dynamics are maintained in the second section paired with Rulfo's monologue beginning at twenty-four minutes into the film, which opens with the men scrambling up the hillside after nightfall. Like the peasants of 'Nos han dado la tierra', who undertake an arduous but fruitless journey to reach an elevated plot of land (44), the subsequent shots of their bodies strewn corpse-like on the plain suggest the futility of their efforts to reach higher ground. While both sequences appear to signal the peasants' demise, such an interpretation is complicated by Rulfo's poetic imagery. The harmonious interrelation between the peasant collective and the land presented in Rivera's mural evolves into a more violent alliance towards the end of the first part of the monologue, as Sabines insists that their voices, which drone like a swarm of wasps, will be heeded and speculates whether their transformation into a destructive natural force might liberate them from their present circumstances:

> Alguien tendrá que oírnos.
> Cuando dejemos de gruñir como avispas en enjambre,
> o nos volvamos cola de remolino
> [...]
> tal vez
> nos llegue a todos
> el remedio (I. 46–55)
>
> [Someone will have to hear us.
> When we stop droning like a swarm of wasps,
> or turn into the tail of a whirlwind
> ...
> perhaps
> the solution
> will reach us all]

This prophecy is played out through the audio elements of the second episode, which evoke the transformation of the *campesinado* into a series of threatening natural and animal entities. Over the sound of rolling thunder and howling winds, Sabines's reverberating voice imagines them dissolving into foam and being consumed by the ash-filled air and darkness. Although Rulfo's sparse prose is rarely associated with the baroque, these images resonate with its thematic focus on decay, instability and metamorphosis. Recurring imagery of smoke, foam, dust, ash, rubble and shadow and a concern with the interplay between life and death and dreams and reality in

Rulfo's literature carry subtle echoes of Hispanic baroque poets such as Quevedo, Góngora and Sor Juana Inés de la Cruz. Such literary influences are not implausible when we consider Rulfo's evaluation of José Gorostiza, a leading member of the Contemporáneos who drew inspiration from these earlier writers, as the greatest Mexican poet of the twentieth century.[126]

Rulfo's poetic images of dissolution and transformation draw attention to the neo-baroque quality of Gámez's cinematography which manipulates shadow to render human forms open and mutable. As Wölfflin explains in his chapter 'Clearness and Unclearness', the interplay of light and shadow in baroque composition results in a blurring of limits and the collapse of stable Renaissance forms.[127] In Gámez's scene, the indistinct figures of the men oscillate between form and formlessness in the darkness as they merge with the landscape, animating it with their movements. The tenebrous quality of the scene and the shifting surface of the plain evoke the fluidity and mobility of smooth space and its particular demands on the viewing eye. Smooth space replaces the 'long-distance' vision encouraged by striated territories with a 'haptic' and 'close' vision that, according to Deleuze (following the art historian Aloïs Riegl) 'allows the eye to function like the sense of touch'.[128] In the cinematic context, Laura U. Marks describes haptic visuality as a form of spectatorship that is grounded in the body and draws 'from other forms of sense experience, primarily touch and kinesthetics'.[129] Marks explains that haptic visuality involves 'gradually discovering what is in the image rather than coming to the image already knowing what it is [...] such works represent the point of view of a disoriented traveller unsure how to read the world in which he has found himself'.[130] As the camera shifts to the gloomy hillside in *La fórmula secreta*, the viewing eye gropes for the human forms or visual coordinates that might lend sense to these images. By destabilising the spectator's sense of place in relation the screen, Gámez's cinematography visually evokes the sense of disorientation described in Rulfo's text, leaving the viewer 'yendo a tientas entre la revuelta oscuridad' [groping around in the turbulent darkness] (II. 63–64). This cinematic imagery reflects a concern with the limitations of visual perception that I have so far identified across Rulfo's corpus. Given that Gámez affirmed his intention to cinematically recreate Rulfo's literary aesthetic, it is possible that these grainy sequences, shot before Rulfo had composed his poetic monologue, were inspired by the previously discussed descriptions of disorientation and blindness found in *Pedro Páramo*.

The volatile mutations of the peasantry in *La fórmula secreta* suggest connections with Deleuze's discussion of seventeenth-century baroque thought and aesthetics in *The Fold*, where he identifies its endless production of forms or 'folds' as a means of conceptualising alternative and, in particular, non-human modes of subjectivity.[131] Building on Wölfflin's interpretation of the baroque as an 'uninterrupted flow of becoming', Deleuze uses the mobile fold as a tool for analysing contemporary aesthetics and as the conceptual basis for a migratory or 'nomadic' mode of existence that resides in a liminal, in-between space known as the *intermezzo*.[132] Deleuze's 'nomadology' provides a useful bridging concept for understanding Rulfo's representation of the body across his literary, photographic and cinematic corpora. Like Comala's nomadic ghosts (241) and the indistinct migratory subjects of his urban photographs, the wandering *campesinos* of his cinematic monologue display a striking mobility in both their navigation of physical space and their bodily composition. Recalling the images of corporeal fragmentation and overflow discussed in Chapters 2 and 3 respectively, Rulfo's monologue presents a vision of the human body in extremis that suggests new creative possibilities. Although for Deleuze and Guattari 'becoming' involves a process through which 'all forms are undone', they underline its regenerative capacity by aligning it with the botanical metaphor of the rhizome as a decentralised mode of thought and political practice. In contrast to vertical arborescent structures, which stand for stratified authoritarian totalities, the rhizome endlessly proliferates outwards in nomadic 'lines of flight' from established identities and systems of relations.[133] As the rhizome can be 'broken, shattered at a given spot, but will start up again on one of its old lines, or on new lines', it represents a creative intermediary state ('between things, interbeing') defined by flux, movement and change.[134] In Rulfo's monologue, the image of the peasants' bodies collectively spilling out across the plain like a 'relámpago de muertos' [lightning bolt of corpses] appears to enact Deleuze's and Guattari's notion of becoming as a 'line of escape' towards new zones of creation, while the intermingling elemental and organic images of their annihilation and re-composition strongly points to a rhizomatic process of rupture and regeneration.

Upholding the consistent link in Rulfo's literature between the image of the swarm and collective human sound, the droning mass of insects described in the first section of the monologue is aurally evoked as Sabines's invocations to God and specific saints are interspersed with a chorus of voices monotonously repeating the refrain 'ruega por nosotros' [pray for us]. As the chant grows more insistent, the poetic voice appeals to St Anthony, protector of animals, before launching into a profane litany:

> Atajo de malvados, punta de holgazanes.
> *Ruega por nosotros.*
> Sarta de bribones, retahíla de vagos.
> *Ruega por nosotros.*
> Cáfila de bandidos.
> *Ruega por nosotros* (II. 87–91)
>
> [Herd of villains, bunch of layabouts.
> *Pray for us*
> Pack of miscreants, string of idlers
> *Pray for us*
> Throng of bandits
> *Pray for us*]

On the annual feast day of St Anthony, animals are traditionally adorned with flowers and ribbons and brought into church spaces to be blessed. Rulfo's allusion to the saint and his description of the peasants as an 'atajo' [herd], directly recalling his comparison of the peasants of 'Nos han dado' to an 'atajo de mulas' [herd of mules], seems to grotesquely parody the *agrarista* notion of the *campesinado* as the 'blessed meek' by imagining the peasant collective as an animalised religious procession.

In view of the film's explicitly political agenda, Rulfo's reimagining of the peasant group as a swarm or herd can be illuminated by Deleuze and Guattari's conception of becoming-animal, a manifestation of 'becoming' that sees humans leave the realm of stable forms and enter a 'zone of indiscernibility' with the animal. Deleuze and Guattari draw their key examples of this process of nomadic deterritorialisation from literature and cinema but also underline its social significance by defining it as a collective impulse ('it always involves a pack, a band, a population, a peopling') that affects 'minoritarian' social groups located on 'the fringe of recognised institutions'.[135] For both thinkers, the subversive potential of 'demonic' animal collectives such as swarms, herds and packs is revealed through their rhizomatic composition.[136] As these assemblages lack a clear centre and operate along fluid horizontal connections, the collective becoming-animal of the peasantry suggests the possibility of their breaking away from the vertical power relations established with the angels in the first episode. This movement is also reflected in the typographic composition of the monologue. While the first section of the text adheres to a narrow vertical structure, it becomes unfixed in the second part where the lines begin to lurch horizontally across the page. Working against the strategies of collective subordination and immobilisation operating in Rivera's classically inspired fresco, the collapsing of the *campesinado* collective into a mobile, centreless mass in Rulfo's text gestures towards the possibility of an anarchic and pluralist mode of political organisation.

The decay of the muralist's orderly angelic congregation into the unstable animalised multitude of *La fórmula secreta* recalls the transition described by Wölfflin from the 'heavenly calm and content' of Renaissance composition to the baroque 'feeling of anticipation, of something yet to come, of dissatisfaction and restlessness'.[137] This sense of anticipation and agitation, this 'yet to be' of the baroque, acquires a more urgent and ominous dimension through the film's apocalyptic allusions. As biblical destruction prefigures the creation of a more just world, the film's apocalyptic imagery and soundscape underscore the political significance of the baroque pursuit of new forms. The threatening image of the swarm recalls numerous biblical descriptions of insect plagues inflicting divine retribution (Revelation 9:10, Exodus 23:28, Exodus 18:24), while their anticipated transformation into a 'lightning bolt of corpses' and a 'remolino de muertos' [whirlwind of death], calls to mind images of apocalyptic elemental destruction from the Books of Jeremiah (23:19), Isaiah (29:6) and Revelation (4:5). These descriptions of natural unrest, and the recurring image of the whirlwind in particular, capture the baroque's sublime intent to plunge the viewer into an 'abyss of infinity'.[138] The baroque motif of the whirlwind, described by Deleuze as 'a vortical form always put in motion by a renewed turbulence', is further evoked by the sound of howling winds and Sabines's booming voice which contribute to the film's attempt to create the sensation of falling through a vortex: 'surgen sueños incoherentes algunas veces a un ritmo violento, como si hubiera caído en la sonda de un remolino' [incoherent dreams rise up, sometimes at a violent pace, as if (the patient) had fallen into depths of a whirlwind].[139] These disorienting sound elements and the decentring shifts between low and high camera angles, and close-up and long shots, harness cinema's particular capacity to suggest the perceptual disintegration of the screen's boundaries. Discussing expressions of the neo-baroque in modern media, Ndalianis explains how sound and movement can be used to create a virtual *trompe l'oeil* effect that dynamically engages the viewer and thus destabilises classical spatial relations based on stable viewpoints and clear boundaries.[140] The unstable visual space created in Gámez's film and the nomadic mutating peasants inhabiting it, provide a counterpoint to the correlation between aesthetic and bodily composition previously analysed in *El reparto de tierras*. Signalling a move away from Rivera's concern with physical immobility and formal containment, the smooth cinematic space of *La fórmula secreta* articulates an emancipation of both aesthetic and collective bodily forms by sensorially evoking the eruption of the peasant mass from the confines of the screen.

As noted in the introduction to this chapter, the baroque emerged in seventeenth century Europe as a response to the collapse of the utopian project of the Renaissance. The turn towards baroque aesthetics in Gámez's film and more broadly in mid-century visual and literary expression in Mexico can also be viewed, in part, as a reaction to the crisis of the institutionalised Revolution and its established aesthetic models. As Paz later commented, muralism produced a sacralised iconography that granted divine authority to the state's interpretation of national reality: 'La gente mira sus pinturas como los devotos las imágenes sagradas [...] El Gobierno mexicano ha hecho del muralismo un culto nacional y, claro, en todos los cultos se proscribe la crítica' [People look at their paintings the way devotees look at sacred images... the Mexican government has turned muralism into a national cult and of course criticism is forbidden in all cults].[141] By appropriating religious forms and symbols in his early state-commissioned work, Rivera articulated a vision of collective post-revolutionary salvation based on collaboration between the state and a cooperative peasant population. With the onset of post-revolutionary disenchantment during the latter part of the twentieth century, however, muralism became the focus of revisionist assessment amongst writers and intellectuals. In a 1967 essay comparing the artistic traditions of muralism and the revolutionary novel, Revueltas challenged the leftist credentials of the movement, exposing its fundamental ideological contradictions. In revolutionary Mexican painting, he writes, 'el Estado, que representa a la burguesía, aparece flotando por encima de las contradicciones históricas y sociales, como la Divina Providencia flotaba encima de las aguas' [the State, which represents the bourgeoisie, floats over historical and social contradictions like God floating over the waters].[142] Revueltas claimed that through this collusion with the state, the movement had produced an 'espejo deformante' [distorting mirror] of Mexican reality.[143] Alongside Paz's account of the movement, Revueltas's bitter critique reveals the extent to which the iconography of the muralists weighed on a subsequent generation of artists reflecting on the Revolution's legacy into the 1960s. Considered in light of these comments, the abundance of inverted biblical images presented in Revueltas's own literature can perhaps be seen as an intentional strategy to produce a distorted vision of the already deformed images of the muralists.

Situating Rulfo's works within the same revisionist moment as Revueltas and Paz, the grim biblical parable of 'Luvina' and the profane litany of *La fórmula secreta* can also be understood as an attempt to actively disfigure the visual narratives of revolutionary redemption produced by Rivera and other nation-builders in the optimistic years that immediately followed the armed Revolution. A comparative analysis of these representations in the context of the post-revolutionary state's educational and agrarian reform programmes has revealed how both artists drew from strikingly similar iconographic vocabularies to illustrate the peasantry's response to state intervention or neglect in the countryside. By analysing a broad range of media including literature, muralism, illustration and cinema in the context of changing political discourses of agrarian reform, I have used their works to trace an evolution in aesthetic interpretations of the *campesino* collective from a receptive, malleable and docile collective to a resistant and potentially subversive entity.

Despite the clear political undercurrents to his representations of the peasantry, Rulfo denied the existence of any critical content in his work, asserting that 'una crítica se hace cuando uno se tiene (sic) una solución' [a criticism is made when there is a solution].[144] As an artist who came of age in a cultural sphere dominated by the muralists, Rulfo's resolute anti-didacticism suggests a conscious desire to move away from the sweeping political statements and visual rhetoric of the previous decades. His later turn to baroque aesthetics is indicative of such a shift. As Umberto Eco notes, the openness of the baroque can be perceived on both formal and interpretative levels, as it replaces the 'unquestionable definitiveness' of closed classical Renaissance form with a poetics of multiplicity and indeterminacy that invites multiple interpretations.[145] This move from Renaissance to baroque figuration in Rivera's and Rulfo's works again underlines a shift from a didactic to a more interrogative body aesthetic, or to recall Fuentes's description of the 'new novel', a transition 'de la seguridad de las respuestas a la impugnación de las preguntas' [from the security of answers to the impugnation of questions].[146] While, as Rulfo insists, his work offers no concrete solutions or strategies of resistance for the real counterparts of his disenfranchised *campesinos*, his images of corporeal instability and indeterminacy invite questions about the possibility of imagining alternative realities.

Notes to Chapter 4

1. 'Constitución política de los Estados Unidos Mexicanos', *Diario Oficial de la Federación*, 5 February 1917, art.27.
2. Guillermo Palacios, *La pluma y el arado: Los intelectuales pedagogos y la construcción sociocultural del 'problema campesino' en México, 1932–1934* (Mexico City: Colegio de México, 1999), p. 149; Adrian A. Bantjes, 'Idolatry and Iconoclasm in Revolutionary Mexico: The De-Christianization Campaigns, 1929–1940', *Mexican Studies/Estudios Mexicanos*, 13 (1997): 87–120 (p. 90).
3. Esther Acevedo and Fausto Ramírez, 'Introduction', in *Los pinceles de la historia: La fabricación del estado, 1864–1910*, ed. by Esther Acevedo and others (Mexico City: Museo Nacional de Arte, 2003), pp. 17–33 (p. 18).
4. Adrian A. Bantjes, 'Saints, Sinners and State Formation', in *The Eagle and the Virgin: Nation and Cultural Revolution in Mexico, 1920–1940*, ed. by Mary K. Vaughan and Stephen E. Lewis (Durham: Duke University Press, 2006), pp. 137–56 (p. 146).

5. Ilene V. O'Malley, *The Myth of Revolution: Hero Cults and the Institutionalization of the Mexican State, 1920–1940* (London: Greenwood, 1986), p. 130.
6. Ibid., p. 130.
7. Álvaro Obregón, quoted in Narciso Bassols Batalla, *El pensamiento político de Álvaro Obregón* (Mexico City: Ediciones 'El Caballito', 1970), p. 112.
8. Henríquez Ureña, 'La influencia de la Revolución en la vida intelectual de México', in *La utopía de América*, ed. by Ángel Rama and Rafael Gutiérrez Giradot (Caracas: Biblioteca Ayacucho, 1978), pp. 367–77 (p. 373).
9. Luis A. Marentes, *José Vasconcelos and the Writing of the Mexican Revolution* (Amherst: University of Massachusetts Press, 2000), p. 13.
10. Richard Stites, *Revolutionary Dreams: Utopian Vision and Experimental Life in the Russian Revolution* (Oxford: Oxford University Press, 1989), p. 102.
11. José Vasconcelos, 'Discurso en la Universidad (Con motivo de la toma de posesión del cargo de rector)', in *Obras completas*, vol.2 (Mexico City: Libreros Mexicanos Unidos, 1958), pp. 773–76 (p. 775).
12. José Vasconcelos, 'Invitación a los intelectuales y maestros para que se inscriban como misioneros', *Boletín de la Secretaría de Educación Pública*, 1 (1922), pp. 177–78 (p. 177).
13. Narciso Bassols, quoted in Francisco Manríquez, 'El ejido y el maestro rural', *MR*, 1 February 1933, p. 33.
14. Rivera shared this view of religion: 'Considero la religión una forma de neurosis colectiva. No soy enemigo de los católicos, así como no soy enemigo de los tuberculosos, los miopes o los paralíticos' [I consider religion to be a form of collective neurosis. I am not an enemy of Catholics, just as I am not an enemy of tuberculosis patients, the blind or paralytics]. Diego Rivera, quoted in Raquel Tibol, *Diego Rivera: Luces y sombras* (Barcelona: Lumen, 2007), p. 239. Consistent with the post-revolutionary discourses on motherhood discussed in Chapter 3, rural women were targeted by public health policy-makers to improve nutrition and hygiene levels within families. Margarita Velázquez, *Políticas sociales, transformación agraria y participación de las mujeres en el campo: 1920–1988* (Cuernavaca: UNAM, 1992), p. 42.
15. Prof. J. Lamberto Moreno, 'Himno a las comunidades infantiles escolares', *MR,* 15 November 1935, p. 58–59; 'Los apóstoles modernos', *MR*, 15 October 1932, p. 23; 'Maestros distinguidos de Oaxaca: Los doce mandamientos de la higiene', *MR*, 15 December 1935, p. 27.
16. Marte R. Gómez, 'Marte R. Gómez, agrarista', interviewed by James W. Wilkie, in *México visto en el siglo XX*, ed. by James W. Wilkie and Edna Monzón de Wilkie (Mexico City: Instituto Mexicano de Investigaciones Económicas, 1969), pp. 75–139 (p. 89).
17. 'Informe del Delegado del Ejido de San José de Santa Engracia', in *Tercera convención de la Liga de Comunidades Agrarias y Sindicatos Campesinos del Estado de Tamaulipas*, ed. by Marte R. Gómez (Mexico City: Editorial Cultura, 1928), pp. 180–83 (p. 180).
18. Dimitri Hazzikostas, 'Arms Raised', in *Encyclopedia of Comparative Iconography: Themes Depicted in Works of Art*, ed. by Helene E. Roberts (Chicago: Fitzroy Dearborn, 1998), pp. 50–58 (p. 54).
19. Comparisons can be also drawn with Anatolii Sokolov's poster *Let the Ruling Classes Shudder* (1922), where Lenin, enveloped by the stylised rays of a rising sun, raises his hand in a sign of benediction. As Bonnell notes, the positioning of the worker and peasant on either side of him recalls standard depictions of Christ and his apostles. Bonnell, p. 146.
20. My sincere thanks to Olga Kenton for this translation.
21. See, for example, Ephesians 1:18.
22. Matthew 6:22–23.
23. Magdaleno Aguilar, 'Discurso pronunciado por el Señor Magdaleno Aguilar', in *Segunda convención de la Liga de Comunidades Agrarias y Sindicatos Campesinos*, ed. by Marte R.Gómez (Mexico City: Editorial Cultura, 1926), pp. 87–89 (p. 88); Miguel Martínez Rojo, 'Discurso pronunciado por el C. Miguel Martínez Rojo', in *Segunda convención*, pp. 331–34 (p. 332).
24. Francisco Monterde, 'Libros para los campesinos', *MR*, 1 September 1933, p. 3–4.
25. Álvaro Yunque, 'Sé como este farol', *MR*, 1 May 1932, p. 17.
26. Matthew 13.14–23.
27. José Vasconcelos, 'Se convoca a las mujeres para la campaña contra el analfabetismo', in *José*

Vasconcelos y el espíritu de la Universidad, ed. by Javier Sicilia (Mexico City: UNAM, 2001) pp. 103–05 (p. 104); Gabriela Mistral, 'A un sembrador', in *Gabriela Mistral: Su prosa y poesía en Colombia, Vol. 3* (Santafé de Bogotá: Convenio Andrés Bello, 2002), p. 45.

28. Portes Gil, 'Discurso pronunciado por el señor lic. Emilio Portes Gil, Gobernador constitucional del estado de Tamaulipas y apertura de los trabajos de la convención', in *Primera convención de la Liga de Comunidades Agrarias y Sindicatos Campesinos*, ed. by Marte R. Gómez (Mexico City: Editorial Cultura, 1926), pp. 69–77 (p. 74); Aguilar, p. 88.
29. Melanie Huska, 'Historically Themed Comic Books as Civic Education in 1980s Mexico', in *Comics as History, Comics as Literature: Roles of the Comic Book in Scholarship, Society, and Entertainment*, ed. by Annessa Ann Babic (Madison: Fairleigh Dickinson University Press, 2013), pp. 65–78 (p. 67).
30. On the theme of hygiene in *El sembrador*, see María Rosa Gudiño, 'Educación higiénica y consejos de salud para campesinos en el sembrador y el maestro rural, 1929–1934', in *Curar, sanar y educar: Enfermedad y sociedad en México, siglos XIX y XX*, ed. by Claudia Agostoni (Mexico City: UNAM/Benemérita Universidad Autónoma de Puebla, 2008) pp. 71–97.
31. 'Los apóstoles modernos', p. 23.
32. Ángel Cifuentes, 'El maestro rural', *MR*, May–June, 1940, p. 18.
33. 'Cursos para correspondencia — organización escolar a cargo del Profesor Felipe de J. Espinosa, Lección 18: Horarios', *MR*, 15 May 1932, p. 29; Wenceslao Rodríguez, 'El maíz', *MR*, 1 December 1932, p. 10.
34. 'Proyecto de bases para la liga de comunidades agrarias del estado de Tamaulipas, Tamps', in *Primera convención*, pp. 231–37 (p. 278)
35. Gerald V. O'Brien and Autumn Molinari, 'Religious Metaphors as a Justification for Eugenic Control: A Historical Analysis', in *Disability in Judaism, Christianity, and Islam: Sacred texts, Historical traditions, and Social Analysis*, ed. by Darla Schumm and Michael Stoltzfus (Basingstoke: Palgrave Macmillan, 2011), pp. 141–65 (p. 147).
36. Stepan, p. 136.
37. Luther Burbank, *The Training of the Human Plant* (New York: Century Company, 1907), p. 48.
38. Karin Alejandra Rosemblatt, *The Science and Politics of Race in Mexico and the United States, 1910–1950* (Chapel Hill: The University of North Carolina Press, 2018) p. 22.
39. Samuel Morales Pereira, *Algunas consideraciones sobre las causas que motivan la gran mortalidad de la primera infancia y recursos que deben oponerse para combatirlas* (Mexico City Oficina Tip. de la Secretaría de Fomento, 1888), p. 50.
40. Ángel Zimbrón, 'Odontología en Relación con la Higiene', *Revista Mexicana de Ciencias Medicas*, 7 (1932), 1659 –73, (p. 1660); Dr Fermín Viniegra, 'Capítulo de un libro de obstetricia: Diagnóstico de la infección puerperal', *Pasteur: Revista mensual de medicina*, 11 (1938), 85–87 (p. 86).
41. Engracia Loyo, 'La educación del pueblo', in *Historia mínima de la educación en México*, ed. by Dorothy Tanck de Estrada (Mexico City: El Colegio de México, 2010), pp. 154–87 (p. 167).
42. Paul Gillingham and Benjamin T. Smith, 'Introduction', in *Dictablanda: Politics, Work, and Culture in Mexico, 1938–1968* (Durham: Duke University Press, 2014), p. 1–44 (p. 12).
43. Matthew Butler, *Popular Piety and Political Identity in Mexico's Cristero Rebellion: Michoacán, 1927–29* (Oxford: Oxford University Press for the British Academy, 2004), p. 90.
44. Raby identifies 139 incidents of violence or threats of violence against rural teachers between 1931 and 1940. David L. Raby, 'Los maestros rurales y los conflictos sociales en Mexico (1931–1940)', *Historia Mexicana*, 18 (1968), 190–226 (p. 191). To mark this wave of violence, the SEP commissioned the artist Leopoldo Méndez to produce a portfolio of seven lithographs entitled *En nombre de Cristo: Han asesinado más de 200 maestros* (1939).
45. Rulfo described pro-Cristero communities as 'pueblos muy reaccionarios, pueblos con ideas muy conservadoras, fanáticos' [very reactionary communities, communities with very conservative and fanatical ideas]. Juan Rulfo, quoted in Luis Harss, *Los nuestros* (Buenos Aires: Editorial Sudamericana, 1969), p. 308.
46. Rulfo stated: 'Nosotros somos bautizados, hemos ido a la Iglesia, hemos hecho la primera comunión, hemos practicado la religión hasta cierta edad [...] entonces, hemos abandonado bastante la cosa del catolicismo' [We are baptised, we went to church, we made our first

communion, we practised religion up until a certain age ... then we more or less abandoned Catholicism]. Juan Rulfo, quoted in García Bonilla, p. 10–11.

47. Despite the narrator's encouragement, his interlocutor notably never drinks his beer (p. 126)
48. 'Me sonaba a nombre de cielo aquel nombre' [That name sounded like a heavenly name to me] (p. 132). In a footnote, Thakkar links the name Luvina to the phrase 'Luz Divina'. Thakkar, *The Fiction of Juan Rulfo*, p. 76.
49. Ibid., p. 77.
50. The town's full name (San Juan Luvina) also prefigures that of Susana San Juan who, as noted in the previous chapter, is profoundly linked to water imagery in *Pedro Parámo.*
51. Yvette Jiménez de Báez, *Juan Rulfo, del Páramo a la esperanza: Una lectura crítica de su obra* (Mexico City: Colegio de México: Fondo de Cultura Económica, 1990), p. 109.
52. 'Los mirará pasar como sombras, repegados al muro de las casas, casi arrastrados por el viento' [you will see them pass by like shadows, sticking close to the walls of the houses, almost dragged by the wind] (131). 'Mujeres sin fuerzas, casi trabadas de tan flacas' [Weak women, so thin they are just skin and bone] (130).
53. Boldy, p. 38. The regular hygiene bulletins in *El maestro rural* indicate that rural teachers frequently acted as community physicians and dentists. Dr Ernesto León Nogueira, 'Orientación de higiene rural un programa de salud dental en el medio rural', *MR*, May–June 1940, p. 13.
54. The term *ejido* refers to an area of land farmed communally under a state-supported system. The system is discussed in greater detail in the second part of this chapter.
55. Matthew 13:12–13.
56. Matthew 13:15.
57. Palacios, p. 43.
58. Dan La Botz, *Democracy in Mexico: Peasant Rebellion and Political Reform* (Boston: South End Press, 1995), p. 96.
59. Hubert Carton de Grammont and Horacio Mackinlay, 'Campesino and Indigenous Social Organizations Facing Democratic Transition in Mexico, 1938–2006', *Latin American Perspectives*, 36 (2009), 21-40 (pp.23-24).
60. Howard J. Wiarda, *The Soul of Latin America: The Cultural and Political Tradition* (New Haven: Yale University Press, 2001), p. 260–62.
61. Saint Thomas Aquinas, *Sermon-Conferences of St. Thomas Aquinas on the Apostles Creed*, ed. Nicholas Ayo (Notre Dame: University of Notre Dame Press, 1988), p. 135.
62. Wiarda, *The Soul of Latin America*, p. 260–62.
63. Howard J. Wiarda, 'Corporatist Theory and Ideology: A Latin American Development Paradigm', *Journal of Church and State*, 20 (1978), 29–56 (p. 33–34).
64. Lázaro Cárdenas, 'Discurso del presidente del partido nacional revolucionario sobre el programa de trabajo para el año de 1931', in *Palabras y documentos públicos de Lázaro Cárdenas: 1928–1970*, pp. 98–101, (p. 99).
65. Gladys McCormick, 'The Forgotten Jaramillo: Building a Social Base of Support for Authoritarianism in Rural Mexico', in *Dictablanda*, pp. 196–215 (p. 199).
66. John M. Hart, 'Agrarian Reform', in *Twentieth-Century Mexico*, ed. by. William H. Beezley and Dirk W. Raat (Lincoln: University of Nebraska Press, 1986), pp. 6–16 (p. 14).
67. Fred S. Kleiner, *Gardner's Art through the Ages: The Western Perspective* (London: Cengage Learning, 2010), p. 407.
68. Heinrich Wölfflin, *Principles of Art History: The Problem of the Development of Style in Early Modern Art*, trans. by Jonathan Blower (California: Getty Publications, 2015), p. 83–99.
69. Heinrich Wölfflin, *Renaissance and Baroque*, trans. by Kathrin Simon (London: Collins, 1964), p. 58.
70. Lois Parkinson Zamora and Monika Kaup, 'Categories and Concepts', in *Baroque New Worlds: Representation, Transculturation, Counterconquest*, ed. by Lois Parkinson Zamora and Monika Kaup (Durham: Duke University Press, 2010), pp. 1–14.
71. Severo Sarduy, *Barroco* (Buenos Aires: Editorial Sudamericana, 1974), p. 184.
72. José Vasconcelos, 'José Vasconcelos por Ortega', *El Universal Ilustrado*, 23 November 1923, p. 35.
73. José Clemente Orozco, quoted in Alma M. Reed, *Orozco* (New York: Oxford University Press, 1956), p. 179. This is not to say that the muralists never incorporated baroque elements into

their works. Fuentes identifies Siqueiros as the first of *los tres grandes* to initiate a transition away from the 'privileged vision' of Renaissance composition towards baroque forms. Carlos Fuentes, *Viendo visiones* (Mexico City: Fondo de Cultura Económica, 2003), p. 384.

74. Jean Charlot, *El renacimiento del muralismo mexicano 1920–1925* (Mexico City: Editorial Domés, 1985); Dr Atl, 'Colaboración artística: ¿Renacimiento artístico?', *El Universal*, 13 July 1923, p. 3.
75. Marte R. Gómez, quoted in de Pina García, p. 42.
76. Louis Gillet, 'L'art dans l'Amérique latine', in *Histoire de l'art*, ed. by André Michel (Paris: Colin, 1929), pp. 1023–96 (p. 1093).
77. Jeffrey T. Schnapp, 'Mob Porn', in *Crowds*, ed. by Jeffrey T. Schnapp and Matthew Tiews (Stanford: Stanford University Press, 2006), pp. 1–46 (p. 5).
78. Richard Offner, 'Giotto, Non-Giotto', in *Giotto: The Arena Chapel Frescoes*, ed. by James H. Stubblebine (London: Thames and Hudson, 1969), pp. 135–55 (p. 139).
79. Jonathan B. Reiss, 'Justice and the Common Good in Giotto's Arena Chapel Frescoes', in *The Arena Chapel and the Genius of Giotto: Padua*, ed. by Andrew Ladis (London: Garland, 1998), pp. 233–44 (p. 237).
80. Ibid., p. 329.
81. This motto is emblazoned on one of the panels in the Patio del Trabajo of the SEP.
82. Emilio Zomzet, 'Diego Rivera en el pueblo cooperativo en Chapingo', *Cultura urbana*, 3 (2007), pp. 70–71 (p. 70). Silva Herzog writes that the cooperative project failed due to poor land quality. Jesús Silva Herzog, *Una vida en la vida de México y Mis últimas andanzas, 1947–1972* (Mexico City: Siglo Veintiuno Editores, 1973), p. 81.
83. Álvaro Obregón quoted in Emilio Portes Gil, *Autobiografía de la Revolución Mexicana: Un tratado de interpretación histórica* (Mexico City: Instituto Mexicano de Cultura, 1964), p. 330; Emilio Portes Gil, 'Discurso pronunciado por el señor lic. Emilio Portes Gil, gobernador constitucional del estado', in *Segunda convención*, pp. 81–86 (p. 81–82).
84. Vicente Lombardo Toledano, 'El reparto de tierras a los pobres no se opone a las enseñanzas de nuestro señor Jesucristo y de la santa madre iglesia', in *Obra histórico-cronológica* (Mexico City: Centro de Estudios Filosóficos, Políticos y Sociales Vicente Lombardo Toledano, 1994), pp. 117–21 (p. 118).
85. Ibid., p. 118.
86. Matthew Butler, 'God's Campesinos? Mexico's Revolutionary Church in the Countryside', *Bulletin of Latin American Research*, 28 (2009), 165–84 (p. 170).
87. Charette Blaine, *The Theme of Recompense in Matthew's Gospel* (London: Bloomsbury, 2015), p. 86; Thomas Watson, *The Beatitudes: An Exposition of Matthew 5:1–12* (London: Banner of Truth Trust, 1971), p. 48.
88. Antonio Soto y Gama, 'El milagro del ejido', in *El pensamiento de Antonio Soto y Gama a través de 50 años de labor periodística 1899–1949*, ed. by Ramón Iglesias González (Mexico City: UNAM, Instituto de Investigaciones Jurídicas, 1997), pp. 124–26, (p. 124).
89. María Rosa Gudiño and Guillermo Palacios, 'Peticiones de tierra y estrategias discursivas campesinas: procesos, contenidos y problemas metodológicos', in *Estudios campesinos en el Archivo General Agrario*, ed. by Antonio Escobar Ohmstede (Mexico City: Registro Agrario Nacional: Centro de Investigaciones y Estudios Superiores en Antropología Social, 1998), pp. 75–118 (p. 108).
90. Ignacio Gutiérrez Ruvalcaba, 'Aproximación visual al mundo campesino', in *La memoria agraria mexicana en imágenes: Cuatro ensayos*, ed. by Ignacio Gutiérrez Ruvalcaba (Mexico City: Registro Agrario Nacional, 2002), pp. 13–62 (p. 33).
91. Ibid., p. 24.
92. Schnapp, p. 5.
93. Gilles Deleuze and Félix Guattari, *A Thousand Plateaus: Capitalism and Schizophrenia*, trans. by Brian Massumi (London: Continuum, 2004), p. 18.
94. Moshe Barasch, *Giotto and the Language of Gesture* (Cambridge: Cambridge University Press, 1987), p. 42.
95. Ibid., p. 46. Rivera's *La liberación del peón* (1923) in the SEP is also based on this fresco.
96. Deleuze and Guattari, p. 545.

97. Friedrich Schuler, *Mexico Between Hitler and Roosevelt: Mexican Foreign Relations in the Age of Lázaro Cárdenas, 1934–1940* (Albuquerque: University of New Mexico Press, 1998), p. 175.
98. José Abel Ogaz Pierce, 'El pensamiento agrario del joven Vicente Lombardo Toledano', in *Personajes, cuestión agraria y Revolución Mexicana*, ed. by Mónica Blanco and Esperanza Fujigaki (Mexico City: INHERM, 2004), pp. 311–42 (p. 329).
99. Tanalís Padilla, *Rural Resistance in the Land of Zapata: The Jaramillista Movement and the Myth of the Pax-Priísta, 1940–1962* (Durham: Duke University Press, 2008).
100. Vicente Lombardo Toledano, 'Capitalismo agrícola contra reforma agraria', in *Escritos en Siempre!* (Mexico City: Ediciones CEFPSVLT, 1994), pp. 195–99, (p. 195).
101. Jesús Silva Herzog, *El agrarismo mexicano y la reforma agraria: exposición y crítica* (Mexico City: Fondo de Cultura Económica, 1959); Moisés T. de la Peña, *El pueblo y la tierra: Mito y realidad de la reforma agraria en México* (Mexico City: Cuadernos Americanos, 1964).
102. José Revueltas, *Ensayo sobre un proletariado sin cabeza* (Mexico City: Ediciones Era, 1980).
103. Elena Garro, 'El problema agrario sigue en pie después de 50 años de revolución', *Siempre!* (*La cultura en México* supplement), 1 September 1965, pp. 2–12; Carlos Fuentes, 'Carlos Fuentes', in *Los narradores ante el público*, ed. by Rubén Marín (Mexico City: Joaquín Mortiz, 1966), pp. 137–55 (p. 153).
104. Rulfo's text was first published independently in the 'La cultura en México' supplement of the magazine *Siempre!* in 1976.
105. Rulfo, 'Juan Rulfo examina su narrativa', p. 460.
106. Ibid., p. 460.
107. It also worth noting that while the film criticises the linguistic implications of U.S. cultural influence in Mexico, it was originally released with English subtitles.
108. Patrick Iber, 'The Cold War Politics of Literature and the Centro Mexicano de Escritores', *Journal of Latin American Studies*, 48 (2016), 247–72 (p. 267).
109. Raúl Anguiano, *Raúl Anguiano, remembranzas* (Toluca: Universidad Autónoma del Estado de México, 1995), p. 80; Adolfo Lopéz Mateos, *Pensamiento en acción: Discursos y declaraciones*, vol. 2 (Mexico City: Oficina de Prensa, 1963); Marco Aurelio Carballo also claims that Rulfo was a speech writer for López Mateos, see 'Los discursos de López Mateos, escritos por Juan Rulfo', *Siempre!*, 27 May 1987, pp. 30–31.
110. Elena Poniatowska, 'Entrevista: Elena Poniatowska, "No tengo más que preguntas sobre las cosas"', interviewed by Jacobo G. García, *El Mundo*, 18 April 2014.
111. Rubén Gámez, 'Rubén Gámez: Mi pretensión es crear un cine realmente mexicano', interviewed by Emilio Garcia Riera, in *La fórmula secreta: Rubén Gámez*, ed. by Damián Ortega (Mexico City: Alias, 2014), pp. 182–84 (p. 182). Gámez notably also borrowed Rulfo's original title for *Pedro Páramo* for his 1974 film *Los murmullos*.
112. Niamh Thornton, *Revolution and Rebellion in Mexican Film*, (New York: Bloomsbury Academic, 2013), p. 35.
113. Andrea Noble, *Mexican National Cinema*, (London: Routledge, 2005), p. 18.
114. El Grupo Nuevo Cine, 'Manifiesto del Grupo Nuevo Cine', in *Hojas de cine: Testimonios y documentos del nuevo cine latinoamericano*, ed. by Fundación Mexicana de Cineastas (Mexico City: Secretaría de Educación Pública: Universidad Autónoma Metropolitana, 1988), pp. 33–35.
115. Carlos Monsiváis, 'El peñón de las ánimas: A 35 años de un feliz aniversario', *Siempre!*, 12 January 1966, pp. xvi–xvii (p. xvii).
116. Rubén Gámez, 'Conversaciones con Rubén Gámez', interviewed by Alejandro Pelayo Rangel, in *La fórmula secreta*, pp. 362– 371 (p. 371).
117. John A. Ochoa, *The Uses of Failure in Mexican Literature and Identity* (Austin: University of Texas Press, 2004), p. 145.
118. Fuentes, *La nueva novela hispanoamericana*, p. 32.
119. Carlos Fuentes, 'La violenta identidad de José Luis Cuevas', in *Casa con dos puertas* (Mexico City: Joaquín Mortiz, 1970), pp. 239–80 (p. 240–41).
120. Jesse Lerner, 'Rubén Gámez: Cine neobarroco en tiempos de cambio', in *La fórmula secreta: Rubén Gámez*, ed. by Damián Ortega (Mexico City: Alias, 2014), pp. 310–21.
121. Angela Ndalianis, 'From Neo-Baroque to Neo-Baroques?', *Revista Canadiense de Estudios Hispánicos*, 33 (2008), 265–80 (p. 267).

122. In the monologue's opening description of this debilitated community (I. 13–14) Rulfo uses the common idiomatic expression 'no tener dónde caerse muerto' meaning 'to not have a penny to one's name' which translates literally as 'to not have a place to drop dead'.
123. Juan Rulfo, 'La fórmula secreta', in Juan Rulfo, *El gallo de oro; La fórmula secreta*, ed. by José Carlos González Boixo and Douglas Weatherford (Mexico City: Ediciones RM, 2010), pp. 151–55 (I. 13–14). Further references to this edition are given after quotations in the text.
124. Rulfo's decision to structure the monologue as a cry for divine assistance was likely influenced by Rainer Maria Rilke's *Duino Elegies*, which he translated into Spanish between 1945 and 1953. The first of Rilke's elegies opens with the despairing poetic voice appealing to a chorus of terrifying angels to take heed of human suffering. Rainer Maria Rilke, *Elegías de Duino*, trans. by Juan Rulfo (Madrid: Sexto Piso España, 2015).
125. Jean Charlot, 'Mexican Ex-Votos', *Magazine of Art*, 42 (1949), 139–42 (p. 141).
126. Juan Rulfo, 'España en el corazón', in *Toda la obra*, pp. 381–83 (p. 381).
127. Wölfflin, *Principles of Art History*, pp. 274–304.
128. Gilles Deleuze, *Francis Bacon* (London: Continuum, 2005), p. 85.
129. Laura U. Marks, *The Skin of the Film: Intercultural Cinema, Embodiment, and the Senses* (London: Duke University Press, 2000), p. 163.
130. Ibid., p. 178.
131. Simon O'Sullivan, 'Fold', in *Deleuze Dictionary Revised Edition*, ed. by Adrian Parr (Edinburgh: Edinburgh University Press, 2010), pp. 107–09 (p. 107).
132. Deleuze and Guattari, *A Thousand Plateaus:*, p. 380.
133. Ibid., p. 36.
134. Ibid., p. 23; p. 10.
135. Ibid., p. 239, p. 272.
136. Ibid., p. 23.
137. Wölfflin, *Renaissance and Baroque*, p. 38.
138. Ibid., p. 86.
139. Gilles Deleuze, *The Fold*, trans. by Tom Conley (London: Continuum: 2006), p. 4; Juan Rulfo, 'Sinopsis', in *Toda la obra*, pp. 363–64 (p. 364). In this quote Rulfo is referring to the anonymous patient depicted at the beginning of the film.
140. Angela Ndalianis, *Neo-baroque Aesthetics and Contemporary Entertainment* (Cambridge, MA: MIT Press, 204), p. 28.
141. Octavio Paz, 'Visión e ideología sobre el muralismo mexicano', *Vuelta*, 1 December 1986, p. 14.
142. José Revueltas, 'Escuela Mexicana de Pintura y novela de la Revolución', in *Cuestionamientos e intenciones* (Mexico City: Ediciones Era, 1981), pp. 241–74 (p. 261).
143. Ibid., p. 261.
144. Juan Rulfo, 'He dejado de publicar, pero nunca dejaré de escribir: Juan Rulfo', interviewed by Dimas Lidio Pitty, *El Gallo Ilustrado*, 5 July 1970, p. 3.
145. Umberto Eco, *The Role of the Reader: Explorations in the Semiotics of Texts* (London: Hutchinson, 1981), p. 52.
146. Fuentes, *La nueva novela hispanoamericana*, p. 13.

CONCLUSION

The Nuevo Cine movement in Mexico emerged against a backdrop of mounting social and political unrest during the 1960s that is often seen as culminating in the eruption of the student movement in Mexico City at the end of that decade. While the student demonstrations of 1968 were arguably no more significant than political mobilisations instigated by rural and working-class groups earlier in that decade, their violent suppression marked a turning point in public perception and dealt a mortal blow to the illusion of the Mexican state as protector of the nation's revolutionary values. Mobilising the slogans and symbols of the Mexican Revolution, the students sought to repossess the revolutionary discourse of a PRI government that after four decades of electoral hegemony had started to face accusations of neo-Porfirian authoritarianism. On 2 October, ten days before the Summer Olympics were to begin in the capital, the military opened fire on several thousand students congregating at the Plaza de las Tres Culturas in the Tlatelolco district of Mexico City, killing a still undefined number. Although the violent silencing of the protesters prevented the movement from achieving the radical democratic change it demanded, the massacre and the cycle of protests that followed produced a crisis of legitimacy for the PRI that gradually eroded its authority, giving way to limited political pluralism in the subsequent decades.[1]

Elena Poniatowska noted the parallels between the student uprising and the events that unfolded between 1910 and 1917 but underlined a fundamental difference: 'La movilización en la calle no era de campesinos ni obreros. Se trataba de una marcha de leídos y escribidos que se rebelaban' [The protests in the streets were not led by peasants or workers. This was a demonstration of well-read people and writers who were rebelling].[2] Just as visual art had been instrumental to its consolidation, literature was bound up in the attempted dismantling of the institutionalised Revolution. Rulfo pledged his support for the students along with several other writers including Vicente Leñero, Monsiváis and Revueltas, a figure commonly identified as one of the movement's intellectual architects. Lines of Paz's poetry were emblazoned on banners during marches and subsequently read by imprisoned protesters.[3] Alongside other poetic and prose works by Paz, Luis González de Alba and María Luisa Mendoza, Poniatowska's *La noche de Tlatelolco* (1971), a text combining testimonial fragments and graphic images of the protesters' mutilated bodies, played a critical role in challenging state-authorised accounts of the event in its aftermath.

The subtle interplay between textual and bodily fragmentation established in Poniatowska's work also emerges in Paz's poem 'Totalidad y fragmento' (1970), where the poet engages in a broader meditation on how artists respond to moments of national trauma. Dedicated to the Ruptura artist José Luis Cuevas, the poem concludes with the line: 'José Luis dibuja nuestra herida' [José Luis sketches our wound].[4] Throughout this poem, artistic expression is conceived as an act of violence inflicted on the blank page by instruments of visual and literary production:

contra la hoja
desgarra acribilla pincha sollama atiza
acuchilla apuñala traspasa abrasa calcina
pluma lápiz pincel (12–15)

[Against the page
rips, riddles, pricks, singes, jabs,
gashes, stabs, pierces, burns, scorches
pen, pencil, paintbrush]

The resulting 'wound' is figured as a 'pueblo de líneas' [nation of lines], which in turn is linked to the lines sketched by the artist and those verbally constructed by the poet. The acts of writing and drawing produce a wound that is 'ours' — a mark on both the surface of the page and the collective body of the nation. This collapsing of poetic and pictorial forms is registered in the text's striking visual composition: multiple fragmented lines combine to form both the aesthetic whole of the poem and the imagined nation. Through these interlinked elements, the body, the artwork and the nation converge to form a single entity whose meaning is inscribed by the visual artist and the writer. This book has explored how post-revolutionary artists and thinkers used the body to narrate the Mexican nation during moments of societal transition and crisis, from the chaotic but optimistic years immediately following the end of the revolutionary conflict to the disillusionment of the 1960s. Examining mobilisations of the body across a range of artistic, political and intellectual contexts, its historically situated comparative analysis has shed light for the first time on its function as a locus for the articulation of specific aspirations and anxieties regarding the revolutionary project across Rivera's and Rulfo's works, and its broader centrality, in both metaphorical and material terms, to post-revolutionary formulations of national identity during these decades.

The interplay between visual and literary forms in Paz's poem also highlights the close interactions between these media in post-revolutionary artistic production. This book has significantly expanded our understanding of this dynamic relationship by establishing a sustained and comprehensive dialogue between visual and verbal forms of representation in Mexico over an extended historical period. By analysing the treatment of common themes across literary and visual texts spanning from the 1920s to the 1960s, I have demonstrated how artistic practitioners operating in a range of media contributed to ongoing debates on national identity during these decades and how their works were influenced by or responded to concepts and images circulating within a shared artistic sphere. This interartistic approach, which acknowledges the fluid interactions and exchanges that existed between visual media and literature during this period, provides a productive way forward for future studies of post-revolutionary cultural production.

Throughout this book, I have embraced an expansive intermedial interpretation of 'the visual' that could be fruitfully employed by researchers carrying out comparative studies of visual and literary works in other cultural and historical contexts. Looking beyond a simple comparative reading of visual and textual images, I have explored how visuality is constructed in and experienced through painted images, illustrations, photographs, literary texts, films and architectural spaces. My discussion of Rivera's muralism has drawn attention to the manner in which pictorial content and architectural setting work together to shape the visual experience of the spectator, often with the aim of generating a sense of visual control or mastery. In addition to documenting his photographic and cinematic production and interest in painting, my analysis of Rulfo has also spotlighted his profound literary preoccupation with issues relating to sight and vision. Through its comparative and historically grounded approach, the book has sought to illuminate and contextualise the unique forms of vision and ways of seeing that are embedded in and invited by these works. While Rivera privileges totalising forms of vision and frequently links seeing and knowledge in his murals and illustrations, Rulfo's work reflects a consistent concern with the limitations of visual perception, from his literary descriptions of impaired vision and perceptual crisis to his photographic interest in ambiguous subjects that challenge or unsettle the eye of the beholder. I have suggested how these distinct models might be interpreted in historical terms, arguing that while Rivera's model reflects the enduring influence of a Porfirian visual regime that embraced positivism's faith in the observation of phenomena, Rulfo's work signals a mid-century movement away from this privileging of the eye and confidence in visual forms of knowing.

By situating Rivera and Rulfo within a wider network of thinkers and artists who shaped the national imaginary during these decades, *Post-Revolutionary Body Politics* has spotlighted the profound but previously underexplored links between intellectual and artistic spheres during these decades. In exploring both artists' works in the context of contemporary developments in the fields of philosophy, historiography, anthropology and architecture, and against the shifting landscapes of twentieth-century intellectual and political history, it has illuminated the specific conditions that harvested their aesthetic visions, as well as previously unexamined patterns in how the Revolution and its outcomes were understood in political, intellectual and artistic spheres. Identifying and analysing the treatment of common themes and metaphors in their work reveals how certain aspects of national identity continued to preoccupy artists and intellectuals and the extent to which perspectives on such concepts evolved during these critical decades of societal transformation.

My discussion has already indicated several avenues for further interdisciplinary inquiry. By incorporating previously explored archival material, the final chapter drew attention to the use of religious motifs and iconography in government visual propaganda during the rural education campaigns of the 1920s and 30s. This intersection between revolutionary politics and religious symbolism within the domains of visual and literary culture demands further scholarly attention, particularly in the context of the religiously motivated Cristero War. It has also attempted to stimulate further discussion of Rulfo's still understudied visual corpus. By exploring the political dimensions of Rulfo's photographs and highlighting the formal, rather than solely thematic, parallels between his textual and visual works, the book signals a way forward for future studies of this corpus. Rulfo's photographs, along with his screenplays and writings on architecture, remain a largely untapped resource that can provide greater insight into his aesthetic and political concerns, as well as his complex relationship with the Mexican government. Although only briefly addressed in this project, further research into Rivera's work as both an architect and theorist of building design would also provide a new perspective from which to assess this canonical artist and the creative exchanges that took place between muralism and architecture during this period.

Building on previous studies on depictions of the body in post-revolutionary literary and visual culture by scholars like Janzen and Dalton, the book has sought to deepen our historical appreciation of such representations by offering the first comprehensive account of how corporeal metaphors were mobilised for political purposes from the late nineteenth century through to the mid-twentieth century. More broadly, this analysis has also sought to expand traditional investigative approaches to the corporeal in art and literature by examining not only visual and textual representations of the body but also the embodied forms of engagement they elicit, from embodied reading and haptic cinematic spectatorship to the physical negotiation of mural sites.

Throughout *Post-Revolutionary Body Politics*, I have argued that Rivera's and Rulfo's corporeal imaginaries embody two distinct visions of revolutionary nationhood in the twentieth century, of its utopian possibilities and devastating realities, that nevertheless converse with each other. These visions continue to inhabit the present. Although somewhat eclipsed today by his wife Frida Kahlo, Rivera's murals remain integral to the official image of Mexico that is promoted both domestically and internationally. During his presidency, Enrique Peña Nieto routinely welcomed political leaders at the Palacio Nacional by offering an explanatory tour of Rivera's *Epopeya del pueblo mexicano*. In June 2018, Peña Nieto announced the opening of a new history museum in the palace that would inspire national pride in Mexicans and function as 'un valioso instrumento para la difusión de la historia y de los valores cívicos entre los mexicanos' [a valuable instrument for disseminating history and civic values amongst Mexicans].[5] In his inaugural speech, Minister of Finance José Antonio González Anaya positioned the museum within a tradition of public cultural dissemination in Mexico initiated by Vasconcelos and Rivera's fresco programme at the SEP.[6] It is perhaps unsurprising then that Peña Nieto's successor, Andrés Manuel López Obrador, who pledged during his presidential campaign to eradicate corruption and usher in a new era in Mexican politics, has emphasised the role of literature in shaping his understanding of politics and listed *Pedro Páramo* among the three books to have had the greatest impact on his life.[7] To mark the bicentenary of the end of the War of Independence in 2021, López Obrador pledged to reprint special editions of 'classic' works of Mexican literature including texts by Rulfo, Fuentes and Poniatowska.[8]

These examples demonstrate how works of art continue to function as valuable tools of legitimacy for contemporary politicians. They also reveal that while Rivera's visual narratives remain closely intertwined with institutionalised discourses of national identity, Rulfo's literature still appears to resonate with an alternative political perspective. Tributes and commemorative events marking the centenary of the writer's birth in 2017 confirmed his status as a monumental figure in the field of Mexican letters and prompted reflection on the resonance of his bleakest narratives in a contemporary Mexico facing persistent inequality, state corruption and increasing levels of violence. For the essayist and writer Jorge Volpi, the reverberations of Rulfo's novel reveal the lack of any significant change in the political landscape since its original publication: 'nos habla tanto de su tiempo como del nuestro' [it speaks to us as much about his time as about our own].[9]

How can these seemingly irreconcilable images co-exist within the cultural imagination? The potent afterlives of these two artistic corpora suggest, to recall Alan Knight, that the Revolution continues to be 'many revolutions'.[10] Historians and non-specialists alike remain divided on whether the events that unfolded between 1910 and 1917 ultimately gave rise to a genuinely egalitarian democratic society or the consolidation of an authoritarian state that has still failed to address the problems of corruption, violence and social inequality. The political legacy of the Revolution is most powerfully embodied by the PRI, a party that retained hegemonic rule from 1929 to 2000 and experienced a resurgence with the presidency of Peña Nieto from 2012 to 2018. The centenary of the promulgation of the Mexican Constitution in 2017 provided an opportunity to reassess the party's material achievements in upholding the Revolution's supposed social ideals. Addressing the nation at the official commemorative ceremony to mark one hundred and seven years since the outbreak of the Revolution in November 2017, Peña Nieto defended the government from criticism of its democratic failings by insisting that 'las instituciones son entidades vivas, inmersas en un proceso permanente de transformación y perfeccionamiento' [institutions are living entities, immersed in an ongoing process of transformation and improvement].[11] The analogy is significant, not only because it indicates that body metaphors are alive and well in contemporary Mexican politics, but because of the line of continuity it reveals with Porfirian organicist theories. Peña Nieto's description of state institutions as living entities engaged in an ongoing process of 'transformation and improvement' echoes the biological metaphors of societal evolution used by Justo Sierra to justify the authoritarianism of the Díaz regime. By conceptualising societal development in physiological terms, the Científicos promoted a gradual and orderly process of change directed by a centralised state as opposed to sudden revolutionary transformation. In his 1879 essay 'Positivismo político', quoted in the Introduction to this book, Sierra explains that 'society, like every organism, is subject to the necessary laws of evolution' and argues that the gradual development of this organism's constitutive parts will result in 'a process of continuous improvement, which in societies is called progress'.[12] The paradoxical correlation between these statements, uttered almost one hundred and forty years apart, reveals the importance of examining bodily metaphors to understand the contradictions and complexities of Mexico's recent political history. While this book has focused on the corporeal images produced by Rivera and Rulfo in the period spanning from the 1920s to the 1960s, it has indicated the need for a historically expanded exploration of political bodies in Mexico and their parallel lives within the artistic and cultural spheres.

Notes to the Conclusion

1. Dolores Trevizo, *Rural Protest and the Making of Democracy in Mexico, 1968–2000* (University Park: Pennsylvania State University Press, 2011), p. 195.
2. Elena Poniatowska, 'El movimiento estudiantil de 1968', in *Fuerte es el silencio* (Mexico City: Ediciones Era, 1980), pp. 34–48 (p. 35).
3. Claire Brewster, 'Mexico 1968: A Crisis of National Identity', in *Memories of 1968: International Perspectives*, ed. by Ingo Cornils and Sarah Waters (Bern: Peter Lang, 2010), pp. 149–80 (p. 156–57).
4. Octavio Paz, 'Totalidad y fragmento', in *Poemas (1935–1975)* (Barcelona: Seix Barral, 1979), pp. 613–15 (p. 165), 53.
5. Enrique Peña Nieto, *Palabras del Presidente, licenciado Enrique Peña Nieto, durante la Inauguración del Museo Histórico del Palacio Nacional*, 22 June 2018, <https://www.gob.mx/presidencia/prensa/palabras-del-presidente-de-los-estados-unidos-mexicanos-162554?idiom=es> [accessed 15 July 2018].
6. José Antonio González Anaya and Cristina García Cepeda, *Diversas intervenciones durante la Inauguración del Museo Histórico del Palacio Nacional*, 22 June 2018, <https://www.gob.mx/presidencia/prensa/diversas-162553?idiom=es> [accessed 1 July 2018].
7. Roberto Gallardo, *Amlo responde sobre tres libros que han marcado su vida*, online video recording, Youtube, 14 December 2011, <https://www.youtube.com/watch?v=HxwzSrhAf7A> [accessed 14 June 2020].
8. This move was likely influenced by his wife Beatriz Gutiérrez Müller, a writer with a doctorate in literary theory, who has stressed the importance of literature in understanding Mexican history and identity.
9. Jorge Volpi, quoted in Javier Lafuente, 'La mirada de Rulfo al México actual', *El País*, 16 May 2017.
10. Knight, 'Interpreting the Mexican Revolution', p. 8.
11. Enrique Peña Nieto, *Proteger a las instituciones fortalece a México, vulnerarlas nos debilita a todos: Enrique Peña Nieto*, 22 November 2017, <https://www.gob.mx/presidencia/prensa/proteger-a-las-instituciones-fortalece-a-mexico-vulnerarlas-nos-debilita-a-todos-enrique-pena-nieto> [accessed 10 June 2018].
12. Sierra, 'Positivismo político', p. 238.

BIBLIOGRAPHY

Archival Sources

El maestro rural (1932–1940): Biblioteca Gregorio Torres Quintero, Universidad Pedagógica Nacional, Mexico City

Archivo Frida Kahlo y Diego Rivera, Museo Frida Kahlo, Mexico City

Fundación Juan Rulfo, Mexico City

Hemeroteca Nacional de México, Universidad Nacional Autónoma de México, Mexico City

Biblioteca Juan Rulfo, Comisión Nacional para el Desarrollo de los Pueblos Indígenas, Mexico City

Works Cited

ACEVEDO ESCOBEDO, ANTONIO, 'La vida en el multifamiliar', *Arquitectura*, 33 (1952), 181–84

ACEVEDO, ESTHER and FAUSTO RAMÍREZ, 'Introduction', in *Los pinceles de la historia: La fabricación del estado, 1864–1910*, ed. by Esther Acevedo and others (Mexico City: Museo Nacional de Arte, 2003), pp. 17–33

AGOSTONI, CLAUDIA, *Monuments of Progress: Modernization and Public Health in Mexico City 1876–1910* (Calgary: University of Calgary Press, 2003)

AGUILAR CAMÍN, HÉCTOR, and LORENZO MEYER, *In the Shadow of the Mexican Revolution: Contemporary Mexican History, 1910–1989* (Austin: University of Texas Press, 1993)

AGUILAR, MAGDALENO, 'Discurso pronunciado por el señor Magdaleno Aguilar', in *Segunda convención de la Liga de Comunidades Agrarias y Sindicatos Campesinos*, ed. by Marte R. Gómez (Mexico City: Editorial Cultura, 1926), pp. 87–89

ALATORRE, ANTONIO, 'La persona de Juan Rulfo', *Literatura Mexicana*, 10 (1999), 225–47

ALONSO, ANA MARÍA, 'Conforming Disconformity: "Mestizaje", Hybridity, and the Aesthetics of Mexican Nationalism', *Cultural Anthropology*, 19 (2004), 459–90

AMAT, NÚRIA, *Juan Rulfo* (Barcelona: Ediciones Omega, 2003)

ANDERSON, BENEDICT, *Imagined Communities: Reflections on the Origin and Spread of Nationalism* (London: Verso, 2006)

ANGUIANO, RAÚL, *Raúl Anguiano, remembranzas* (Toluca: Universidad Autónoma del Estado de México, 1995)

'Los apóstoles modernos', *MR*, 15 October 1932

ANREUS, ALEJANDRO, and OTHERS, eds., *Mexican Muralism: A Critical History* (University Park: Pennsylvania State University Press, 2006)

AQUINAS, SAINT THOMAS, *Sermon-Conferences of St. Thomas Aquinas on the Apostles Creed*, ed. by Nicholas Ayo (Notre Dame: University of Notre Dame Press, 1988)

ARNHEIM, RUDOLF, *Visual Thinking* (London: Faber, 1970)

ASCENCIO, JUAN, *Un extraño en la tierra: Biografía no autorizada de Juan Rulfo* (Mexico City: Debate, 2005)

AZUELA, ALICIA, *Arte y poder: Renacimiento artístico y revolución social: México, 1910–1945* (Mexico City: Fondo de Cultura Económica, 2005)

——'Rivera and the Concept of Proletarian Art', in *Diego Rivera: A Retrospective*, ed. by Stanton L. Catlin (Detroit: Detroit Institute of the Arts, 1986), pp. 125–29

BAKHTIN, MIKHAIL, *Problems of Dostoevsky's Poetics*, ed. and trans. by Caryl Emerson (Minneapolis: University of Minnesota Press, 1984)

BANTJES, ADRIAN A., 'Idolatry and Iconoclasm in Revolutionary Mexico: The De-Christianization Campaigns, 1929–1940', *Mexican Studies/Estudios Mexicanos*, 13 (1997), 87–120.

——'Saints, Sinners and State Formation', in *The Eagle and the Virgin: Nation and Cultural Revolution in Mexico, 1920–1940*, ed. by Mary K. Vaughan and Stephen E. Lewis (Durham: Duke University Press, 2006), pp. 137–56

BARASCH, MOSHE, *Giotto and the Language of Gesture* (Cambridge: Cambridge University Press, 1987)

BASSOLS BATALLA, NARCISO, *El pensamiento político de Álvaro Obregón* (Mexico City: Ediciones 'El Caballito', 1970)

BECKER-LECKRONE, MEGAN, *Julia Kristeva and Literary Theory* (Basingstoke: Palgrave Macmillan, 2005)

BELL, LUCY, *The Latin American Short Story at its Limits: Fragmentation, Hybridity and Intermediality* (London: Routledge, 2017)

——,'Photography, Punctum and Shock: Re-Viewing Juan Rulfo's Short Stories', *Bulletin of Hispanic Studies*, 91 (2014), 437–52

BENÍTEZ, FERNANDO, 'Conversaciones con Juan Rulfo', in *La ficción de la memoria: Juan Rulfo ante la crítica*, ed. by Federico Campbell (Mexico City: UNAM, 2003), pp. 541–50

——,'Diego Rivera y su visión de la historia de México', in *Diego Rivera y los escritores mexicanos: Antología tributaria*, ed. by Elisa García Barragán and Luis Mario Schneider (Mexico City: UNAM, 1986), pp. 25–37

BENJAMIN, THOMAS, 'Mexico's Monument to the Revolution', in *Latin American Popular Culture: An Introduction*, ed. by William H. Beezley (Wilmington: SR Books, 2000), pp. 169–79

BENJAMIN, WALTER, *The Origin of German Tragic Drama*, trans. by John Osborne (London: Verso, 1998)

——'On Some Motifs in Baudelaire', in *Illuminations*, ed. by Hannah Arendt and trans. by Harry Zorn (London: Cape, 1970), pp. 157–202

——'Theses on the Philosophy of History', in *Illuminations*, pp. 255–66

——'The Work of Art in the Age of Mechanical Reproduction', in *Illuminations*, pp. 219–54

——'The Work of Art in the Age of its Technological Reproducibility' (Second Version), in *Walter Benjamin: Selected Writings*, 4 vols., trans. by Rodney Livingstone, ed. by Michael W. Jennings and others (Cambridge, MA: Belknap, 2002), pp. 101–33

BERGHAUS, GÜNTER, *Futurism and the Technological Imagination* (New York: Rodopi, 2009)

BERNDTSON, ARTHUR, 'Mexican Philosophy: The Aesthetics of Antonio Caso', *The Journal of Aesthetics and Art Criticism*, 9 (1951), 323–29

BEST, SUE, 'Sexualizing Space', in *Sexy Bodies: The Strange Carnalities of Feminism*, ed. by Elizabeth Grosz and Elspeth Probyn (London: Routledge, 1995), pp. 181–94

BLAINE, CHARETTE, *The Theme of Recompense in Matthew's Gospel* (London: Bloomsbury, 2015

BLANCO AGUINAGA, CARLOS, 'Prólogo', in Roberto García Bonilla, *Un tiempo suspendido: Cronología de la vida y obra de Juan Rulfo* (Mexico City: Centauro, 2009), pp. 13–17

BLANCO, MARÍA DEL PILAR and ESTHER PEEREN, 'Haunted Historiographies/ Introduction', in *The Spectralities Reader: Ghosts and Haunting in Contemporary Cultural Theory*, ed. by María del Pilar Blanco and Esther Peeren (New York: Bloomsbury Academic, 2013), pp. 481–87

Boccioni, Umberto, 'Manifesto of Futurist Sculpture', in *Futurism: An Anthology*, ed. by Lawrence S. Rainey and Christine Poggi (New Haven: Yale University Press, 2009), pp. 113–18

Boldy, Steven, *A Companion to Juan Rulfo* (Woodbridge: Tamesis, 2016)

Bonfil Batalla, Guillermo, *México profundo: Una civilización negada* (Mexico City: Grijalbo, 1989)

Bonnell, Victoria E., *Iconography of Power: Soviet Political Posters Under Lenin and Stalin* (Berkeley: University of California Press, 1997)

Bowskill, Sarah, *Gender, Nation and the Formation of the Twentieth-Century Mexican Literary Canon* (New York: Routledge, 2017)

Boym, Svetlana, 'Ruins of the Avant Garde, From Tatlin's Tower to Paper Architecture', in *Ruins of Modernity*, ed. by Julia Hell and Andreas Schönle (London: Duke University Press, 2010), pp. 58–85

Bradu, Fabienne, *Ecos de Páramo* (Mexico City: Fondo de Cultura Económica, 1989)

Breton, André, Diego Rivera and Leon Trotsky, 'Towards a Free Revolutionary Art', in *Theories of Modern Art: A Source Book by Artists and Critics*, ed. by Herschel Browning Chipp and Peter Selz (Berkeley: University of California Press, 1968), pp. 483–86

Brewster, Claire, 'Mexico 1968: A Crisis of National Identity', in *Memories of 1968: International Perspectives*, ed. by Ingo Cornils and Sarah Waters (Bern: Peter Lang, 2010), pp. 149–80

Brighenti, Andrea Mubi, 'Introduction', in *Urban Interstices: The Aesthetics and the Politics of the In-Between*, ed. by Andrea Mubi Brighenti (Farnham: Ashgate Publishing, 2013), pp. xv–xxiv

Brushwood, John, *Mexico in Its Novel: A Nation's Search for Identity* (Austin: University of Texas Press, 1966)

Buck-Morss, Susan, 'Aesthetics and Anaesthetics: Walter Benjamin's Artwork Essay Reconsidered', in *Walter Benjamin: Critical Evaluations in Cultural Theory*, ed. by Peter Osborne (London: Routledge, 2005), pp. 291–331

Buffington, Robert, 'Architecture', in *Mexico: An Encyclopedia of Contemporary Culture and History*, ed. by Don M. Coerver and others (Santa Barbara: ABC-CLIO, 2004), pp. 21–26

Burbank, Luther, *The Training of the Human Plant* (New York: Century Company, 1907)

Burian, Edward, 'The Architecture of Juan O'Gorman: Dichotomy and Drift', in *Modernity and The Architecture of Mexico*, ed. by Edward Burian (Austin: University of Texas Press, 1997), pp. 127–50

Burns, Archibaldo, '*Pedro Páramo* o la unción y la gallina', *Novedades*, May 1955

Butler, Matthew, 'God's Campesinos? Mexico's Revolutionary Church in the Countryside', *Bulletin of Latin American Research*, 28 (2009), 165–84

——*Popular Piety and Political Identity in Mexico's Cristero Rebellion: Michoacán, 1927–29* (Oxford: Oxford University Press for the British Academy, 2004)

Caminos de México. Guía Goodrich-Euzkadi (Mexico City: Goodrich-Euzkadi, 1958)

Cantú, Roberto, ed., *Mexican Mural Art: Critical Essays on a Belligerent Aesthetic* (Newcastle: Cambridge Scholars Publishing, 2021)

Carballo, Emmanuel, 'Arreola y Rulfo, cuentistas', *Revista de la Universidad de México*, 8 March 1954, pp. 28–32

Carballo, Marco Aurelio, 'Los discursos de López Mateos, escritos por Juan Rulfo', *Siempre!*, 27 May 1987

Cardona Peña, Alfredo, *Conversaciones con Diego Rivera (el monstruo en su laberinto)* (Mexico City: Editorial Diana, 1980)

Cárdenas, Lázaro, 'Discurso del candidato del PNR a la presidencia de la República', in *Palabras y documentos públicos de Lázaro Cárdenas: 1928–1970*, ed. by Javier Romero, (Mexico City: Siglo Veintiuno Editores, 1978), pp. 121–22

——'Discurso del presidente del partido nacional revolucionario sobre el programa de trabajo para el año de 1931', in *Palabras y documentos públicos de Lázaro Cárdenas: 1928–1970*, pp. 98–101

——'Mensaje a la nación del Presidente de la República', in *Palabras y documentos públicos de Lázaro Cárdenas: 1928–1970*, pp. 225–32

Carton de Grammont, Hubert and Horacio Mackinlay, 'Campesino and Indigenous Social Organizations Facing Democratic Transition in Mexico, 1938—2006', *Latin American Perspectives*, 36 (2009), 21-40

Castañeda, Jorge, 'The Intellectual and the State in Latin America', *World Policy Journal*, 10 (1993), 89–95

Castellanos, Rosario, *Poesía no eres tú: Obra poética: 1948–1971* (Mexico City: Fondo de Cultura Económica, 1972)

Castillo, Debra A., *Easy Women: Sex and Gender in Modern Mexican Fiction* (Minneapolis: University of Minnesota Press, 1998)

Cézanne, Paul, *Conversations with Cézanne*, ed. by Michael Doran and trans. by Julie Lawrence (Berkeley: University of California Press, 2001)

Charlot, Jean, 'Mexican Ex-Votos', *Magazine of Art*, 42 (1949), 139–42

——*El renacimiento del muralismo mexicano 1920–1925* (Mexico City: Editorial Domés, 1985)

Chumacero, Alí, 'La primera novela de Juan Rulfo', *La Gaceta del Fondo de Cultura Económica*, 15 March 1955

Cifuentes, Ángel, 'El maestro rural', *MR*, May–June, 1940

Clark, Meri L, 'The Emergence and Transformation of Positivism', in *A Companion to Latin American Philosophy*, ed. by Susana Nuccetelli, Ofelia Schutte, and Otávio Bueno (Oxford: Wiley-Blackwell, 2009), pp. 53–67

Coffey, Mary K. *How a Revolutionary Art Became Official Culture: Murals, Museums, and the Mexican State* (Durham: Duke University Press, 2012)

——'Mural Art and Popular Reception: The Public Institution and Cultural Politics in Post-Revolutionary Mexico', in *La imagen política: XXV Coloquio Internacional de Historia del Arte*, ed. by Cuahtémoc Medina (Mexico City: UNAM, 2006), pp. 362–72

——'The "Mexican Problem": Nation and "Native" in Mexican Muralism and Cultural Discourse', in *The Social and the Real: Political Art of the 1930s in the Western Hemisphere*, ed. by Alejandro Anreus and others (University Park: Pennsylvania State University Press, 2006), pp. 43–70

Cohn, Deborah, 'The Mexican Intelligentsia, 1950–1968: Cosmopolitanism, National Identity, and the State', *Mexican Studies/Estudios Mexicanos*, 21 (2005), 141–82

Colín, José R., 'La Revolución Mexicana: R.I.P', *Excélsior*, 21 November 1950

Conjunto urbano 'Presidente López Mateos' (Nonoalco-Tlatelolco): Una realización del Presidente Adolfo López Mateos (Mexico City: Banco Nacional Hipotecario Urbano y de Obras Públicas, 1963)

Connor, Steven, *Beckett, Modernism and the Material Imagination* (Cambridge: Cambridge University Press, 2014)

——*Beyond Words: Sobs, Hums, Stutters and Other Vocalizations* (London: Reaktion Books, 2014)

'Constitución política de los Estados Unidos Mexicanos', *Diario Oficial de la Federación*, 5 February 1917, pp. 50–54

Contreras, Carlos, 'Editorial (Respecto a la necesidad de un plano regulador para la ciudad y Valle de México)', in *Planificación y urbanismo visionarios de Carlos Contreras: Escritos de 1925 a 1938*, ed. by Rafael López Rangel (Mexico City: UNAM, 2003), pp. 75–78

Cornejo Polar, Antonio, 'La novela indigenista: Un género contradictorio', *Texto Crítico*, 14 (1979), 58–70

Cortázar, Julio. *Rayuela*, ed. by Julio Ortega and Saúl Yurkiévich (Madrid: C.S.I.C, 1991)

Cortés Gutiérrez, Laura, *Diego Rivera* (Mexico City: SEP, Dirección General de Publicaciones y Medios, 1988)

Cosío Villegas, Daniel, 'La crisis de México', *Cuadernos Americanos*, March–April 1947

Cottington, David, *Cubism and its Histories* (Manchester: Manchester University Press, 2004)

Craib, Raymond B., *Cartographic Mexico: A History of State Fixations and Fugitive Landscapes* (Durham: Duke University Press, 2004)

Craven, David, *Art and Revolution in Latin America, 1910–1990* (New Haven: Yale University Press, 2002)

—— *Diego Rivera: As Epic Modernist* (New York: G.K. Hall, 1997)

Cruz Porchini, Dafne, 'Formando el cuerpo de la nación: el imaginario del deporte en el México posrevolucionario (1920–1940)', in *Formando el cuerpo de una nación: El imaginario del deporte en el México posrevolucionario (1920–1940)*, ed. by Monserrat Sánchez Soler (Mexico City: INBA, 2012), pp. 33–56

Cuevas, José Luis, 'La cortina del nopal', in *Ruptura 1952–1965: Catálogo de la exposición, Museo de Arte Alvar y Carmen T. de Carrillo Gil* (Mexico City: Museo Carrillo Gil, 1988), pp. 84–91

'Cursos para correspondencia — organización escolar a cargo del Profesor Felipe de J. Espinosa, Lección 18: Horarios', *MR*, 15 May 1932

Dalton, David S., *Mestizo Modernity: Race, Technology, and the Body in Postrevolutionary Mexico* (Gainesville: University of Florida Press, 2018)

Danius, Sara, *The Senses of Modernism: Technology, Perception, and Aesthetics* (London: Cornell University Press, 2002)

Davis, Colin, 'The Skeptical Ghost: Alejandro Amenábar's *The Others* and the Return of the Dead', in *Popular Ghosts: The Haunted Spaces of Everyday Culture*, ed. by María del Pilar Blanco and Esther Peeren (London: Continuum, 2010), pp. 64–74

Dr Atl, 'Colaboración artística: ¿Renacimiento artístico?', *El Universal: El gran diario de México*, 13 July 1923

de Certeau, Michel, *Heterologies: Discourse on the Other*, trans. by Brian Massumi (Manchester: Manchester University Press, 1986)

—— 'Walking in the City', in *The Cultural Studies Reader*, ed. by Simon During (London: Routledge, 1999), pp. 126–33

—— *The Writing of History*, trans. by Tom Conley (New York: Columbia University Press, 1998)

de la Peña, Moisés, *El pueblo y su tierra: Mito y realidad de la reforma agraria en México* (Mexico City: Cuadernos Americanos, 1964)

de Pina García, Juan Pablo, *Diego Rivera en los años radicales* (Chapingo: Universidad Autonoma de Chapingo, 1990)

de la Torriente, Loló, *Memoria y razón de Diego Rivera* (Mexico: Renacimiento, 1959)

Deleuze, Gilles, *The Fold*, trans. by Tom Conley (London: Continuum: 2006)

—— *Francis Bacon* (London: Continuum, 2005)

Deleuze, Gilles and Félix Guattari, *A Thousand Plateaus: Capitalism and Schizophrenia*, trans. by Brian Massumi (London: Continuum, 2004)

'El departamento de Salubridad Pública hace una obra educativa acerca de los problemas de higiene racial', *Eugenesia, Higiene y Cultura Física para el Mejoramiento de la Raza*, 3 (1935), 33–34

de Valdés, María Elena, *The Shattered Mirror: Representations of Women in Mexican Literature* (Austin: University of Texas Press, 1998)

Dickerman, Leah and others, *Diego Rivera: Murals for the Museum of Modern Art* (New York: Museum of Modern Art: 2011)

DOMÍNGUEZ-RUVALCABA, HÉCTOR *Modernity and the Nation in Mexican Representations of Masculinity: From Sensuality to Bloodshed* (New York: Palgrave Macmillan, 2007)

DOREMUS, ANNE T., *Culture, Politics and National Identity in Mexican Literature and Film, 1929–1952* (New York: Peter Lang AG, 2000)

DORON, GIL M., 'The Dead Zone and the Architecture of Transgression', *City*, 4 (2000), 247–63

DOUGLAS, MARY, *Purity and Danger: An Analysis of Concepts of Pollution and Taboo* (London: Routledge, 2018)

DOVE, PATRICK, *The Catastrophe of Modernity: Tragedy and the Nation in Latin American Literature* (Lewisburg: Bucknell University Press, 2004)

DR. ATL, 'Colaboración artística: ¿Renacimiento artístico?', *El Universal: El gran diario de México*, 13 July 1923

DREYFUS, HUBERT L. and PAUL RABINOW, *Michel Foucault: Beyond Structuralism and Hermeneutics* (Chicago: University of Chicago Press, 1983)

EAGLETON, TERRY, 'Peter Brooks on Bodies', in *Figures of Dissent: Critical Essays on Fish, Spivak, Žižek and Others* (London: Verso, 2003), pp. 129–35

ECO, UMBERTO, *The Role of the Reader: Explorations in the Semiotics of Texts* (London: Hutchinson, 1981)

'Editorial: La Higiene, base de la Economía Nacional', *Salubridad*, 1 (1930), 9–10

ELLMANN, MAUD, *The Hunger Artists: Starving, Writing, and Imprisonment* (London: Virago, 1993)

'En el umbral', *Savia Moderna: Revista mensual de arte*, March 1906

ESPEJEL Y ÁLVAREZ, MANUEL, *Miguel Alemán, biografía de su obra: Reportaje de la acción constructiva del régimen* (Mexico City: Taller Gráfico de la Nación, 1952)

FABELA, ISIDRO, 'Diego Rivera: Ensayo en miniatura', in *Diego Rivera y los escritores: Antología tributaria*, pp. 73–75

FAERNA, JOSÉ MARÍA, *Léger*, trans. by Alberto Curotto (New York: Abrams, 1996)

FERNÁNDEZ, JUSTINO, *Arte moderno y contemporáneo de México* (Mexico City: UNAM, 1952)

——*A Guide to Mexican Art: From its Beginnings to the Present*, trans. by Joshua C. Taylor (Chicago: University of Chicago Press, 1969)

FINNEGAN, NUALA, *Monstrous Projections of Femininity in the Fiction of Mexican Writer Rosario Castellanos* (Lewiston: Edwin Mellen Press, 2000)

NUALA FINNEGAN and DYLAN BRENNAN, eds., *Rethinking Juan Rulfo's Creative World: Prose, Photography, Film* (London: Routledge, 2016)

FLORES, TATIANA, *Mexico's Revolutionary Avant Gardes: From Estridentismo to ¡30–30!* (New Haven: Yale University Press, 2013)

FLORESCANO, ENRIQUE, *Historia de las historias de la nación mexicana* (Mexico City: Taurus, 2002)

—— *Imágenes de la patria a través de los siglos* (Mexico City: Santillana Ediciones Generales, 2006)

——*El mito de Quetzalcoatl* (Mexico City: Fondo de Cultura Económica, 1995)

FOLGARAIT, LEONARD, *Mural Painting and Social Revolution in Mexico, 1920–1940: Art of the New Order* (Cambridge: Cambridge University Press, 1998)

——'Revolution as Ritual: Diego Rivera's National Palace Mural', *Oxford Art Journal*, 14 (1991), pp. 18–33

FOSTER, HAL, *Prosthetic Gods* (Cambridge: MIT Press, 2004)

FOUCAULT, MICHEL, *Discipline and Punish: The Birth of the Prison*, trans. by Alan Sheridan (London: Allen Lane, 1995)

——*The History of Sexuality*, 3 vols, trans. by Robert Hurley (New York: Vintage, 1990)

——*Society Must Be Defended: Lectures at the Collège de France, 1975–76*, trans. by David Macey (London: The Penguin Press, 2003)

Fraser, Howard M., '*Inframundo*: Juan Rulfo's Photographic Companion to *El Llano en llamas*', *Chasqui*, 17 (1988), 56–74

Fraser, Valerie, *Building the New World: Studies in the Modern Architecture of Latin America, 1930–1960* (London: Verso, 2000)

Frías, José D., 'La obra genial del pintor Diego M. Rivera', *El Universal Ilustrado*, 19 February 1924

Fry, Roger, 'The Post-Impressionists-II', in *Post-Impressionists in England*, ed. by J. B. Bullen (London: Routledge, 1988), pp. 130–31

Fuentes, Carlos, 'Aclarar los humos del pasado, volver el pasado presentable', interviewed by Margarita García Flores, *La cultura en México*, 27 August 1969

——'Carlos Fuentes', in *Los narradores ante el público*, ed. by Rubén Marín (Mexico City: Joaquín Mortiz, 1966), pp. 137–55

——*La muerte de Artemio Cruz* (Mexico City: Fondo de Cultura Económica, 1962)

——*La nueva novela hispanoamericana* (Mexico: Editorial Joaquín Mortiz, 1969)

——*Viendo visiones* (Mexico City: Fondo de Cultura Económica, 2003)

——'La violenta identidad de José Luis Cuevas', in *Casa con dos puertas* (Mexico City: Joaquín Mortiz, 1970), pp. 239–80

Galeana, Patricia, 'Origen y actualidad del Instituto Nacional de Estudios Históricos de las Revoluciones de México', in *60 años: Historia del Instituto Nacional de Estudios Históricos de las Revoluciones de México*, ed. by Patricia Galeana (Mexico City: INHERM, 2013), pp. 15–24

Gallardo, Roberto, *Amlo responde sobre tres libros que han marcado su vida*, online video recording, Youtube, 14 December 2011, <https://www.youtube.com/watch?v=HxwzSrhAf7A> [Accessed 14 June 2020]

Gallese, Vittorio, 'Embodied Simulation: From Neurons to Phenomenal Experience', *Phenomenology and the Cognitive Sciences*, 4 (2005), 23–48

Gallo, Rubén, *Mexican Modernity: The Avant-garde and the Technological Revolution* (Cambridge: MIT, 2005)

Gámez, Rubén, 'Conversaciones con Rubén Gámez', interviewed by Alejandro Pelayo Rangel, in *La fórmula secreta: Rubén Gámez*, ed. by Damián Ortega (Mexico City: Alias, 2014), pp. 362–71

——'Rubén Gámez: Mi pretensión es crear un cine realmente mexicano', interviewed by Emilio García Riera, in *La fórmula secreta: Rubén Gámez*, pp. 182–84

Gamio, Manuel, *Forjando patria* (Mexico City: Librería de Hermanos Porrúa, 1916)

García Bonilla, Roberto, *Un tiempo suspendido: Cronología de la vida y la obra de Juan Rulfo* (Mexico City: CONACULTA, 2008)

García Canclini, Néstor, *La ciudad de los viajeros: travesías e imaginarios urbanos, México, 1940–2000* (Mexico City: Universidad Autónoma Metropolitana, 1996)

Gillingham, Paul, and Benjamin T. Smith, 'Introduction', in *Dictablanda: Politics, Work, and Culture in Mexico, 1938–1968*, ed. by Paul Gillingham and Benjamin T. Smith (Durham: Duke University Press, 2014), pp. 1–44

Garro, Elena, 'El problema agrario sigue en pie después de 50 años de revolución', *Siempre!* (*La cultura en México* supplement), September 1965

Gillet, Louis, 'L'art dans l'Amérique latine', in *Histoire de l'art*, ed. by André Michel (Paris: Colin, 1929), pp. 1023–96

Gleizes, Albert and Jean Metzinger, 'Cubism', in *Art in Theory, 1900–1990: An Anthology of Changing Ideas*, ed. by Charles Harrison and Paul Wood (Oxford: Blackwell, 1992), pp. 187–96

Goizueta, Roberto S., *Caminemos con Jesús: Towards a Hispanic/Latino Theology of Accompaniment* (New York: Orbis Books, 1995)

Goldfarb, Jeffrey, *Civility and Subversion: The Intellectual in Democratic Society* (Cambridge: Cambridge University Press, 1998)

Gómez, Marte R., 'Marte R. Gómez, agrarista', interviewed by James W. Wilkie, in *Mexico visto en el siglo XX*, ed. by James W. Wilkie and Edna Monzón de Wilkie (Mexico City: Instituto Mexicano de Investigaciones Económicas, 1969), pp. 75–139

Gómez Villalpando, Armando, 'Presentación' in Emilio Uranga, *Ensayos* (Mexico City: Gobierno del Estado de Guanajuato, 1991), pp. 7–14

Gonzales, Michael J., 'Imagining Mexico in 1910: Visions of the Patria in the Centennial Celebration in Mexico City', *Journal of Latin American Studies*, 39 (2007), 495–533

González, José Eduardo, *Algunas consideraciones sobre eugenética* (Mexico City: Companía Editora Latino Americana, 1923)

González y González, Luis, *Pueblo en vilo: Microhistoria de San José de Gracia* (Mexico City: El Colegio de México, 1968)

González Anaya, José Antonio and Cristina García Cepeda, *Diversas intervenciones durante la Inauguración del Museo Histórico del Palacio Nacional*, www.gob.mx>, 22 June 2018. <https://www.gob.mx/presidencia/prensa/diversas-162553?idiom=es> [Accessed 1 July 2018]

González Boixo, José Carlos, 'Aclaraciones de Juan Rulfo a su novela *Pedro Páramo*', in *Pedro Páramo* (Madrid: Cátedra, 2000), pp. 247–51

——'Esteticismo y clasismo', in *Tríptico para Juan Rulfo: Poesía, fotografía, crítica*, ed. by Víctor Jiménez and others (Mexico City: Editorial RM, 2006), pp. 249–87

——'Juan Rulfo, fotógrafo', in *Territorios de la Mancha: Versiones y subversiones cervantinas en la literatura hispanoamericana: Actas del VI Congreso Internacional de la Asociación Española de Estudios Literarios Hispanoamericános*, ed. by Matías Barchino Pérez (Cuenca: Ediciones de la Universidad de Castilla-La Mancha, 2007), pp. 365–72

González del Rivero, Leticia, 'Tiempo de la iglesia versus tiempo del estado: México en la década de los treinta', in *Un haz de reflexiones en torno al tiempo, la historia y la modernidad*, ed. by María Dolores Illescas Nájera (Mexico City: Universidad Iberoamericana, Dirección de Investigación y Posgrado, Centro de Integración Universitaria, 1995), pp. 177–210

González-Stephan, Beatriz, 'Forms of Historic Imagination: Visual Culture, Historiography, and the Tropes of War in Nineteenth-Century Venezuela', in *Building Nineteenth-century Latin America: Re-rooted Cultures, Identities, and Nations*, ed. by Juan Carlos González Espitia and William G. Acree (Nashville: Vanderbilt University Press, 2009), pp. 101–32

Grau, Oliver, *Virtual Art: From Illusion to Immersion* (Cambridge, Mass: MIT Press, 2003)

Greeley, Robin Adèle, 'Muralism and the State in Post-Revolutionary Mexico 1920–1970', in *Mexican Muralism: A Critical History*, ed. by Alejandro Anreus and others (Berkeley: University of California Press, 2012), pp. 13–16

Grosz, Elizabeth, *Architecture from the Outside: Essays on Virtual and Real Space* (Cambridge, Mass: MIT Press, 2001)

——'Notes Towards a Corporeal Feminism', *Australian Feminist Studies*, 5 (1987), 1–16.

——*Space, Time, and Perversion: Essays on the Politics of Bodies* (London: Routledge, 1995)

——'Woman, *Chora*, Dwelling', in *Gender Space Architecture: An Interdisciplinary Introduction*, ed. by Iain Borden and others (London: Routledge, 2002), pp. 210–22

El Grupo Nuevo Cine, 'Manifiesto del Grupo Nuevo Cine', in *Hojas de cine: testimonios y documentos del nuevo cine latinoamericano*, ed. by Fundación Mexicana de Cineastas (Mexico City: Secretaría de Educación Pública: Universidad Autónoma Metropolitana, 1988), pp. 33–35

Gudiño, María Rosa and Guillermo Palacios, 'Peticiones de tierra y estrategias discursivas campesinas: Procesos contenidos y problemas metodológicos', in *Estudios campesinos en el Archivo General Agrario*, ed. by Antonio Escobar Ohmstede (Mexico City: Registro Agrario Nacional: Centro de Investigaciones y Estudios Superiores en Antropología Social, 1998), pp. 75–118

GUDIÑO, MARÍA ROSA, 'Educación higiénica y consejos de salud para campesinos en el sembrador y el maestro rural, 1929–1934', in *Curar, sanar y educar: Enfermedad y sociedad en México, siglos XIX y XX*, ed. by Claudia Agostoni (Mexico City: UNAM/Benemérita Universidad Autónoma de Puebla, 2008) pp. 71–97

GUTIÉRREZ RUVALCABA, IGNACIO, 'Aproximación visual al mundo campesino', in *La memoria agraria mexicana en imágenes: cuatro ensayos*, ed. by Ignacio Gutiérrez Ruvalcaba (Mexico City: Registro Agrario Nacional, 2002), pp. 13–62

GUTIÉRREZ SILVA, MANUEL, 'Aesthetic Rivalries in Avant-Garde Mexico: Art Writing and the Field of Cultural Production', in *Pierre Bourdieu in Hispanic Literature and Culture*, ed. by Ignacio M. Sánchez Prado (Basingstoke: Palgrave Macmillan, 2018), pp. 87–131

GYURKO, LANIN A., 'Twentieth Century Fiction', in *Mexican Literature: A History*, ed. by David William Foster (Austin: University of Texas Press, 1994), pp. 243–304

HANSEN, MIRIAM, 'Unstable Mixtures, Dilated Spheres: Negt and Kluge's The Public Sphere and Experience, Twenty Years Later', *Public Culture*, 5 (1993), 179–212

HARRIS, MAX, *Aztecs, Moors, and Christians: Festivals of Reconquest in Mexico and Spain* (Austin: University of Texas Press, 2010)

HARSS, LUIS, *Los nuestros* (Buenos Aires: Editorial Sudamericana, 1969)

HART, JOHN M., 'Agrarian Reform', in *Twentieth–Century Mexico*, ed. by William H. Beezley and Dirk W. Raat (Lincoln: University of Nebraska Press, 1986), pp. 6–16

HARTE, TIMOTHY, *Fast Forward: The Aesthetics and Ideology of Speed in Russian Avant-Garde Culture, 1910–1930* (Madison: University of Wisconsin Press, 2010)

HAZZIKOSTAS, DIMITRI, 'Arms Raised', in *Encyclopedia of Comparative Iconography: Themes Depicted in Works of Art*, ed. by Helene E. Roberts (Chicago: Fitzroy Dearborn, 1998), pp. 50–58.

HELL, JULIA and ANDREAS SCHÖNLE. 'Introduction', in *Ruins of Modernity*, ed. by Julia Hell and Andreas Schönle (London: Duke University Press, 2010), pp. 1–14

HELLIER-TINOCO, RUTH, *Embodying Mexico: Tourism, Nationalism and Performance* (Oxford: Oxford University Press, 2011)

HENRÍQUEZ UREÑA, PEDRO, 'Diego Rivera', *El Mundo*, 6 July 1923

——'La influencia de la Revolución en la vida intelectual de México', in *La Utopía de América*, ed. by Ángel Rama and Rafael Gutiérrez Giradot (Caracas: Biblioteca Ayacucho, 1978), pp. 367–77

——'La revolución y la cultura en México', in *Ensayos*, ed. by José Luis Abellán and Ana María Barrenechea (Madrid: ALLCA XX: 2000), pp. 254–61

HILLMAN, DAVID and ULRIKA MAUDE, 'Introduction', in *The Cambridge Companion to The Body in Literature*, ed. by David Hillman and Ulrika Maude (Cambridge: Cambridge University Press, 2015), pp. 1–9

EMILY, HIND, *Dude Lit: Mexican Men Writing and Performing Competence, 1955–2012* (Tucson: The University of Arizona Press, 2019)

HUTCHEON, LINDA, *The Politics of Postmodernism* (London: Routledge, 2001)

HUSKA, MELANIE, 'Historically Themed Comic Books as Civic Education in 1980s Mexico', in *Comics as History, Comics as Literature: Roles of the Comic Book in Scholarship, Society, and Entertainment*, ed. by Annessa Ann Babic (Madison: Fairleigh Dickinson University Press, 2013), pp. 65–78

IBER, PATRICK, 'The Cold War Politics of Literature and the Centro Mexicano de Escritores', *Journal of Latin American Studies*, 48 (2016), 247–72

INDYCH-LÓPEZ, ANNA, 'An Abstract Courbet: The Cubist Spaces of Rivera's Murals', in *Diego Rivera: The Cubist Portraits 1913–1917*, ed. by Sylvia Navarrete (London: Philip Wilson Publishers, 2009), pp. 150–54

——*Muralism Without Walls: Rivera, Orozco, and Siqueiros in the United States, 1927–1940* (Pittsburgh: University of Pittsburgh Press, 2009)

'Informe del Delegado del Ejido de San José de Santa Engracia', in *Tercera convención de la Liga de Comunidades Agrarias y Sindicatos Campesinos del Estado de Tamaulipas*, ed. by Marte R. Gómez (Mexico City: Editorial Cultura, 1928), pp. 180–83

ITO, TOYO, 'El prodigio de la vanguardia y la pureza: Las casas de Diego Rivera y Frida Kahlo y la casa del arquitecto Juan O'Gorman', in *Casa O'Gorman 1929*, ed. by Xavier Guzmán Urbiola and others (Mexico City: Editorial RM, 2015), pp. 79–85

ITURRIAGA, JOSÉ, 'México y su crisis histórica', *Cuadernos Americanos*, May–June 1949

JACOBS, KAREN, *The Eye's Mind: Literary Modernism and Visual Culture* (Ithaca: Cornell University Press, 2001)

JANZEN, REBECCA, *The National Body in Mexican Literature: Collective Challenges to Biopolitical Control* (New York: Palgrave Macmillan, 2015)

JENKS, CHRIS, 'The Centrality of the Eye in Western Culture: An Introduction', in *Visual Culture*, ed. by Chris Jenks (London: Routledge, 2002), pp. 1–25

JIMÉNEZ, VÍCTOR, 'Introduction', in Juan Rulfo, *Arquitectura de México: Fotografías de Juan Rulfo* (Mexico City: Consejo Nacional para la Cultura y las Artes, 1994), p. 1

——'Introduction', in *Nuevos indicios sobre Juan Rulfo: Genealogía, estudios, testimonios*, ed. by Jorge Zepeda (Mexico City: Fundación Juan Rulfo: Juan Pablos Editor, 2010), pp. 1–5

——'Juan Rulfo: Literatura, fotografía e historia', in *Juan Rulfo: Letras e imágenes*, ed. by Víctor Jiménez (Mexico City: Editorial R.M, 2002), pp. 22–19

JIMÉNEZ DE BÁEZ, YVETTE, *Juan Rulfo, del Páramo a la esperanza: Una lectura crítica de su obra* (Mexico City: Colegio de México: Fondo de Cultura Económica, 1990)

JIMÉNEZ RUEDA, JULIO, 'El afeminamiento en la literatura mexicana', *El Universal*, 21 December 1924

JOLLY, JENNIFER, *Creating Pátzcuaro, Creating Mexico: Art, Tourism, and Nation Building under Lázaro Cárdenas* (Austin: University of Texas Press, 2018)

KAHLO, FRIDA, 'Retrato de Diego', in *Escrituras*, ed. by Raquel Tibol (Mexico City: Coordinación de Humanidades, Programa Editorial, UNAM, 2001), pp. 305–16

KETTENMANN, ANDREA, *Diego Rivera, 1886–1957: A Revolutionary Spirit in Modern Art* (London: Taschen, 1997)

KLEINER, FRED S., *Gardner's Art through the Ages: The Western Perspective* (London: Cengage Learning, 2010)

KNIGHT, ALAN, 'Interpreting the Mexican Revolution', in *Texas Papers on Mexico* (Austin: Institute of Latin American Studies, 1988), no. 88–02.

——*Mexican Revolution Vol.2: Counter-Revolution and Reconstruction* (Cambridge: Cambridge University Press, 1986)

——'The Peculiarities of Mexican History: Mexico Compared to Latin America, 1821-1992', *Journal of Latin American Studies*, 24 (1992), 99–144

——'Popular Culture and the Revolutionary State in Mexico, 1910–1940', *The Hispanic American Historical Review*, 74 (1994), 393–444.

KOLODNY, ANNETTE, *The Lay of the Land* (Chapel Hill: University of North Carolina Press, 1975)

KRACAUER, SIEGFRIED, *The Mass Ornament: Weimar Essays*, ed. and trans. by Thomas Y. Levin (London: Harvard University Press, 1995)

KRISTEVA, JULIA, *Desire in Language: A Semiotic Approach to Literature and Art*, ed. by Leon S. Roudiez and trans. by Thomas Gora and Alice A. Jardine (Oxford: Basil Blackwell, 1981)

——*Revolution in Poetic Language*, trans by Margaret Waller (New York: Columbia University Press, 1974)

KUHN, ANNETTE, 'The Body and Cinema: Some Problems for Feminism', in *Writing on the Body: Female Embodiment and Feminist Theory*, ed. by Katie Conboy and others (New York: Columbia University Press, 1997), pp. 195–207

LA BOTZ, DAN, *Democracy in Mexico: Peasant Rebellion and Political Reform* (Boston: South End Press, 1995)

LAFUENTE, JAVIER, 'La mirada de Rulfo al México actual', *El País*, 16 May 2017

LAMBERTO MORENO, PROF. J., 'Himno a las comunidades infantiles escolares', *MR*, 15 November 1935

LAVERY, JANE, 'The Physical and Textual Body in the Works of Ángeles Mastretta and Elena Poniatowska', *Romance Studies*, 19 (2001), 173–86

LEAL, LUIS, *Mariano Azuela* (New York: Twayne Publishers, 1971)

LEAR, JOHN, *Picturing the Proletariat: Artists and Labor in Revolutionary Mexico, 1908–1940* (Austin: University of Texas Press, 2017)

LE CORBUSIER, *The Four Routes* (London: D. Dobson, 1947)

—— *Towards a New Architecture*, trans. by Frederick Etchells (London: Rodker, 1931)

LEE, ANTHONY W., *Painting on the Left: Diego Rivera, Radical Politics, and San Francisco's Public Murals* (Berkeley: University of California Press, 1999)

——'Workers and Painters: Social Realism and Race in Diego Rivera's Detroit Murals', in *The Social and the Real: Political Art of the 1930s in the Western Hemisphere*, ed. by Alejandro Anreus and others (University Park: Pennsylvania State University Press, 2006), pp. 201–22

LEON NOGUEIRA, DR ERNESTO, 'Orientación de higiene rural un programa de salud dental en el medio rural', *MR*, May–June 1940

LERNER, JESSE, 'Rubén Gámez: Cine neobarroco en tiempos de cambio', in *La fórmula secreta: Rubén Gámez*, pp. 310–32

LESLIE, ESTHER, 'Walter Benjamin: Traces of Craft', *Journal of Design History*, 11 (1998), 5–13

LESSING, GOTTHOLD EPHRAIM, *Laocoon: An Essay Upon the Limits of Painting and Poetry*, trans. by Ellen Frothingham (Boston: Roberts Brothers, 1887)

LIEKENS, ENRIQUE, 'Archivo fónico de la Revolución: Grabaciones históricas', *El legionario órgano de la legión de honor mexicana*, 28 February 1959

STEPAN, NANCY LEYS, *The Hour of Eugenics: Race, Gender and Nation in Latin America* (London: Cornell University Press, 1991)

LISSITZKY, EL, *Russia: An Architecture for World Revolution*, trans.by Eric Dluhosch (Cambridge, Mass: MIT Press, 1970)

LOMBARDO TOLEDANO, VICENTE, 'Capitalismo agrícola contra reforma agraria', in *Escritos en Siempre!* (Mexico City: Ediciones CEFPSVLT, 1994), pp. 195–99

—— 'El reparto de tierras a los pobres no se opone a las enseñanzas de nuestro señor Jesucristo y de la santa madre iglesia: El pueblo Mexicano peleó y sufrió diez años queriendo hallar la palabra de nuestro señor Jesucristo', in *Obra histórico-cronológica* (Mexico City: Centro de Estudios Filosóficos, Políticos y Sociales Vicente Lombardo Toledano, 1994), pp. 117–21

——'La Revolución Mexicana de ayer y la de hoy', *Futuro*, 3 (1936), 1

LÓPEZ, NACHO, *Los pueblos de la bruma y el sol* (Mexico City: INI: FONAPAS, 1981)

LÓPEZ, RICK A., *Crafting Mexico: Intellectuals, Artisans, and the State After the Revolution* (Durham, N.C: Duke University Press, 2010)

LOPÉZ MATEOS, ADOLFO, *Pensamiento en acción*, 2 vols (Mexico City: Oficina de Prensa, 1963)

LÓPEZ RANGEL, RAFAEL, *Diego Rivera y la arquitectura mexicana* (Mexico City: SEP, Dirección General de Publicaciones y Medios, 1986)

López Sánchez, Oliva, *Enfermas, mentirosas y temperamentales: La concepción médica del cuerpo femenino durante la segunda mitad del siglo XIX en México* (Mexico City: Plaza y Valdés Editores, 1998)

Loyo, Engracia, 'La educación del pueblo', in *Historia mínima de la educación en México*, ed. by Dorothy Tanck de Estrada (Mexico City: El Colegio de México, Seminario de la Educación en México, 2010), pp. 154–87

Lozano, Luis-Martín, 'Song to The Earth and Those Who Labour Thereon: Universidad Autónoma de Chapingo Mexico', in *Diego Rivera: The Complete Murals*, ed. by Luis-Martín Lozano and Juan Coronel Rivera (London: Taschen, 2008), pp. 136–45

Majumdar, Margaret A., 'Orientalism and the Problematic of Vision: A Contemporary Perspective', in *Eastern Voyages, Western Visions: French Writing and Painting of the Orient*, ed. by Margaret Topping (New York: Peter Lang, 2004), pp. 347–66

'Maestros distinguidos de Oaxaca: Los doce mandamientos de la higiene', *MR*, 15 December 1935

Manríquez, Francisco, 'El ejido y el maestro rural', *MR*, 1 February 1933

Maples Arce, Manuel, 'Actual No 1: Hoja de Vanguardia:. Comprimido Estridentista', in *El Estridentismo: México, 1921–1927*, ed. by Luis Mario Schneider (Mexico City: UNAM, 1985), pp. 41–48

——. *El arte mexicano moderno* (London: A. Zwemmer, 1946)

Marentes, Luis A., *José Vasconcelos and the Writing of the Mexican Revolution* (Amherst: University of Massachusetts Press, 2000)

'María Izquierdo vs. Los Tres Grandes', *El Nacional*, 2 October 1947

Marks, Laura U., *The Skin of the Film: Intercultural Cinema, Embodiment, and the Senses* (London: Duke University Press, 2000)

Marnham, Patrick, *Dreaming with His Eyes Open: A Life of Diego Rivera* (London: Bloomsbury, 1998)

Martínez Rodríguez, Fabiola, 'Representing the Nation: Art and Identity in Porfirian Mexico', *National Identities*, 15 (2013), 333–55

Martínez Rojo, Miguel, 'Discurso pronunciado por el c. Miguel Martínez Rojo', in *Segunda convención de la Liga de Comunidades Agrarias y Sindicatos Campesinos*, pp. 331–34

Massey, Doreen, *Space, Place and Gender* (Cambridge: Polity, 1994)

Matute, Álvaro, 'Orígenes del revisionismo historiográfico de la revolución mexicana', *Signos Históricos*, 1 (2000), 29–48

McCabe, Susan, *Cinematic Modernism: Modernist Poetry and Film* (Cambridge: Cambridge University Press, 2005)

McCormick, Gladys, 'The Forgotten Jaramillo: Building a Social Base of Support for Authoritarianism in Rural Mexico', in *Dictablanda*, pp. 196–215

Merrim, Stephanie, 'The Existential Juan Rulfo: *Pedro Páramo*, Mexicanness, and the Grupo Hiperión', *MLN*, 129 (2014), pp. 308–29.

Meyer, Jean, 'Revolution and Reconstruction in the 1920s', in *Mexico since Independence*, ed. by Leslie Bethell (Cambridge: Cambridge University Press, 1991), pp. 201–40

Meza Márquez, Consuelo, *La utopía feminista: Quehacer literario de cuatro narradoras mexicanas contemporáneas* (Aguascalientes: Universidad Autónoma de Aguascalientes, 2000)

Millán, Paulina, 'A Journey Through Juan Rulfo's Photographs', in *Rethinking Juan Rulfo's Creative World: Prose, Photography, Film*, pp. 51–65

——'Juan Rulfo entre vías y trenes', in *En los ferrocarriles: Juan Rulfo: Fotografías*, ed. by Víctor Jiménez (Mexico City: UNAM, Editorial RM, 2014), pp. 29–34

Miller, Nicola, *In the Shadow of the State: Intellectuals and the Quest for National Identity in Twentieth-century Spanish America* (London: Verso, 1999)

Minna Stern, Alexandra, 'Responsible Mothers and Normal Children: Eugenics, Nationalism, and Welfare in Post-revolutionary Mexico, 1920–1940', *Journal of Historical Sociology*, 12 (1999), 369–97

GABRIELA MISTRAL, 'A la mujer mexicana', in *La tierra tiene la actitud de una mujer*, ed. by Pedro Pablo Zegers (Santiago de Chile: RIL Editores, 1999), pp. 129–31
——*Lecturas para mujeres* (Mexico City: Porrúa, 1997)
——'Una nueva organización del trabajo', in *La tierra tiene la actitud de una mujer*, pp. 55–58
——'A un sembrador', in *Gabriela Mistral: Su prosa y poesía en Colombia*, 3 vols (Santafé de Bogotá: Convenio Andrés Bello, 2002), p. 45
MITCHELL, W. J. T., *Picture Theory* (Chicago: The University of Chicago Press, 1994)
MOLINA ENRÍQUEZ, ANDRÉS, *Los grandes problemas nacionales* (Mexico City: Imprenta de A. Carranza e Hijos, 1909)
MOLINA ENRÍQUEZ, RENATO, 'Un libro de México: *Pedro Páramo*', *Boletín Bibliográfico de la Secretaría de la Hacienda*, August 1955
MONSIVÁIS, CARLOS, 'Diego Rivera: Creador de públicos', *Historias* (April–June 1986)
——'Sí, tampoco los muertos retoñan. Desgraciadamente', in Federico Campbell, *La ficción de la memoria: Juan Rulfo ante la crítica*, pp. 187–202
——'El peñón de las ánimas: A 35 años de un feliz aniversario', *Siempre!*, 12 January 1966
MONTERDE, FRANCISCO, 'Existe una literatura viril', *El Universal*, 25 December 1924
——'Libros para los campesinos', *MR*, 1 September 1933
MORALES PEREIRA, SAMUEL, *Algunas consideraciones sobre las causas que motivan la gran mortalidad de la primera infancia y recursos que deben oponerse para combatirlas* (Mexico City Oficina Tip. de la Secretaría de Fomento, 1888)
MORSON, GARY SAUL, *Mikhail Bakhtin: Creation of a Prosaic* (California: Stanford University Press, 1990)
MOYSSÉN ECHEVARRÍA, XAVIER, *La crítica de arte en México, 1896–1921* (Mexico City: UNAM, 1999)
MRAZ, JOHN, *Looking for Mexico: Modern Visual Culture and National Identity* (Durham: Duke University Press, 2009)
MUÑIZ, ELSA, *Cuerpo, representación y poder: México en los albores de la reconstrucción nacional, 1920–1934* (Mexico City: Universidad Autónoma Metropolitana, 2002)
MURIÀ, JOSÉ MARÍA, *Historia de Jalisco* (Jalisco: Gobierno de Jalisco, Secretaría General, Unidad Editorial, 1982)
NAVARRO, FRANCISCO, 'México y Diego Rivera', *El Nacional*, 2 March 1922
NDALIANIS, ANGELA, 'From Neo-Baroque to Neo-Baroques?', *Revista Canadiense de Estudios Hispánicos*, 33 (2008), 265–80
——*Neo–baroque Aesthetics and Contemporary Entertainment* (Cambridge, MA: MIT Press, 204), p. 28
NEAD, LYNDA. *The Female Nude: Art, Obscenity and Sexuality* (London: Routledge, 1992)
NIBLO, STEPHEN R., *Mexico in the 1940s: Modernity, Politics, and Corruption* (Wilmington, Del: Scholarly Resources, 1999)
NOBLE, ANDREA, *Mexican National Cinema* (London: Routledge, 2005)
NOCHLIN, LINDA, *The Politics of Vision* (New York: Harper and Row, 1989)
OBREGÓN, ÁLVARO, *Discursos del General Álvaro Obregón*, 2 vols (Mexico City: Talleres Gráficos de la Nación, 1932)
O'BRIEN, GERALD V., and AUTUMN MOLINARI, 'Religious Metaphors as a Justification for Eugenic Control: A Historical Analysis', in *Disability in Judaism, Christianity, and Islam: Sacred texts, Historical traditions, and Social Analysis*, ed. by Darla Schumm and Michael Stoltzfus (Basingstoke: Palgrave Macmillan, 2011), pp. 141–65
OCHOA, JOHN A., *The Uses of Failure in Mexican Literature and Identity* (Austin: University of Texas Press, 2004)
OFFNER, RICHARD, 'Giotto, Non-Giotto', in *Giotto: The Arena Chapel Frescoes*, ed. by James H. Stubblebine (London: Thames and Hudson, 1969), pp. 135–55
OGAZ PIERCE, JOSÉ ABEL, 'El pensamiento agrario del joven Vicente Lombardo Toledano', in *Personajes, Cuestión Agraria y Revolución Mexicana*, ed. by Mónica Blanco and Esperanza

Fujigaki (Mexico City: Instituto Nacional Estudios Históricos Revolución Mexicana, 2004), pp. 311–42

O'GORMAN, EDMUNDO, ALFONSO CASO and RAMÓN IGLESIA, 'Sobre el problema de la verdad histórica (1945)', in *La teoría de la historia en México 1940–1973*, ed. by Álvaro Matute (Mexico City: Secretaría de Educación Pública, 1974), pp. 32–65

O'GORMAN, JUAN, 'Abstracción y realismo en la arquitectura de hoy en México', in *Juan O'Gorman: Autobiografía, antología, juicios críticos y documentación exhaustiva sobre su obra*, ed. by Antonio Luna Arroyo (Mexico City: Cuadernos Populares de Pintura Mexicana Moderna, 1973), pp. 275–85

——'Conferencia en la Sociedad de Arquitectos Mexicanos', in *La palabra de Juan O'Gorman: Selección de textos*, ed. by Ida Rodríguez Prampolini (Mexico City: UNAM, Instituto de Investigaciones Estéticas, 1983), pp. 108–12

——'Escuelas Nuevas', *Imagen*, 1 (1933), n.p

——'Más allá del funcionalismo (II)', in *Juan O'Gorman, arquitecto y pintor*, ed. by Ida Rodríguez Prampolini (Mexico City: UNAM, 1982), pp. 107–10

——'Notas sobre arquitectura', in *La Palabra de Juan O'Gorman: Selección de textos*, ed. by Ida Rodríguez Prampolini (Mexico City: UNAM, Instituto de Investigaciones Estéticas, 1983), pp. 132–40

O'MALLEY, ILENE V., *The Myth of Revolution: Hero Cults and the Institutionalization of the Mexican State, 1920–1940* (London: Greenwood, 1986)

OLES, JAMES, *Diego Rivera, David Alfaro Siqueiros, José Clemente Orozco: The Mexican Muralists* (New York: Moma Artist Series, 2011)

OLIN, MARGARET, 'Gaze', in *Critical Terms for Art History*, ed. by Robert S. Nelson and Richard Shiff (Chicago: University of Chicago Press, 2003), pp. 208–19

OLIVER, KELLY, *Reading Kristeva: Unravelling the Double-bind* (Bloomington Indiana University Press, 1993)

OLWIG, KENNETH, *Landscape, Nature, and the Body Politic: From Britain's Renaissance to America's New World* (Madison: University of Wisconsin Press, 2000)

OROZCO, JOSÉ CLEMENTE, *Autobiografía* (Mexico City: Ediciones Era, 1999)

ORTEGA Y GASSET, JOSÉ, 'La doctrina del punto de vista', in *El tema de nuestro tiempo: El ocaso de las revoluciones: El sentido histórico de la teoría de Einstein* (Madrid: Revista de Occidente, 1966), pp. 188–201

——'Verdad y perspectiva', in *Obras completas de José Ortega y Gasset*, 11 vols (Madrid: Alianza, 1983), pp. 15–21

O'SULLIVAN, SIMON, 'Fold', in *Deleuze Dictionary Revised Edition*, ed. by Adrian Parr (Edinburgh: Edinburgh University Press, 2010), p. 107–09

OZENFANT, AMÉDÉE and CHARLES-EDOUARD JEANNERET, 'After Cubism', in *L'Esprit Nouveau: Purism in Paris, 1918–1925*, ed. by Carol Eliel (Los Angeles: Los Angeles County Museum of Art, 2001), pp. 134–39

PADILLA, TANALÍS, *Rural Resistance in the Land of Zapata: The Jaramillista Movement and the Myth of the Pax-Priísta, 1940–1962* (Durham: Duke University Press, 2008)

PALACIOS, GUILLERMO, *La pluma y el arado: los intelectuales pedagogos y la construcción sociocultural del 'problema campesino' en México, 1932–1934* (Mexico City: Colegio de México, 1999)

PANI, MARIO, 'Penicilina para la ciudad', *Arquitectura/México*, 30 (1950), 309–12

'La patria reconocida', in *La crítica de arte en México en el siglo XIX: Estudios y documentos III (1879–1902)*, ed. by Rodríguez Prampolini (Mexico City: UNAM, Instituto de Investigaciones Estéticas, 1997), pp. 245–46

PARTRIDGE, WILLIAM L. and DAVID B. HALMO, *Resettling Displaced Communities: Applying the International Standard for Involuntary Resettlement* (Lanham: Lexington Books, 2020)

PAZ, OCTAVIO, *El laberinto de la soledad* (Mexico City: Fondo de Cultura Económica, 1959)

——'Los muralistas a primera vista', in *Obras completas de Octavio Paz*, 8 vols (Barcelona: Galaxia Gutenberg, 2001), pp. 709–15

——'En París, encuentro con Octavio Paz', interviewed by Claude Couffon, *La Gaceta del Fondo de Cultura Económica*, March 1959

——*Las peras del olmo* (Mexico City: Imprenta Universitaria, 1957)

——'Visión e ideología sobre el muralismo mexicano', *Vuelta*, 1 December 1986

——'Totalidad y fragmento', in *Poemas (1935–1975)* (Barcelona: Seix Barral, 1979), pp. 613–15

Peña Nieto, Enrique, *Palabras del Presidente, licenciado Enrique Peña Nieto, durante la inauguración del Museo Histórico del Palacio Nacional*, www.gob.mx, 22 June 2018, <>https://www.gob.mx/presidencia/prensa/palabras-del-presidente-de-los-estados-unidos-mexicanos-162554?idiom=es> [Accessed 15 July 2018]

——*Proteger a las instituciones fortalece a México, vulnerarlas nos debilita a todos: Enrique Peña Nieto*, www.gob.mx, 22 November 2017, <https://www.gob.mx/presidencia/prensa/proteger-a-las-instituciones-fortalece-a-mexico-vulnerarlas-nos-debilita-a-todos-enrique-pena-nieto> [Accessed 10 June 2018]

Pérez Montfort, Ricardo, 'Representación e historiografía en México 1930–1950: "Lo mexicano" ante la propia mirada y la extranjera', *Historia Mexicana*, 62 (2013), 1651–94

Perus, Françoise, *Juan Rulfo: El arte de narrar*, with an introduction by José Pascual Buxó (Mexico City: RM–UNAM, 2012)

Plato, *Timaeus*, trans. by Donald J. Zeyl (Indianapolis, IN: Hackett Publishing, 2000)

Poniatowska, Elena, 'Entrevista: Elena Poniatowska, 'No tengo más que preguntas sobre las cosas', interviewed by Jacobo G. García, *El Mundo*, 18 April 2014.

——'El movimiento estudiantil de 1968', in *Fuerte es el silencio* (Mexico City: Ediciones Era, 1980), pp. 34–48

Poole, Deborah, *Vision, Race, and Modernity: A Visual Economy of the Andean Image World* (Princeton: Princeton University Press, 1997)

Portes Gil, Emilio, *Autobiografía de la Revolución Mexicana: Un tratado de interpretación histórica* (Mexico City: Instituto Mexicano de Cultura, 1964)

——'Discurso pronunciado por el señor lic. Emilio Portes Gil, Gobernador constitucional del estado', in *Segunda convención de la Liga de Comunidades Agrarias y Sindicatos Campesinos*, pp. 81–86

——'Discurso pronunciado por el señor lic. Emilio Portes Gil, Gobernador constitucional del estado de Tamaulipas y apertura de los trabajos de la convención', in *Primera convención de la Liga de Comunidades Agrarias y Sindicatos Campesinos*, ed. by Marte R. Gómez (Mexico City: Editorial Cultura, 1926), pp. 69–77

——*En memoria de Zapata: Un balance social político del momento actual en México* (Mexico City: PNR, Biblioteca de Cultura Social y Política, 1936)

'Proyecto de bases para la liga de comunidades agrarias del estado de Tamaulipas, Tamps', *Primera convención*, pp. 231–37

Puig Casauranc, José Manuel, 'La educación integral', *Boletín de la Secretaría de Educación Pública*, 5 (1925), 74–80

——*Páginas viejas con ideas actuales* (Mexico City: Talleres Gráficos de la Nación Editorial, 1925)

Raby, David L., 'Los maestros rurales y los conflictos sociales en Mexico (1931–1940)', *Historia Mexicana*, 18 (1968), 190–226

Ramírez, Arthur, 'Spatial Form and Cinema Techniques in Rulfo's *Pedro Páramo*', *Revista de Estudios Hispánicos*, 15 (1981) 233–49

—— 'Style and Technique in Juan Rulfo' (unpublished doctoral thesis, University of Texas at Austin, 1973)

Ramírez, Hugo Hernán, 'El personaje femenino en los cuentos de Juan Rulfo', *Iberoamericana: América Latina-España-Portugal*, 8 (2008), 47–63

RAMÍREZ, MARIO TEODORO, 'Estadios de la otredad en la reflexión filosófica de Luis Villoro', *Diánoia*, 52 (2007), 143–75

RAMÍREZ MORENO, SAMUEL, 'Concepto actual sobre la neurastenia y su patogénesis', *Medicina Revista Mexicana*, 25 May 1940

RAMOS, SAMUEL, 'Diego Rivera', in *Obras completas III: Estudios de estética*, ed. and intro. by Raúl Cardiel Reyes (Mexico City: UNAM, 1991), pp. 41–74.

——*Hacia un nuevo humanismo programa de antropología filosófica* (Medellín: Canal Ramírez Antares, 1940)

——'La mecanización de la vida humana', *Hoy*, 20 August 1938

——*El perfil del hombre y la cultura en México* (Buenos Aires: Espasa-Calpe Argentina, 1951).

REAGAN, PATRICIA, *Deconstructing Paradise: Inverted Religious Symbolism in Twentieth-Century Latin American Literature* (Lanham: Lexington Books, 2016)

REED, ALMA M., *Orozco* (New York: Oxford University Press, 1956)

REISS, JONATHAN B., 'Justice and The Common Good in Giotto's Arena Chapel Frescoes', in *The Arena Chapel and the Genius of Giotto: Padua*, ed. by Andrew Ladis (London: Garland, 1998), pp. 233–44

REVUELTAS, JOSÉ, 'El hijo tonto', in *Dios en la tierra* (Mexico City: Editorial Novaro, 1973), pp. 95–106

——*Ensayo sobre un proletariado sin cabeza* (Mexico City: Ediciones Era, 1980)

——'Escuela Mexicana de Pintura y novela de la revolución', in *Cuestionamientos e intenciones* (Mexico City: Ediciones Era, 1978), pp. 241–74

REYES, ALFONSO, 'Literatura Mexicana', in *Obras completas I: Cuestiones estéticas, Capítulos de literatura mexicana* (Mexico City: Letras Mexicanas: Fondo de Cultura Económica, 1996), pp. 468–72

——'Pasado inmediato', in *Pasado inmediato y otros ensayos* (Mexico City: El Colegio de México, Fondo de Cultura Económica, 1914), pp. 3–64

——*Tres puntos de exegética literaria* (Mexico City: El Colegio de México, 1945)

——'Visión de Anáhuac', in *Última Tule y otros ensayos* (Caracas: Biblioteca Ayacucho, 1991), pp. 3–17

RILKE, RAINER MARIA, *Elegías de Duino*, trans. by Juan Rulfo (Madrid: Sexto Piso España, 2015)

RIVERA, DIEGO, *Confesiones*, ed. by Luis Suárez (Mexico: Editorial Grijalbo, 1975)

——'La cuestión del arte en México', in *Palabras ilustres: 1921–1957*, ed. by Roberto Pliego, Magdalena Zavala and Juan Coronel Rivera (Mexico City, INBA: Editorial RM, 2007), pp. 305–22

——*Diego Rivera: Arte y revolución* (Mexico City: Consejo Nacional para la Cultura y las Artes, 1999)

——'Diego Rivera opina', in *Diego Rivera y la arquitectura mexicana*, ed. by Rafael López Rangel (Mexico City: SEP, Dirección General de Publicaciones y Medios), pp. 123–24

——'El espíritu revolucionario en el arte moderno', in *Textos de Arte*, ed. by Xavier Moyssén Echeverría (Mexico City: UNAM, 1986), pp. 159–72

——'Las formas puras', in *Palabras ilustres*, pp. 155–56

——'De la libreta de apuntes de un pintor mexicano', in *Textos de arte*, pp. 71–77

——*Mi arte, mi vida: Una autobiografía hecha con la colaboración de Gladys March* (Mexico City: Herrero, 1963)

——*My Life, My Art: An Autobiography (with Gladys March)* (New York: Dover Publications, 1957)

——'The New Mexican Architecture: A House by Carlos Obregón /La nueva arquitectura mexicana: Una casa de Carlos Obregón', *Mexican Folkways*, 2 (1926), 19–29

——'La obra del pintor Diego Rivera', in *Textos de arte*, pp. 118–24

——'Un pintor opina', in *Diego Rivera y la arquitectura mexicana*, pp. 116–19

——'Los primeros murales', in *Arte y política*, ed. with notes by Raquel Tibol (Mexico City: Grijalbo, 1979), pp. 49–54
——'Retrato de América', in *Textos de arte*, pp. 213–17
——'The Revolutionary Spirit in Modern Art', *Modern Quarterly*, 6 (1932), 51–57
——, Unpublished interview with Diego Rivera, interviewed by Rafael Heliodoro Valle, Archivo Frida Kahlo y Diego Rivera, Museo Frida Kahlo, 23 May 1938
——'Volver a nacer', in *Palabras ilustres*, pp. 367–68
RIVERA MARÍN, GUADALUPE, *Encuentros con Diego Rivera* (Mexico City: BNCI, 1993)
ROCHFORT, DESMOND, *Pintura mural mexicana: Orozco, Rivera, Siqueiros* (Mexico City: Limusa, Grupo Noriega Editores, 1993)
RODRÍGUEZ, ANTONIO, *Canto a la tierra: Los murales de Diego Rivera en la capilla de Chapingo* (Chapingo: Universidad Autónoma Chapingo, 1986)
——*Guía de los murales de Diego Rivera en la Secretaría de Educación Pública* (Mexico City: SEP Cultura, 1984)
——'Literatura contra pintura: La pintura mexicana a la zaga de la literatura', *Claridades Literarias: Suplemento Cultural de los Jueves*, April 1959
RODRÍGUEZ, WENCESLAO, 'El maíz', *MR*, 1 December 1932
RODRÍGUEZ PRAMPOLINI, IDA, *La crítica de arte en México en el siglo XIX: La crítica de arte en México en el siglo XIX: Estudios y documentos III (1879–1902)* (Mexico City: UNAM, Instituto de Investigaciones Estéticas, 1997)
ROGGIANO, ALFREDO A., *Pedro Henríquez Ureña en México* (Mexico City: Facultad de Filosofía y Letras, UNAM, 1989)
ROH, FRANZ, 'Magic Realism, Post-impressionism', in *Magical Realism: Theory, History, Community*, ed. by Lois Parkinson Zamora and Wendy B. Faris and trans. by Wendy B. Faris (London: Duke University Press, 1995), pp. 15–30
ROMANELL, PATRICK, *The Making of the Mexican Mind: A Study in Recent Mexican Thought* (Lincoln: University of Nebraska Press, 1952)
ROSEMBLATT, KARIN ALEJANDRA, *The Science and Politics of Race in Mexico and the United States, 1910–1950* (Chapel Hill: The University of North Carolina Press, 2018)
ROSENBLUM, ROBERT, *Cubism and Twentieth-Century Art* (New York: Harry N. Abrams, 2001)
ROWE, WILLIAM, *Rulfo, El Llano en llamas* (London: Grant & Cutler, 1987)
RULFO, JUAN, *Aire de las colinas: Cartas a Clara*, ed. by Alberto Vital (Buenos Aires: Editorial Sudamericana, 2000)
——'Charlando con Juan Rulfo: Voz de la tierra en llamas', interviewed by Elena Poniatowska, *Excelsiór*, 15 January 1954
——'He dejado de publicar, pero nunca dejaré de escribir: Juan Rulfo', interviewed by Dimas Lidio Pitty, *El Gallo Ilustrado*, 5 July 1970, p. 3
——'El desafío de la creación', in *Toda la obra*, ed. by Claude Fell (Paris: ALLCA XX, 1996), pp. 388–91
——'Donde quedó nuestra historia', in *Toda la obra*, pp. 421–28
——'España en el corazón', in *Toda la obra*, pp. 381–83
——*En los ferrocarriles: Juan Rulfo: Fotografías*, ed. by Víctor Jiménez (Mexico City: UNAM, Editorial RM, 2014)
——'Fotografías de Nacho López: De cuántas amarguras está hecha la dura vida', in *Toda la obra*, pp. 435–36
——'La fórmula secreta', in *El gallo de oro: La fórmula secreta*, ed. by José Carlos González Boixo and Douglas Weatherford (Mexico City: Ediciones RM, 2010), pp. 151–55
——'Juan Rulfo examina su narrativa', in *Toda la obra*, pp. 451–62
——'Juan Rulfo y Fernando Benítez hablan sobre los indios', interviewed by Fernando Benítez, *México Indígena*, December 1978, pp. 259–60

——*Juan Rulfo: Letras e imágenes*, ed. by Víctor Jiménez (Mexico City: Editorial RM, 2002)
——*Juan Rulfo's Mexico*, trans. by Margaret Sayers Peden (Washington, D.C.: Smithsonian Institution Press, 2002)
——'La literatura es una mentira que dice la verdad: Una Conversación con Ernesto González Bermejo', in *Toda la obra*, pp. 462–69
——*El Llano en llamas, Pedro Páramo, Castillo de Teayo* (Barcelona: RM Verlag, 2011)
——'México y los mexicanos', in *Toda la obra*, pp. 443–45
——'No puedo escribir sobre lo que veo', interviewed by Juan Cruz, *El País*, 19 August 1979
——'Notas sobre la literatura indígena en México', in *Toda la obra*, pp. 412–16
——,'Sinopsis', in *Toda la obra*, pp. 363–64
——'Tutotepec', in *Juan Rulfo: Letras e imágenes*, p. 34
Russek, Dan, *Textual Exposures: Photography in Twentieth Century Spanish American Narrative Fiction* (Calgary: University of Calgary Press, 2015)
Sáenz, Moisés, *México íntegro* (Lima: Imprenta Torres Aguirre, 1929)
Said, Edward, *Orientalism* (London: Routledge and Kegan Paul, 1978)
Salazar Mallén, Rubén, 'El mensaje en la obra', *El Universal*, 21 June 1955
Samuels, Maurice, *The Spectacular Past: Popular History and the Novel in Nineteenth-century France* (Ithaca: Cornell University Press, 2004)
Sánchez, Carlos Alberto, '20th Century Mexican Philosophy: Features, Themes, Tasks', *Inter-American Journal of Philosophy*, 1 (2016), 1–25
Sánchez Prado, Ignacio, 'La destrucción de la escritura viril y el ingreso de la mujer al discurso literario: *El libro vacío* y *Los recuerdos del porvenir*', *Revista de Crítica Literaria Latinoamericana*, 32 (2006), 149–67
——*Naciones intelectuales: Las fundaciones de la modernidad literaria mexicana, 1917–1959* (Indiana: Purdue University Press, 2009)
Santí, Enrico Mario 'Introduction', in Octavio Paz, *El laberinto de la soledad*, ed. by Enrico Mario Santí (Madrid: Cátedra, 1993), pp. 11–137
Sarduy, Severo, *Barroco* (Buenos Aires: Editorial Sudamericana, 1974)
Scarry, Elaine, *The Body in Pain: The Making and Unmaking of the World* (New York: Oxford University Press, 1985)
Schell, Patience A., 'Eugenics, Policy and Practice in Cuba, Puerto Rico, and Mexico', in *The Oxford Handbook of the History of Eugenics*, ed. by Alison Bashford and Philippa Levine (Oxford: Oxford University Press, 2010), pp. 477–92.
Schnapp, Jeffrey T., 'Mob Porn', in *Crowds*, ed. by Jeffrey T. Schnapp and Matthew Tiews (Stanford: Stanford University Press, 2006), pp. 1–46
Schuler, Friedrich, *Mexico Between Hitler and Roosevelt: Mexican Foreign Relations in the Age of Lázaro Cárdenas, 1934–1940* (Albuquerque: University of New Mexico Press, 1998)
Schwartz, Diana Lynn, 'Displacement, Development and the Creation of a Modern *Indígena* in the Papaloapan, 1940s –1970s', in *Beyond Alterity: Destabilizing the Indigenous Other in Mexico*, ed. by Paula López Caballero and Ariadna Acevedo-Rodrigo (Tucson: University of Arizona Press, 2018), pp. 222–43
Segre, Erica, 'The Complicit Eye: Directorial and Ocular Paradigms in Luis Buñuel's Mexican Films and Interdisciplinary Visuality', in *A Companion to Luis Buñuel*, ed. by Rob Stone and Julián Daniel Gutiérrez-Albilla (Oxford: Wiley-Blackwell, 2013), pp. 205–25
——*Intersected Identities: Strategies of Visualisation in Nineteenth- and Twentieth-Century Mexican Culture* (Oxford: Berghahn Books, 2007)
Shields, Kathryn M., 'Masking', in *Encyclopedia of Twentieth-Century Photography*, 3 vols, ed. by Lynne Warren (London: Routledge, 2006), pp. 1014–16

SIERRA, JUSTO, 'Respuesta del Presidente del Congreso, Lic. Justo Sierra', in *Informes y manifiestos de los poderes ejecutivo y legislativo de 1821 a 1904*, ed. by José A. Castillón (Mexico City: Imprenta del Gobierno Federal, 1905), pp. 479–80

—— 'Positivismo político', in *Obras completas*, 14 vols (Mexico: UNAM, 1977), pp. 238–39

SILVA HERZOG, JESÚS, *El agrarismo mexicano y la reforma agraria: Exposición y crítica* (Mexico City: Fondo de Cultura Económica, 1959)

——'La revolución mexicana es ya un hecho histórico', *Cuadernos Americanos*, September–October 1949

——*Una vida en la vida de México y, Mis últimas andanzas, 1947–1972* (Mexico City: Siglo Veintiuno Editores, 1973)

SIQUEIROS, DAVID ALFARO, *Cómo se pinta un mural* (Mexico City: Ediciones La Rana, 1998)

——'Manifiesto del Sindicato de Obreros, Técnicos, Pintores y Escultores', in *Palabras de Siqueiros*, ed. by Raquel Tibol (Mexico City: Fondo de Cultura Económica, 1996), pp. 23–26

——'The Mexican Experience in Art', in *Artists against War and Fascism: Papers of the First American Artists' Congress*, ed. by Matthew Baigell and Julia Williams (New Brunswick, N.J.: Rutgers University Press, 1985), pp. 208–12

——'Rivera's Counter-Revolutionary Road', *New Masses*, 29 May 1934

——'Tres llamamientos de orientación actual a los pintores y escultores de la nueva generación Americana', *Vida Americana: Revista norte centro y sudamericana de vanguardia*, May 1921

SLEVIN, TOM, *Visions of the Human: Art, World War I and The Modernist Subject* (London: I.B. Tauris, 2005)

SLUIS, AGEETH, *Deco Body, Deco City: Female Spectacle and Modernity in Mexico City, 1900–1939* (London: University of Nebraska Press)

SMITH, STEPHANIE J., *The Power and Politics of Art in Postrevolutionary Mexico* (Chapel Hill: The University of North Carolina Press, 2017)

SOMMER, DORIS, *Foundational Fictions: The National Romances of Latin America* (Berkeley: University of California Press, 1991)

SONTAG, SUSAN, *On Photography* (Harmondsworth: Penguin, 1979)

SOTO Y GAMA, ANTONIO, 'El milagro del ejido', in *El pensamiento de Antonio Soto y Gama a través de 50 años de labor periodística 1899–1949*, ed. by Ramón Iglesias González (Mexico City: UNAM, Instituto de Investigaciones Jurídicas, 1997), pp. 124–26

STITES, RICHARD, *Revolutionary Dreams: Utopian Vision and Experimental Life in the Russian Revolution* (Oxford: Oxford University Press, 1989)

STOLL, ANDRÉ, 'Iniciación fotográfica en la mexicanidad: Los desconcertantes mundos surrealistas de Juan Rulfo, visitados por un peregrino europeo', *Los murmullos: Boletín de la Fundación Juan Rulfo*, 1 (1999), 54–65

TARICA, ESTELLE, *The Inner Life of Mestizo Nationalism* (Minneapolis: University of Minnesota Press, 2008)

TENORIO-TRILLO, MAURICIO, *Mexico at the World's Fairs: Crafting a Modern Nation* (Berkeley: University of California Press, 1996)

THAKKAR, AMIT, *The Fiction of Juan Rulfo: Irony, Revolution and Postcolonialism* (Woodbridge: Tamesis, 2012)

——'Studium and Punctum in Juan Rulfo's "Puerta del cementerio de Janitizio"', in *Rethinking Juan Rulfo's Creative World*, pp. 82–101

THORNTON, NIAMH, *Revolution and Rebellion in Mexican Film* (New York: Bloomsbury Academic, 2013)

TIBOL, RAQUEL, *Diego Rivera: Luces y sombras* (Barcelona: Lumen, 2007)

——,'Palacio Nacional en el torrente muralista riveriano', in *Los murales del Palacio Nacional*, ed. by Raquel Tibol (Mexico City: INBA, 1997), pp. 27–38

Tirres, Christopher D., *The Aesthetics and Ethics of Faith: A Dialogue Between Liberationist and Pragmatic Thought* (New York: Oxford University Press, 2014)

Trevizo, Dolores, *Rural Protest and the Making of Democracy in Mexico, 1968–2000* (University Park: Pennsylvania State University Press, 2011)

Turner, Victor W., 'Are there Universals of Performance in Myth, Ritual, and Drama?', in *By Means of Performance*, ed. by Richard Schechner and Willa Appel (Cambridge, Cambridge University Press, 1990) pp. 8–18

Uranga, Emilio, and Carlos Alberto Sánchez, *Emilio Uranga's Analysis of Mexican Being: A Translation and Critical Introduction* (London: Bloomsbury Academic, 2021)

Urías Horcasitas, Beatriz, *Historias secretas del racismo en México (1920–1950)* (Mexico City: Tusquets, 2007)

Vargas Llosa, Mario, 'La dictadura perfecta', in *Desafíos a la libertad* (Madrid: El País, 1994), pp. 171–76

Vasconcelos, José, 'Se convoca a las mujeres para la campaña contra el analfabetismo', in *José Vasconcelos y el espíritu de la Universidad*, ed, by Javier Sicilia (Mexico City: UNAM, 2001) pp. 103–05

——'Discurso inaugural del edificio de la SEP', in *Obras completas*, 4 vols (Mexico City: Libreros Mexicanos Unidos, 1957) pp. 796–92

——'Discurso en la Universidad (Con motivo de la toma de posesión del cargo de rector)', in *Obras completas*, pp. 773–76

——'Don Gabino Barreda y las ideas contemporáneas', in *Conferencias del Ateneo de la Juventud*, ed. by Juan Hernández Luna (Mexico City: UNAM, 1984), pp. 97–113

——'The Race Problem in Latin America', in *Aspects of Mexican Civilization: Lectures on the Harris Foundation*, ed. by José Vasconcelos and Manuel Gamio (Chicago: University of Chicago, 1926), pp. 75–102

——*Indología: El pensamiento latinoamericano* (Mexico: Editorial Limusa, 1958)

——'Invitación a los intelectuales y maestros para que se inscriban como misioneros', *Boletín de la Secretaría de Educación Pública*, 1 (1922), 177–78

——'José Vasconcelos por Ortega', *El Universal Ilustrado*, 23 November 1923

——*Pitágoras: Una teoría del ritmo* (La Habana: Imprenta, 1916)

——*La raza cósmica: Misión de la raza iberoamericana: Notas de viajes a la América del Sur* (Barcelona: Agencia Mundial de librería, 1928)

Vaughan, Mary Kay, *The State, Education and Social Class in Mexico* (De Kalb: Northern Illinois U.P., 1982)

Vázquez, Josefina Zoraida, *Nacionalismo y educación en México* (Mexico City: Colegio de México, 1970)

Velázquez, Margarita, *Políticas sociales, transformación agraria y participación de las mujeres en el campo: 1920–1988* (Cuernavaca: UNAM, 1992)

Vilhauer, Ruvanee P., 'Inner reading voices: An Overlooked Form of Inner Speech', *Psychosis: Psychological, Social and Integrative Approaches*, 8 (2016), 37–47

Villa Rojas, Alfonso, *Los Mazatecos y el problema indígena de la cuenca del Papaloapan* (Mexico City: Ediciones del Instituto Nacional Indigenista, 1955)

Villegas, Abelardo, *La filosofía de lo mexicano* (Mexico City: FCE, 1960)

Villoro, Luis, *Los grandes momentos del indigenismo* (Mexico City: Ediciones de la casa chata, 1979)

Viniegra, Fermín, 'Capítulo de un Libro de Obstetricia Diagnóstico de la Infección Puerperal', *Pasteur: Revista mensual de medicina*, 11 (1938), 85–87

Vital, Alberto, *Noticias sobre Juan Rulfo, 1784–2003* (Mexico City: Editorial RM, 2004)

——*Palabra clave: Géneros inesperados y personajes esenciales de la literatura* (Mexico City: Taurus, 2012)

Vitruvius. *On Architecture*, trans. by Frank Granger, vol 1 (London: W. Heinemann, 1931)

VON MOOS, STANISLAUS, *Le Corbusier, Elements of a Synthesis* (Cambridge, Mass: MIT Press, 1979)
WARMAN, ARTURO and OTHERS, *De eso que llaman antropología mexicana* (Mexico City: Editorial Nuestro Tiempo, 1970)
WATSON, THOMAS, *The Beatitudes: An Exposition of Matthew 5:1–12* (London: Banner of Truth Trust, 1971)
WHITE, HAYDEN, *Metahistory: The Historical Imagination in Nineteenth-Century Europe* (London: Johns Hopkins University Press, 1975)
WIARDA, HOWARD J., 'Corporatist Theory and Ideology: A Latin American Development Paradigm', *Journal of Church and State*, 20 (1978), 29–56
—— *The Soul of Latin America: The Cultural and Political Tradition* (New Haven: Yale University Press, 2001)
WILLIS, BRUCE DEAN, *Corporeality in Early Twentieth-Century Latin American Literature: Body Articulations* (Basingstoke: Palgrave Macmillan, 2013)
WOLFE, BERTRAM, *The Fabulous Life of Diego Rivera* (London: Barrie & Rockliff, 1968)
WÖLFFLIN, HEINRICH, *Principles of Art History: The Problem of the Development of Style in Early Modern Art*, trans. by Jonathan Blower (California: Getty Publications, 2015)
—— *Renaissance and Baroque*, trans. by Kathrin Simon (London: Collins, 1964)
WOOLF, VIRGINIA, 'Walter Sickert', in *The Captain's Death-Bed and Other Essays*, ed. by Leonard Woolf (New York: Harcourt, Brace, 1950), pp. 187–203
YUNQUE, ÁLVARO, 'Sé como este farol', *MR*, 1 May 1932
ZAMORA, LOIS PARKINSON, *The Inordinate Eye: New World Baroque and Latin American Fiction* (Chicago: The University of Chicago Press, 2006)
ZAMORA, LOIS PARKINSON and MONIKA KAUP, 'Categories and Concepts', in *Baroque New Worlds: Representation, Transculturation, Counterconquest*, ed. by Lois Parkinson Zamora and Monika Kaup (Durham: Duke University Press, 2010), pp. 1–14
ZENDEJAS, FRANCISCO, 'Carta a los intelectuales de México: deberes de la inteligencia en esta hora y ante los problemas del país', *Revista de América*, August 1955
ZIMBRÓN, ÁNGEL, 'Odontología en Relación con la Higiene', *Revista Mexicana de Ciencias Médicas*, 7 (1932), 1659–73
ZOMZET, EMILIO, 'Diego Rivera en el pueblo cooperativo en Chapingo', *Cultura urbana*, 3 (2007), 70–71
ZOZAYA, JOSÉ, 'Higiene Mental', *Medicina, Revista Científica Mensual*, 6 (1926), 208–13

INDEX

www.ingramcontent.com/pod-product-compliance
Lightning Source LLC
LaVergne TN
LVHW081258100826
845148LV00005B/911